The Ultimate
JOKE
ENCYCLOPAEDIA

GUINNESS BOOKS

Editor: Honor Head
Design and Layout: Alan Hamp

© Victorama Ltd and Guinness Superlatives Ltd, 1986

Published in Great Britain by Guinness Superlatives Ltd,
33 London Road, Enfield, Middlesex

Typeset in Linotron Souvenir
by Input Typesetting Ltd, London SW19 8DR
Printed and bound in Great Britain by
Richard Clay Ltd, Bungay, Suffolk

British Library Cataloguing in Publication Data

Brandreth, Gyles
    The ultimate joke encyclopaedia.
    1. English wit and humor
    I Title
    828'.02   PN6175
    ISBN 0–85112–408–9 (cased edition)
    ISBN 0–85112–409–7 (limp edition)

Introduction

This is the Ultimate Joke Encyclopaedia.

What does that mean?

Well, 'Ultimate', according to the dictionary, means 'last, final, supreme, beyond which no other exists or is possible'. And that fits, because this is certainly the last joke book you will ever need, the final word on the subject, the supreme collection. We know no bigger or better joke book exists. We believe none is possible.

Everybody knows what the word 'Joke' means. The dictionary says that it's 'a thing written or said or done to excite laughter', but that's not one hundred per cent correct because not every joke will make you laugh. A lot of them will make you groan. And some of the ones in this collection will have you running out of the house screaming!

The dictionary can't quite make its mind up about the word 'Encyclopaedia' either. For a start it says you can spell the word in one of two ways: Encyclopaedia or Encyclopedia. (We can't spell it at all.) According to the dictionary, however you spell it, the word means 'a book giving information on all branches of knowledge, arranged alphabetically'. That's definitely what we've got here: every kind of joke – elephant jokes, knock knocks, waiter waiter jokes, doctor doctor jokes, mini jokes, monster jokes, shaggy dog stories, the lot! – and they are all arranged alphabetically, from A to Z.

If truth be told we had a bit of a problem with X. You see, there just aren't that many jokes about xylophones and X-rays. But don't worry, we solved the problem. X began as the thinnest chapter in the book. Now it's one of the fattest because whenever we couldn't decide where to put a joke we gave it to X.

Deciding the categories for all the jokes hasn't been easy. Where would you file this one? Under D for Dentist? Or C for Cake? Or F for Filling?

Question: What did the dentist say when his wife baked a cake?

Answer: Can I do the filling?

And how about this one? Should it go under B for Banana? Or W for Washing Machine? Or even Y for Yellow?

Question: What's yellow and goes round and round?

Answer: A banana in a washing machine.

We think the next one belongs under V for Vampire. On second thoughts, perhaps it should be under S for Soup. Or what about T for Tomato?

Question: What is a vampire's favourite soup?

Answer: Scream of tomato.

With most of the jokes, we're happy to say, it's not been much of a problem deciding to which category they belong:

Apples
Why wouldn't the man eat apples?
Because he'd heard his grandmother had died of apple-plexy.

Music
What music can you hear in a field?
Popcorn.

Nut

What nut has no shell?
A doughnut.

You will find 5,555 jokes in this book and they come in all shapes and sizes. There are very short ones:

What sugar sings?
I-sing sugar.

And rather longer ones:

At a family gathering, a man was talking to an aunt he hadn't seen for a long time when his son started to tug his coat. 'Don't interrupt me,' said the father, 'I'm talking.' So the boy waited, and when the man had finished talking he said, 'Now, what was it you wanted?'
'It doesn't matter now,' replied the boy. 'I was trying to tell you there was a slug on your lettuce, but you've eaten it.'

There are old ones:

What do bees do with their honey?
They cell it.

And modern ones:

What do scientists eat for supper?
Microchips.

And quick ones:

What sort of food do fighter pilots like?
Scrambled eggs.

And slow ones:

1st farmer: Why has your pig got a wooden leg?
2nd farmer: It's a great pig, it saved my life once!
1st farmer: How?
2nd farmer: The farm caught fire, and it rang the fire brigade.
1st farmer: But that still doesn't explain why it's got a wooden leg.
2nd farmer: You don't think I'd eat such a great pig all at once, do you?

There are ones that rhyme:

There was a young lady named Rose
Who had a big wart on her nose,
    When she had it removed
    Her appearance improved
But her glasses slipped down to her toes!

And ones that don't:

1st little boy: Can you fight?
2nd little boy: No.
1st little boy: Put them up, then – you coward!

We hope that we have included your favourite joke and that by the time you've read the book frontwards and backwards and learnt it off by heart, you will agree that *The Ultimate Joke Encyclopaedia* is indeed *THE ULTIMATE JOKE ENCYCLOPAEDIA!*

Acknowledgements

The jokes in this unique collection come from all over the world, from Africa, America, Australia, Europe and Milton Keynes. They have been compiled by a remarkable team of jokers of all shapes and sizes and several ages. The youngest contributor was Sally Thompson from Baltimore, Maryland, aged five ('What's green, covered in custard and unhappy?' *Apple grumble!*) and the oldest was Mr Nathaniel Herbert of Accrington in Lancashire, aged 87 ('Why did the orange visit the doctor?' *Because it wasn't peeling very well!*) (Mr Herbert's grandmother also sent us a joke but we decided not to include it because it really wasn't funny enough.)

Our special thanks goes to the project's chief researcher Jacqueline Bayes (who is currently in hospital with a fractured funny bone) who typed the manuscript single-handedly (she had to, of course, because of the fractured funny bone) and Lizzie Woolfenden who photocopied it. Lizzie also offered us this gem:

Breeding frogs for profit
  Is a very sorry joke.
How can you make money
  When so many of them croak?

Accident

Doctor: So tell me how it happened that you burnt both your ears.

Patient: I was ironing when the telephone went and I answered the iron by mistake.

Doctor: But you burnt them both!

Patient: Well, as soon as I put the phone down it rang again.

★

Policeman: Now, sir, how did you come to have this accident?

Motorist: Well, the sign just there says, 'Stop – Look – Listen'. And while I was doing that the train hit me.

★

Why couldn't the motorist help the police at the scene of the accident?

Because he'd had his eyes shut at the time.

★

A man cut his hand at work and was told by the doctor that it would have to be stitched.

'Oh, that's fine,' said the injured man. 'Sew this button back on to my shirt at the same time, would you?'

★

Mother: Be careful, Billy, most home accidents happen in the kitchen.

Silly Billy: I know, I have to eat them.

★

A farmer was interviewing a young man for the job of assistant farmhand.

'You'll need to be fit,' said the farmer. 'Have you ever had any illnesses? Any accidents?'

'No, sir,' replied the young man proudly.

'But you're on crutches. You must have had an accident!' said the farmer.

'Oh, the crutches!' said the young man. 'A bull tossed me last week. But that wasn't an accident! He did it on purpose!'

Acid Indigestion

What is the best way to cure acid indigestion?
Stop drinking acid.

Acorns

How many acorns grow on the average pine tree?
None – acorns don't grow on pine trees!

★

What is an acorn?
An oak in a nutshell.

Acoustics

The acoustics in this concert hall are wonderful.
Pardon?

Acquaintance

Amy: What is an acquaintance?

Zoe: Someone you know well enough to borrow from, but not well enough to lend to.

Acrobat

Amy: What made you marry an acrobat?
Zoe: He was head over heels in love with me.

★

When are circus acrobats needed in restaurants?
    When the owner wants tumblers on the table.

★

Jack: My best friend is an acrobat.
Jill: How come?
Jack: Because he'll always do me a good turn and will bend over backwards to help me.

Acting

A bit-part actor finally got his first leading role in a major film. In one scene the actor had to jump off a high diving board in to a swimming pool. He climed to the top of the board, looked down and promptly climbed down again.
'What's the matter?' asked the director.
'I can't jump from that board!' said the actor. 'Do you know there's only one foot of water in that pool?'
'Yes,' said the director. 'We don't want you to drown, you know.'

★

Amy: I'd love to be an actress.
Zoe: Break a leg then!
Amy: Whatever for?
Zoe: Then you'd be in a cast for weeks.

★

An actor went to see a new agent one day and said, 'You must have a look at my act, it really is innovative.' So saying, he flew up to the ceiling, circled the room a few times and landed smoothly on the agent's desk.
'So you do bird impressions,' said the agent, 'what else can you do?'

★

Why does an actor enjoy his work so much?
    Because it's all play.

★

Who stars in cowboy films and is always broke?
    Skint Eastwood.

Actors

An actor is someone who tries to be everybody but himself.

★

Why do actors like snooker halls?
    Because that's where they get their best cues.

★

Jack: I met a really conceited actor the other day.
Jill: Why do you say he's conceited?
Jack: Well, every time there was a thunderclap during the storm, he went to the window and took a bow.

★

Andy: Who was the most popular actor in the Bible?
Zak: Samson. Why?
Andy: Because he brought the house down.

Actress

Producer: Would you call your leading lady ugly?
Director: Let's just say she'd look better on radio than on TV.

Adam

At what time of day was Adam born?
    Just before Eve.

★

Adam and his son Cain were walking in the fields one evening.
'Who was that lady I saw you with last night?' asked Cain.
'That wasn't night, that was Eve,' answered Adam.

★

What did Adam do when he wanted some sugar?
He raised Cain.

★

Who is the fastest runner in history.
Adam – because he was the first in the human race.

Adam and Eve

Why did Adam and Eve have to stop gambling?
Because their paradise was taken from them.

★

Did Adam and Eve have a date?
No, they had an apple.

★

What didn't Adam and Eve have that everyone else has?
Parents.

★

Adam (naming the animals): And finally, that is a hippopotamus.
Eve: Why is it called a hippopotamus?
Adam: Because it looks like a hippopotamus, stupid!

Adam and Eve Party

Rick: Do you want to come to an Adam and Eve party?
Nick: Oh, yes!
Rick: Right, leaves off at eleven.

Adding

Which sea creature can add up?
An octoplus.

Address

A lady walked in to the post office to buy stamps and as she was short-sighted the clerk offered to stick the stamps on for her. 'Wait a minute,' he said, 'you've written the address upside down.'
'I know,' said the little old lady, 'the letter is going to Australia.'

Admiral

What's higher than an admiral?
His hat.

Adult

When is a grown man like a child?
When he's a miner.

★

What's another name for an adult?
Someone who's stopped growing except around the waist.

Adults

Why are adults boring?
Because they're groan-ups.

Advertisement

Andy: Have you seen the new advertisement put up by old man Lang?
Zak: No, I haven't.
Andy: Everyone's calling it Old Lang's Sign.

★

Job advertisement:
Wanted: Young assistant to club manager.

Lady on the phone: I'd like to put an advertisement in your newspaper.
Telephone sales girl: In the Small Ads, madam?
Lady on the phone: Oh, no! I'm selling an elephant.

Aeroplane

Why is an aeroplane like a con man?
  Because neither has any visible means of support.

★

Two wrongs don't make a right.
But what did two rights make?
  The first aeroplane.

Affection

How does a boat show its affection?
  It hugs the shore.

Afford

What is the meaning of afford?
  It's the car most sales representatives drive.

After-Dinner Speech

The after-dinner speaker had been boring his audience for about an hour when one of the guests, fighting a losing battle against sleep, turned to his neighbour and said, 'Can't anything be done to shut him up?' To which the lady replied, 'I'd like to know if there is. I'm his wife, and I've been trying to shut him up for years.'

Aftermath

Teacher: Sam, can you tell me what aftermath means?
Sam: Yes, sir! The lesson that follows arithmetic.

Age

Where did Queen Victoria go in her 70th year?
  Into her 71st.

Paul: How old are your grandparents?
Saul: I don't know – but we've had them ever such a long time.

★

Mother: Billy, go next door and see how old Mrs Able is, please.
Silly Billy (later): Mrs Able is very cross with you – she says it's none of your business how old she is.

★

The teacher noticed Soppy Poppy was staring out of the window, not paying attention, and decided to catch her out.
'Poppy,' she said, 'if India has the world's biggest population and apples are thirty pence a pound, how old does that make me?'
'Thirty-two,' said Soppy Poppy straight away.
'How did you know that?' said the teacher, going red.
'Easy,' said Soppy Poppy. 'My brother is sixteen and he's only half-mad.'

★

What goes up and never comes down?
  Age.

★

How do you know when you're getting old?
  When the cake costs less than the candles.

★

What one thing is everybody in the world doing at exactly the same time?
  Growing older.

★

Visitor: And how old are you, Sam?
Sam: Nine.
Visitor: And what are you going to be?
Sam: Ten.

★

Rick: How old is your brother?
Nick: He's one.
Rick: Well! I've got a dog that's a year old and he can walk twice as well as your brother.
Nick: I should hope so – he's got twice as many legs!

Mr Able: How old is your wife?
Mr Cable: Approaching forty.
Mr Able: From which direction?

★

An eminent old man was being interviewed, and was asked if it was correct that he had just celebrated his ninety-ninth birthday.
'That's right,' said the old man. 'Ninety-nine years old, and I haven't an enemy in the world. They're all dead.'
'Well, sir,' said the interviewer, 'I hope very much to have the honour of interviewing you on your hundredth birthday.'
The old man looked at the young man closely, and said, 'I can't see why you shouldn't. You look fit and healthy to me!'

★

Mrs Able: How old are you?
Mrs Cable: Twenty-six. But I don't look it, do I?
Mrs Able: No, but you used to!

Agony
What is agony?
   A one-armed man hanging on to a window sill whose palm starts to itch.

Air Pollution
Bill: How can we lick this air pollution?
Ben: Well, we could go outside and stick our tongues out!

Alarm Clock
Bill: Why did you throw your alarm clock away?
Ben: Because it always went off when I was asleep.

★

Mother: Sam! Time to get up! It's 7.15.
Sam: Who's winning?

Foreman: Why were you late for work?
Silly Billy: Well, there are eight of us in the family and the alarm was set for seven.

Algebra
Who invented algebra?
   A clever X-pert.

Algy and the Bear
Did you hear the story about Algy and the Bear?
It's very short:
Algy met a bear.
The bear was bulgy.
The bulge was Algy.

Ali Baba
Interviewer: What's it really like, Ali Baba, flying on your magic carpet?
Ali Baba: Rugged.

Aliens
Two aliens landed in the remote countryside and went walking from the flying saucer along a narrow lane. The first thing they saw was a red pillar box.
'Take us to your leader,' said the first alien.
'Don't waste time talking to him. Can't you see he's only a child?' said the second alien.

Allergy
Jack: I went to the doctor and he says I'm allergic to horses.
Jill: Does that have a medical name?
Jack: Yes – bronchitis!

Allocate

Jack: What is allocate?
Jill: That's how I say hello to my friend Catherine.

Alphabet

Amy: I bet I can say the alphabet faster than you.
Zoe: Bet you can't.
Amy: The alphabet – beat you!

★

How many letters are there in the alphabet?
Eleven – T – H – E A – L – P – H – A – B – E – T.

★

What goes A, B, C, D, E, F, G, H, I, J, K, L, M, N, O, P, Q, R, S, T, U, V, W, X, Y, Z, Slurp?
Someone eating alphabet soup.

★

Why did the man ask for alphabet soup?
So that he could read while he was eating.

★

Tom: Why did Dick put his hands in the alphabet soup?
Harry: Because he was groping for words.

American Cow

Where does an American cow come from?
Moo York.

American Drawing

What do you call an American drawing?
A Yankee Doodle.

American Stoats

What happened when the American stoats got married?
They became the United Stoats (States) of America.

Ammonia

What's the difference between ammonia and pneumonia?
One comes in bottles and the other comes in chests.

★

1st court reporter: What happened to the man who threw a bottle of ammonia over the officer?
2nd court reporter: He was charged with a bleach of police.

Anaesthetist

What did the patient say to the anaesthetist?
'Because of you I am considerably put out.'

Analyse

Rick: Anna lies.
Nick: Analyse what?
Rick: Anna lies about everything.
Nick: Don't be silly, you can't analyse *about* everything.

Ancestors

Nick: My great-grandfather fought with Napoleon, my grandfather fought with the Americans and my father fought with the Australians.
Rick: How come your family could never get on with anybody?

★

Johnny: I've traced my ancestors right back to royalty.
Jenny: King Kong?

★

English boy: My grandfather was touched on the shoulder by Queen Victoria, and that made him a knight.
American boy: That's nothing! My grandfather was touched on the head with a tomahawk by an Apache and that made him an angel.

Anchor
What does every ship weigh, whatever its size?
Anchor.

Ancient History
Bill: I'm learning ancient history.
Ben: So am I! Let's go for a walk and talk about old times.

Anemones
A man went in to a florist's shop to buy his wife anemones for their first wedding anniversary because they were her favourite flowers. But it was late and the shop only had a variety of ferns left. The man bought several bunches of these rather than go home empty-handed and gave them to his wife rather sheepishly.

'Never mind, darling,' she said, 'with fronds like these who needs anemones?'

Angels
Why did the angel lose her job?
She had harp failure.

★

Amy: I think Jenny is a real angel.
Zoe: Yes, she does harp on things, doesn't she.

★

How do angels greet each other?
They say, Halo.

Anger
Andy: Why are you so angry?
Zak: Don't you know? It's all the rage now.

Angler
What's the difference between an angler and a dunce?
One baits his hooks while the other hates his books.

Animals
Which animal has the highest intelligence?
A giraffe.

★

Teacher: Mary, name six animals of the Arctic.
Mary: Three walruses and three polar bears.

★

Which animal has a chip on his shoulder?
A chipmunk.

★

A puppy called June was always picking fights with larger animals. One day she got into an argument with a lion. The next day was the first of July. Why?
Because that was the end of June.

★

What animal's eye should you always aim for?
A bull's eye.

★

Why are four-legged animals such poor dancers?
Because they have two left feet.

★

What animal hibernates standing on its head?
Yoga Bear.

Anniversary
Rick: Today is my twenty-fifth wedding anniversary.
Nick: Really!

Rick: Yes, I've been married twenty-five times.

Anonymous Letter
Rick: I got an anonymous letter today.
Nick: Oh, really — who was it from?

Ant
What is an ant dictator?
  A tyrant.

★

What is an ant?
  A hard-working insect that takes time off to go to all the picnics.

★

Which is the smallest ant in the world?
  An infant.

★

How many legs does an ant have?
  Two, same as an uncle.

★

What do you call a stupid ant?
  Antwerp.

★

What are ants called when they run away very fast to get married?
  Ant-elopers.

★

What do ants take when they're ill?
  Antibiotics.

★

Customer: I'd like some ant powder, please.
Chemist: Shall I wrap it for you?
Customer (sarcastically): No, I'll send the ants down here.

★

What happens to the ant when he stops running around all day?
  He gets stepped on at night.

★

What's the biggest ant in the world?
  A Gi-ant.

Antelope
Why did the ant elope?
  Nobody gnu.

Ant Hill
What do you get when you cross an ant hill with a window box?
  Ants in your plants.

Antifreeze
How do you make antifreeze?
  Hide her nightdress.

★

Why did the mean man buy five pints of antifreeze?
  To avoid having to buy a winter coat.

Antique Collector
Mr Able: I'm a well-known antique collector.
Mr Cable: That's right! I've seen your wife.

Apaches
How can you tell an Apache car?
  By its red engine.

Ape
Why did the ape put a hamburger on his head?
  Because he thought he was a griller.

Appearance

Did you hear about the school boy who was reprimanded for his careless appearance?

He hadn't appeared at school for half a term.

Appendicitis

Doctor: Have you ever had trouble with appendicitis?

Patient: Only when I tried to spell it.

Appendix

Amy: My doctor specializes in taking out appendixes.

Zoe: Makes money on the side, does he?

★

Bill: I've just had my appendix out.

Ben: Have a scar?

Bill: No, thanks, I don't smoke.

Appetite

Which country has a good appetite?

Hungary

The Appian Way

When should a hitchhiker take the Appian Way?

When he starts to Rome.

Apple

How do you make an apple puff?

Chase it round the garden

★

How does an apple a day keep the doctor away?

When you take careful aim.

★

What is red and goes putt, putt, putt?

An outboard apple.

★

Once upon a time there were five apples – which was the cowboy?

None – because they were all redskins.

★

What can a whole apple do that half an apple can't do?

It can look round.

★

How do you make an apple turnover?

Push it down hill.

★

What's worse than biting in to an apple and finding a worm?

Finding half a worm.

★

If an apple a day keeps the doctor away, what does an onion do?

Keeps everyone away.

Apricots

What are apricots,

Where monkeys sleep.

Arab

What do you call an Arab dairy farmer?

A milk sheik.

Arab Dance

How do Arab women dance?

Sheik to sheik.

Archaeologist

An archaeologist is someone whose career is in ruins.

Argument

Paul: I had an argument with my girl-friend last night. I wanted to go to football and she wanted to go to the cinema.
Saul: What film did you see?

★

Did you hear about the lady who is so argumentative that she won't eat anything that agrees with her?

Arithmetic

Maths teacher: If I slice two oranges and two apples into ten pieces each, what will that make?
Soppy Poppy: Fruit salad.

★

Teacher: Who can tell me what five and five make?
Smart Alec: Ten!
Teacher: Good.
Smart Alec: Good? That's perfect!

★

Teacher: If you add 2,506 and 6,205, multiply that by 6 and divide by 22, what would you get?
Soppy Poppy: The wrong answer.

★

In Old Testament times, how did people do arithmetic?
    They listened to the Lord when he told them to multiply.

★

Teacher: Johnny, if I gave you three hamsters, and the next day gave you three more, how many would you have?
Johnny: Seven, miss.
Teacher: Seven?
Johnny: Yes, I've got one already.

★

Trainee accountant: I've added these figures ten times.
Chartered accountant: Well done!
Trainee: And here are my ten answers.

Father: Maths was my best subject at school. I can't understand why you don't get better marks.
Sam: But, Dad, I did get 9 out of 10.
Father: Yes, but 60 per cent isn't good enough.

★

Rick: Why are you taking your arithmetic homework to the gym?
Nick: I have to reduce some fractions.

★

Teacher: Sam, if one and one makes two, and two and two makes four, what does four and four make?
Sam: Why do you always answer the easy ones and ask me the hard ones?

★

What are arithmetic bugs?
Mosquitoes — because they add to misery, subtract from pleasure, divide your attention, and multiply quickly.

★

Teacher: Sam, if you had a pound and you asked your mother for another pound, how many pounds would you have?
Sam: One.
Teacher: You don't know your arithmetic.
Sam: You don't know my mother.

Army

Recruiting sergeant: So you want to join the army. What's your name?
Recruit: Fish, sir.
Recruiting sergeant: OK, you can go in the Tank Regiment.

★

Paul: I was in the army for five years.
Saul: Commission?
Paul: No, straight salary.

★

Did you hear about the recruit who was asked what he was before he joined the army and said, 'Happy, Sergeant'?

Rick: Russia has a standing army of over two million soldiers.
Nick: I never knew Russia was so short of chairs.

★

Paul: How long were you in the Army?
Saul: Oh, about six feet two.

★

Who has the biggest boots in the British Army? The soldier with the biggest feet.

★

Paul: Did you hear about the accident at the Army base?
Saul: No, what happened?
Paul: A truck ran over a tin of corn and killed two kernels.

Art and Artists

An artist at an exhibition was approached by a foolish woman. 'Oh, how wonderful to meet you!' she said. 'I'd like to buy one of your paintings. Do they have a big sale?'

'Only when I draw big boats,' said the artist.

★

What is an artist's favourite subject for drawing?
   His wages.

★

Mrs Able: What a rare work of art!
Mrs Cable: I'd agree it's not well done.

★

Why are a lot of famous artists Dutch?
   Because they were born in Holland.

Did you hear about the artist who was so bad he couldn't even draw breath?

★

How can you tell when an artist is unhappy? When he draws a long face.

★

A snobbish lady was being shown around a London art gallery.
'I suppose you call *that* painting a work of art,' she said to the gallery owner.
'No,' he replied,' I call that a mirror.'

★

Rick: I met an artist the other day who is never short of money.
Nick: How's that? I thought all artists were poor.
Rick: Not this one — he's always drawing cheques.

Artificial Respiration

Paul: Have you ever had artificial respiration?
Saul: No, I prefer the real thing.

Arrows

I shot an arrow in the air.
It fell to earth
I know not where.
I lose all my arrows that way!

Asparagus

Customer: Have you got some asparagus?
Waiter: No, we don't serve sparrows and my name is *not* Gus.

Asthma

Jenny: I'm having some trouble with asthma, miss.
Teacher: I'm sorry to hear that Jenny. What's the matter?
Jenny: I can't spell it.

Astronaut

What's an astronaut's favourite meal?
  Launch.

★

Why did the boy become an astronaut?
  Because he was told he was no earthly good.

★

What do astronauts wear to keep warm?
  Apollo-neck jumpers.

★

Where do astronauts leave their spaceships?
  At parking meteors.

★

Why didn't the astronauts stay on the moon?
  Because it was a full moon and there was no room.

★

Why don't astronauts keep their jobs very long?
  Because as soon as they start they get fired.

★

Two astronauts were in a space ship circling high above the earth. One had to go on a space walk while the other stayed inside. When the space walker tried to get back inside the space ship, he discovered that the cabin door was locked, so he knocked. There was no answer. He knocked again, louder this time. There was still no answer. Finally he hammered at the door as hard as he could and heard a voice from inside the space ship saying, 'Who's there?'

Athlete

Which athlete keeps warmest in winter?
  The long jumper.

★

Did you hear about the world's worst athlete?
  He ran a bath and came in second.

★

Why did the athlete blame his losing the race on his socks?
  Because they were guaranteed not to run.

★

What's the best diet for athletes?
  Runner beans.

★

If an athlete gets athlete's foot, what does an astronaut get?
  Missile-toe.

At Home

Salesman seeing little girl in the garden: Hello, is your mother home?
Soppy Poppy: Yes, she is.
Salesman (having knocked and received no reply): I thought you said your mother was at home?
Soppy Poppy: Yes, she is. But I live next door.

Atlantic

What do you get if you cross the Atlantic with the Titanic?
  Half-way.

Atom

Teacher: What is an atom, Billy?
Silly Billy: Wasn't he the man who went around with Eve?

Attack

What is the definition of attack?
  A small nail.

Attention

Teacher: Please pay a little attention!
Silly Billy: I'm paying as little as I can.

Auctioneer

What knowledge do you need to be an auctioneer?
    Lots.

★

What is an auctioneer?
    A man who looks forbidding.

Audience

What's the difference between a disappointed audience and a sick cow?
    One boos madly and the other moos badly.

Auntie

Amy: I don't like my Auntie Adeline.
Zoe: Oh, are you anti-Auntie too?

Au Pair

A young Finnish girl arrived in England to work as an *au pair*. The family welcomed her and Mrs White sat down with her to explain what work she would be doing. 'In the morning, you should make the beds,'
    'Oh, Mrs White,' said the *au pair*, I not know how to make beds.'
    'Oh. Well, never mind. When the children come home from school you can have tea ready.'
    'Oh, Mrs White, I not know how to cook.'
    'Ah. Well, you can vacuum and dust the house.'
    'Oh, Mrs White, what is vacuum and dust?'
    'You don't know how to vacuum? Tell me,' said Mrs White, fast losing patience, 'what do you know?'
    'I know how to milk a reindeer.'

Australia

Bruce: In Australia, I used to chase kangaroos on horseback.
Benny: Well, I never. I didn't know kangaroos rode horses.

★

Sam: But I don't want to go to Australia, Mum.
Mother: Shut up and keep swimming.

What was the largest island in the world before Australia was discovered?
    Australia.

Author

Have you heard about the author who made a fortune because he was in the write business?

Autobiography

What is an autobiography?
    The life story of an automobile.

Autograph

What is an autograph?
    A chart which shows car sales.

Autumn

Why do soldiers like autumn so much?
    Because of all the leaves.

There was a young fellow named Hall
Who fell in the spring in the fall.
    'Twould have been a sad thing
    If he died in the spring,
But he didn't – he died in the fall.

Avoidance

What is avoidance?
    A dance for people who hate each other.

Axe

What did the tree say to the axe?
    I'm stumped.

What happened when an axe fell on a car?
    There was an axe-i-dent.

What is an axe?
    A chop-stick.

Babies

Proud father: My new baby is the image of me.
Visitor: Never mind, as long as it's healthy . . .

★

Paul: My mum's having a new baby.
Saul: What's wrong with the old one?

★

Mother: Would you rather have a baby brother or a baby sister?
Little boy: I'd much rather have a jelly baby.

★

Who is bigger – Mrs Bigger or Mrs Bigger's baby?
Mrs Bigger's baby, because he's a little Bigger.

★

Visitor: Do you like your new baby sister, Sam?
Sam: She's all right.
Visitor: Do you play with her?
Sam: No, and we can't even send her back because she's been here more than 28 days.

★

Mrs Able: Today I saw a baby who had put on five stone in weight in two weeks by drinking elephant's milk.
Mrs Cable: Whose baby was it?
Mrs Able: The elephant's!

★

Visitor: And is your baby sister all soft and pink?
Smart Alec: No, she's a horrible yeller!

★

A man rang the maternity home where his wife had been admitted to see how she was and whether she'd had their baby yet.
'Is this her first child?' asked the nurse.
'No, this is her husband,' he replied.

★

How do you get a baby astronaut to sleep?
You rock-et.

★

Polly: Is your new baby brother going to stay here?
Little Holly: I think so – he's taken all his clothes off.

★

Why are babies always gurgling with joy?
Because it's a nappy time.

★

Mother: Sam! How could you have dropped the baby!
Sam: The lady next door said he was a bouncing baby and I wanted to see for myself.

★

How do you get a paper baby?
Marry an old bag.

Baboons

The large group of baboons in the Safari Park were playing on the grass beside the entrance gate, watching a carful of tourists drive in. 'Isn't wicked,' said one baboon, 'to keep them locked up like that.'

Baby Birds

Did you hear about the baby chick who found an orange in his nest and said:
Look what marmalade!

★

What did the baby birds day to the miser?
　Cheap, cheap.

Baby Corn

What did Baby Corn say to Mother Corn?
　Where's Pop Corn?

Baby Duck

Why does a baby duck walk softly?
　Because it's a baby and can't walk, hardly.

Baby — Emerald

Why is a baby like an emerald?
　Because it's a dear little thing.

Baby Food

When a baby is learning to eat, shouldn't he have an L-plate?

Baby Goat

How should you treat a baby goat?
　Like a kid.

Baby Hippo

Visitor: What's the new baby hippo's name?
Hippopotamus keeper: I don't know, he won't tell me.

Baby Lion

Who do you think was sent to cover the story of the baby lion born in the zoo?
　A cub reporter.

Baby Monsters

What brings the monster's babies?
　The Frankenstork.

★

Why did the baby monster put his father in the freezer?
　Because he wanted frozen pop.

Baby Rabbit

As soon as she could talk, the baby rabbit started to ask her mother where she'd come from. But the mother rabbit was far too busy to tell her. The baby rabbit kept on asking until the mother rabbit couldn't stand it any more. 'All right,' she said, 'if you must know, 'you were pulled out of a magician's hat.'

Baby Sister

Johnny: Mum, is it true my baby sister came from Heaven?
Mother: Yes, that's right.
Johnny: Well, I don't blame God for chucking her out.

Baby-Sitter

Did you hear about the baby-sitter who put the TV to bed and watched the baby?

Baby Snake

How can you tell a baby snake?
　By its rattle.

Baby Whale

What's a baby whale called?
　A little squirt.

20

Bachelor

What is the definition of a bachelor?
  A man who never Mrs anyone.

★

Why is a bachelor such a smart man?
  Because he is never miss-taken.

Backseat Driver

Bill: You know all that talk about backseat driving? Well, I've been driving all my life and can safely say that I've never heard a word from the back seat.
Ben: What kind of car do you drive?
Bill: A hearse!

Back-Stroke

Jack: Why do you always do the back-stroke?
Jill: It's too soon after lunch to swim on a full stomach.

Bacon and Eggs

What's the best day to eat bacon and eggs?
  Fry-day.

Bacteria

One bacterium, floating through the system, came across another one who appeared to be very poorly.
'What's the matter?', he asked.
'Oh – keep away from me!', replied the other.
'I think I've caught penicillin.'

★

Science teacher: What are bacteria?
Silly Billy: The rear entrances of cafeterias.

Bad Driver

Paul: My sister's a really bad driver.
Saul: What makes you say that?
Paul: Every time she goes out in the car, Dad puts a glass panel in the floor so that she can see who she's run over.

Bad Joke

Why is a bad joke like an unsharpened pencil?
  Because it has no point.

Bad Luck

Bad luck is finding a four-leaf clover and being attacked by poison ivy as you bend down to pick it up.

★

When is it bad luck to have a black cat follow you?
  When you're a mouse.

Badminton

When is badminton mentioned in the Bible?
In the story of Joseph serving in Pharoah's court.

Bagpipes

Rick: I've borrowed my neighbour's bagpipes.
Nick: But you can't play them!
Rick: I know, but neither can he when I've got them.

Baked Apples

Soppy Poppy: Dad, do you like baked apples?
Father: Yes, why?
Soppy Poppy: The orchard's on fire.

Baked Beans

What do you call baked beans on toast?
  Skinheads on a raft.

Bakers

Why are bakers silly?
  Because they sell what they knead.

★

Why did the baker work so hard?
  To earn an honest crust.

★

Andy: Why did you leave your job at the bakery, Zak?
Zak: Oh, the work was too crummy.

★

Why does Ben work in the bakery?
  Because he kneads the dough.

★

Mr Able: There was trouble at the bakery last night!
Mr Cable: Yes, I heard – two stale buns tried to get fresh.

Baker's Dozen?

Customer: I ordered twelve rolls from you, and you delivered thirteen.
Baker: Ah, yes, madam, but one was only half-baked.

Baldness

Why do bald-headed men never use keys?
  Because they've lost their locks.

Ball

What does a ball do when it rolls to a halt?
  Looks round.

★

In what ball can you carry your shopping?
  A basketball.

Ballet

Why is ballet like fresh milk?
  Because it strengthens the calves.

Balloon

What did the balloon say to the pin?
  Hi, buster!

Ball Point Pen

Mother: Doctor, come quickly! The baby has swallowed a ball-point pen.

Doctor: I'll be right there. What are you doing in the meantime?
Mother: Using a pencil.

Banana

What do you do if you see a blue banana?
  Try to cheer it up.

★

What's yellow and writes?
  A ball-point banana.

★

What's yellow on the inside and green on the outside?
  A banana disguised as a cucumber.

★

Teacher: What is $Ba + Na_2$?
Silly Billy: Banana.

★

What is yellow and goes bzzzzzz?
  An electric banana.

★

Two men took a train ride to a big city, taking a bunch of bananas with them to eat on the journey. One man took a bite of his banana just as the train approached a tunnel.
'Have you tasted your banana yet?' he asked his friend, very frightened.
'No, I haven't,' replied the friend.
'Well, don't!' said the first man. 'I did, and went blind.'

★

What's yellow and always points to the north?
A magnetic banana.

★

Why did the man lose his job in a fruit packing firm?
He kept throwing the bent bananas away.

★

How did the Mother Banana spoil the Baby Banana?
She left him out in the sun too long.

★

Why did the banana go out with the prune?
Because he couldn't find a date.

★

Bill: Why isn't Jamaica growing bananas any longer?
Ben: Because they're long enough already.

★

Why are bananas never lonely?
Because they go around in bunches.

★

Did you hear about the unlucky man who bought some bananas?
They were empty.

★

Why don't bananas snore?
Because they don't want to wake up the rest of the bunch.

Banana Skin
Andy: Why are you eating a banana with the skin on?
Zak: Oh, it's all right. I know what's inside.

Banana Split
What's the easiest way to make a banana split?
Cut it in half.

Bandage
Amy: That dress fits you like a bandage.
Zoe: Yes, I bought it by accident.

Bandeau
What is a bandeau?
A stretch of water the French aren't allowed to swim in.

Bandstand
What's the easiest way to make a bandstand?
Take all the chairs away.

Bank Account
Bank manager: I'm sorry, sir, you can't open an account with this sort of money. They're wooden pieces!
Lumberjack: But I only want to open a shavings account.

Bank Balance
What's the best way to increase the size of your bank balance?
Look at it through a magnifying glass.

Banker
Paul: Our bank manager can't ride a bike any more.
Saul: Why not?
Paul: He lost his balance.

Why was the banker bored?
Because he lost interest in everything.

Bank Loan
A man went in to the bank and asked to see the man who arranged the loans.

'I'm sorry, sir,' said a cashier, 'the loan arranger is out to lunch.'
'Can I speak to Tonto, then?' asked the man.

Bank Notes
Silly Billy (in the bank): Who dropped a wad of notes with an elastic band round them?
Customers: I did!
Silly Billy: Well, here's the elastic band.

Bank Robbery
A bank had just been robbed and there were police and police cars everywhere.
'I just don't understand how the robbers got away,' said the Detecitve Inspector. 'We had all the exits covered.'
'Well, sir,' said a police constable, 'they must have gone out by the entrance.'

Bar
Why did the man cry out when he walked into the bar?
　　It was an iron bar.

★

A man walked into a pub and asked the landlord, 'Do you serve Americans?'
'Yes, of course, sir,' replied the landlord.
'Good. I'll have a gin and tonic, and two Americans for my lion here, please.'

Barbecue
What's a barbecue?
　　A row of men waiting to get their hair cut.

Barbed Wire
Why did the little boy who rode his bike over a barbed wire fence miss his music lesson?
　　Because he'd already done the sharps and flats.

Barber
What's a barber's favourite kind of holiday?
　　Cruising on a clipper.

Why does a barber never shave a man with a wooden leg?
　　Because he always uses a razor.

★

Is a barber's training long?
　　Not if he takes short cuts.

★

Barber: Your hair is getting grey, Sir.
Customer: I'm not surprised — hurry up, will you?

★

Customer: What do you charge for a shave?
Barber: 50p.
Customer: And what for a shave?
Barber: 40p.
Customer: All right, then — shave my head, please.

★

Barber: And how old are you, little man?
Sam: Eight.
Barber: And do you want a haircut?
Sam: Well, I certainly didn't come in for a shave!

★

Nick: My barber is a specialist in road map shaves.
Rick: How come?
Nick: When he's finished, your face is full of short cuts.

★

Barber: Were you wearing a red scarf when you came in?
Customer: No.
Barber: Oh dear! Then I must have cut your throat.

Bareback Riding
Why did the bareback performer ride his horse?
Because it got too heavy to carry.

Bargain

Bill: She's a real bargain.
Ben: How come?
Bill: Fifty per cent off.

Bark

Teacher: Who can tell me what the outside of a tree is called? Sam? Billy? Poppy? Anybody? . . . Bark, class, bark!
Class: Bow, wow, wow!

Barking Dog

How do you stop a dog barking in the back seat of the car?
Let him sit in the front seat.

Barometer

What does it mean when the barometer is falling?
Someone hasn't nailed it to the wall properly.

★

Businessman: I bought a barometer in Tokyo.
Unimpressed office boy: Who wants to know if it's raining in Japan?

Barrel

What do you call a man in a barrel in the Atlantic?
Bob!

Barrel of Beer

Why wasn't the brewer hurt when a barrel of beer fell on him?
Because it was full of light ale.

Barrel Organ

What's musical and holds gallons and gallons of beer?
A barrel organ.

Baseball Park

Why is a baseball park cool?
Because there's a fan in every seat.

Basketball

A father and son were watching a basketball match on television. The father was getting more and more angry as a player on the team he supported kept giving away fouls.
'What an idiot!' he shouted. 'What on earth is he doing playing in such an important game!
His son sat quietly for a while and then said, 'Daddy, maybe it's his ball.'

Bat

What did the baby mouse say when he saw a bat for the first time?
Mummy, I've just seen an angel.

Bath

Doctor: Your system needs freshening up a bit. I suggest you take a cold bath every morning.
Patient: Oh, but I do, doctor.
Doctor: You do?
Patient: Yes, every morning I take a nice cold bath and fill it with nice hot water!

★

Doctor: The best time to take a bath is before retiring.
Silly Billy: You mean I don't need another bath until I'm sixty-five?

★

Why did the bank robber take a bath?
So he could make a clean getaway.

Adam: How did Mummy know you hadn't had a bath?
Eve: I forgot to dirty the towel/wet the soap/flood the bathroom.

★

Nick: Can you tell me the way to Bath?
Rick: I use soap and water, personally.

★

Mother: Are you going to take a bath, Billy?
Silly Billy: No, Mum, I'm leaving it where it is.

★

My mother says I look just like an animal when I'm in the bath – a little bear.

Bathing Beauty
Paul: My girl's a real bathing beauty.
Saul: She must be worth wading for!

Bathroom
Jenny: Mum, does God use the bathroom?
Mother: No, what a funny question!
Jenny: Then why did Dad say this morning, 'Oh, God, are you still in there?'

Bathroom Scales
Amy: What are bathroom scales for?
Zoe: I don't know, but when you stand on them they make you cross!

Batman and Robin
Why couldn't Batman go fishing?
　　Because Robin had eaten all the worms.

★

What's Robin's favourite game?
　　Batmanton.

★

What do you call Batman and Robin if they're run over by a steamroller?
　　Flatman and Ribbon.

★

What made Batman sad in the autumn?
　　Robin flew south.

★

Why did Batman go to the pet shop?
　　To buy a robin.

★

Why does Batman go looking for worms?
　　To feed his Robin.

Battery
Silly Billy: Dad, did you manage to fix my robotic toy?
Father: No, Billy; it's not broken, the battery's flat.
Silly Billy: Well, what shape should it be?

Batting
A player received a telephone call just as he was going in to bat. 'He can't come to the phone now,' said the captain. 'He's batting.' 'Oh,' said the caller, 'in that case I'll hang on.'

Beach
Why should you never starve on a beach?
　　Because you can eat the sand-which-is-there.

★

What is the best day to go to the beach?
　　Sun-day.

Beans
What did the bean plant say to the farmer?
　　Stop picking on me.

★

Paul: I once lived on a tin of beans for a whole week.
Saul: Weren't you afraid of falling off?

Bear
Andy: If you were walking through the jungle and a bear was coming towards you, would

you keep on walking or run back to camp?
Zak: I'd run back to camp.
Andy: With a bear behind?

★

What's white, furry, and smells of peppermint?
   A polo bear.

★

Game hunter: Have you ever hunted bear?
Traveller: No, but I've been fishing in my
   shorts.

★

How can you tell where a bear lives?
   Look for his Den mark.

★

What have Rupert the Bear and Winnie the
Pooh got in common?
   Their middle names.

★

Why do bears have fur coats?
   Well, they'd look silly in plastic macs,
wouldn't they!

Beard

Bill: Why does your Dad keep shaving off his
   beard every time it looks nice?
Ben: Mum makes him do it – she's stuffing a
   cushion.

★

Mrs Able: A man came to see you this
   morning with a really bushy beard.
Mr Able: Naval?
Mrs Able: No, it was on his chin.

★

Why did the dishonest man grow a beard?
   So that no one could call him a bare-faced
liar.

Bear Tracks

Two hunters were in a forest and came across
some bear tracks.

'Right,' said one, 'you see where they go and
I'll look to see where they come from.'

Beating

What did the little boy say when his teacher
said, 'This is going to hurt me more than it will
you'?
   'Can I beat you, then, sir?'

Beautiful

The rain makes all things beautiful,
The grass and flowers too.
If rain makes all things beautiful
Why don't it rain on you?

★

Where is everyone beautiful?
   In the dark.

★

Amy: Johnny keeps telling me that he's going
   to marry the most beautiful girl in the world.
Zoe: Oh, what a shame! And you've been
   engaged for such a long time.!

★

Amy: People keep telling me I'm beautiful.
Zoe: What vivid imaginations some people
   have.

Beaver

What did the beaver say to the tree?
   It's been nice gnawing you.

Bed

What is the softest bed for a baby to sleep on?
   Cot-on-wool.

Mother: Jenny, you can't have any more chocolates tonight. It's not good for you to go to bed on a full stomach.
Jenny: Oh, Mum. I promise I'll lay on my side.

★

Soppy Poppy: I'd like to buy a bed, please.
Saleslady: Certainly, madam. Spring mattress?
Soppy Poppy: Oh, no! I want to be able to use it all year.

★

Three boys were sharing the same bed on holiday, but it was so crowded that one of them decided to sleep on the floor. After a while, one of his friends told him he might as well get in to bed again. 'There's lots of room now,' he said.

★

How can you shorten a bed?
Don't sleep long in it.

★

Mrs Able: I'd love you to stay the night, but I'm afraid you'll have to make your own bed.
Mrs Cable: Oh, that's all right, I don't mind at all.
Mrs Able: Right. Here's a hammer, a saw, and some nails. The wood's in the garage.

★

I have four legs, but only one foot. What am I?
A bed.

★

A neighbour bumped into Jenny playing outside her house after dark.
'Hello, Jenny,' said the neighbour. 'Isn't it time for little girls to be in bed?'
'How would I know?' asked Jenny. 'I haven't got any little girls.'

★

Why did the girl put her bed in the fireplace?
Because she wanted to sleep like a log.

Why do people go to bed?
Because the bed won't come to them.

★

Shall I tell you the joke about the bed?
No, because it hasn't been made up yet.

Bed Spread
Why did the bed spread?
Because it saw the pillow slip.

Bee
What's the difference between a sick horse and a dead bee?
One is a seedy beast and the other is a bee deceased.

★

What do you get if you cross a bee and chopped meat?
A humburger.

★

What's even better than a talking dog?
A spelling bee.

★

What do you call a bee with a low buzz?
A mumble bee.

★

Why do bees have sticky hair?
Because they have honey combs.

★

Why do bees hum?
Because they don't know the words.

★

Mother: Who's that at the door, Johnny?
Johnny: It's a man selling bees, Mum.
Mother: Tell him to buzz off — we don't want any.

★

Visitor: I've just been stung by one of your bees.

Apiarist: Show me which one and I'll punish it.

★

What do you call a bee born in May?
A maybe.

★

Rick: What did the bee say to the rose?
Nick: I don't know.
Rick: Hi, bud!
Nick: And then what did the rose say to the bee?
Rick: I don't know!
Nick: Buzz off!

Beer
How do frogs make beer?
Like everybody else – they start with some hops . . .

★

What happened to the lady who spilled some beer on her stove?
She got foam on the range.

Beetle
What do you call a beetle from outer space?
Bug Rogers.

Beetroot
Bill: I went out to dinner the other night and all there was to eat was a beetroot.
Ben: What did you say?
Bill: That beet's all.

Bell
Teacher: Poppy, don't you know the bell has gone?
Soppy Poppy: I haven't got it, miss!

★

What do you get when you cross a bell with a bee?
A humdinger.

★

What did the bell say when it fell in the water?
I'm wringing wet.

Benign
When is someone benign?
The year after they be-eight!

Bias
Mr Able: I've never known anyone to have such a biased outlook as my wife!
Mr Cable: Why do you say that?
Mr Able: When we go shopping, it's always bias this, bias that.

Bible
Examiner: I think you know very little, if anything at all, about the Bible. Can you quote any passage?
Student: 'Judas departed and went and hanged himself.'
Examiner: Well, that's a surprise. Can you quote another?
Student: 'Go thou and do likewise.'

★

Jill: Have you read the Bible?
Jack: No, I'm waiting for the film to come round.

Bicycle
Which is the cheapest bicycle you can buy?
A penny-farthing.

★

Do you hear about the bike that went round and round biting people?
It was known as the vicious cycle.

★

What did the silly boy take his bicycle to bed with him?

Because he didn't want to walk in his sleep.

★

Why couldn't the bicycle stand up for itself?

Because it was two-tyred.

★

A little boy out riding his bicycle knocked down an old lady. She was a bit shaken, but got up, dusted herself off, then turned to the little boy and said, 'Don't you know how to ride a bike?' 'Yes,' he answered, 'but I don't know how to ring the bell yet.'

★

Jack and Jill were riding a tandem up a hill, but making heavy weather of it. At the top, Jack said:

'I didn't think we'd make it!' Jill replied, 'Nor did I – what a good thing I kept the brakes on, or we'd have slid all the way back down!'

★

Andy: I went on a long bicycle ride yesterday.
Zak: Farcical?

★

What's the hardest thing about learning to ride a bicycle?

The road.

★

Johnny was racing around the garden on his new bicycle and called out to his mother to watch his tricks.

'Look, Mum! No hands! Look, Mum! No feet! Waaah! Look, Mum! No teeth!'

Big Game Hunter

What's a big game hunter?

Someone who's lost his way to the match.

Big Head

Sam: Mum! The kids all call me Big head at school.

Mother: Never mind that, go out to the orchard and pick up all the windfalls in your cap, like I asked you.

Billiard Ball

A poor pharmacist once concocted a solution that put hair on a billiard ball, but it didn't make him rich. Who would want to buy a billiard ball with hair on it?

Billy Goat – Pig

What do you get when you cross a pig with a billy goat?

A crashing bore.

Bills

Father: All our bills have gone up this quarter – gas, telephone, food. Why doesn't anything *ever* go down!

Son: Dad, I got my exam results today . . .

Bird-Cage

Teacher: Poppy, do you know why there is a hyphen in a bird-cage?

Soppy Poppy: So the bird has somewhere to perch.

Bird in Hand

A bird in the hand makes it difficult to tie your shoelaces.

Birds

What bird is always out of breath?

A puffin.

★

Little birdie flying high
Dropped a message from the sky.
'Oh,' said the farmer, wiping his eye.
'Isn't it a good thing cows don't fly!'

★

Which bird can lift the heaviest weight?
  The crane.

★

What kinds of birds are found in captivity?
  Jail-birds.

★

What do you give a sick bird?
  Tweetment.

★

A baby bird fell out of its nest and went bumping through the leaves and branches towards the ground.
'Are you all right?' called out another bird from its nest in the tree.
'So far,' said the baby bird.

★

What builds nests down pit shafts?
  Miner birds.

Why do birds fly south in winter?
  Because it's too far to walk.

Which birds are always unhappy?
  Bluebirds.

★

Amy: What do birds eat when the bird table's empty?
Zoe: Whatever they can find.
Amy: What if they can't find anything?
Zoe: Then they eat something else.

Bird Seed
Silly Billy: I'd like a packet of bird seed, please.

Pet shop owner: How many birds have you got?
Silly Billy: None, but I'd like to grow some.

Bird Show
Adam: My cat took the first prize in the local bird show.
Eve: How could your cat get a prize in a bird show!
Adam: He ate the prize canary.

Birds in the Nest
Why do birds in the nest always agree?
  Because they don't want to fall out.

Birth
When my grandfather was born, they passed out cigars. When my father was born, they passed out cigarettes. When I was born, they passed out.

Birthday
A kindly old lady came across a little boy sitting on the pavement crying his eyes out.
'What's the matter?' she asked.
'It's my birthday!' he hollered. 'And I had a bicycle and a new tracksuit and this afternoon there's to be a party with crisps and jelly and a birthday cake and a disco afterwards ...' and he had to stop talking because he was crying so hard.
'But that's lovely,' said the old lady. 'Why are you crying?'
'Because I'm lost!'

★

Rick: What did you get for your birthday?
Nick: Another year!

★

Paul: When is your birthday?
Saul: 17th January.
Paul: What year?
Saul: Every year!

★

Sam's girlfriend's birthday was the same day as his father's. He bought his girlfriend a bottle of perfume and his father a pistol. He wrapped the perfume and wrote a note to his girlfriend, saying, 'Use this all over yourself and think of me.' Unfortunately he put the note on his father's present.

★

Sam: Something happened to me yesterday that will never, ever, happen to me again.
Teacher: How can you be so sure?
Sam: I was 10 years old yesterday.

★

Visitor: How old were you on your last birthday, Sam?
Sam: Eight.
Visitor:: And how old will you be on your next birthday?
Sam: Ten.
Visitor: Oh, I don't think that's possible.
Sam: Oh, yes it is – I'm nine today.

★

Sam: Grandma, is it exciting being 99?
Grandma: It certainly is! If I wasn't 99 I'd be dead.

★

Rick: I forgot my brother's birthday last month.
Nick: What did he say?
Rick: Nothing, yet.

Birthday Party

Jack: Will you come to my party on Saturday, Jill?
Jill: Yes, please, Jack. What's the address?
Jack: 25 The High Street. Just push the bell with your elbow.
Jill: Why with my elbow?
Jack: Well, you won't be empty-handed, will you!

Birthday Present

Mr Able: I've been shopping for my wife's birthday present.
Mr Cable: What did you get her?

Mr Able: A bottle of expensive toilet water. It cost £20.
Mr Cable: £20! Why didn't you come to my house – you could have had some of ours for free!

★

Amy: Dad bought Mum a bone-china tea set for her birthday.
Zoe: How lovely!
Amy: Yes, but he only did it so as not to have to do the washing-up. Mum's too frightened he'll break it!

★

What's the greatest birthday present?
Hard to say – but a drum takes a lot of beating.

Birthplace

Amy: How come you were born in Venice?
Zoe: Because my mother wanted to be near me.

★

Amy: Where were you born?
Zoe: In hospital.
Amy: Oh, how awful! What was the matter with you?

Biscuit

What's the difference between a biscuit and a monster? You can dip a biscuit in your tea, but a monster is too big to fit in the cup.

★

Why did the biscuit cry?
   Because its mother had been a wafer so long.

★

Smart Alec: Have you got any broken biscuits?
Shopkeeper: Yes, I have.
Smart Alec: Well, you shouldn't be so clumsy!

★

Why do idiots like biscuits?
   Because they're crackers.

★

What did the biscuit say when it saw two friends knocked down?
   Crumbs!

★

What did the biscuits say to the almonds?
   You're nuts and we're crackers!

Biscuit Factory
Amy: Why did your brother give up his job in the biscuit factory?
Zoe: Because he went crackers.

Bishop
Mrs Able: I hear our Bishop is keeping very doubtful company.
Mrs Cable: Yes, Mrs Sable told me she saw him with a crook.

Bison
Teacher: What's the difference between a buffalo and a bison?
Cockney Charlie: You can't wash your hands in a bison, Miss.

Black
Paul: I bet I can make you say 'black'.
Saul: OK, try it.
Paul: What are the colours of the Union Jack?
Saul: Red, white and blue.

Paul: I told you I'd make you say 'black'.
Saul: I didn't say 'black'.

★

What is big, black and eats boulders?
   A big, black, boulder-eater.

Black and White
What's black and white and red all over?
   A sunburned zebra.

★

What is black and white and goes round and round?
   A zebra caught in a revolving door.

★

What is black and white and goes about on eight wheels?
   A nun on roller skates.

Blackbird
What do you get when you cross a blackbird with a mad dog?
   A raven maniac!

Blackboard
What's black when clean and white when dirty?
   A blackboard.

Black Cat
Jenny: Mum, there's a black cat in the kitchen.
Mother: That's all right, Jenny. Black cats are lucky.
Jenny: Not this one – he's just eaten our lunch.

Black Eye
Mother: Just wait until I find out who gave you that black eye!
Sam: No one gave it to me, Mum. I had to fight for it!

Blackmail

Rick: What's blackmail?
Nick: A letter the postman dropped in the mud.

Black Prince

Who was the Black Prince?
   The son of Old King Coal.

Black, Red and Grey

What is black when you get it, red when you use it and grey when you've finished with it?
   Coal.

Black, White and Noisy

What's black and white and noisy?
   A zebra playing the drums.

Blancmange

Why did the blancmange wobble?
   Because it saw the milk shake.

Blarney Stone

Bill: I find it really difficult to believe all that I hear about the Blarney Stone.
Ben: Why's that?
Bill: Well, there *are* a lot of sham rocks in Ireland.

Blind Man

What is the difference between a blind man and a sailor in prison?
   One can't see to go, the other can't go to sea.

Blinds

Mrs Able: Are your blinds drawn?
Mrs Cable: No, they're real.

★

The lady of the house was having a shower when she heard the front doorbell ring.
'Who is it?' she shouted.

'Blind man,' came the reply.
'I'll be right there,' said the lady, and got out of the bath and went downstairs without stopping to put on any clothes.
She opened the door to a very startled man who said, 'Where do you want the Venetian blinds fitted?'

Blockhead

Adam: Everyone in my block asks for my advice, and follows it.
Eve: I believe you. You're a natural-born blockhead.

Blood and Water

Paul: They say blood is thicker than water.
Saul: So what? So's toothpaste.

Blood Cells

Did you hear about the two blood cells who loved in vein?

Blood Donor

Two men were having a rest and a cup of tea after giving blood. One was a Sioux Indian, the other a local man. The local stared at the Indian for a while and then plucked up the courage to ask him, 'Is it true you're a full-blooded Indian?'
'I was,' came the reply, 'but now I'm a pint short.'

Bloodhound

Andy: My dog is a terrible bloodhound.
Zak: Why?
Andy: I cut my finger the other day and he fainted.

Blood Vessels

Biology teacher: There are 60,000 miles of blood vessels in the body. . . .
Silly Billy: No wonder I have tired blood.

Blotting Paper

Andy: Have you ever studied blotting paper?
Zak: No, why?
Andy: You should – you'd find it very absorbing.

Blue-Blood

What are blue-blooded, live in a palace, and go 'woof'?
  The Queen's corgis.

Blushing

Why did the windowpane blush?
  Because it saw the weather-strip.

Boasting

A Texan visiting London was seeing the sights from the top of an open bus. Each time the guide pointed out an historic building, the Texan would say, 'The Tower of London, eh? Why, back home we could put up a building like that in two weeks.'
The guide was becoming very annoyed so when they passed St Paul's Cathedral the guide remained silent.
'Say, what's that building?' asked the Texan.
'I don't know, sir,' said the guide. 'It wasn't there this morning.'

★

Mrs Able: My next door neighbour is so old, she knew Madame Butterfly when she was still a cocoon.
Mrs Cable: That's nothing! There's a woman in my street who's so old she knew Eve when she was still a rib.

★

1st boy (boasting): My Dad dug the Panama Canal.

2nd boy: That's nothing. *My* Dad killed the Dead Sea.

Boats

Boat attendant: Come in number 9 – your time's up.
Assistant: We've only got eight boats.
Boat attendant: Oh, dear, number 6 must be in trouble then.

★

When is a boat like a fall of snow?
  When it is adrift.

Bobby and J.R.

How did Bobby really escape from JR?
  He swam back to Atlantis.

Body Building

A body builder was boasting about the weight he could lift.
'That's nothing,' said a scrawny on-looker, 'I know a woman who can lift over a thousand pounds.'
'Never!' said the amazed body builder.
'Oh yes, I do,' said the little man. 'The cashier at my bank!'

★

Bill: I bought a best-selling book on body building and I've been doing the exercises every day for a month.
Ben: Is it having any effect?
Bill: I should say so – now I can lift the book above my head.

Body Snatchers

Jack: Have you heard the story about the body snatchers?
Jill: No, tell me!
Jack: No, you might get carried away.

Boiled Egg

I've boiled this egg for 15 minutes, and it still isn't soft.

Boiling Over

Angry Mother:: Poppy! I thought I asked you to watch the milk pan and see when it boiled over?

Soppy Poppy: But, Mum, I did. It boiled over at 8.30!

Boil-Wash

Customer: Is it all right to boil-wash this cardigan?

Shop assistant: Yes, as long as you boil it in warm water.

Bone

Rick: I just swallowed a bone.
Nick: Are you choking?
Rick: No! I'm serious!

Bongo Drums

Interviewer: What are those little bongos hanging from your ears?

Punk Rock star: Oh, those? They're just my ear-drums.

Booby Prize

The booby prize at a nudist camp competition was a clothes brush.

Book-Keepers

What sort of people make the best book-keepers?

The people who borrow your books and never return them.

Books

What did one arithmetic book say to the other? I've got a big problem.

★

Amy: My father always gives me a book for my birthday.

Zoe: What a wonderful library you must have!

Book Titles

How to Feed Elephants by P. Nutts

Aches and Pains by Arthur Ritis

The Spicy Sausage by Della Katessen

The Flower Garden by Polly Anthus

The Punished Schoolboy by Major Bumsaw

The Long Walk Home by Miss D. Buss

How I Crossed the Desert by Rhoda Camul

Round the Mountain by Sheelagh B. Cummin

Is this Love? by Midas Wellbee

Dancing at the Party by Hans Neesanboompsadaisy

Who Saw Him Go? by Wendy Leeve

All You Need to Know about Explosives by Dinah Mite

Army Jokes by Major Laugh

The Ugly Hag by Ida Face

The Post Script by Adeline Extra

Grow Your Own Vegetables by Rosa Carrotts

Never Give Up! by Percy Vere

The Greatest Party by Maud D. Merrier

The Joys of Horse-riding by Jim Karna

How to Diet Successfully by M. T. Cupboard

Outsize Clothes-buying by Ellie Fant

How to Make an Igloo by S. K. Mow

Neck Exercises by G. Rarff

Peek-a-Boo! by I. C. Hugh

My Years in a Lunatic Asylum by I. M. Nutty

Falling from a Window by Eileen Dowt

Monster-making as a Hobby by Frank N. Stine

Why You Need Insurance by Justin Case

The Art of Button-collecting by Zipporah Broaken

What's Up, Doc? by Howie Dewin

The Joys of Hitch-hiking by Marsha Long

Parachute Jumping by Hugo Furst

How I Won the Pools by Jack Potts

Silence is Golden by Xavier Brethe

The Greatest Detective Stories Ever Told by Watts E. Dunn

The Steel Band by Lydia Dustbin

At the South Pole by Anne Tarctic

Food on the Table by E. Tittup

One Hundred Metres to the Bus Stop, by Willy Makit, illustrated by Betty Wont

Solving the Mystery by Ivor Clew

Strong Winds by Gail Force

Nothing's Ever Right by Mona Lott

The Untamed Tiger by Claudia Armoff

I'm Absolutely Certain by R. U. Sure

End of the Week by Gladys Friday

My Favourite Sweets by Annie Seedball

Improve Your Target Shooting by Mr Completely

Noisy Nights by Constance Norah

The New Drum by Major Headache

The Embarrassing Moment by Lucy Lastic

I've Been Bitten! by A. Flea

The Lost Bet by Henrietta Hatt

The Insomniac by Eliza Wake

The Escaping Herd by Gay Topen

Horror Stories by R. U. Scared

Hit on the Head by I. C. Stars

The World of Vegetables by Artie Choak

The Millionaire by Ivor Fortune

Looking Forward by Felix Ited

Using an Electric Drill by Andy Gadget

The Economic Breakfast by Roland Marge

The Naughty Schoolboy by Enid Spanking

How to Get There by Ridya Bike

School Meals by R. E. Volting

All Aboard! by Abel Seamann

The Barber of Seville by Aaron Floor

Apologising Made Simple by Thayer Thorry

Bookworm
What did the bookworm say to the librarian?
Can I burrow this book?

Boots
Mother: Billy, you've got your boots on the wrong feet.

37

Silly Billy: No, Mum, these are the only feet I've got.

★

Silly Billy (crying his eyes out): Please, Miss, I can't find my boots in the cloakroom – and I've searched everywhere!
Teacher: Are you sure this pair isn't yours, Billy? They're the only pair left.
Silly Billy: Quite sure, Miss – mine had snow on them.

Bores

Amy: I hear you've been going around telling everyone I'm a bore!
Zoe: Oh, I'm sorry, I didn't know it was a secret.

★

What's the difference between a boring man and a bad book?
  You can shut up the book.

Borrowing and Lending

Andy: But why won't you lend me a dollar?
Zak: Because I don't believe in passing the buck.

★

Tom: Dick, you always remind me of Harry.
Dick: I'm not a bit like Harry!
Tom: Oh yes, you are. You both owe me £5.

Boxers

Boxers sometimes give each other a paunch on the nose.

★

What is a boxer's favourite read?
  Scrap books.

Boxing

Rick: My brother's a boxer.
Nick: What's his fighting name?
Rick: Rembrandt – because he's always on the canvas.

Paul: My uncle was a boxer.
Saul: Heavyweight?
Paul: No, featherweight. He used to tickle his opponents to death.

★

Manager: Keep on swinging – the draught might give him a cold.

Boy

Amy: That boy's annoying me.
Zoe: But he's not even looking at you.
Amy: I know. That's what's annoying me.

★

What happened to the boy who said he was listening to the match?
  He burnt his ear.

Boyfriend

Amy: What's your new boyfriend like?
Zoe: Mean, low-down, dirty, . . . and they're just his good points.

Boy Next Door

Amy: When I grow up, I've got to marry the boy next door.
Zoe: Why?
Amy: Because I'm not allowed to cross the road.

Boy Scout

Why is a boy scout like a TV dinner?
  Because they're both prepared.

★

38

Why was the boy scout dizzy?
Because he'd spent all day doing good turns.

★

What's a boy scout's favourite good deed?
Letting someone do a good deed to him.

★

A troop of boy scouts was hiking through the woods when one stopped and sighed.
'What's the matter?' said the leader.
'Nothing, really,' replied the boy scout. 'But I do wish we had brought a book on etiquette along with us.'
'What on earth for?' asked the leader.
'Because I think we took the wrong fork.'

Braces
Why did the fireman wear spotted pink braces?
To hold his trousers up.

★

Why did the fireman have red braces?
Because he was a sloppy spaghetti eater.

Brain
Andy: When I die I'm going to leave my brain for science.
Zak: Well, every little helps.

★

Paul: How long can someone live without a brain?
Saul: I don't know exactly. How old are you?

Brain Transplant
What happened when the idiot had a brain transplant?
The brain rejected him.

Brass
What's the brass section of a French orchestra called?
Le Toot Ensemble.

Bread
Andy: Have you heard the story about the loaf of bread?
Zak: No.
Andy: Oh, crumbs.

★

Mr Able: Why can't you make bread like my mother?
Mrs Able: I would if you could make dough like your father!

★

What looks just like half a loaf of bread?
Its other half.

Breakfast
What two things should you never eat before breakfast?
Lunch and supper.

★

Why is breakfast in bed so easy?
It's just a few rolls and a turnover.

Breakage
Silly Billy: Mum, remember that special plate you were always so worried I would break?
Mother: Yes – why?
Silly Billy: Well, your worries are over.

Break-In
Why is it easy to break in to an old man's house?
Because his gait is broken, and his locks are few.

Breath
What's lighter than a feather but much harder to hold?
Your breath.

Breathing

Patient: I'm having trouble breathing.
Doctor: Well, I think I can give you something to stop that.

Brick

Why is a brick like an egg?
    Because they both have to be laid.

★

Why did the brick cry?
    Because his mother was up the wall and his father was round the bend.

Bricklayer

What happened to the bricklayer who fell into the cement mixer?
    He became a very hard man.

★

A man was walking by a building-site when a brick fell and hit him on the head, ruining his new hat.
'Hey, you up there!' he shouted to the men on the scaffold.
'One of those bricks hit me!'
'You're lucky!' one man shouted back. 'Look what happened to the ones that didn't.'

Bride and Groom

Here comes the bride,
Short, fat and wide.
See how she wobbles
From side to side.

Here comes the groom,
All full of gloom.
He's as thin as a broom
Going to meet his doom.

Bridge

What's the shortest bridge in the world?
    The bridge of your nose.

Broken Arm

Jack: Dad's off work because Mum broke an arm.
Jill: Why can't your Dad work if your Mum broke an arm?
Jack: It was his arm she broke.

Broken Bones

When are broken bones useful?
    When they start to knit.

Broken Leg

Critic: Why have you called your new play *The Broken Leg*?
Playwright: Because it needs a strong cast.

★

If you broke your leg in two places, what would you do?
    Stay away from those two places.

★

A little old lady who broke her leg had to have a plaster cast on for several months, but at last the time came for the doctor to take it off.
'Can I go up the stairs again?' she asked excitedly.
'Yes, of course,' said the doctor.
'Oh good!' said the little old lady. 'I've had such trouble shinning up and down the drainpipe.'

★

Adam: How did you manage to break your leg?
Eve: See those steps by the fishpond?
Adam: Yes.
Eve: Well, I didn't.

Broken Neck

Hospital visitor: But how did you break your neck?
Patient: I just followed my doctor's prescription.
Hospital visitor: How could you break your neck doing that?

Patient: It blew down the stairs — and I followed it.

Broken Window
Sam: Jenny broke a window.
Mother: How did that happen?
Sam: I threw a brick at her — and she ducked.

Broom
How does a broom make itself understood?
  By sweeping gestures.

★

Why does a witch ride on a broom?
  Because a vacuum cleaner is too heavy.

★

What did one broom say to the other broom?
  Have you heard the latest bit of dirt?

Brothers
Paul: Why is your brother so small?
Saul: He's my half-brother.

★

When a girl slips on the ice, why can't her brother help her up?
  Because he can't be a brother and assist her (a sister) too.

★

'What do you mean you only have one brother?' demanded the judge. 'Your sister has testified under oath that she has two.'

★

Wouldn't it be fun if Charles Toomey had a brother called Socket?

Brown, Brown, Brown and Brown
Caller: Good morning, Brown, Brown, Brown and Brown?
Voice on phone: Yes, madam.
Caller: May I speak to Mr Brown, please?
Voice on phone: I'm so sorry, Mr Brown is away sick today.
Caller: Oh, then may I speak to Mr Brown, please?
Voice on phone: Mr Brown is on holiday.
Caller: It's very important, may I speak to Mr Brown?
Voice on phone: Mr Brown is away from the office on business.
Caller: Oh, no! Then I'll have to speak to Mr Brown, it's a matter of life or death!
Voice on phone: Mr Brown speaking.

★

What's brown and can see just as well from either end?
  A walrus with his eyes shut.

Bruises
Paul: How did you get all those bruises?
Saul: I started to go through a revolving door, and then I changed my mind.

Bubble
What's very light, but you still can't lift it?
  A bubble.

Budgie
What do you get if you mow over a budgie?
  Shredded tweet.

Buffalo

What did the buffalo say to his son when he went on holiday?
  Bison!

Buffalo Bill

What will the 200th anniversary of Buffalo Bill's birthday be called?
  The Bison-tennial.

Bug

What is black, has six legs, wears a disguise and listens to people?
  A telephone bug.

Building Site

Nick: How many people work on this building site?
Rick: Only about half of them.

★

The foreman on a building site was always hurrying his workmen to do their jobs more quickly. One man couldn't stand the pace any more and said to the foreman, 'Let's slow down a bit, Rome wasn't built in a day, you know!' 'Ah, well,' said the foreman, 'I wasn't foreman on that job!'

★

A foreman was walking around a building site one morning, keeping an eye on the work in progress. He came across one man who appeared to be doing only half the work of the others, so he asked him, 'Why are you only carrying one plank when all the other men are carrying two?'
'Well,' replied the workman, 'they're just too lazy to make a double journey like I do.'

Bulbs

What sort of bulbs should you never water?
  Light bulbs.

Bull

What did the bull say after he visited the china shop?
  I've had a smashing time.

★

Paul: I paid £50 for that dog – part alsatian and part bull.
Saul: Which part's the bull?
Paul: The part about the £50.

★

What did the bull say to the cow?
  When I fall in love, it will be for heifer.

Bulldogs

Why do bulldogs have flat faces?
  From chasing parked cars.

Bullfight

A tourist was watching his first bullfight in Spain.
After a while he suddenly burst out, 'Hold the red flag still or he'll never run into it!'

★

Interviewer (to famous matador): Will you confirm for the listeners the old story that the bull is incensed by your red cape?
Matador: Well, really it's the cows. The bull is incensed because he doesn't like being mistaken for a cow.

★

Paul: Bullfighting is the most popular pastime in Spain.
Saul: Bullfighting? Isn't that revolting?
Paul: No, revolting *used* to be their favourite pastime.

Bun

Why did the lady have her hair in a bun?
    Because she had her nose in a cheeseburger.

Burglar

What did the burglar say to the watchmaker as he tied him up?
    Sorry to take so much of your valuable time.

★

Judge: Why did you steal that bird?
Prisoner: For a lark, sir.

★

Mrs Able: We were burgled last week and they took everything except the soap and towels.
Mrs Cable: Why, the dirty crooks!

★

Judge: You claim you robbed the grocery store because you were starving. So why didn't you take the food instead of the cash out of the till?
Burglar: Your Honour! I'm a proud man, sir, and I make it a rule to pay for *everything* I eat.

★

Lady of the manor: I think I hear burglars, dear. Are you awake?
Lord of the manor: No.

★

Judge: Tell me your occupation.
Prisoner: I'm a locksmith, Your Honour.
Judge: Then what were you doing in a jewellery shop in the middle of the night when the police saw you?
Prisoner: Making a bolt for the door!

What did the burglar give his wife for her birthday?
    A stole.

Burglary

Reporter: My editor sent me to do the burglary.
Policeman: You're too late – it's already been done.

Burial

Did you hear about the undertaker who buried someone in the wrong place and was sacked for the grave mistake?

★

Paul: Why do you want to be buried at sea?
Saul: Because my wife says she wants to dance on my grave.

★

Man: I want you to bury my wife.
Undertaker: But I buried your wife last year.
Man: Yes, but I remarried.
Undertaker: Oh, congratulations, sir.

★

Mrs Able: I was so sorry to hear you buried your mother last week.
Mrs Cable: Well, we had to, you know, she was dead.

Bus

As the bus came to the stop, the man at the front of the queue took out his *eye*, threw it up in the air and caught it before getting on the bus. An amazed conductor said, 'What on earth did you do that for?'
'I wanted to know if there was room on top,' replied the man.

★

Paul: When you go for a bus ride, do you like sitting upstairs or downstairs?
Saul: I prefer to ride on top, but it's very hard getting the horse up the stairs.

A man trying to get on an overcrowded bus was pushed off by the people inside. 'There's no room,' they said. 'It's full up!'

'But you must let me on!' shouted the man.

'Why, what's so special about you?' they asked.

I'm the driver,' replied the man.

★

Why did the bus stop?

Because it saw the zebra crossing.

★

What do you call a bloke with a bus on his head?

Dead.

★

Passenger: Does this bus go to London?

Conductor: No.

Passenger: But it says London on the front.

Conductor: There's an advertisement for baked beans on the side, but we don't sell them!

★

Sam left work after a tiring day.

'Take the bus home,' suggested a friend.

'My mother would only make me take it back,' Sam said.

★

What's big, red, and lies upside-down at the side of the road?

A dead bus.

Bill: Did you say that you fell over fifty feet but didn't hurt yourself?

Ben: Yes – I was trying to get to the back of the bus.

★

Fat passenger getting off bus: Conductor, this bus was very slow!

Conductor: Oh, I expect we'll pick up speed now you're getting off!

★

Rick: Have you heard that all the buses and trains are stopping today?

Nick: No. Is there a strike?

Rick: No, they're stopping to let the passengers off.

★

Rick: What have I got in my hands?

Nick: A double decker bus!

Rick: You looked!

★

Paul: Do buses and trains run on time?

Saul: Usually, yes.

Paul: No, they don't. Buses run on wheels and trains run on the tracks.

★

Passenger: Does this bus stop at the river?

Conductor: If it doesn't there'll be a very big splash.

★

Passenger: Conductor, do you stop at the Savoy Hotel?

Conductor: I should say not, on my salary!

★

'Is everyone in the bus?' asked the driver before he closed the door.

'No,' called a lady, 'wait until I get my clothes on.'

All the passengers in the bus turned towards the door to look at the woman. She got on with a bag full of laundry.

Bus Driver

What is the difference between a bus driver and a cold?

One knows the stops, the other stops the nose.

Business

What did the ruthless businessman tell his sales team?

If at first you don't succeed – you're fired!

★

On the first day his son joined the family firm, the founder took him on to the roof of the factory building and said, 'I am going to give you your very first lesson in business. Stand on the edge of the roof.' Reluctantly, the boy went to stand on the edge of the roof.

'Now,' said his father, 'when I say, "Jump," I want you to jump off the roof.'

'But, Dad,' said the boy, 'there's a huge drop!'

'Do you want to succeed in business?'

'Yes, Dad.'

'And you trust me, don't you?'

'Yes, Dad.'

'So do as I say and jump.'

The boy jumped. He crashed to the ground and lay there, winded and bruised. His father went racing down the stairs and ran up to him. 'That was your first lesson in business, son. Never trust anyone.'

★

There was once a high-powered businessman who insisted on taking his three secretaries everywhere with him – a tall one for writing longhand, a short one for taking down shorthand, and a very small one for adding footnotes.

Bus Journey

Bus passenger: I'd like a ticket to New York, please.

Ticket seller: By Buffalo?

Bus passenger: Of course not, I'm in the bus queue, aren't I?

Butcher

Butcher: We had some lovely pork in today.

His wife: Don't start talking chop!

★

Customer: I'd like a nice piece of bacon. And make it lean.

Butcher: Certainly madam, which way?

★

Mrs Able: How much are your chickens?

Butcher: A pound a pound.

Mrs Able: Did you raise them yourself?

Butcher: That's right. This morning they were 80p a pound.

Butterfly

What's green, hairy, and turns into a heavyweight butterfly?

A caterpillar tractor.

★

What is pretty, has teeth and flies?

A killer butterfly.

★

What is very beautiful, has wings, rests on flowers and is highly dangerous?

A man-eating butterfly.

Button

What would you do if you got a button wedged in your nose?

Breathe through the button's four little holes.

Buttress

What is a buttress?

A female goat.

By-Pass

What do the Welsh call a by-pass?

A Dai-version.

Cabbages

What do you call a rude cabbage?
   A fresh vegetable.

★

What's green and goes, 'Boing, boing, boing'?
   Spring cabbage.

★

What do you call two rows of cabbages?
   A dual cabbageway.

Cad

What do you call a small cad?
   A caddy.

Caesar

Amy: When did Caesar reign?
Zoe: I didn't know he rained.
Amy: Of course. 'Didn't they hail him?

Caffeine

Did you hear about the parents who called their baby 'Caffeine' because she kept them awake all night?

Cake

What kind of cake would most children not mind going without?
   A cake of soap.

★

Paul: Have you heard the joke about the heavyweight cake?
Saul: No, tell me.
Paul: Well, it'll take some swallowing.

★

Mr Able: This cake tastes funny.
Mrs Able: Oh dear. I followed the recipe exactly! It said, separate two eggs, so I put one on the kitchen table and the other on top of the washing machine.

★

Jill: Do you like my pound cake?
Jack: Well, perhaps you over-pounded it a little.

★

Jenny: Why are you mopping up your tea with your cake?
Johnny: Well, it's sponge cake, isn't it?

Mr Able stood up on the occasion of his Golden Wedding anniversary to make a short speech.

'The beautiful cake which we are about to cut to celebrate our anniversary was made by my dear wife. Each year on our anniversary she has made a cake, and I like to think of them as milestones of our journey through life together.'

★

Mr Able: How did you make these cakes?
Mrs Able: I cut out the recipe from this magazine.
Mr Able: Are you sure you read the right page? The other side tells you how to make a rock garden.

★

Mother: What would you like to eat?
Jenny: Cake.
Mother: Cake what?
Jenny: Cake first.

★

Wife to minister in restaurant: Don't be put off. If you want to order angel cake, order it!

★

Which cake wanted to rule the world?
    Attila the Bun.

★

What do elves have for tea?
    Fairy cakes.

★

Bill: I can't decide whether to ask Kate or Edith to marry me.
Ben: Well, you can't have your Kate and Edith too!

★

How can you make cakes light?
    Use paraffin.

★

What jumps from cake to cake and tastes like almonds?
    Tarzipan.

Eve: Try one of my freshly-baked cakes.
Adam (tasting one): They're awful!
Eve: You have no taste. The recipe says they're delicious.

Calculator
Rick: What did the calculator say to its owner?
Nick: I don't know.
Rick: You can count on me.

Calendar
Why did the little boy put a calendar in his piggy bank?
    Because he wanted to save time.

Calendar Girl
What did the girl calendar say to her friend?
    I have more dates than you do.

Caller
Mrs Able: A man called to see you earlier.
Mr Able: Did he have a bill?
Mrs Able: No, just an ordinary nose.

Camel
What do you call a camel that's got three humps?
    Humphrey.

★

Who rides a camel and carries a lamp?
    Florence of Arabia.

★

What is a camel?
    An animal designed by committee.

Camelot
For what was Camelot famous?
Its knight-life.

★

What was Camelot famous as?
    A parking space for camels.

Cameras

Judge: What is this prisoner charged with?
Lawyer: He's a camera enthusiast, m'lud.
Judge: But taking photographs isn't a criminal offence!
Lawyer: He doesn't take photographs, m'lud, just cameras.

Campers

What is the definition of intense?
    It's where campers sleep.

Canary

Bill: My canary drank some of Dad's lighter fuel yesterday.
Ben: What happened?
Bill: It zoomed out of the room, upstairs, flew around my bedroom, out of the window, back through the front door and straight into a kitchen cupboard.
Ben: Was he dead?
Bill: No, just run out of petrol.

★

Adam: I've lost my canary! What shall I do?
Eve: Get in touch with the Flying Squad.

Candidate

What's the difference between a candidate and an elected politician?
    You can eat a candied date.

Candle

What did one candle say to the other candle?
    Are you going out tonight?

★

What did one candle say to the other?
    You're getting on my wick.

★

What made the baby candle feel warm all over?
    Glowing pains.

★

Do you know that workers in a candle factory are paid by the wick?

★

Why is a burning candle like thirst?
    Because a drop of water puts and end to both of them.

★

Paul: How long does a candle take to burn down?
Saul: About one wick.

★

Candles make light meals.

★

Rick: Which burn longer – the candles on a boy's birthday cake or the candles on a girl's birthday cake?
Nick: Neither! Candles burn shorter, not longer!

★

Mrs Able: Do you know that the price of candles has doubled?
Mrs Cable: That's candleous!

Cannibal

A cannibal bold of Penzance
Ate an uncle and two of his aunts,
A cow and her calf,
An ox and a half –
And now he can't button his pants.

★

The cannibal was just about to cook his latest captive for the chief's lunch when he decided to ask him what work he did.
'I'm an assistant editor,' replied the man.
'Oh,' said the cannibal, 'soon you'll be an editor in chief.'

★

How could you help a starving cannibal?
    Give him a hand.

★

Did you hear about the cannibal who liked to stop where they serve lorry drivers?

★

What is a cannibal?
A man who goes into a restaurant and orders the waiter.

★

What was the cannibal who ate his mother's sister?
An aunt-eater.

★

Why did the cannibal get thrown out of school?
Because he kept buttering up the teacher.

★

1st cannibal: I don't know what to make of my husband nowadays.
2nd cannibal: What about hotpot?

★

What is a cannibal?
Someone who is fed up with people.

★

Did you hear about the cannibal who went for a luxury cruise?
At dinner on the first night he refused the menu and asked to see the passenger list.

★

Do you like beans?
Yes, I do!
What sort do you like best?
Human bein's.

What did the cannibal say to the famous missionary?
Dr Livingstone, I consume.

★

A cannibal mother and her little boy looked up above the trees in the jungle at the sound of an aeroplane. It was the first time the little boy had seen an aeroplane, and he asked his mother what it was.
'Well,' she said, 'the best way to explain it is that it's like a tin of sardines. You open it up and eat what's inside.'

★

Young cannibal: Mummy, mummy, I don't like my auntie.
Mother cannibal: Well just eat the chips then, dear.

★

1st cannibal: How do you know our new missionary has been eaten?
2nd cannibal: I have inside information.

★

What happened to all the cannibals?
Somebody ate them.

★

What is a cannibal's favourite kind of soup?
One with plenty of body!

★

Most cannibal jokes are in poor taste.

★

1st cannibal: We had burglars last night.
2nd cannibal: Nice?
1st cannibal: Yes, but they don't taste as good as missionaries.

★

What did the cannibal say when he saw his wife chopping up a snake and a little man?
Not snake and pigmy pie again?

★

Little cannibal: Mummy, Mummy, why is Daddy so tough?

Mother cannibal: I don't know dear, but if he's that bad leave him on the side of your plate.

★

What happened to the cannibals when they ate a comedian?
  They had a feast of fun.

★

What do cannibals do at a wedding?
  They toast the bride and groom.

★

1st cannibal: How did the missionary go down?
2nd cannibal: Very well. So good in fact that we've ordered another one for Easter.

★

What is a cannibal's favourite book?
  'How to Serve Your Fellow Man'.

Cannon
Why did the little boy aim a cannon at the peas?
  Because his mother told him to shell them.

Canoeing
Paul: Why are you taking that water pistol canoeing with you?
Saul: I'm going to shoot the rapids.

Can't and Don't
If can't is short for cannot, what is don't short for?
  Doughnut.

Capital
Teacher: Do you know the capital of Alaska?
Student: Juneau?
Teacher: Yes, but I'm asking you.

★

Which capital city cheats at exams?
  Peking.

Captain
How does the captain of a ship address his crew?
  He makes a decoration.

Captain Kidd
Adam: Who was Captain Kidd?
Eve: He was an acrobat.
Adam: What do you mean, he was an acrobat?
Eve: It says in this book that he often sat on his chest.

Car
Paul: What kind of car does your dad drive?
Saul: I can't remember, but it starts with T.
Paul: How strange! Ours starts with petrol.

★

A man walked in to a garage and asked to see the mechanic.
'Can you have a look at my car? I think the engine's flooded.'
'Yes, sir, is it on the road outside?'
'No,' replied the man, 'it's at the bottom of the river.'

★

Angry buyer: You told me this car was a good one, and it won't go up hills.
Second-hand car dealer: On the level, it's a good car.

★

When can a car drive on water?   When it's on a bridge.

★

What goes at 200 mph on a washing line?
  Honda pants.

★

When is a car not a car?
  When it turns into a driveway.

★

Rick: Hello, old top! New car?
Nick: No, old car. New top.

What would happen if everyone in the country had a pink car?

We'd be a pink car-nation.

★

Chauffeur: Your car is at the door sir.
Car owner: I didn't hear it knocking.

★

Why do large cars go so quickly?

Because they've got a big boot behind.

★

Which part of a car is the laziest?

The wheels – because they're always tyred.

★

What do you call snakes on your car windscreen?

Windscreen vipers.

★

What car do hot dogs like driving?

A Rolls.

★

What did the vintage Bentley say to the brand-new Ford?

I'm feeling rather tyred.

★

Rick: Why have you painted your car different colours each side?
Nick: So if I ever have an accident the witnesses will spend all their time contradicting each other.

★

What would you have if your car's motor caught fire?

A fire engine.

★

Why is a car out of petrol like dividing 21 by 2?

It won't go.

★

Nick: My sister's just bought a baby car.
Rick: A baby car?

Nick: That's right – it doesn't go anywhere without a rattle.

★

What is dense?

What a car gets if it crashes in thick fog.

Car Accident

1st motorist: You drove straight in to my car. Why?
2nd motorist: I saw the sticker in your window that says 'Give Blood', so I decided to let you have some of mine.

★

What's the best thing to do if you're run down?

Take the number of the car that hit you.

★

A man was driving his new car to work one morning in very icy conditions when he skidded in to a lamp post. He got out to have a look at the damage and a friend stopped to see if he could help. The friend was horrified at the state of the car and started to commiserate but the car owner shook his head and said, 'I guess that's the way the Mercedes-Benz.'

Carbuncle

Did you know that a carbuncle was a car crash?

Car Driver

Why did the motorist drive his car in reverse?

Because he knew the rules of the road backwards.

★

Andy: I've been driving for twenty years and I've never had an accident.
Zak: I suppose we should call you a wreckless driver.

★

Why can't a car play football?

Because it's only got one boot.

Which cars do rich funnymen drive?
Droll's Royces.

★

How do we know there were cars nearly 2000 years ago?
Because Moses came over the hill in Triumph.

Cards

Bill: Do you know why card games are so popular?
Ben: No, why?
Bill: Because whoever plays holds hands.

★

Why is it dangerous to play cards in the jungle?
Because of all the cheetahs.

★

Why couldn't the sailors play cards?
Because the captain was standing on the deck.

Careers

Mr Able: And what do you do for a living?
Mr Cable: I write.
Mr Able: Oh! What a coincidence! I read.

★

Father: Do you think we should have a discussion about your future?
Sam: I've decided that when I grow up I want to be a bus driver.
Father: Well, son, I won't stand in your way.

Cargo

What's the difference between cargo and shipment?
Cargo goes by ship and shipment goes by car.

Car Horn

What did the broken car horn say?
I don't give a hoot.

Car Lights

One evening after a long day's drive to his holiday destination, a motorist was stopped by a policeman in the West Country.
'I'll have to report you, sir, for driving without rear lights.'
'Oh, no!' said the distraught driver, getting out of the car for a look. 'This is terrible.'
'It'll probably only be a small fine, sir,' the policeman reassured him.
'Never mind that,' said the driver, 'where's my trailer?'

Carpenter

Adam: Did you hear about Chippy the blind carpenter who regained his sight?
Eve: How?
Adam: He picked up his chisel and saw.

★

Why is a carpenter like a pilot?
Because they both know all the drills.

★

Amy: Why do you call your dog Carpenter?
Zoe: Because he's always doing odd jobs around the house.

★

What finally killed the ship's carpenter who made poop decks?
He was all pooped out.

★

Why do people become carpenters?
Because they think it's all plane sailing.

Carpet

Mrs Able: At the jumble sale today, I bought a carpet in mint condition.
Mrs Cable: As good as new, do you mean?
Mrs Able: No, it has a hole in the middle.

★

What did the carpet say to the desk?
I can see your drawers.

Two workmen were laying a new living room carpet. When they'd finished they stood back to admire their work and to their horror noticed a small bump in the middle of the carpet. 'It must be my cigarettes,' said one fitter. 'Well, we're certainly not going to take the carpet up and relay it, so I'll just flatten it.' He went to the bump and jumped up and down until the carpet was flattened out. At that moment the lady of the house came in to the room.
'I've made you both a cup of coffee,' she said. 'And here are your cigarettes, I found them in the kitchen. There's just one problem, I can't find my hamster anywhere.'

★

What do you buy by the yard, but wear by the foot?
    A carpet.

Carrots
Paul: Why do people say carrots are good for the eyesight?
Saul: Well, have you ever seen a rabbit wearing glasses?

★

What's long and thin, orange, and shoots grouse?
    A double-barrelled carrot.

Carving
What's the best way to carve wood?
    Whittle by whittle.

Car Wash
A lady took her old banger car to the carwash and asked, 'Can you improve my car's looks?' 'Sorry, madam,' said the attendant, 'we only wash cars here, we don't iron them as well.'

Cashier
Mr Able: How's business?
Mr Cable: I'm advertising for a new cashier.

Mr Able: I thought you had a new one start last week?
Mr Cable: That's the one I'm advertising for!

Cat
How does a cat go down the motorway?
    Mee-OWW-OWW!

★

Bill: I wish I had the money to buy a pedigree Persian cat.
Ben: What on earth do you want a pedigree Persian cat for?
Bill: I don't — I just wish I had that much money.

★

Paul: Our cat is really smart.
Saul: What does it do that makes it so smart?
Paul: It eats a piece of cheese and then breathes down a mousehole.

★

What do you get when you cross an alley cat with a budgie?
    A peeping tom.

★

Jack: Have you heard about the cat who won a milk-drinking context?
Jill: No, how did it win?
Jack: It lapped the field.

★

Mrs Able: Did you put the cat out?
Mr Able: No, was it on fire again?

★

Visitor: What's your cat's name, Johnny?
Johnny: Ben Hur.
Visitor: What a strange name for a cat. Why is he called that?
Johnny: Well, he was just Ben until she had kittens.

★

Jack: Have you ever seen the Catskill Mountains?
Jill: No, but I've seen them chase mice.

Jack: What's the difference between a cat and a flea?
Jill: Easy — a cat can have fleas, but a flea can't have cats.

★

What happened when the cat swallowed a pound coin?
  There was money in the kitty.

★

What do cats strive for?
  Purrfection.

★

What do cats put their heads on when they're asleep?
  Caterpillars.

★

How does a cat cross the road?
  It uses a purrdestrian crossing.

★

Andy: My cat joined the Red Cross.
Zak: Why?
Andy: Because it wanted to be a first-aid kit.

★

What do cats read each morning?
  Mewspapers.

★

What happened to the cat that swallowed a ball of wool?
  She had mittens.

★

What sort of cat loves swimming, and has eight arms?
  An octopuss.

★

What do cats eat for breakfast?
  Mice Crispies.

★

What did the cat who had no money say?
  I'm paw.

★

Jack: We bought a cat the other day and the pet shop said it would purr more than any other cat.
Jill: Why's that?
Jack: Because it's a purrsian cat.

★

A black and white cat crossed my path this morning.
  Since then, my luck has been very patchy.

★

What do you call a cat that's swallowed a duck?
  A duck-filled fatty puss.

★

Why is a cat sitting on a fence like a coin?
  Because she has a head on one side and a tail on the other.

★

What's a cat from the Wild West called?
  A posse.

★

Baker: Here's a nice cake.
Shopper: It looks as if the mice have been eating it.
Baker: That's impossible. The cat's been lying on it all night.

★

Why is a cat longer at night than in the morning?
  Because he's let out every night and taken in again every morning.

★

Lady of the manor: Jeeves, there's a mouse in the west wing.
Butler: Very good, madam. I'll ascertain if the cat is available to dine.

★

Patient: Doctor, I think there must be something wrong with me — I keep thinking I'm a cat.
Doctor: How long has this been going on?
Patient: Since I was a kitten.

54

What did the cat do when he'd swallowed the cheese?
    Waited for the mouse with baited breath.

★

What cat is most useful in a library?
    A catalogue.

★

What is the definition of a catalogue?
    A four-legged animal sitting on a tree trunk.

Catamaran
What moves when it's not fast and doesn't move when it's fast?
    A catamaran that's tied up.

Catapult
Father: How did this window get broken?
Silly Billy: My catapult went off while I was cleaning it.

Cat Burglar
Supersleuth: I'm after a cat burglar.
Police Constable: How do you know it was a cat burglar?
Supersleuth: Because all that's missing is a pint of milk and a saucer.

Caterpillar
Teacher: What is a caterpillar?
Soppy Poppy: A worm with a sweater on.

What's the definition of a caterpillar?
    A worm rich enough to buy a fur coat.

★

What made the caterpillar late for the football match kick-off?
    Putting his boots on.

★

Why is hot bread like a caterpillar?
    Because it's the grub that makes the butterfly.

★

What did one caterpillar say to the other when they saw a butterfly?
    You'll never get me up in one of those things!

★

What does a caterpillar do on New Year's Day?
    Turns over a new leaf.

Catfish
Paul: Have you ever seen a catfish?
Saul: Yes.
Paul: How did it hold the rod?

Cat Food
How is cat food sold?
    Usually purr can.

Cats and Dogs
Andy: What did the dog say when the cat scratched it?
Zak: Nothing — dogs can't talk, silly!

★

Why do cats and dogs turn around and around before they go to sleep?
    Because one good turn deserves another.

Cattle Thief
What do you call a man who steals cattle?
    A beefburglar.

Cellar

What would you find in a haunted cellar?
  Whines and spirits.

Cement Mixer

What do you get if you cross a cement mixer with a hen?
  A bricklayer.

Cemetery

What makes a cemetery such a noisy place?
  All the coffin.

★

Rick: I went to the cemetery today.
Nick: Oh, somebody died?
Rick: Yes, all of them.

Censorship

Andy: Do you think censorship is a good thing or a bad thing?
Zak: That depends on whether the end product makes censor not.

Census

Census-taker: But you have to tell me your age, Mrs Cable. Everyone does!
Mrs Cable: Do you mean that Miss Annabelle and Miss Beatrice Hill who live down the road told you their age?
Census-taker: Yes, they did.
Mrs Cable: Well, I'm the same age as them, then.
Census-taker: I see, as old as the Hills.'

★

How do you take a census of monkeys in the zoo?
  Use an ape recorder.

Cent

French boy: I can pick up a cent with my toes.
English boy: So what? My dog can pick up a scent with his nose.

Centimetre

Teacher: Can someone give me a sentence containing the word 'centimetre'?
Soppy Poppy: When my little sister comes out of school I'm centimetre.

Centipede

What did the boy centipede say to the girl centipede?
  You sure have a nice pair of legs, pair of legs, pair of legs. . . .

★

What goes 99-thump, 99-thump, 99-thump?
  A centipede with a wooden leg.

★

What lies on the ground, 100 feet up in the air?
  A centipede on its back.

Chair

What is a chair?
  Headquarters for hindquarters.

★

When is a chair like a fabric?
  When it is sat in.

Chandelier

Why did the man go to sleep on the chandelier?
  Because he was a light sleeper.

Channel Swim

'C'est magnifique!' exclaimed the Frenchman, welcoming the Channel swimmer to the Calais shore. 'It is a very grand foot!'
'Actually,' said the English swimmer, 'it's feat.'
'Incroyable!' said the Frenchman. 'That you 'ave swum it both ways!'

56

Chatterbox

What box can never keep a secret?
  A chatterbox.

Cheddar Gorge

What is the Cheddar Gorge?
  A very large cheese sandwich.

Cheer Up

Paul: Guess what happened after I saw you yesterday and you said, 'Cheer up, things could be worse'?
Saul: What happened?
Paul: Things got worse.

Cheese

There's a new kind of cheese on the market, called 'two-handed cheese' – because you eat it with one hand and hold your nose with the other.

★

What musical instrument goes with cheese?
  Pickle-o.

★

How do Welsh people eat cheese?
  Caerphilly.

Cheeseburger

If cheese comes on top of a hamburger, what comes after cheese?
  A mouse.

Cheese on Toast

What's yellow, brown and hairy?
  Cheese on toast dropped on the carpet.

Cheetah

Where do you find a cheetah?
  Depends where you leave him.

Chef

Did you hear about the chef who was so feeble that when he tried to whip the cream, the cream won?

Chemistry Class

In chemistry class one day the teacher was demonstrating how acids work. He took a glass container of acid and dropped a £1 coin in to it.
'Now,' he said, 'will that £1 coin dissolve in the acid?'
'No, sir, it won't,' said one of the class.
'Quite right,' said the teacher, 'but how did you know?'
'Because, sir,' said the boy, 'if that £1 coin was going to dissolve, I know you would never have dropped it in.'

Chemistry Set

Baby skunk: Can I have a chemistry set for Christmas?
Mother: And smell the house out?

Chess

A man was sitting quietly in the corner of a pub playing chess with his dog. A customer who was watching could hardly contain himself, and said, 'That dog could make you a fortune!'
  'He's not that good,' replied the dog's owner, 'I've beaten him in the last three games.'

★

When is a chess-player happiest?
  When he takes a knight off.

Chess Set

Where is the best place to buy a second-hand chess set?
  At a pawnbroker's.

Chest Cold

How can you stop a cold going to your chest?
  Tie a knot in your neck.

Chewing Gum

A young man was sitting on a train carriage staring in to space, chewing gum. Suddenly the old man sitting opposite him shouted, 'It's no good your talking to me. I'm deaf!'

Chicken

Why did the chicken go half-way across the road?

Because it wanted to lay it on the line.

★

Adam: Why did the chicken cross the road?
Eve: I don't know.
Adam: Neither do I. But you can be sure it had some fowl reason.

★

A lady walked in to a butcher's shop late one afternoon, wanting to buy a chicken. The butcher weighed the very last chicken in the shop and said: 'That'll be £3.50.'
'That's too small,' said the lady, 'haven't you a bigger one?'
The crafty butcher took the chicken back to the cold store, plumped it up a little, and brought it out again.
'This is £4.50,' he said.
'Oh, good,' said the customer, 'I'll take both of them, please.'

★

Why does a chicken lay an egg?

Because if she dropped it, it would break.

★

Why did the chicken cross the road?

To escape from Colonel Sanders.

★

Wife: I've made the chicken soup.'
Husband: 'Oh, good – I thought it was for us.'

★

Customer: I'd like a chicken, please.
Butcher: Do you want a pullet?
Customer: No, I want to carry it home in my basket.

Why did the chicken run on to the football pitch?

Because the referee had whistled for a fowl.

★

Why did the idiot put a chicken in to a hot bath?

So she'd lay hard-boiled eggs.

★

Mr Able: Your neighbour's chickens are all in a run, now. How did you persuade him not to let them run loose?
Mr Cable: I hid a dozen eggs in my garden last night, and this morning I made sure he saw me collect them and take them indoors!

★

What goes cluck, cluck, bang!?

A chicken in a minefield.

★

What would you get if you crossed Rhode Island Reds with waiters?

Hens that lay tables.

★

Rick: My uncle's a farmer, and when we visited yesterday he was really worried about how to get his chickens to lay faster.
Nick: Has he tried giving them Castrol GTX?

★

What do you call a greasy chicken?

A slick chick.

★

Why did the chicken refuse to lay eggs?

Because she was tired of working for chicken feed.

★

Why is a black chicken smarter than a white chicken?

★

Because a black chicken can lay a white egg, but a white chicken can't lay a black egg.

A chicken that was fed on saw-dust by mistake still managed to lay a dozen eggs. Eleven chicks hatched out with a wooden leg and the last was a woodpecker.

★

Paul: Why were all your chickens in the front garden yesterday?

Saul: Oh, they heard that the council were laying a pavement, and they wanted to see how it was done.

★

Jack: Isn't it wonderful how little chicks get out of their shells?

Jill: It's even more wonderful how they get in.

★

How do baby hens dance?
　Chick to chick.

★

Why is it a waste of time holding a party for chickens?
　Because it's hard to make hens meet.

★

Who tells chicken jokes?
　Comedihens.

★

Where do all good chickens go when they die?
　To oven.

★

Why did the lady blush when she walked past the chicken coop?
　Because she heard fowl language.

Why does the chicken go to the theatre?
　For hentertainment.

Chicken Feathers

On which side does a chicken have most of its feathers?
　The outside.

Chicken Pox

Paul: I'm going to tell you a joke about chicken pox.

Saul: Please don't, you know how these things spread.

Children

Son: Dad, can I use your car?

Father: What are your feet for?

Son: One for the accelerator and one for the brake!

★

Andy: Parents shouldn't have children – they don't know anything about us!

Zak: What makes you say that?

Andy: Because Mum and Dad always put me to bed when I'm wide awake and wake me up when I'm sleeping.

★

How many children does a man have if he has ten sons and each son has a sister?
　Eleven – the daughter is each son's sister.

★

Why are children like denim?
　Because they shrink from washing.

★

Visitor: What is your son going to be when he passes all his examinations?

Father: Old.

★

A young father was wheeling a pushchair in which sat a screaming child. As he walked along, he muttered to himself, 'Keep calm,

Harry; steady on, now. Calm down, everything will be all right, Harry.'
A lady paused as she walked past, saying, 'You're doing so well, talking to your crying child so quietly.' She leaned over and said to the child, 'What's the matter, Harry?'
'I'm Harry,' said the father. 'He's Stephen!'

★

Two old friends met after having lost touch since they left school. The conversation went like this:
'Are you married now?'
'Yes.'
'Any children?'
'Three boys and five girls.'
'Eight altogether!'
'No, I had them one at a time.'

★

Why is it true that children always brighten a home?
Because they never turn the lights off.

★

Mr Able: Do you believe in striking children?
Mr Cable: Only in self-defence.

★

Mother heard her children scream
So she pushed them in the stream
Saying, as she pushed the third,
'Children should be seen, not heard.'

★

What children live in the ocean?
Buoys.

Chimney
1st factory chimney: How come you smoke day and night?
2nd factory chimney: I've got a twenty-four hour flue.

★

What happened when the chimney got angry?
It blew its stack.

★

What did one chimney say to the other chimney?
I'm going out tonight – can I borrow your soot?

★

What did the big chimney say to the little chimney?
You're too young to smoke.

Chimpanzee
How did the chimpanzee escape from his cage?
He used a monkey wrench.

★

What was the chimps' favourite book?
'The Monkey House' by Bab Boone.

China
What is purple and 4,000 miles long?
The Grape Wall of China.

China Cat
Who wrote the 'Thoughts of a China Cat'?
Chairman Miaow.

Chinaman
What's yellow and goes 'Clunch, clunch'?
A Chinaman eating potato crisps.

Chinese
What did the 14th-century Chinese people wear to keep out the cold?
Ming coats.

★

Where do the Chinese make motor-car horns?
Hong King.

★

A Chinese boy who had just arrived in England telephoned his brother from the airport. He was speaking very broken English, trying to explain which train he would be catching, when the brother said, 'Why don't you speak Chinese?'

'Oh,' said the new arrival, 'do English telephones speak Chinese?'

★

What is Chinese and deadly?
  Chop sueycide.

Chinese Food
Should you eat chinese food on an empty stomach?
  No, you should eat it on a plate.

Chinese Take Away
A masked man burst in to a Chinese restaurant and demanded that the owner give him all the money in the till. The owner looked inscrutable and said, 'To take away, sir?'

Chip Pan
What do you call a foreign body in a chip pan?
  An Unidentified Frying Object.

Chips
What are hot, greasy and romantic?
  Chips that pass in the night.

Chip Shop
Paul: Did you hear about the fight in the chip shop?
Saul: No. What happened?
Paul: A lot of fish got battered.

Chiropodist
Which famous chiropodist ruled over England?
William the Corn Curer.

Chocolate
What's chocolate on the outside, peanut inside and sings hymns?
  A Sunday School Treet.

What did the chocolate say to the lollipop?
  Hi there, sucker!

★

What's made of chocolate and is found on the sea bed?
  An oyster egg.

Choir Boys
Where do military choir boys get their uniforms?
  At an Army surplice store.

Choo Choo
Sam: I want a choo choo for Christmas!
Father: A what?
Sam: A choo choo. A CHOO CHOO!
Father: Are you getting a cold, Sam?

Chopin
Paul: Do you like Chopin?
Saul: No, I get tired walking from shop to shop.

Christening
Did you hear about the baby who was christened 'Glug-glug' – the vicar fell in the font!

Christmas Cracker
What did the Christmas cracker say to a friend?
  My pop's bigger than your pop!

Christmas

What's Christmas called in England?
  Yule Britannia.

★

What happens to you at Christmas?
  Yule be happy.

Christmas Decorations

What happens to you if you eat Christmas decorations?
  You get tinselitis.

Christmas Dinner

Young cannibal: Mummy, are we having Great Uncle Arthur over for dinner this Christmas?
Mummy cannibal: No, dear, turkey as usual.

Christmas Eve

Silly Billy insisted on being born on Christmas Eve.
  He said he wanted to be home in time for Christmas.

★

Overheard one Christmas Eve:
  'I don't care who you are, fat man, get those reindeer off my roof!'

Christmas Present

Father: What would you like for Christmas, Sam?
Sam: I've got my eye on a new bike.
Father: Well, keep your eye on it, son. Because you'll never get your bottom on it!

Christmas Shopping

Burglar: The police arrested me for doing my Christmas shopping early.
Lawyer: They can't do that!
Burglar: It seems they can — they caught me in the shop at three in the morning.

Christopher Columbus

Why was Christopher Columbus an economical explorer?
  Because he travelled 30,000 miles on a galleon.

Church

In some churches the seats on the right are for women and the ones on the left are for men. What is the gangway called?
  The aisle of Man.

★

What did the fireman say when he saw the church on fire?
  Holy Smoke!

★

What do you get when you cross a church with a fish?
  Holy mackerel.

Church Bells

Johnny: Have you got many church bells in your town?
Jenny: About twenty, all tolled.

★

Why do the church bells ring on Sundays?
  Because the bell ringers pull the ropes!

★

What's the difference between a church bell and a pickpocket?
  One peals from the steeple, the other steals from the people.

CID.

Father: Do you know what CID stands for?
Son: Yes — coppers in disguise.

Cigarette

How do you make a cigarette lighter?
  Take out the tobacco.

Cinderella

What kind of clothes did Cinderella wear?
　Wish-and-wear.

★

Why was Cinderella thrown out of the England rugby team?
　Because she kept running away from the ball.

★

Why is Cinderella such a bad footballer?
　Because her coach is a pumpkin.

★

Why didn't the baseball catcher meet Cinderella?
　Because he missed the ball.

Cinema

Ticket seller: That's the sixth ticket you've bought, sir.
Customer: I know – but there's a girl inside who keeps tearing them up.

★

Bill: What's on at the cinema this week?
Ben: Same old thing, the roof.

★

Amy: We went to the cinema last night.
Zoe: Oh, how lovely! Did you enjoy it?
Amy: No, I cried.
Zoe: Why, was it a sad story?
Amy: No, we couldn't get in.

★

Johnny (at the cinema): Can you see all right?
Jenny: Yes, thank you.
Johnny: No one blocking your view?
Jenny: No, no one.
Johnny: And is your seat comfortable?
Jenny: Yes, everything's fine.
Johnny: Mind changing places?

★

Eve: What a frightening film! It sent a shiver down my spine.
Adam: So that's where my ice-cream went.

Circle

Why were seven wooden planks standing in a circle?
　They were having a board meeting.

Circus

A circus owner found his animal trainer beating one of the ten performing elephants. 'Stop that this minute!' he shouted.
'What do you think you're doing, beating a valuable animal like that?'
'He slipped this afternoon, coming out of the ring,' replied the trainer.
'That's no reason to beat him!'
'No? When he slipped he pulled the tails off your other nine elephants!'

★

A little girl went on her very first trip to the circus. When she saw the horses she gasped and said, 'Dad, where are their rockers?'

★

The most popular sideshow in the circus was a horse that played the trumpet. A farmer who saw the show was amazed and asked the horse's trainer how the horse had learned to play.
'No mystery,' said the trainer, 'he took lessons for years.'

★

Paul: My uncle has a leading position in the circus.
Saul: That must be exciting! What does he do?
Paul: He leads in the elephants.

Citrus Fruit

How can you help deaf citrus fruit?
　Give them a lemon aid.

City

Did you hear about the man who went to live in the city because he heard the country was at war?

Classroom

Paul: I'm the most advanced boy in my class.
Saul: How do you know?
Paul: I sit at the front!

Sam was falling off his chair in the classroom and chewing gum. 'Sam!' shouted the teacher, 'take that chewing gum out of your mouth and put your feet in!'

Clean

Mother: Don't come in, Johnny, unless your feet are clean! I've just washed the kitchen floor.
Johnny: My feet *are* clean, Mum. It's just my shoes that are dirty.

★

Why did the cleaning woman stop cleaning?
   Because she found grime doesn't pay.

Cleopatra

Why was Cleopatra so contrary?
   Because she was Queen of denial.

Cliff

Bill: I heard you said you could jump off a cliff and not get hurt – is that true?
Ben: No, it was just a bluff.

Cloak

What is a cloak?
   A Chinese frog's mating call.

Clock

Paul: I wonder why that clock is slow.
Saul: You would be slow, too, if you had to run all day.

★

What part of a clock is always old?
   The second hand.

★

Rick: What time did your clock stop?
Nick: I don't know, I wasn't here.

★

What will a clock be called when it lands on the moon?
   A lunar-tick.

★

When was the clock at its most dangerous?
   When it struck twelve.

★

Why is a clock like a river?
   Because it won't run long without winding.

★

Teacher: What sort of invention would you call the clock?
Soppy Poppy: A timely one.

★

If a man smashed a clock, would he be found guilty of killing time?
   Not if the clock struck first.

★

Grandmother: If you haven't seen it before, Jenny, we'll just sit here and watch the cuckoo come out of the cuckoo clock.
Jenny: Couldn't we sit and watch Grandfather come out of the grandfather clock?

★

When is a clock on the stairs dangerous?
   When it runs down.

★

What did one clock say to another clock who was frightened?
   Don't be alarmed.

What did the big hand of the clock say to the little hand?
  Got a minute?

★

Why did the little old man keep a hundred clocks at home?
  Because he'd heard that time was valuable.

Clockmaker
What do you call a man who makes faces all day?
  A clockmaker.

Clothes
Conceited Charlie: I'd like a blue tie to match my eyes, please.
Salesman: I'm sorry, sir, we don't have a single blue tie left. But we do have some soft hats which would match your head.

★

Clothes may not make a man –
  but a good suit has made many a lawyer.

★

Boasting boutique owner: Last week I sold twenty Victorian dresses.
Rival boutique owner: Early clothing day?

★

Amy: I choose my own clothes.
Zoe: It seems to be moth that chews mine.

Clothesline
What did the shirt say to the trousers?
  Meet me on the clothesline – that's where I hang out.

Clover
What did one clover leaf say to the other clover leaf?
  Take me to your weeder.

Clowns
How do clowns dress on a cold day?
  Quickly.

★

When does a clown become two clowns?
  When he's beside himself.

★

If it takes a dozen clowns half an hour to eat a ham, how long will it take two dozen clowns to eat half a ham?
That depends on whether they're professional clowns or 'am-a-chewers'.

Coal
How is it that, whoever the buyer;
coal is always delivered to the cellar (seller).

Coat
What kind of coat can you only put on when it's wet?
  A coat of paint.

★

What coat has the most sleeves?
  A coat of arms.

Cobbler
What did the cobbler say when a flock of chickens came into his workshop?
  Shoo!

Cock-a-Doodle-Do

What's the opposite of cock-a-doodle-do?
  Cock-a-doodle-don't.

Cockerel

Jack: How do you stop a cockerel crowing on a Monday morning?
Jill: I don't know.
Jack: Eat him for Sunday lunch!

★

Why did the farmer name his rooster Robinson?
  Because he Crusoe.

★

Where could a cockerel with no knees go?
  To London – where there are lots of cockneys.

Coconut

What's brown, hairy, and wears dark glasses?
  A coconut in disguise.

★

What's a coconut?
  Someone who loves drinking chocolate.

Coconut Milk

How can you tell that coconut milk is nutty?
  Because it lives in a padded cell.

Codfish

Adam: Do you like codfish balls?
Eve: I don't know. I've never been to one.

Coffee

Customer: Waiter – this coffee tastes like mud!
Waiter: Well, sir, it was ground only ten minutes ago.

Tramp: Give us a pound for a cup of coffee?
Passer-by: Coffee doesn't cost £1!
Tramp: I'm expecting company!

Coffee Pot

Amy: How does a coffee pot feel when it's full?
Zoe: I don't know.
Amy: Perky!

Coffin

Rick: What's another name for a coffin?
Nick: A snuff box.

Coin

Amy: I've got the perfect way to get out of doing my homework.
Zoe: How's that?
Amy: I toss a coin. If it lands on the edge, I do my homework.

Coincidence

Rick: What does coincidence mean?
Nick: Funny, I was just going to ask you that.

Coke and Coal

What did the coke say to the coal?
  What kind of fuel am I?

Cold War

What is a cold war?
  A snowball fight.

Collar

Customer: I'd like some shirts for my husband, please.

Sales assistant: Certainly, madam, what size collar?

Customer: Oh, I'm not sure — but I can just about get both hands around his neck.

Collection Plate

Mother: Weren't you nicely behaved in church today, Poppy?

Soppy Poppy: Yes! And when that nice man offered me a whole plate of money I said, 'No, thank you.'

★

A little boy went off to church one morning with a 20 pence piece for the collection plate and a 20 pence piece to buy sweets with on the way home. Unfortunately he tripped as he stepped off the pavement, and one of the coins fell out of his pocket and disappeared down the grating. He looked up to heaven, and said, 'Sorry, God. That was your 20 pence piece.'

★

A Rabbi and a Catholic priest were having a discussion on the way they disposed of the collection plate.

The priest said, 'We divide our collection into thirds — one-third for the Pope in Rome, one-third for the bishop and one-third we keep for the parish.'

'Oh, I see,' said the Rabbi. 'Our way is a little different. When everyone has left the synagogue, my wife, my two sons and I put the collection into a blanket. We each take a corner, and I lead the prayers. Then we toss the money into the air. Whatever God wants he keeps, and whatever falls back into the blanket we keep!'

Collectors

Paul: My Dad's a great collector. He has Sir Walter Raleigh's cloak.

Saul: That's nothing. My Dad doesn't collect anything but he still has an Adam's apple.

Collision

What is the result of a collision in a school playground?

A fight.

Comb

What do you often part with, but never give away?

A comb.

Comedian

What's the difference between a comedian and a clock-maker?

One takes the mick, the other makes the tick.

★

What do you get when you cross an ocean and a comedian?

Waves of laughter.

Common Cold

Amy: What do you want for your cold?

Zoe: I'm not sure. What will you give me?

★

Why do you feel cold when you lose your two front teeth?

No central heating.

★

What can you still keep even if you give it away?

A cold.

★

What kind of transport gives people colds?

A-choo-choo trains.

★

Paul: I run much faster when I have a cold.

Saul: That's odd.

Paul: No, it's easy — because I've a racing pulse and a running nose.

Commuting

A very tired commuter came home late one evening complaining of how ill riding backwards in the train made him feel.

'Well,' said his wife, 'why didn't you ask the person sitting opposite you to change seats?'

'Oh, I couldn't do that,' said the commuter. 'There wasn't anyone sitting opposite me.'

Company

Amy: Sam asked me last night if I liked his company.

Zoe: What did you say?

Amy: I told him I didn't know which company he worked for.

Compass

Paul: Why do you always carry a compass around with you?

Saul: So I know whether I'm coming or going.

Complaint

Customer: I have a complaint.

Bank clerk: This is a bank, sir, not a hospital.

Composer

Why couldn't anyone find the famous composer?

Because he was Haydn.

★

Did you hear about the composer who took so many baths that he began to write soap operas?

Computer

What do you get if you cross a computer and an elastic band?

A computer that makes snap decisions.

Computer Programmer

Sheriff: Which way did the computer programmer go?

Modern cowboy: Data way!

Concorde

What is huge, hairy, and flies to New York at Mach 1?

King Kongcorde.

★

What goes mooz?

Concorde flying backwards.

★

When do you go as fast as Concorde?

When you're in it.

★

What do you get if you cross Concorde with a kangaroo?

A plane that makes quick hops.

Conductor

Johnny: I hear your brother is a conductor. Musical or on the buses?

Jenny: Electrical. He was struck by lightning.

Confession

Young priest: A man has just confessed to me that he stole a crate of whisky. What shall I tell him?

Old priest: Tell him we don't pay more than £1 a bottle.

Conquered

History teacher: Having conquered North Africa Julius Caesar went on to conquer Gaul and then conquered Britain. Why did he stop?

Silly Billy: He ran out of conkers!

Contentment

Quiz master: I'll give a £10 note to any one of the panel who's contented.

Contestant: I'm quite contented.

Quiz master: If you're quite contented, why do you want £10?

Conversion Table

What's a conversion table?

A piece of very adaptable furniture.

Convictions

Judge: This is your sixth conviction for the same crime. Aren't you ashamed of yourself?

Prisoner: No, sir. My mother always told me never to be ashamed of my convictions.

Cooker

What did the cooker say to the saucepan?

I can make things hot for you.

Cooking

Rick: My sister's taking cookery lessons. Yesterday she gave us cold boiled ham.

Nick: That's nice.

Rick: Hers wasn't – she just dipped the boiled ham in cold water.

★

Soppy Poppy: Teacher says I can't go to cookery classes any more because I burnt something.

Mother: And what did you burn?

Soppy Poppy: The kitchens.

★

Mr Able: What's your wife's cooking like?

Mr Cable: Terrible! She even burns the washing up water.

★

Amy: Mum says she'll never let Dad cook again!

Zoe: Why not?

Amy: Last night he burnt the salad.

★

Cookery tip – to prevent rice from sticking, boil each grain separately!

★

Why are cooks cruel?

Because they whip cream and beat eggs.

Copying

Teacher: I hope I didn't see you copying just then, Alec.

Smart Alec: I hope so too!

Cork

What did the cork say to the bottle?

Behave or I'll plug you.

Corn

Two ears of corn were running a race. What were they when they'd finished?

Puffed wheat.

★

Andy: Why does your brother put corn in his shoes?

Zak: Because he's got pigeon toes.

Cornfield

What size is a cornfield?

As big as from ear to ear.

★

Why should you never tell secrets in a cornfield?

Because corn has ears and is bound to be shocked.

Cornflakes

What do cornflakes wear on their feet?
  K-logs (clogs).

Cost

Jenny: How much are those little dolls?
Shop keeper: 25p for two or 15p for one.
Jenny: Here's 10p. I'll have the other one.

Cough

Did you know that people who cough loudly never go to the doctor – they go to the theatre.

★

What cuts through metal and has a bad cough?
  A hacksaw.

Count Dracula

Where do you address a letter to Count Dracula?
  The dead-letter office.

★

Where is Count Dracula's New York office?
  On the 13th floor of the Vampire State Building.

Counterfeit Money

Why might you be arrested if you walked by a counterfeit five pound note lying on the pavement?
  Because you passed counterfeit money.

Counting

How does a card sharp count?
  One, two, three, four, five, six, seven, eight, nine, ten, Jack, Queen, King.

★

Did you hear about the little girl who wanted to count higher than ten?
  She counted on her fingers with her hands above her head.

Counting Sheep

One morning an accountant complained bitterly to his wife that he hadn't slept a wink all night.
'You should have counted sheep,' said his wife.
'I did,' said the accountant. 'But I made a mistake in the first hour, and it took me until this morning to correct.'

Country Air

If country air is so good –
why don't they build cities in the country?

Court

Mr Able and Mr Cable had to appear in court for fighting, and Mr Able was fined £20.
'Twenty pounds!' he exclaimed. 'But I only acted in self-defence! Cable bit half my ear off!'
The magistrate ignored this outburst, and turned to Mr Cable.
'You,' he said, 'are bound over to keep the peace for a year.'
'Oh, your honour, I can't do that,' said Mr Cable. 'I threw it away!'

★

Judge: I shall throw out the next person who raises his voice in my court.
Prisoner loudly: Hip, hip, hooray!

Cows

What happens if you walk under a cow?
  You could get a pat on the head.

★

A farmer once called his cow 'Zephyr'
She seemed such a breezy young heifer.
When the farmer drew near

She kicked off his ear
And now the old farmer's much deafer.

★

A farmer's prize dairy cow fell over a cliff, but the farmer didn't cry – why?
　Because it's no good crying over spilt milk.

★

Where would you go to see a prehistoric cow?
　To a Moo-seum.

★

What will you get if you feed a cow pound coins?
　Rich milk that jangles.

★

A farmer's cows started mooing very early one morning and, try as he might, he couldn't ignore the noise. Eventually he got up to go and milk them, calling out loudly, 'I herd you!'

★

Did you hear about the cow who was so cold one winter she produced nothing but ice cream?

★

If you had 20 cows and a man gave you 30 more cows, what would you have?
　A dairy herd.

★

What games do cows most like playing?
　Moo-sical chairs.

★

Nick: What a lovely colour that cow is!
Rick: It's a Jersey.
Nick: Really? I thought it was her skin.

★

What has four legs, horns, and goes OOM, OOM?
　A cow walking backwards.

★

How do you count cows?
　With a cowculator.

What do you get from nervous cows?
　Milk shakes.

★

Why do cows have bells?
　For when their horns don't work.

★

Where do cows go for a night out?
　To the moo-ooo-vies.

★

A man's car stalled in the countryside and a cow walked past and suggested he checked the petrol tank. The startled man ran to a nearby farmhouse and told the story to the farmer.
'Was it a Jersey cow?', asked the farmer.
'Yes,' replied the man.
'Don't take any notice – Jerseys don't know a thing about cars.'

★

What do you call a cow that eats grass?
　A lawn-mooer.

★

Why did the cow jump off the cliff?
　Because her calf wanted a milk-shake.

★

Why did the farmer take his cow to the vet?
　Because she was moo-dy.

★

What do you get when you cross a cow with a camel?
　Lumpy milkshakes.

★

When was beef at its highest?
　When the cow jumped over the moon.

★

Bill: Look at that bunch of cows.
Ben: Not bunch – herd.

Bill: Heard what?
Ben: Herd of cows.
Bill: Of course I've heard of cows.
Ben: I mean a cowherd.
Bill: I don't care if a cow heard. I haven't said anything wrong.

★

Why did the cow jump over the moon?
  Because she couldn't crawl underneath.

Coward
Adam: Show me a medieval knight's cowardly helper . . .
Eve: . . . and I'll show you a Yellow Page.

Cowboys
Where do cowboys keep their water supply?
  In their ten-gallon hats.

★

1st cowboy: Did you know they call you 'Pale-face' on the reservation?
2nd cowboy: No – why's that?
1st cowboy: Because you've got a face like a bucket.

★

Why do cowboys die with their boots on?
  So as not to stub their toes when they kick the bucket.

★

A city man was surprised to see a cowboy walking towards him in town one day, complete with stetson and jangling spurs.
'Pardon me,' said the city man. 'Are you a real cowboy?'
'That's right,' said the cowboy. 'And my name's Tex.'
'Oh, from Texas, eh?' asked the man.
'Nope,' replied the cowboy, 'from Louisiana.'
'Louisiana? But why are you called Tex?'
'Would you want to be called Louise?'

★

What did the cowboy say when his dog fell over the cliff?
  Dawg gone.

Why did the cowboy call his horse Hot-head?
  Because it had a blaze on its forehead.

★

Why does a cowboy take a hammer to bed?
  So that he can hit the hay.

★

Who has eight guns and terrorises the ocean?
  Billy the Squid.

★

Why was the cowboy a lot of fun?
  Because he was always horsing around.

★

A cowboy on a Wild West ranch stood watching a city slicker trying to saddle a horse. Trying to be helpful, he said, 'Excuse me, pardner, but you're putting that saddle on the wrong way round.' 'How do you know?' snapped the city slicker, 'you don't even know which direction I'm going to take.'

Cowboys and Indians
One evening some cowboys were sitting around their camp fire telling stories. One said: 'I know an Indian chief who never forgets anything. May the Devil take my soul if I lie.' That night the Devil appeared to the cowboy and said,
'I heard what you said earlier and I'm ready to take your soul for lying.'
'But,' said the cowboy, 'I was telling the truth. Come with me and I'll show you.'

The two of them went and found the Indian chief and the Devil asked him just one question:
'Do you like eggs?'
'Yes,' replied the Indian.
Then the Devil and the cowboy went their separate ways. Many years later the Devil heard that the cowboy had died and, anxious to claim his soul, went to find the Indian again. The Devil greeted him in the traditional Indian way, raising his right arm and saying, 'How!'
'Scrambled,' replied the Indian.

★

Why wouldn't the little boy play cowboys and indians with his grandfather?
    Because his grandfather had already been scalped.

Cowhide
What is cowhide most used for?
    Holding cows together.

Cow Horns
Paul: Do cows change their horns?
Saul: No, but they switch their tails.

Cowslip
Paul: Have you ever seen a cowslip under a bush?
Saul: No, but I once saw a horsefly over the hedge.

Coyote
What is the difference between a coyote and a flea?
    One howls on the prairie, the other prowls on the hairy.

Crabs
Customer: Do you serve crabs here?
Waiter: We serve anyone, sir.

★

Why was the crab arrested?
    For pinching things.

Crawling
Teacher: Why are you crawling in to the class-room, Billy?
Silly Billy: Because on the first day of term you told us that no one ever walked in to your class late.

Crayons
Teacher: Where is your crayon, Jenny?
Jenny: I haven't got none.
Teacher: Oh, Jenny. I've told you over and over again not to say that. Listen carefully: I do not have a crayon, you do not have a crayon, she does not have a crayon. Now do you understand?
Jenny: No – who's got all the crayons?

Crazy
Why have you got to be crazy to get by?
    Because otherwise you'd go nuts.

Crazy Clock
What kind of clock is crazy?
    A cuckoo clock.

Crazy Lady
Why did the lady who mended pottery go crazy?
    Because she was with crackpots too long.

Cream
Soppy Poppy: Please may I have a cup of coffee without cream.
Waitress: I'm sorry, we're out of cream. Will you have it without milk?

Cricket Essay

The sports master was taking a lesson in the absence of the English teacher, and asked the class to write an essay entitled, 'A Game of Cricket'. Smart Alec thought for a while, wrote a sentence and handed in his piece of paper. The sports master looked at it, smiled, and allowed Smart Alec to go out and play. On the piece of paper he had written, 'Rain stopped play.'

Cricket Lesson

Two boys at a cricket lesson:
1st boy: How do you hold the bat?
2nd boy: By the wings, of course.

Cricket Team

Andy: I have a chance on the cricket team.
Zak: Nobody told me they were raffling it.

Criminal

Why did the teacher suggest one of her pupils take up criminal law?
  Because she thought he had a criminal mind.

★

Have you heard about the criminal who came out of prison and went straight back behind bars?
  He bought a pub!

Crisps

Who was rich and famous and invented flavoured crisps?
  Sultan Vinegar.

Croak

What goes croak! croak! when it's misty?
  A frog-horn.

★

Grandson: Can you croak, Grandad?
Grandfather: I don't think so, why?

Grandson: Because Dad says we'll get thousands when you do.

★

What goes 'da-dit-dit croak, da-dit-dit croak'?
  A Morse toad.

Crocodile

What's a crocodile's favourite game?
  Snap!

★

Jack: What do you get if you cross a crocodile with a rose?
Jill: I don't know, but I wouldn't try smelling it.

★

Bill: What's worse than a crocodile with toothache?
Ben: I don't know!
Bill: A centipede with bunions.

★

What do you get if you cross a crocodile and a lettuce?
  A big green salad that eats you.

Crocodile Shoes

Amy: Would you ever wear crocodile shoes?
Zoe: No, I never wear secondhand things.

★

Customer in shoe shop: I'd like some crocodile shoes, please.
New salesman: Yes, madam — what size is your crocodile?

Cross-Eyed

How can you tell if you're cross-eyed?
  If you can see eye to eye with yourself.

Crossing the Road

Old lady: Excuse me, little boy, can you see me across the road?

Silly Billy: Just a minute, I'll go over and if I can see you I'll wave.

Crossword
Crossword fan: I've been trying to think of a word for two weeks!
Friend: How about a fortnight?

★

Why is a crossword puzzle like an argument?
Because one word leads to another.

Crowbar
What is a crowbar?
A place where birds drink.

Crowds
1st passenger: Would you mind taking your elbow out of my ribs?
2nd passenger: Of course, if you'll take your pipe out of my mouth!

Crunchbird
A lady went in to a pet shop to buy a bird and was intrigued by one sitting on the cash register.
'What kind of bird is that?' she asked.
'That's a crunchbird,' replied the pet shop owner. 'I'll let him show you what he can do. Crunchbird, my pen!' And the bird flew to the man's pocket, took out his pen and ate it.
'Crunchbird, my paper!' And the bird flew to the desk and devoured the newspaper.
'Oh,' said the lady, 'that's a marvellous bird.' She bought the bird and took it home and proudly showed it to her husband.
'This,' she said to him, 'is a crunchbird.'
'Crunchbird, my foot!' said her husband.

Crusts
Visitor: I see you've left all your crusts, Poppy. When I was a little girl I ate every single one.
Soppy Poppy: Do you still like them?
Visitor: Oh, yes.
Soppy Poppy: You can have mine then.

Cry for Help
Drowning man: Help! Help! I can't swim.
Drunk on shore: So what? I can't play the violin but I'm not shouting about it.

Crying
A little boy went indoors crying to tell his mother that the next door neighbour's son had hit him.
'When did he hit you?' asked his mother.
'Oh, a while ago,' replied the boy.
'But I didn't hear you crying then,' said his mother.
'No, I thought you were out,' said the boy.

★

Sam: Mum, can I have some money for the man who's crying outside?
Mother: Yes, of course, Sam. What's he crying about?
Sam: He's crying, 'Ice creams! Ice creams!'

Cucumber
What fruit plays snooker?
A cue-cumber.

Cups
What cups can't you drink out of?
Buttercups and hiccups.

Cured Ham
Customer: Waiter, are you sure this ham is cured? From the taste of it I think it's still very sick.

Curlers
Why do women wear curlers at night?
Because they want to wake curly in the morning.

Cushion

What's the best way to cover a cushion?
  Sit on it!

Custard

What's yellow and stupid?
  Thick custard.

Customer's Rights

The manager of a large department store was reprimanding one of his staff.
'Please don't let me see you arguing with a customer again,' he said. 'In this store, the customer is always right.'

'Yes, sir,' said the sales assistant.
'Now, what was the argument about?'
'Well, sir, he said you were a fool.'

Cyclist

A man driving along the motorway was over-taken by a cyclist. He didn't like this at all, so accelerated away, past the cyclist. Soon the cyclist passed him again, pedalling hard. The driver was incensed, and pulled off the motorway at the next exit.
'Thank goodness!' said the cyclist. 'My braces were caught in your rear bumper.'

Cyclops

Why did the cyclops stop teaching?
  It wasn't worth going on with just one pupil.

Why did the two cyclops always fight?
  Because they never saw eye to eye on anything.

Dachshund

The Dachshund's a dog of German descent;
Whose tail never knew where his front end went.

Dad

Rick: My little brother's called Dad.
Nick: Why's that?
Rick: They named him after my father.

Dallas

Two Italian friends living in the USA were filling in their income tax returns. 'Taxes!' said one.
'Thatsa where my brother Sergio lives,' said the other.
'No,' said the first man. 'Not Texas – taxes. You know, the dollars we have to pay the government.'

'Thatsa right,' replied the other. 'Dallas, Texas.'

Dance
What dance should you do when the summer is over?
  The tan-go.

Adam: You'd make a wonderful dancer, except for two things.
Eve: What?
Adam: Your feet.

Describe 100 dancing cakes in one word.
  Abundance.

Dancing
Have you heard about the new dance called the 'Lift'?
  It hasn't got any steps.

★

Why couldn't the butterfly go to the dance?
  Because it was a moth-ball.

★

What's the best place for dancing in California?
  San Frandisco.

Dandruff
Amy: I think I've got a bit of dandruff.
Zoe: Oh, will I catch it?
Amy: Only if you've got very quick fingers.

Dark
Paul: Why did you wake me up? It's still dark.
Saul: Open your eyes, then.

Mother: Sam, there were three cakes in the pantry before I went out – now there's only one. Why is that?
Sam: I don't know, Mum – maybe because it was so dark in there I didn't see the last one.

Why did the teacher wear dark glasses?
  Because the class was so bright.

What is there more of the less you see?
  Darkness.

★

Juggler: Aren't you afraid to put your head in the lion's mouth?
Lion tamer: Yes. I'm afraid of the dark.

Dark Ages
Teacher: Why are the years between AD500 and AD1200 always known as the Dark Ages?
Soppy Poppy: Because those were the days of the (k)nights!

Dark Glasses
Why did the man wear sunglasses on rainy days?
  To protect his eyes from umbrellas.

Darth Vader
Mrs Able had to take her son Sam with her when she went to the hairdressers, and he was all dressed up in a Darth Vader outfit, twirling his laser and shouting 'Die!' to everyone. One of the apprentices offered to look after him while Mrs Able had her hair washed, but was a little nervous that she wouldn't be able to fully occupy him.

'Oh, don't worry,' said Mrs Able. 'Just disintegrate for him a few times and he'll be happy.'

Dates
If a man eats dates could he be said to be consuming time?

Daughter
Mrs Able: I'm really worried about my daughter. That new doctor keeps pursuing her.
Mrs Cable: Why don't you give her an apple a day?

★

Mrs Able: Why do you call your *daughter* Sonny?
Mrs Cable: Because she's so bright.

Davy Crockett
Andy: Did you know Davy Crockett had three ears?
Zak: No, how was that?
Andy: He had a right ear, a left ear, and a wild frontier.

Dawn
Andy: I'm going to get up at dawn tomorrow to see the sunrise.
Zak: If you'd picked a better time I'd have come with you.

Days
Rick: Can you name five days of the week without saying Monday, Tuesday, Wednesday, Thursday or Friday?
Nick: Oh yes! The day before yesterday, yesterday, today, tomorrow and the day after tomorrow!

★

What is the strongest day of the week?
Sunday – all the rest are week days.

★

Why is one day never complete?
Because it always begins by breaking.

★

What has gone forever and you can never get back?
Yesterday.

Dead
If a man was born in Italy, raised in Australia, came to England, and died in America, what is he?
Dead.

Dead Fly
Customer: Waiter, there's a dead fly in my soup.
Waiter: How sad! He was too young to die!

Dead Potato
Did you hear that the potato died?
There was a huge turnip at his funeral.

Dead Sea
Teacher: Tell me all you know about the Dead Sea, please Billy.
Silly Billy: The Dead Sea? I didn't know it was ill.

Deaf
Three somewhat deaf friends met one afternoon.
The first said, 'Windy, isn't it?'
'No, it's Thursday,' said the second.
Up piped the third, 'So am I, let's all go and have a cup of tea.'

★

Rick: The most intelligent person in the world is going deaf!
Nick: Sorry, what did you say?

★

A judge in London decided to let a deaf man go free yesterday, even though he was found guilty. The judge said afterwards that he couldn't convict a man without a hearing.

Deaf and Dumb
Bill: How dare you call me deaf and dumb!
Ben: I never said you were deaf.

Death
What's the last thing you do before you die?
    You bite the dust.

★

What animal does death never really affect?
    A pig, because as soon as you kill him you can cure him and save his bacon.

Debt-Collecting
Why is debt-collecting a pleasant job?
    Because people always ask you to call again!

December
What do you call a tug-of-war on 24 December?
    Christmas 'Eave.

Decimals
The maths master wrote 11.40 on the blackboard and then rubbed it out to show the class the result of multiplying the number by ten.
'Where is the decimal point now, Billy?'
'On the duster, sir!'

★

Did you hear about the schoolgirl who hated decimals?
    She couldn't see the point.

Decorator
Did you hear about the decorator who died after drinking Supa-Gloss paint?
    They say he had a lovely finish.

Deer
Have you heard the story of the three deer?
    Oh, dear, dear, dear.

Defeat
What is defeat?
    What you walk on.

Defoe
Rick: Who was Daniel Defoe?
Nick: I don't know about Daniel, but Defoe was the author everyone hated.

Dentist
A man burst in to a dentist's surgery waving a gun in the air. He pointed the gun at the dentist's head and shouted:
'Take out all my teeth!'
'But there's nothing wrong with your teeth!' said the dentist, trying to stay calm.
'Never mind that, take them all out,' said the man.
'I'll give you an injection first,' said the dentist.
'No, no injection, no gas, no anaesthetic whatso-ever! Just take out all my teeth,' said the man, still waving the gun. So very slowly and nervously the dentist started to take out the man's teeth, without any anaesthetic. When he had pulled out the last tooth, the man leapt out of the chair, pulled the trigger of the gun – and out popped a flag which said 'Bang!'
'April Fool!' shouted the man, 'I only wanted to buy a toothbrush!'

★

Sam: You said the dentist would be painless – well, he wasn't.
Father: Why? Did he hurt you?
Sam: No, but he screamed when I bit his finger.

★

Dentist: Now calm down, I haven't touched your tooth yet.
Patient through clenched teeth: Maybe not, but you're standing on my foot.

Dentist: Oh, sorry. Now say 'Ah' so that I can get my finger out of your mouth.

★

How long should a dentist practise?
Until he gets it right.

★

Patient: I'd like to make an appointment with the dentist.
Receptionist: Dr Brown is out at the moment.
Patient: Oh good – when do you expect him to be out again?

★

Paul: My dentist is very artistic.
Saul: How's that?
Paul: He draws teeth all the time.

★

Dentist: Open wide, please, Mrs Cable. Oh, my! You've got the biggest cavity I've ever seen, the biggest cavity I've ever seen.
Mrs Cable: You don't have to repeat it.
Dentist: I didn't. That was an echo.

★

Why did the man hit the dentist?
Because he got on his nerves.

★

Rick: What time did the Chinese man go to the dentist?
Nick: I've no idea.
Rick: Tooth-hurty.

★

The phone rang in the dentist's surgery just as he was about to leave for an afternoon's golf. 'I have terrible toothache,' said the caller. Can you please see me this afternoon?'
'Well,' said the dentist. You can come to the surgery and wait. But I do have eighteen other cavities to fill first.'

★

Mrs Able: Why are your charges for Jenny's visit so high? This bill is for £40 instead of your usual £10.
Dentist: To make up for her last visit – she made such a noise that she drove three of my other patients away.

★

Andy: I went to the dentist today.
Zak: Is he nice?
Andy: No, he bores me to tears.

★

'I told you not to swallow!' shouted the dentist. 'That was my last pair of pliers.'

★

Army dentist: I'll need a drill before I can tackle your tooth.
Patient: What! Even you need a rehearsal!

★

News report:
Morale amongst dentists is very low. They are so badly paid for their work that they're pulling out in droves.

★

Why are dentists always unhappy?
Because they always look down in the mouth.

Deodorant
Amy: Have you heard about the newest deodorant on the market called 'Vanish'?
Zoe: Is it any good?
Amy: I'll say! You spray it on and disappear. That way no one knows where the smell is coming from.

Desert
What should you always take into the desert?
A thirst-aid kit.

Detective
When is a detective like a bird of prey?
When he watches you like a hawk.

★

What did the dective say when he tracked down the crook?

I'm policed to meet you.

★

Which famous detective takes bubble baths?
Sherlock Foams.

★

What are private detectives called in Fairyland?
Sherlock Gnomes.

Diamond

What is even harder than a diamond?
Paying for it.

★

Where's the easiest place to find diamonds?
In a pack of cards.

★

Jill: Why did you buy me such a small diamond?
Jack: Because I didn't want the glare to hurt your eyes.

Diamond Ring

Jill: Did you really manage to buy a diamond ring for only £1.50?
Jack: Yes, it didn't have a stone in it, though.

Dictator

Who was one of the strongest dictators?
Muscle-ini.

Dictionary

What do you call someone who keeps a dictionary in their Wellingtons?
Smarty-boots.

Dieting

What do seven days of dieting do?
They make one weak.

★

Did you hear about the fat lady who went on a special diet?
She ate only coconuts and bananas for six months. She didn't lose any weight – but you should see her swing through the trees!

★

Mrs Able: My doctor put me on a seafood diet.
Mrs Cable: Oh really?
Mrs Able: Yes, the more I see, the more I eat.

★

Paul: My Dad's been on a diet.
Saul: Why's that?
Paul: Because he was thick to his stomach.

★

What's the dieter's motto?
If at first you don't recede, diet again.

Digital Watch

What did the digital watch say to its mother?
Look, Ma – no hands!

Dimes

Why isn't a dime worth as much as it used to be?
Because dimes have changed.

Dinner

Paul: Have you had your dinner yet?
Saul: Yes, I was so hungry at seven fifty-nine that I eight o'clock.

★

Late husband: Is my dinner hot?
Angry wife: It should be! It's been on the fire since seven!

★

During dinner at the Ritz
Father kept on having fits,
But something made me really ill —
I was left to pay the bill.

★

Mrs Cable: We're having mother for dinner on Sunday.
Mr Cable: Oh, I'd rather have a nice chicken.

Diplomat

A diplomat is someone who thinks twice before saying nothing.

Diploma

What is a diploma?
   Someone you call on when there's a leak in the pipes.

Dinosaurs

How do dinosaurs pass exams?
   With extinction.

Directions

Motorist: Could you tell me how to get to Grantham from here?
Countryman: Well, go back along this road for a few miles and then take the first turning on the left. No, wait, maybe it's the second turning on the left. Come to think of it, if I was trying to get to Grantham, I wouldn't start from here at all.

Dirty Mind

What's the best way to clean up a dirty mind?
   Think a litter bit less.

Dirty Window

Have you heard the story about the dirty window? No?
   You wouldn't see through it.

Disco

Bill: Was it crowded at the disco last night?
Ben: Not under my table.

★

Who's tall, dark and discos all night?
   Darth Raver.

Discovery

Teacher: Rick, can you point out Canada on the globe, please?
Rick: There, sir!
Teacher: Right — now, Nick, can you tell me who discovered Canada?
Nick: Rick, sir!

★

What did Columbus see on his right hand after he discovered America?
   Five fingers.

Dishwasher

Mrs Able: I should think you'd need an automatic dishwasher with the size of your family!
Mrs Cable: But we don't have automatic dishes yet.

Disinfectant

What has tracks and should be sprayed with disinfectant?
   A septic tank.

Diver

What does a diver get if he works extra hours?
   Under-time payments.

★

Who is always let down by his work mates?
   A deep-sea diver.

Divorce

1st girl: Last week I took my first step towards a divorce.
2nd girl: You left your husband?
1st girl: No, I got married.

Mr Able: I'm divorcing my wife.
Mr Cable: Oh, why?
Mr Able: She smokes in bed.
Mr Cable: Smoking cigarettes in bed isn't *that* bad.
Mr Able: She doesn't smoke cigarettes – she smokes kippers.

★

Did you hear that the comedian's wife sued him for divorce – on the grounds that he was trying to joke her to death!

★

Why did Jane divorce Tarzan?
  He became too big a swinger.

Doctor
Doctor: What have you done for your cold?
Patient: Nothing.
Doctor: Why not?
Patient: Why should I? It hasn't done anything for me.

★

Mr Able: Doctor, please come over quickly. My wife's broken a leg.
Doctor: But I'm a doctor of music.
Mr Able: That's OK – it's the piano leg.

★

Patient: Doctor, why are you writing on my toes?
Doctor: Just adding a footnote.

★

Patient: Doctor, I have flat feet. Can you give me something?
Doctor: How about a bicycle pump.

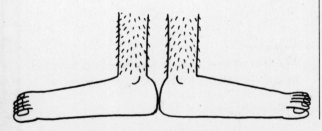

Mrs Cable: Doctor, my husband mistook the medicine you gave me for engine oil.
Doctor: Do you want some more, then?
Mrs Cable: No, but would you come over and shake the car?

★

A short-sighted man went to see the doctor, who told him to eat lots of carrots. A month later the man was back, complaining about the diet.
'Last night,' said the man, 'I went out of the back door and I fell over in the dark.'
'Couldn't you see properly?' asked the doctor.
'Oh, yes, I could see. But I tripped over my ears.'

★

Patient: Doctor, I think I'm shrinking.
Doctor: Well, you'll just have to be a little patient.

★

Patient: Doctor, please help me, I'm boiling.
Doctor: Just simmer down, now.

★

Patient: I've just swallowed four red, three pink and two brown snooker balls.
Doctor: Eat some greens and you'll soon be all right.

★

Patient: Tell me honestly, doctor, is it serious?
Doctor: Well, I wouldn't advise you to start watching any new serials.

★

Patient: Doctor, I feel like a needle.
Doctor: I see your point.

★

A man charged in to a doctor's surgery, jumped on the doctor, and shouted, 'One, two, three, four. . . .'
The doctor fought to get rid of the man. 'What on earth are you doing? Get off!'
'Well,' said the deranged man, 'everyone said I could count on you.'

★

Mr Cable: I'm sorry to be a nuisance, doctor. But can you come and see my old Dad? He keeps saying that he wants to die.
Doctor: You did the right thing by calling me.

★

Paul: That new doctor's no good.
Saul: Why not?
Paul: Sam went to see him last week. He tapped Sam's knee with his little hammer and his leg fell off.

★

Patient: Doctor, how can I avoid this run-down feeling?
Doctor: Look both ways before you cross the street.

★

A man was waiting nervously in the doctor's waiting room, fidgeting and pulling down his hat. People started to stare and he burst out, 'I do hope that the ringing in my ears isn't disturbing you?'

★

A patient was advised by his doctor to go away for a long weekend for a rest and a change. The man went back to see the doctor after the weekend, and was very annoyed.
'Didn't the rest and the change do you any good, then?' asked the doctor.
'No, not a bit,' replied the man. The porter got my change and the hotel got the rest.'

★

Patient: Doctor, have you got something for my liver?
Doctor: Certainly, here's some bacon.

★

Patient: Doctor, I feel like a racehorse.
Doctor: Take these pills every two furlongs.

★

Patient: Doctor, I think I'm a bee.
Doctor: Buzz off, will you? I'm busy.

★

Patient: Doctor, will these little pink pills really help?
Doctor: Well no one I've given them to has ever come back.

★

Patient: Doctor, I keep thinking I'm a fridge.
Doctor: Shut your mouth, will you? Your light is shining right in my eyes.

★

Patient: Doctor, I keep thinking I'm a doorknob.
Doctor: All right. There's no need to fly off the handle.

★

Doctor: I feel like a bar of soap.
Doctor: That's life, boy.

★

Patient: Doctor, I keep thinking I'm a fly.
Doctor: Well, come down off the ceiling and we'll discuss it.

★

Doctor: How are those pills I prescribed to improve your memory working?
Doctor: Which pills?

★

Patient: Doctor, every bone in my body hurts.
Doctor: My, my – aren't you glad you're not a sardine?

★

Patient: Doctor, I keep on thinking I'm a strawberry.
Doctor: You really are in a jam, aren't you.

★

Doctor: You must take things quietly.
Patient: I do – I'm a cat burglar!

★

Patient: Doctor, I've just swallowed a bullet.
Doctor: Point the other way, would you?

★

Patient: I've just swallowed my flute!
Doctor: Just be thankful you don't play the organ!

★

What kind of doctor would you take a sick duck to see?
A quack doctor.

★

Marathon runner: Doctor, there's something wrong with my feet.
Doctor: Yes, indeed, it looks like athlete's foot.

★

Patient: Please help me, doctor, I prefer cotton vests to thermal ones.
Doctor: I don't see a problem here. Lots of people do, even me.
Patient: Oh, good! How do you like yours — roast or barbecued?

★

Doctor: There's nothing wrong with you. You're just lazy.
Patient: Can you give me the medical term for that so I can tell my boss what I'm suffering from?

★

Doctor: How did you get that splinter in your finger?
Patient: I scratched my head!

★

Patient: Doctor I keep feeling like a sheet of glass.
Doctor: I thought so. Next time don't come through the window.

★

Patient: Doctor, I feel like a doorbell.
Doctor: Take these pills and I'll give you a ring.

★

Patient: Doctor, I feel like a guitar.
Doctor: Wait while I make some notes.

★

Doctor: Say 'one hundred', please.
Patient: Why not ninety-nine?
Doctor: Inflation, you know.

★

Patient: Doctor, I keep thinking I'm a dog.
Doctor: Why do you say that?
Patienrt: Here, feel my nose.

★

Patient: Doctor, I can't seem to stop stealing things.
Doctor: Take these pills, they should help you.
Patient: But what if they don't?
Doctor: Pick up a Rolls for me, would you?

★

Fat patient: What can I do? I'm so worried about losing my figure.
Doctor: You'll just have to diet.
Fat patient: Yes, but what colour?

★

Doctor: You should have sent for me sooner, Mrs Able. Your husband is seriously ill.
Mrs Able: I thought I'd give him a chance to get better first.

★

Caller: Doctor, can you come over straight away?
Doctor: Why, what's the matter?
Caller: We can't get in to our house.
Doctor: Well, call the police. That's nothing to do with me.
Caller: Oh, yes, it is. The baby's swallowed the front door key.

★

Patient: Doctor, I think I need glasses!
Cashier: You certainly do, sir, this is a bank!

★

Patient: Doctor, I think I'm really ill.
Doctor: What are the symptoms — do you have spots?
Patient: Yes, all over.
Doctor: Do your eyes ache?
Patient: Oh, yes.
Doctor: And your colour's not too good, is it.

Patient: No.
Doctor: I'm the same – I wonder what we've got?

★

Patient: Doctor, I feel like a goat.
Doctor: Well, now, how are the kids?

★

A man who went to see his doctor for a check-up was passed perfectly fit, but the doctor suggested he take more exercise.
'Try walking about three miles a day,' he said.
'I'd get dizzy if I walked three miles a day!' said the patient.
'Why would you get dizzy walking?' asked the doctor.
'Because I'm a lighthouse keeper.'

★

Patient: Doctor, I feel like an onion.
Doctor: Well, what a pickle to be in!

★

Patient: Doctor, I feel like a car.
Doctor: Park over there a moment, will you?

★

Patient: Doctor, I think I've got chicken pox.
Doctor: That's a rash thing to say.

★

Pretty patient: Doctor, I have a pain in my right side.
Doctor (after examination): You have acute appendicitis.
Pretty patient: Don't get fresh with me! Just tell me what's wrong, will you?

★

Patient: Doctor, please will you treat me?
Doctor: Certainly not! I'll have to charge you the same as my other patients.

★

Patient: Help me, doctor. My head feels stuffed up, my nose is running and my chest feels like lead.
Doctor: You need a plumber, not a doctor.

Patient: Well, doctor, you were certainly right when you said you'd have me up on my feet and walking around.
Doctor: Good! When did you start walking?
Patient: Straight after I sold my car to pay your bill.

★

Patient: I'm sorry to call you out so late, doctor.
Doctor: Don't worry about it at all. I was seeing another patient down the road and might just as well kill two birds with one stone.

★

What do you call a doctor who has greasy fingers?
A medicine dropper.

★

Patient: Doctor, I've had stomach ache since eating a dozen oysters yesterday.
Doctor: Were they fresh?
Patient: I don't know.
Doctor: Well, how did they look when you opened them up?
Patient: You mean you're supposed to open the shells?

★

Receptionist: The new doctor's very funny – he'll have you in stitches!
Patient: I hope not! I've only come in for a check-up.

★

A doctor was examining a little boy in his surgery. He went in to the waiting room and asked the receptionist for a pair of pliers. She gave him one and he went back in to the surgery. A little while later he came out again and asked for a screwdriver.
'For goodness' sake! cried the little boy's mother. 'What is the matter with my son?'
'I don't know yet,' said the doctor. 'I can't get my instrument cupboard open.'

★

Doctor: What seems to be the trouble?
Patient: I get the feeling that nobody can hear what I say.
Doctor: I said, what seems to be the trouble?

★

Patient: Doctor, I feel like an apple.
Doctor: Don't worry, I won't bite you.

★

Patient: Doctor, you think I'm overweight, don't you?
Doctor: What makes you say that?
Patient: Well, when you were doing my check up, you said, 'Open your mouth and say Moo. . . .'

★

Why was the unemployed doctor angry? Because he had no patients.

★

Patient: Doctor, I feel half dead.
Doctor: I'll see if I can make arrangements for you to be buried up to your waist.

★

Patient: I must tell you, doctor, I feel like my old self again.
Doctor: In that case you need further treatment.

★

Doctor: Well, Sam, how's the broken rib coming along?
Sam: I keep getting a stitch in my side, doctor.
Doctor: That's good – it shows the bones are knitting.

★

Patient: Doctor, I think there's something wrong with my stomach.
Doctor: Well keep your coat buttoned up and no one will notice.

★

Jack: How's your new doctor?
Jill: Wonderful! He's so sympathetic he makes you feel really ill.

On his hospital rounds, the specialist stopped at the bedside of a very sick man. 'I have to admit that you are seriously ill,' he said solemnly. 'Is there anything you'd like?'
'Yes, please,' said the patient, 'a second opinion.'

★

Doctor: Breathe out three times, please.
Patient: Are you going to check my lungs?
Doctor: No, I'm going to clean my glasses.

★

Patient: Doctor, what can I do to stop my nose running?
Doctor: Put out your foot and trip it up.

★

Patient: Doctor, I keep thinking I'm a dumpling.
Doctor: Well, don't get in such a stew.

★

Patient: Doctor, please help me – I keep stealing things.
Doctor: Have you taken anything for it?

★

Doctor: Hello, there, Mrs Cable. I haven't seen you for ages.
Mrs Cable: That's right, doctor. I've been ill.

★

Patient: Doctor, can you give me something for wind?
Doctor: Yes, take this kite.

★

Patient: Well, doctor, how do I stand?
Doctor: I've no idea – it's a miracle.

★

Patient: Doctor, please help me. I think I'm at death's door.
Doctor: Don't worry, I'll soon pull you through.

★

Patient: Doctor, I keep thinking I'm a bird.
Doctor: Perch over there and I'll tweet you in a moment.

★

Doctor on the telephone: Yes, you're obviously very sick, but I've told you, Mother, I never make house calls.

★

Patient: Doctor, I've got such a sore throat.
Doctor: Go to the window, please, and stick your tongue out.
Patient: Why, will that help?
Doctor: Not a bit, but I don't like the neighbours.

★

Patient: Doctor, I'm very nervous. This is the first operation I've ever had.
Doctor: Don't worry – this is the first operation I've ever performed.

★

Patient: Doctor, I feel like a yo-yo.
Doctor: Sit down, sit down, sit down.

★

Patient: Doctor, these strength pills you gave me aren't doing me any good at all.
Doctor: Why not?
Patient: I can't unscrew the bottle top.

★

Patient: Doctor, I can't seem to stop pulling ugly faces.
Doctor: Well, I can't see that's too serious a problem.
Patient: Tell that to the people with ugly faces!

★

Doctor: And how do you feel today?
Patient: Same as always, Doctor, with my hands.

★

Patient: Doctor, I don't think the pills you gave me are doing any good.
Doctor: Have you been taking two on an empty stomach as I told you?

Patient: Well, I've tried, but they keep rolling off.

★

Doctor: How is your husband's rheumatism?
Wife: Not so good. I rubbed his back with brandy as you suggested, and he broke his neck trying to lick it off.

★

Patient: Doctor, I get the feeling that everyone is taking advantage of me.
Doctor: That's nonsense!
Patient: Oh, that makes me feel much better. Thank you, doctor. What do I owe you?
Doctor: How much have you got?

★

Patient: Doctor, I swallowed a clock last week.
Doctor: That could be serious! Why didn't you come to see me last week?
Patient: I didn't want to alarm anybody.

★

Patient: Doctor, please help me, I eat dates.
Doctor: What's wrong with that.
Patient: I eat them off calendars.

★

Doctor, doctor, I feel like a pair of curtains.
Be quiet and pull yourself together.

★

Patient: Doctor, everyone thinks I'm a cricket ball.
Doctor: How's that?
Patient: Oh no! Not you as well!

Patient: Doctor, I keep thinking I'm a bridge.
Doctor: What has come over you?
Patient: Lorries, buses, cars, bikes. . . .

★

Patient: Doctor, doctor, I keep thinking I'm a dustbin.
Doctor: Don't talk such rubbish.

★

Doctor: You have a bad cold. My advice is that you avoid draughts for the time being.
Patient: Can I play Monopoly instead?

★

Doctor, doctor, I keep thinking I'm invisible.
Who said that?

★

Doctor, doctor, I've only got 59 seconds to live!
Just wait a minute, please.

★

Patient: Doctor, I couldn't sleep a wink last night.
Doctor: Did you try counting sheep?
Patient: Yes, I counted 783, 459 sheep – and then it was time to get up!

★

Patient: Doctor, I keep seeing double.
Doctor: Sit on the couch, please.
Patient: Which one?

★

Patient: Doctor, can you cure my spots?
Doctor: I never make rash promises.

★

Doctor, doctor, I feel like an old sock.
Well, I'll be darned.

Doctor-Nurse
If it takes an apple a day to keep the doctor away, what does it take to get rid of the nurse?

Dodos
A sailing ship was anchored off a desert island and two dodos on the shore watched the crew rowing towards them.
'Quick, we'd better hide,' said one dodo.
'Why? They look friendly,' said his friend.
'We're supposed to be extinct, though,' said the first dodo.

Dog
Andy: I've got a new dog. Come over and play with him.
Zak: Does he bite?
Andy: I don't know, I want you to help me find out.

★

Andy: My dog's bone idle.
Zak: Really? How do you know?
Andy: Yesterday when I was watering the garden he never lifted a leg to help me!

★

Visitor: I don't believe my eyes! There's a dog in the High Street handing out parking tickets.
Local: Is it brown, with pointed ears and a stubby tail?
Visitor: Yes.
Local: Well, no wonder. That's the town police dog.

★

What is the difference between a flea-ridden dog and a bored guest?
—One is going to itch, the other is itching to go.

★

Did you hear about the man who thought the Rover 3500 was a bionic dog?

★

Why did the dog run away from home?
Doggone if I know.

★

A lady went into a restaurant for afternoon tea and sat down at a table with her dog on the chair beside her. The waitress came to take her order, and said,

'I'm so sorry, madam, dogs are not allowed in the restaurant.'

'But mine is a very special dog,' said the lady. 'It's a talking dog.'

'That makes no difference,' said the waitress. 'No dogs are allowed in the restaurant.' But the lady would not leave, so the waitress went to call the manager, who repeated that dogs were not allowed. Still the lady would not leave, insisting that her dog was very special.'

'All right, then,' said the manager, 'if he's so special, let's hear him talk! What's above this restaurant?' he asked the dog.

'R-r-r-oof,' said the dog.

'There!' said the manager. 'I knew he couldn't talk!

Both of you, get out!'

So the lady left with her dog. When they got outside, the dog looked up at her mistress and said,

'Oh! I see what he meant! Above the restaurant is a hairdressing salon!'

★

What sort of clothes does a pet dog wear?
  A petticoat.

★

Andy: Is your dog a good watchdog?
Zak: No, all he ever watches is television.

★

What happened to the stupid dog which lay down to eat its bone?
  When it got up it only had three legs.

★

What do you call a dog in the middle of a muddy road?
  A mutt in a rut.

★

Why did the dog howl?
  Because he barked up the wrong tree.

★

Paul: I tied my dog to a ten-foot lead yesterday and he still managed to reach my Dad's slippers twenty feet away.

Saul: How come?
Paul: I forgot to tie the lead to anything.

★

Amy: What kind of dog do you have?
Zoe: A bird dog.
Amy: Oh, I've never heard him sing.

★

A man walking down the road was stopped by another man asking if he would buy his dog for a few pounds. The man was about to refuse when the dog said, 'Please buy me, sir. You look kind and my master is very cruel to me. He doesn't look after me properly and never feeds me.'

The man was astounded. 'What on earth do you want to sell that wonderful talking dog for?' he asked.

'Because I can't stand a liar,' said the owner.

★

A boy took his dog in to the cinema with him when he went to see 'Watership Down', and the dog sat quietly in the seat beside him. After the film finished and the boy was leaving, the usherette said, 'Fancy your dog enjoying the film.'

'Yes,' replied the boy, 'I was surprised – he didn't like the book at all.'

★

Where do you take a sick dog?
  To the dogtor.

★

A man went in to a pet shop to buy a dog. It was a very hot day and the dog the sales assistant showed him was breathing hard with his tongue hanging out. The man said he didn't want the dog.

'Why sir, isn't his coat good?' asked the assistant.

'The coat's fine,' said the man, 'but I don't like the pants.'

★

1st dog: My name's Rover – what's yours?
2nd dog: I'm not quite sure – but I think it's Down Boy.

Rick: Is your dog fond of children?
Nick: Yes, but he prefers biscuits.

★

Adam: My dog has no nose.
Eve: How does he smell?
Adam: Terrible.

★

What did the dog say when he sat on a sheet of sandpaper?
    Ruff!

★

Mrs Dainty: It's so kind of you to invite me to tea. And haven't you got a friendly dog — just look how he keeps wagging his tail!
Mrs Dirty: That's probably because you're eating out of his bowl.

★

When is a black dog not a black dog?
    When it's a greyhound.

★

Jack: Our dog is just like one of the family.
Jill: Oh really? Which one?

★

Jack: What would you do if your dog was chewing up your favourite book?
Jill: I'd take the words right out of his mouth.

★

Amy: I know a hairdresser who breeds dogs.
Zoe: What kind?
Amy: Shampoodles.

Amy: Why do you call your dog Camera?
Zoe: Because he's always snapping.

★

Bill: Every day my dog and I go for a tramp in the woods.
Ben: Does the dog enjoy it?
Bill: Yes, but the tramp's getting a bit fed up.

★

What goes tick-tock, woof?
    A watchdog.

★

Why did the dog go in to the corner every time the doorbell rang?
    He was a boxer.

★

Rick: My dog has no tail.
Nick: So how do you know when he's happy?
Rick: When he stops biting me.

★

Andy: My dog died of flu.
Zak: I didn't know dogs got flu.
Andy: Mine flew under the car.

★

A man tied his Dobermann to a post outside a supermarket and went inside to do his shopping. As he got to the till to pay, a very distraught lady came in and called, 'Whose Dobermann is that outside?'
'It's mine,' said the man. 'Why?'
'I'm afraid my dog has just killed him,' replied the lady.
'Killed my Dobermann?' cried the man. 'How? What kind of dog do you have?'
'A Dachshund,' said the lady.
'But how could a dog as small as a Dachshund kill a huge Doberman?'
'She got stuck in his throat and he choked to death.'

★

Amy: There's only one thing I hate about my dog.
Zoe: What's that?

Amy: He hides under the bed when there's a thunderstorm.

Zoe: Well, he's frightened. What's wrong with that?

Amy: There isn't enough room for me!

★

What is essential knowledge for anyone trying to teach their dogs tricks?
More than the dog.

★

Andy: What's your dog called?

Zak: Isaiah.

Andy: Why do you call him Isaiah?

Zak: Because one eye's 'igher than the other.

★

What is the last hair on a dog's tail called?
Dog's hairs.

★

Why did the dog stop going to school with his master?
Because the dog had passed all his exams.

★

Rick: Did you know there's a star called the Dog Star?

Nick: You can't be Sirius!

★

Mother: Sam! Stop pulling the dog's tail!

Sam: Mum, he's doing the pulling.

★

Paul: Why do you call your dog Johann Sebastian?

Saul: Have you heard his Bach?

★

Paul: Why do you call your dog Ginger?

Saul: Because Ginger snaps.

★

Mrs Able: I'm entering my poodle in the county dog show.

Mrs Cable: How exciting! Do you think she'll win a prize?

Mrs Able: No, but she'll meet a nice class of dog.

★

Jack: I've lost my dog.

Jill: Well, put an advertisement in the paper.

Jack: Don't be silly – my dog can't read.

★

Jack: My dog is really clever.

Jill: Oh?

Jack: Yes – I ask him to subtract 20 from 20 and he says nothing.

★

Jack: Is your dog a pointer or a setter?

Jill: Neither one. He's a disappointer and an upsetter.

★

What do you get if you cross a terrier with a vegetable?
A Jack Brussel.

★

What do you get if you cross a tractor with a dog?
A Land-Rover.

★

What is the difference between a good-natured dog and a bad scholar?
One rarely bites, the other barely writes.

★

What do you get if you cross a gun dog with a telephone?
A golden receiver.

★

Why does a dog chase its tail?
To make both ends meet.

★

Which dogs have their eyes closest together?
The smallest dogs.

★

Lady in pet shop: I like this dog, but his legs are too short.

Manager: But all four do reach the floor, madam.

Dog and Cat
What would you get if you crossed a dog and a cat?
An animal that chases itself.

Dog Biscuits
What is the main ingredient in dog biscuits?
Collie flour.

Doggerel
A doggerel is a little dog.

Dog Licence
Silly Billy took his dog for a walk one day when he was stopped by a policeman.
'Does your dog have a licence, little boy?' asked the policeman.
'He doesn't need one,' said Silly Billy. 'He's not old enough to drive.'

Dogma
Teacher: Can anyone tell me what dogma is?
Silly Billy: A puppy's mother.

Doll
Have you heard about the new doctor doll?
When you wind it up it operates on batteries.

Dollars and Cents
A dollar and a cent fell out of a pocket. The cent rolled along the gutter and fell down the drain. Why didn't the dollar follow?
Because it had more cents (sense).

Why is a dollar millionaire so clever?
Because he has a lost of cents.

Dolphins
Paul: I bumped in to a dolphin when I went swimming yesterday.
Saul: Did you do it on porpoise?

★

What do you call a school of angry dolphins?
Cross porpoises.

Dominoes
Adam: Can you play dominoes?
Eve: I don't know, I've never tried.

Donkey
A farmer was selling his donkey and a prospective buyer asked him why the donkey was so cheap. The farmer told him, 'It's a good donkey, but it sits on eggs.' The buyer thought about this, decided he didn't often have eggs, so he bought the donkey.
As he was riding it home they reached a stream and, crossing the bridge, the donkey sat down. The new owner dismounted and tugged and pushed the donkey until at last it got up, and they went back to the farmer where the owner explained what had happened.
'Oh,' said the farmer, 'I forgot to mention that he also sits on water.'

★

What do you get if you cross a donkey with a mother?
Ass-ma.

★

What is the difference between a stubborn donkey and a postage stamp?
One you lick with a stick, the other you stick with a lick.

★

Jack was showing Jill his holiday photographs. She admired all the scenery and the pictures of his friends, and then Jack showed her one of him having a donkey-ride on the beach. 'Who's that sitting on your back?' she asked.

★

Rick: If a donkey's head is pointing north, where would its tail be pointing?
Nick: South?
Rick: No — to the ground!

Door

When is a door not a door?
  When it's ajar.

Doorbell

What never asks questions, but gets a great number of answers?
  A doorbell.

★

A little girl was trying to reach up to ring a doorbell. A lady passing by stopped and rang the bell for her.
'Thanks,' said the little girl. 'Now we'd both better run for it!'

★

How do you use an Egyptian doorbell?
  Toot-and-come-in.

★

Electrician: I've come to repair your doorbell, madam.
Lady of the house: You should have come earlier. I'm just going out.
Electrician: Madam, I've been standing on the doorstep all morning ringing your bell!

Door Knockers

What did they give the man who invented door knockers?
  The No Bell Prize.

Doorstep

What relation is a doormat to a doorstep?
  A step farther.

Double Glazing

What is double glazing?
  A man with glasses who's had too much to drink.

Double Negative

Teacher: Billy, can you give me an example of a double negative?
Silly Billy: I don't know none.
Teacher: Well done, Billy!

Double Vision

Adam: That man over there sees everything double.
Eve: Poor man — he must find it hard to get a job.
Adam: No — he's a meter reader for the Gas Board.

★

What's the quickest way to cure double vision?
  Close one eye.

Doughnut

Teacher: If I bought 40 doughnuts for 80 pence, what would each one be?
Silly Billy: Stale!

Dracula

What kind of ship did Dracula captain?
  A blood vessel.

★

Why do people always take advantage of Dracula?
  Because no one ever gives a sucker a break.

★

What is Count Dracula's favourite breakfast?
  Readyneck.

★

What space film stars Count Dracula?
  The Vampire Strikes Back.

★

Why was Count Dracula glad to help young vampires?
  Because he liked to see new blood in the business.

★

Who has feathers, fangs, and goes quack?
  Count Duckula.

★

Was Dracula ever married?
  No – he was a bat-chelor.

★

Tom: There's Dick – he'll know!
Harry: Yes – how do I join Dracula's fan club?
Dick: Send your name, address and blood group!

★

Paul: How would you describe Dracula films?
Saul: Fangtastic!

★

Why is the Dracula family so close?
  Because blood is thicker than water.

★

What is Count Dracula's favourite snack?
  A fangfurter.

Dragon

What games do dragons play at parties?
  Swallow my leader.

★

What did one dragon say to another?
  I keep trying to give up smoking, but I can't.

★

Why do dragons sleep during the day?
  So that they can fight knights.

★

What did the dragon say when he saw St George in all his shining armour?
  Oh, no! Not more tinned food!

★

What do you call a dragon that weighs twenty tonnes and has six heads and breathes fire?
  Sir!

★

What kind of planes do dragons fly?
  Spitfires.

Drama Teacher

Why is a drama teacher like the Pony Express?
  Because he is a stage coach.

Drawing

How can you draw teeth painlessly?
  With a pencil.

★

Amy: What are you doing?
Zoe: I'm drawing my bath.
Amy: I paint too, you know.

★

Why did the boy draw a square when the teacher asked him to draw a ring?
  It was a boxing ring.

Dream

A man went to see his doctor because he hadn't slept properly for over a week. He told the doctor that every night he had the same dream, of a door with a sign on it.
'I push and push the door, but it won't open.'
'What does the sign say?' asked the doctor.
'Pull,' said the patient.

★

Rick: I only ever have one dream. I dream about cricket. I'm always playing one long game of cricket that never ends. Do you think anything's wrong with me?
Nick: Well, don't you ever dream about girls?
Rick: What? And miss my innings?

Dress

What dress does everyone have, but nobody wears?
 Address.

★

Amy: I bought a new dress today. It's already.
Zoe: What's already?
Amy: The dress – it's crimson all over.

★

Mrs Able: How do you like my dress? It's fifty years old.
Mrs Cable: Did you make it yourself?

★

Mrs Cable: I'd like a dress to wear around the house, please.
Saleslady: Certainly, madam, how big is your house?

★

Customer: I'd like to try on that dress in the window, please.
Salesgirl: I'm sorry, madam, you'll have to try it on in the changing-rooms like everyone else.

★

Customer: I'd like a dress to match my eyes.
Sales assistant: I'm sorry, madam, we don't sell bloodshot dresses.

Dressing

What is always dressing?
 Salad cream.

Drink

Lady of the manor: Why do you drink to excess, my man?
Drunken tramp: Because of my problem, lady.
Lady of the manor: And what might your problem be?
Drunken tramp: I'm an alcoholic.

★

Poppy's father's boss was coming to the house for dinner one night. When he arrived, her mother was in the kitchen and Poppy's father asked her to hand the boss his drink. The boss took the drink, but Poppy stood in front of him, staring.
'What's the matter?' asked the boss.
'I'm waiting to see you do your trick,' said Poppy.
'What trick?' he asked.
'Dad says you drink like a fish.'

Driving

A motorist was driving the wrong way down a one-way street. He was stopped by a traffic policeman, who asked him if he knew where he was going.
'Yes,' said the man, 'but I must be very late. Everyone else is coming back!'

★

Lorry driver (to new mate): Step down from the cab, will you, and tell me if my indicators work.
Mate: Yes, no, yes, no, yes, no.

★

Teacher: Can anyone tell me what we call someone who drives a motor car?
Silly Billy: Doesn't that depend on how close he misses you?

★

Tom: Dick drove his car in to the lake last night.
Harry: Why did he do that?
Tom: He was trying to dip his headlights.

★

Silly Billy took a friend for a drive up into the mountains. The friend got quite nervous with all the hairpin bends and said, 'I get really really scared each time you go round the curves.' 'Then do what I do,' said Silly Billy, 'close your eyes.'

★

Rick: What happens when everything's coming your way?
Nick: You're in the wrong lane.

Amy: We bumped into some old friends yesterday.
Zoe: Oh, your Mum was driving again, I guess?

★

Jill: Quick, grab the wheel!
Jack: Why, what's the matter?
Jill: There's a lamp post coming straight for us.

★

Traffic policeman: You were driving at 90 mph, Miss.
Soppy Poppy: Isn't that wonderful! I only passed my test yesterday.

★

1st angel: You can tell that old boy was a careful driver when he was on earth.
2nd angel: How's that?
1st angel: He's asked to be fitted with wing mirrors up here.

★

What animal drives a motor car?
    The road hog.

★

It takes about 2,000 screws to put together a motor car.
    But only one nut to scatter it all over the motorway.

★

Father: Sam! How on earth did you manage to drive into the dining room?
Sam: Easy, Dad. I turned left at the kitchen.

Driving Test
Did you hear about the man who failed his driving test because he opened his door to let the clutch out?

★

Paul: My eldest brother has just passed his driving test.
Saul: Good for him!
Paul: And good for my three brothers and me, too. We can all move up one bike.

Dr Jekyll
Why does Dr Jekyll seek the sun in winter?
    To tan his Hyde.

★

What was Dr Jekyll's favourite game?
    Hyde and Seek.

Drowning
A man related this tail of woe when he got in to work one morning: 'I almost drowned last night! The bed spread, the pillow slipped and I fell in to the spring.'

Drums
What did the parents say when their son wanted to play the drums?
    Beat it!

★

How do drum sets greet each other?
    They say, 'Hit the skin!'

★

What did Sam say when his mother called him in for his drum lesson?
    Smashing!

Drunk
Witness: He was as drunk as a judge.
Judge: Don't you mean 'as drunk as a lord'?
Witness: Yes, my lord.

★

Two drunks went staggering home one night. One looked up to the sky and said, 'Is that the sun or the moon?'
'I don't know,' replied the other, 'I don't live around here either.'

★

A drunken man, locked up in the cells late one night, was singing and shouting at the top of his voice. The policeman on duty knocked him on the head to try and make him quiet.
'What was that?' said the drunk.
'It just struck one,' said the policeman.

'What a good thing I wasn't in here at midnight!' said the drunk.

Duchess
Amy: Have you seen the Duchess?
Zoe: No, but I have seen an English 's'.

Duck
What happens to a duck before it grows up?
    It grows down.

★

Andy: Do you like duck?
Zak: Yes, it's my favourite chicken after turkey.

★

If you gave a lift to a duck, would it be called a viaduct?

★

What do you get if you cross a duck with a fire?
    A firequacker.

★

What is a fast duck?
    A quick quack.

★

What did the duck say as it rushed in to the duckpond?
    Quick-quick!

★

What does every duckling become when it first takes to the water?
    Wet.

City visitor: So this is a duck farm! Is business picking up?
Duck farmer: No, picking down.

★

What do you get when you cross a duck with a cow?
    Milk and quackers.

★

Rick: Which of those ducks would you choose for a pet?
Nick: Eider.

★

What do duck decorators do?
    Paper over the quacks.

★

Some ducks were walking down a path. There was a duck in front of two ducks, a duck behind two ducks, and a duck between two ducks. How many ducks in all?
    Three ducks walking in a line.

★

What are ducks' favourite films?
    Duckumentaries

★

Why do ducks look sad?
    Because when they preen their feathers they get down in the mouth.

Rick: What's the difference between ducks and geese?

Nick: Ducks go 'quack' and geese go 'honk'.
Rick: Right! And if you were out shooting and you saw a flock of birds going 'honk, honk,' what would you do?
Nick: I'd pull in and let them pass me.

★

What happens when ducks fly upside down?
   They quack up.

★

Rick: We ran over a duckway yesterday.
Nick: What's a duckway?
Rick: Oh, about seven pounds.

★

What is a duck's favourite television programme?
   The feather forecast.

Dumbbell

Jack: My doctor told me to exercise with a dumbbell.
Jill: So?
Jack: Come to the gym with me then, will you?

★

Paul: Did your mother ever lift weights?
Saul: No, why?
Paul: I just wondered how she raised a dumbbell like you.

Dumb Blonde

Jack: What happened to that dumb blonde Johnny used to go out with?
Jill: I dyed my hair.

Dunce

What's the difference between an angler and a dunce?
   One baits his hooks while the other hates his books.

Dunce's Cap

Silly Billy was put in the corner wearing the dunce's cap because he got all his test answers wrong. He fidgeted about for a while and then said to the teacher, 'Sir, this dunce's cap is too tight.' 'Well, Billy,' said the teacher, 'that's because it's fool to the brim.'

Dust

Soppy Poppy came home from Sunday School and asked her father whether or not it was true that people really come from dust.
'Yes,' he replied, 'in a way we do.'
'And go back to dust?' asked Poppy.
'Yes, in a way that's true too,' said her father.
Poppy went up to her bedroom and then came bounding down the stairs, shouting, 'Everyone come quickly! Somebody's coming or going under my bed!'

★

Rick: The Bible says we're made of dust, right?
Nick: Right.
Rick: Then how come we don't get muddy in the rain?

Dustbin

The dustman was on his rounds one Monday morning, and realized that one household had forgotten to put out their dustbin. The dustman rang the doorbell and knocked on the door and soon an upstairs window opened and a sleepy head looked out.
'Where's yer bin?' asked the dustman.
'I'se bin asleep,' answered the sleepy head. 'Where's yer bin?'

★

Sam: Mum, I wish we could have a dustbin like all the other families!
Mother: Be quiet and keep eating.

Dustcart

Paul: Have you heard the joke about the dustcart?
Saul: Yes, it's a load of rubbish.

★

What has four wheels and flies?
   A dustcart.

★

Why does a dustman never accept an invitation?
   Because he's a refuseman.

Dutchman

What's the difference between a tube and a mad Dutchman?
   One is a hollow cylinder, the other is a silly Hollander.

Dwarf

What do you call a dwarf novelist?
   A short story writer.

★

What did the dwarf say when the giant asked to borrow some money?
   Sorry, I'm a bit short.

Dynamite

A famous scientist began his speech with the immortal words, 'Everyone laughed when I invented a new kind of dynamite, but when I dropped it they exploded.'

Dying

Husband: Am I really dying?
Wife: Yes, you are.
Husband: Can I have one last request?
Wife: Yes, of course. What is it?
Husband: Can I have a slice of your sponge cake?
Wife: Certainly not! I'm saving that for the funeral.

★

Foreman: You had last week off work, lad, because you told me your mother was dying. But I saw her coming out of the hairdresser's yesterday.
Workman: That's right. She was dyeing there. Now she's doing all the hair-cutting.

Dynamite

What happened when the Royal Navy fed dynamite to hens?
   It got mine layers.

Eagle

Why did the captain refuse to put a sick eagle in the ship's hold?
   Because it would have been an illegal cargo.

Earl

What happened to the earl who was given an OBE?
   He became an earlobe.

Ear Muffs

Teacher: Poppy, why are you wearing your ear muffs indoors?

Soppy Poppy: Because I'm trying to stop everything going in one ear and out the other.

Ears

What did one ear say to the other ear?

Between you and me, we need a haircut.'

★

Silly Billy: Mother! Mother! There's something wrong with my ears. Every time I put my fingers in them, I can't hear a thing.

★

There was a young man of Devizes
Whose ears were of two different sizes.
The one that was small
Was of no use at all,
But the other won several prizes.

★

What did one ear say to the other?

I didn't know we lived in the same block.

Earth

Why was the little girl carrying a bag full of earth?

It was instant mud-pie mix.

★

What do you do with all the earth you dig out of a hole?

Dig another hole to bury it in!

Earthquake

What did one mountain say to another mountain after an earthquake?

That wasn't my fault.

Earwig

If an earwig fell out of a building, what would he say?

'Ere we go.

Easter Egg

What did the mother egg say to her baby on its first Easter?

Don't get over-eggcited.

Eating

Mother: Don't eat your chips so quickly, Sam.

Sam: But I might lose my appetite unless I do.

★

Mother: Now, Poppy, eat up your greens — they're good for growing children.

Soppy Poppy: But who wants to grow children?

★

Where does it cost you £20 a head to eat?

In a cannibal restaurant.

★

Two girls went in to a cafe to eat their sandwiches.

'Hey!' the waitress shouted, 'you can't eat your own food in here!'

So the two girls swapped sandwiches.

★

Tom: Dick shouldn't be eating chips with his fingers, should he.

Harry: No, fingers should be eaten separately.

★

101

A family had finished their meal in a restaurant and the father called over the waiter to ask for the bill. 'Oh,' he said, 'and could we have a bag to take my daughter's leftovers home to the dog, please?'
'Oh, Dad!' cried his daughter, 'are we getting a dog?'

Echo
What speaks every known language, but never went to school?
    An echo.

★

What can you hear but not see, and only speaks when it's spoken to?
    An echo.

Edward
Why did a father call both his sons Edward?
    Because two Eds are better than one.

Eel
If you cross an electric eel with a puffin, what do you get?
    A big electric bill.

Eggs
How can you drop an egg ten feet without breaking it?
    Drop it eleven feet – for the first ten it will stay whole.

★

Old Mother Hen: I'm going to give you some advice.
Young Chick: Yes, what's that?
Old Mother Hen: An egg a day keeps the axe away.

★

What's smooth, oval, and very rich?
    An eggstravaganza.

★

Where does an egg start from if it's seen floating down the Ganges?
    A chicken.

★

What did the egg in the monastery say?
    'Tough luck – out of the frying pan in to the friar.'

★

What's another name for a mischievous egg?
    A practical yolker.

★

What goes up brown or white and comes down yellow and white?
    An egg.

★

A countrywoman walked to her nearby farm every Friday to get eggs. One Friday, as she was watching the farmer put the eggs in to a box, she said, 'They're very small today.'
    'They were only laid yesterday,' said the farmer, 'give them a chance!'

★

What did the Headmaster Egg say to the Pupil Egg?
    I have no choice but to eggspell you.

★

Could you kill someone just by throwing eggs at him?
    Yes – because he would be eggs-terminated.

★

What did the King Egg say to the Bad Egg?
    I'm going to have you eggsecuted.

★

What's as tall as the Post Office Tower and contains one thousand eggs?
    A multi-storey omelette.

★

Amy: My uncle's farm had a chicken that laid a six-inch-long egg. Can your farm beat that?
Zoe: Yes – with an egg-beater!

Boiled egg in saucepan: It's hot in here!
Second egg: Wait until you get out – they'll bash your head in.

★

Jack: Have you heard the joke about the eggs?
Jill: No – tell me.
Jack: Two bad.

★

Teacher: So, class, you understand – you cannot get eggs without chickens.
Silly Billy: Dad can.
Teacher: What do you mean, Billy?
Silly Billy: Dad keeps ducks.

★

How can you eat an egg without breaking its shell?
Ask someone else to break it.

★

Is there anything nutritious in an eggshell?
Yes – an egg.

★

Amy: I hear that egg shampoo is good for your hair.
Zoe: Yes – but how do you get a hen to lay an egg on your head?

★

What would you get if you crossed a hen with an electric organ?
Hammond eggs.

Egg Whisk
What did the egg say to the whisk?
I know when I'm beaten.

Egg White
What do you get if you cross an egg white and some gunpowder?
A boom-meringue.

Egoist
Soppy Poppy: My brother and I know every word in the whole wide world!
Teacher: Oh really! Well, then, tell me what egoist means.
Soppy Poppy: Oh – my brother knows that one.

★

An egotist is one who suffers from 'I' strain.

Egypt
Silly Billy: Have you ever been to Egypt, Dad?
Father: No, Billy.
Silly Billy: Then where did you get Mummy?

★

Name a nervous Egyptian.
The Shake of Araby.

★

How did the Egyptian worm catch a cold?
From its mummy.

★

Why was the young Egyptian girl worried?
Because her daddy was a mummy.

★

Said one Egyptian to another:
I don't remember your name, but your fez is familiar.

Eiffel Tower
Jack: When we were in Paris, we went right to the top of the Eiffel Tower.
Jill: What did you see?
Jack: An eyeful.

Eileen Rose

Sweet little Eileen Rose
Was tired and sought some sweet repose.
But her naughty sister Clare
Placed a pin upon her chair.
And sweet little Eileen rose.

Einstein

What kind of jokes did Einstein make?
  Wise cracks.

Elastic

What is the longest word in the dictionary?
  Elastic, because it stretches.

Elbow

What can you never make right?
  Your left elbow.

Elections

What bird can never vote in an election?
  A mynah bird – because he's too young.

Electric Blanket

An Exeter man slept really badly one night –
he'd plugged his electric blanket into the
toaster by mistake, and spent all night popping
out of bed.

Electric Chair

What did the condemned man say to the
prison governor about to throw the switch on
the electric chair?
  Will you hold my hand?

★

What did the electrician's wife say when he
arrived home late one night?
  Wire you insulate?

★

Why did the man become an electrician?
  He was looking for a bit of light relief.

★

What did Benjamin Franklin say when he
discovered electricity in lightning?
  Nothing – he was too shocked.

★

What happened to the man who discovered
electricity?
  He got a nasty shock.

★

Master electrician to apprentice: Right, lad,
take hold of those two wires and rub them
together. Do you feel anything?
Apprentice: No.
Master electrician: Good. Don't touch the
  other wires – it's those that'll give you a
  shock.

Electrician

What do you call a man who always wires for
money?
  An electrician.

Electricity

A tribal native went to the big city for the first
time in his life and was amazed at the buildings
and the traffic, but most of all he was bemused
by electricity. When he got home he told the
tribe he'd had terrible trouble sleeping.
'Why couldn't you sleep?' they asked.
'Because there was light in my bedroom the
whole time,' he replied.

'Well why didn't you blow it out?'
'Because it was inside a little glass bottle.'

★

What is the most shocking city in the world?
Electri-city.

★

What's golden, sticky and will give you a shock?
Electric syrup.

★

Science teacher: Billy, would you please tell me what a unit of electricity is called?
Silly Billy: What?
Science teacher: That's right!

Electric Shock
Amy: My mum got an electric shock today.
Zoe: How?
Amy: When she was baking she trod on a bun and a current shot up her leg.

Elephant
Why couldn't the elephant travel on the inter-city shuttle?
Because his trunk wouldn't fit under the seat.

★

Andy: If you were in the jungle and being charged by an elephant, what would you do?
Zak: Pay him!

★

What's the best way to raise an elephant?
On a fork-lift truck.

★

How do you get down from an elephant?
You can't get down from an elephant – you get down from a swan.

★

Is it hard to bury a dead elephant?
Yes, it's a huge undertaking.

What has two tails, two trunks and five legs?
An elephant with spare parts.

★

How do you get an elephant in a telephone box?
Open the door.

★

What do you call a fat elephant who drowns in a thin river?
A non-slimmer.

★

What did the elephant say into the microphone?
Tusking, tusking, one, two, three.

★

How do you stop an elephant going through the eye of a needle?
Tie a knot in his tail.

★

Why did the elephant cross the road?
To pick up the squashed chicken.

★

Why did the elephant take two trunks on holiday?
One to drink through, the other to swim in.

★

Why did the elephant sit on the tomato?
Because he wanted to play squash.

★

What do you do if an elephant sneezes?
Get out of the way – fast!

★

Rick: How big is an elephant?
Nick: What kind of elephant?
Rick: A big one.
Nick: How big?

★

Paul: What would you do if you saw an elephant with a broken toe?
Saul: Ring for a tow truck.

How does an elephant know when it's drunk?
  It keeps on seeing pink people.

★

How can you tell when an elephant's in your custard?
  When it's very, very lumpy.

★

What's worse than a giraffe with a stiff neck?
  An elephant with a blocked up nose.

★

Why did the elephant paint her head yellow?
  To see if blondes really do have more fun.

★

Why did the elephant tie a knot in his trunk?
  So that he wouldn't forget.

★

What is an elephant?
  A mouse drawn to government specifications.

★

How do you make an elephant fly?
  Well, you start with a 10-foot zip!

★

Why is an elephant grey, large and wrinkled?
  Because if it was white, small and smooth it would be an asprin.

★

Why did the elephant cross the road?
  Because it was the chicken's day off.

★

What is red on the outside, grey on the inside, and very crowded?
  A bus full of elephants.

★

Amy: What's the difference between an elephant and a banana?
Zoe: I don't know.
Amy: Have you ever tried to put an elephant in your fruit salad?

★

Can an elephant jump higher than a lamp-post?
  Yes – lamp-posts can't jump!

★

Why did the elephant leave the circus?
  Because it was tired of working for peanuts.

★

Why does an elephant have a trunk?
  So that he has somewhere to hide if he sees a mouse.

★

How do you tell an elephant from a monster?
  A monster never remembers.

★

Why did the elephant paint himself all the colours of the rainbow?
  So that he could hide in a paint box.

★

What animal took the most luggage into Noah's Ark?
  The elephant – because he took his trunk.

★

What goes stomp, stomp, stomp, squelch?
  An elephant with wet trainers.

★

Why did the elephant paint his toenails red?
   So that he could hide in the strawberry patch.

★

How can you tell that an elephant has been in the refrigerator?
   You can see his footprints in the butter.

★

What's the difference between an apple and a white elephant?
   An apple is red.

★

What's grey and lights up?
   An electric elephant.

★

What is big, green, and has a trunk?
   An unripe elephant.

★

What did the hotel manager say to the elephant who couldn't pay his bill?
   Pack your trunk and clear out.

★

What do you get an over-active elephant?
   Trunkquillizers.

★

What time is it when an elephant sits on a fence?
   Time to get a new one.

★

How can you tell an elephant from a banana?
   Try to lift it up. If you can't, it's either an elephant or a very heavy banana.

★

What's the difference between an African elephant and an Indian elephant?
   About 3,000 miles!

★

What was the elephant doing on the freeway?
   About five miles per hour.

★

What happens if you cross an elephant with a kangaroo?
   You get great big footprints all over Australia.

★

What's the difference between a flea and an elephant?
   An elephant can have fleas, but a flea can't have elephants.

★

What do you get if you cross an elephant and a computer?
   A huge four-legged know-all.

★

Elephant: Why are you so very weak and tiny?
Mouse: Well, I haven't been very well lately.

★

Adam: What's the difference between an elephant and a matterbaby?
Eve: What's a matterbaby?
Adam: Nothing, but thank you for asking.

★

Jack: Can a person be in love with an elephant?
Jill: No.
Jack: Oh dear. Know anyone who might want to buy a very large engagement ring?

★

Why do elephants wear green felt hats?
   So that they can walk across snooker tables without being seen.

★

How do you stop a herd of elephants from charging?
   Take away their credit cards.

★

Two elephants fell over a cliff —
Boom! Boom!

★

Why can't two elephants go in to the swimming pool at the same time?

Because they've only got one pair of swimming trunks.

★

Why do elephants drink so much water?

Nobody ever thinks to give them anything else.

★

Customer: I'd like to order an elephant sandwich, please.

Waiter: I'm sorry, sir, but we can't do elephant sandwiches.

Customer: Why not?

Waiter: Because we haven't any bread.

★

How powerful is the squirt from an elephant's trunk?

Well, haven't you seen a jumbo jet flying with hundreds of people across the Atlantic?

★

Why do elephants hide behind trees?

So that they can trip up ants.

★

How does an elephant get down from a tree?

It sits on a leaf and waits for autumn.

★

Why do elephants paint the soles of their feet yellow?

So that they can hide upside down in the butter.

★

Have you ever seen an elephant hiding upside down in the butter?

No.

Shows what a good disguise it is!

★

A policeman walked up to a man who was standing in the middle of the road with a box of elephant powder in his hands. The man was spreading the powder all over the road, so the policeman asked him what on earth he was doing. 'Spreading this elephant powder around,' replied the man.

'But there aren't any elephants around here' said the policeman.

'Yes, I know – it really works well,' said the man.

★

Bill: What's the difference between an elephant and a postbox?

Ben: I don't know.

Bill: Well! I certainly shan't ask you to post any of my letters!

★

Why do elephants wear sandals?

To stop themselves sinking in the sand.

★

Why do ostriches bury their heads in the sand?

To look for those elephants who don't wear sandals.

★

What do you get when you cross an elephant with peanut butter?

Either an elephant that sticks to the roof of your mouth or peanut butter that never forgets.

★

Why did the elephant wear pink trainers?

Because he wanted to hide in the cherry tree.

★

Why does an elephant wear sunglasses?

Because he's travelling incognito.

★

How do you cross over an elephant?

Climb up his trunk, sprint across his back and then slide down his tail.

★

News flash from Cleethorpes:

Two elephants were thrown out of the public baths at Cleethorpes yesterday because they couldn't keep their trunks up.

How do you get an elephant in a matchbox?
  Take the matches out first.

★

How do you get four elephants in a Mini?
  Two in the front and two in the back.

★

How do you get four kangaroos in a Mini?
  Take out the elephants and put two in the front and two in the back.

★

Rick: Where can you buy ancient elephants?
Nick: I don't know.
Rick: At a mammoth sale.

★

What did the elephant say to the banana?
  Let's play squash.

★

Why do elephants have wrinkled knees?
  Because they play marbles so often.

★

Why don't elephants ride bicycles?
  Because they can't ring the bells with their thumbs.

★

How can you tell if there's an elephant under your bed?
  The ceiling is very close.

How do you kill a blue elephant?
  With a blue elephant gun.

★

How do you kill a pink elephant?
  Squeeze him until he's blue and then shoot him with a blue elephant gun.

★

What's the difference between a biscuit and an elephant?
  You can't dip an elephant in your tea.

★

What's a jumbo jet?
  A flying elephant.

★

How can you tell if there's an elephant near during a hurricane?
  You can hear his ears flapping in the wind.

★

What is grey and pink and grey and pink and grey and pink . . . ?
  An elephant rolling down a hill with a carnation in its mouth.

★

What games do elephants play in a Mini?
  Squash.

★

Paul: It says in this newspaper that more than 6,000 elephants go each year to make piano keys.
Saul: Isn't it amazing what animals can be trained to do.

★

Why shouldn't you go in to the jungle after six in the evening?
  Because of elephants falling out of the trees.

★

Why do African elephants have Big Ears?
  Because Noddy won't pay the ransom!

★

Elf

What do you call an elf that lives with his grannie?

An old folk's gnome.

★

Where do elves really live?

Gnome, Sweet Gnome.

Encyclopedia

Mother: Johnny's teacher says he should have an encyclopedia.

Father: Why can't he walk to school like I did?

End of the World

Rick: Do you know that the world will never come to an end?

Nick: What makes you say that?

Rick: Because it's round.

Enemies

Why are your handkerchief and your nose such enemies?

Because they always come to blows when they meet.

Engagement

Jill: Now that we're engaged, I hope you plan to give me a ring.

Jack: Of course! What's your telephone number?

English Channel

Teacher: Who can tell me where the English Channel is?

Silly Billy: Not me, miss. We only get the local station on our TV set.

English Language

Sam's English teacher went to his house and asked to see his mother.

'She ain't in,' said Sam.

'Sam!' said the teacher, 'where's your grammar?'

'She ain't in neither,' replied Sam.

Englishman

Why are Englishmen useless at hula-hooping?

Because they all have such stiff upper hips.

Englishman/American

Englishman: I'll have you know, sir, that my father is an English peer (pier).

American: And I'll have you know, buddy, that my father is an American doc (dock).

★

English teacher: 'He was bent on seeing her.' Can you put that sentence another way?

Soppy Poppy: 'The sight of her doubled him up.'

English teacher: No, not quite. Try this one: 'Her beauty was timeless.'

Soppy Poppy: 'Her face would stop a clock.'

★

English teacher: Take this sentence, for example, 'Let the cow be taken to the pasture', now — what mood?

Silly Billy: The cow, sir.

★

Teacher: What is wrong with my saying 'I have went'?

Smart Alec: You're still here!

★

Teacher: Alec, if English is your favourite subject, perhaps you could tell me what tense I am speaking in.

Smart Alec: Pre-tence, miss!

English Sausage

How do you make an English sausage laugh?
  Tell it an American frankfurter joke.

Enlargements

Customer: Do you make life-size colour print enlargements?
Photographic shop assistant: Yes, sir.
Customer: Oh, good. Here's a picture of an elephant.

Equator

Clown: What's the Equator?
Ringmaster: I don't know.
Clown: An imaginary lion running round the earth.

Eraser

'Eraser' said the artist's wife when he drew a beautiful nude.

Envelope

What did the envelope say when the man licked it up?
  It just shut up and said nothing.

Eskimo

An Eskimo mother was sitting in the family igloo, reading nursery rhymes to her little girl:
'Little Jack Horner sat in a corner . . .'
'Mum!' interrupted her daughter, 'what's a corner?'

★

How did the Eskimo boy know his engagement was off?
  The Eskimo girl gave him the cold shoulder.

How do you confuse a naughty Eskimo boy?
  Tell him to stand in the corner of his igloo.

★

Eskimos are God's frozen people.

★

What do Eskimos sing at a 21st birthday party?
  Freeze a jolly good fellow!

★

Eskimo boy to Eskimo girl: What's an ice girl like you doing in a place like this?

★

Why do Eskimos eat whale meat and blubber?
  Well, wouldn't you blubber if you had to eat whale meat?

★

1st Eskimo girl: Where does your Mum come from?
2nd Eskimo girl: Alaska.
1st Eskimo girl: Never mind, I'll ask 'er myself.

★

What do Eskimos call big, formal dances?
  Snowballs.

★

Two Eskimos met at a trading post in the spring.
'It was so cold last winter,' said one, 'our candles froze and we couldn't blow them out.'
'That's nothing,' said the one, 'where I live our words came out frozen and we had to thaw them over the fire to find out what we were saying.'

★

What do Eskimos call their money?
  Iced lolly.

Essay

An English teacher asked her class to write an essay on what they would do if they had £100,000. They all started to write except Poppy. When the teacher collected the work at the end of the lesson, Poppy's sheet of paper was blank.

'Poppy, you haven't done anything. Why is that?' asked the teacher.

'Because that's what I'd do if I had £100,000,' she replied.

Estate

Why didn't it take very long to wind up the old man's estate?

Because he only left a grandfather clock.

★

A widow was complaining about all the trouble she had had dealing with various lawyers. 'My poor dead husband's estate has been so difficult to settle I sometimes wish he hadn't died!'

E.T.

What did E.T.'s mother say to him when he got home?

Where on earth have you been?

Everlasting

What happens if you're good in this life?
You merit everlasting bliss.
And what happens if you're bad in this life?
You merit everlasting blister.

Evolution

Son: Is it true that man is descended from gorillas?:
Father: The scientists seem to think so.
Son: But what about all the gorillas that are still gorillas?
Father: They're the smart ones!

Exaggeration

Mother to son: Sam! How many millions of times have I told you not to exaggerate!

Exam

Mother: Poppy, did you get a good place in your exams?
Soppy Poppy: Oh, yes! Right next to the window.

★

Did you hear about the teacher who marked exam papers so strictly she failed a pupil who wrote full-stops upside down?

★

Father: How did you do in your exams today, Johnny?
Johnny: I did what Queen Victoria did.
Father: What was that?
Johnny: I went down in history.

★

A father and mother went to see round a school where they were thinking of sending their son. They were very pleased with everything and everyone they met was very helpful, and finally they went for an interview with the Headmaster.

'What about exam results?' asked the father. 'Are they good here?'

'Oh, yes,' replied the Headmaster. 'Satisfaction guaranteed — or we return the boy.'

★

Mrs Able: Johnny's taking ten exams this summer.
Mrs Cable: Oh, are you getting a coach?
Mrs Able: No, just a new bike if he passes them all.

Excuses

Teacher (on the phone): I see — Sam can't come to school because he has a cold. To whom am I speaking?
Voice: This is my father.

Exercise

What is the best exercise for losing weight?
Pushing away from the table.

★

Trainer: All right, everybody — lie flat on your backs and circle your feet in the air as though you were pedalling a bike. Sam, move your feet!

Sam: But I'm freewheeling, sir!

Exorcist

What happens to you if you don't pay your exorcist's bill?

You'll be re-possessed.

Exporter

What's an exporter?

A man who used to work on the railways.

Extravagance

Customer to sales assistant: If my husband doesn't like this diamond bracelet, will you refuse to take it back?

Eye

Why is an eye like a man being whipped?

Both are under the lash.

Eyes

Amy: Have your eyes ever been checked?

Zoe: No, they've always been this colour.

★

Amy: You'd better keep your eyes wide open today.

Zoe: Why?

Amy: You'll bump in to things if you don't!

★

Bill: The police are looking for a man with one eye called Neville Macpherson.

Ben: Oh, really? What's his other eye called?

★

When are eyes not eyes?

When the wind makes them water.

Eye Test

A little boy went to the opticians to have his eyes tested. The optician sat him down in front of the chart with lots of big letters on and said, 'Now, cover your right eye with your right hand and read the chart with your left eye.'

But the little boy didn't remember which was his right hand and which was his left, so the optician tried again:

'All right, then, cover your left eye with your left hand and read the chart.'

But the little boy still could not remember which was which. The optician, being a kindly man, decided to make things easier for the little boy and he took a cardboard box and cut a small hole on one side. He put the box over the little boy's head and was just about to ask him to read the chart when he heard the little boy crying.

'What's the matter?' he asked.

'I wanted a pair of metal frames like my brother,' sobbed the little boy.

Face

Mrs Able: My husband always carries a photograph of me over his heart. It saved his life one day when the bank robber shot at him.

Mrs Cable: I'm not surprised. Your face would stop anything.

★

Amy: My friend's got a face like a million dollars.

Zoe: What do you mean?

Amy: It's all green and wrinkled!

★

Amy: Do you think I'll lose my looks as I get older?

Zoe: If you're lucky!

★

Amy: I'll have you know I have the face of a 16-year-old.

Zoe: Well, give it back. You're getting it all wrinkled.

★

Judge: Haven't I seen you before?

DIY man: Probably. So many people owe me money I can't remember all their faces.

★

Autograph hunter: Haven't I seen your face somewhere else?

Television celebrity: I don't think so, it's always been here!

Face Cream

Amy: I know a woman who is black and blue because every night she puts on cold cream, moisturising cream, anti-wrinkle cream, night cream and hand cream.

Zoe: Why does that make her black and blue?

Amy: Because every night she slips out of bed.

Face Lift

Tom: Dick had a face lift last week.

Harry: Good grief! Who on earth would want to steal his face?

Factories

What do you call a lady who is afraid of factories?

Mill-dred.

Fairground

At a fairground a man strolled up to the dart throwing stall to try his luck. He scored double the number of points he needed to win a prize so the stall-holder gave him a very special prize – a tortoise. The man was very pleased and off he went with the tortoise. A short while later he came back, paid his money, and scored even more points with his darts.

'Well!' said the stall-holder, 'you really are good at this. What would you like as a prize this time?'

'Oh,' said the man, 'just give me another of those crusty meat pies.'

Falling

Paul: A friend of mine fell from a window of a skyscraper.
Saul: Was he badly hurt?
Paul: No, he fell indoors.

★

Jack: Last night one of our spies fell out of her bedroom window.
Jill: How awful! Did she hurt herself?
Jack: No, she lives in a bungalow.

★

A lady was in the kitchen preparing dinner when she heard loud banging all the way down the stairs. She rushed into the hall where she saw her daughter spread-eagled on the floor.
'What happened?' she asked. 'Did you miss a step?'
'No,' replied the little girl crossly. 'I caught every single one.'

★

Sam: Mum, Dad's just fallen off the roof.
Mother: I know, Sam. I saw him go past the window.

Falsehood

What is a falsehood?
A fake hat.

False Teeth

A man was dining in a restaurant when suddenly he sneezed so violently that his false teeth flew out of his mouth and smashed into a wall on the opposite side of the room.
'Don't worry, sir,' said the waiter, 'my brother will fix you up with a new set of teeth and he can provide them almost immediately.' The man was naturally very pleased as he couldn't eat anything without his teeth, and he was delighted when the waiter returned in ten minutes with another set of teeth. The Englishman tried them and they fitted perfectly.
'Thank you so much,' he said, 'and thank your brother too. He must be a very clever dentist.'
'Oh, he's not a dentist,' said the waiter. 'He's an undertaker.'

Why are false teeth like stars?
Because they come out at night.

Famous Last Word

What was the famous last word in the operating theatre?
Ouch!

Fancy Dress

A lady who was going to a fancy dress party went to a shop to rent her costume. The shop assistant brought out the most beautiful Cinderella ball gown, with silver slippers and a tiara.
'How much is that?' asked the lady.
'50 pounds,' said the assistant.
'Oh, I'm afraid that's too much,' said the lady. 'Could I see something a little less expensive?'
So the assistant brought out a simple dress and broom, saying,
'You could wear this as Cinderella before her fairy godmother visited. It costs £15 to hire.'
'I'm afraid that's still too much,' said the lady.
'Well,' said the assistant, 'for £1 I'll let you have the broom and a tin of red paint.'
'All right,' said the lady. 'But what do I go as?'
'Take off the broom handle and carry it,' said the assistant, 'pour the red paint over your head, and go as a toffee apple.'

Fans

What do you call it when hundreds of fans gather together?
A fanfare.

Farmer

A farmer was putting up a building adjacent to one of his fields. A passer-by stopped to ask him what it was going to be.
'Well,' replied the farmer, 'if I can let it, it's a rustic cottage. If I can't, it's a cow shed.'

★

1st farmer: What good is your farm? You'll never get a combine harvester in your long, thin fields.

2nd farmer: I don't care, I'm going to grow spaghetti.

★

A farmer loved to eat eggs for breakfast. He didn't keep chickens, nor did his neighbours, and he didn't go into the town to get eggs. Where did he get his eggs from?

His ducks.

★

What is the difference between a farmer and a dressmaker?

One gathers what he sows and the other sews what she gathers.

★

Why is a farmer cruel to his corn?

Because he pulls its ears.

Fast Money

How can you make money fast?

Glue it to the floor.

Fat

A very fat man was going to spend a week at a health farm, so he went to a sports shop to get a smart new tracksuit. He tried one on which fitted perfectly but, as the assistant was wrapping it up, he said, 'I'll have a smaller size tracksuit as well, please. I'm going to be much thinner by the end of the week.'

'That's just as well, sir,' replied the salesman. 'If you shrink as quickly as these do, they'll just about fit you.'

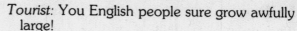

Tourist: You English people sure grow awfully large!

Englishman: What makes you say that?

Tourist: Why, I read in the paper this morning about a lady who lost five hundred pounds.

★

Which country has no fat people?

Finland.

★

Tom: Dick's really fat!

Harry: Yes! Did you know he had mumps for a week before his mother realised.

Fat and Thin

Fat man: You look as though you've lived through a famine.

Thin man: And you look as if you caused it.

Father and Son

There was a farmer who hoped that his son would one day inherit his farm. But the son did not take to farming and went off to the city to seek his fortune. He wrote to his father that he had got a wonderful job as a shoe-shine boy. His father was very disappointed at first, but decided to look at the situation philosophically, and said to himself, 'Oh, well, at least I can say that I make hay while my son shines.'

Father Christmas

Bill: Did you have a nice Christmas?

Ben: Not really, but that's what comes from living in a tough neighbourhood. On Christmas Eve I hung my stocking up over the fireplace and Father Christmas stole it.

Fault

Amy: What would you say your worst fault was?

Zoe: My vanity. I sit in front of the mirror for hours just admiring my beauty.
Amy: That's not vanity! You've just got a vivid imagination!

Favourites
Amy: What's your favourite animal?
Zoe: A cat.
Amy: What's your favourite colour?
Zoe: Pink.
Amy: And what's your favourite number?
Zoe: Six. Why?
Amy: I just wondered if you'd ever seen a six-legged pink cat!

★

Jack: I bought you a present. Your favourite chocolates.
Jill: But the box is half-empty.
Jack: They're my favourites too!

Fear
Rick: Did you hear about the man who didn't know the meaning of the word 'fear'?
Nick: How come?
Rick: He was too afraid to ask.

Feather Bed
Did you hear about the idiot who found a feather in his bed and thought he had chickenpox?

★

What's the difference between a feather bed and a poor man?
One is soft down, the other is hard up.

February
Andy: Can February March?
Zak: No, but April May.

Feet
Show me a man who stands on his own two feet —
and I'll show you a man who can't get his trousers on.

Jack: My bed's too short and every night my feet freeze sticking out from the covers.
Jill: You idiot! Why don't you put them under the covers?
Jack: I'm not putting those cold things in bed with me!

★

Why are feet like ancient tales?
Because they are leg-ends.

★

Andy: We had a letter from my cousin in the army the other day.
Zak: How is he doing?
Andy: Fine. He says he's grown another foot so my auntie knitted him another sock.

★

Mrs Able: My daughter is a very good pianist. She even plays with her feet.
Mrs Cable: How old is your daughter?
Mrs Able: Twelve.
Mrs Cable: Oh, that's nothing. My son plays with his feet and he's only one!

Felon
What is the definition of felon?
Something that dropped on you from above.

Fence
Bill: You remind me of a fence.
Ben: Why's that?
Bill: Because you run around, but you never get anywhere.

★

Angry neighbour: When are you going to fix that fence?
Calm neighbour: When our son comes home from university.
Angry neighbour: What good is that? Your son doesn't know anything about fixing fences!
Calm neighbour: He should do. He's told us he's taking fencing lessons.

Ferry Trip

Amy: We're going on a ferry for our school outing.

Zoe: Every time I go on a ferry it makes me cross.

★

Mr Able: Last year on our ferry crossing my wife and I had four meals.

Mr Cable: Overnight crossing?

Mr Able: No, two down and two up.

Fiend

What does a fiend do every Saturday night?
He sees his girl fiend.

Fighting

Two sisters who were sent to bed early for fighting lay in bed. After about ten minutes the elder sister decided that if they made up, they might be allowed downstairs again.

'Are you awake?' she whispered.

'I'm not telling you,' came the reply.

★

Mother: Sam, have you been fighting again? You've lost your front teeth!

Sam: No I haven't, Mum. They're in my pocket.

★

Mother: Sam! You've been fighting again! Didn't I tell you to count up to 10 so that you wouldn't lose your temper?

Sam: Yes, Mum. But next door's mother only told him to count up to 5 and he hit me first.

Figures

Teacher: Johnny, your figures are badly formed. That 1 looks too much like a 7.

Johnny: It is a 7.

Teacher: Then why does it look like a 1?

Filing

Boss: I can never find what I'm looking for in these files. Are you using any sort of system?

Secretary: Yes, the Biblical system.

Boss: And what's the Biblical system?

Secretary: 'Seek and ye shall find.'

★

What did the secretary say to her boss when he asked her to file some letters?
Wouldn't it be easier to trim them with scissors?

Film

Amy: I finished a film yesterday.

Zoe: Oh, how exciting!

Amy: It should be developed by the end of the week.

★

Amy: How did you like the film?

Zoe: It was dreadful! I hardly knew how to sit through it a second time.

Finder's Keepers

Visitor: Johnny, if you found some money, would you keep it?

Johnny: Oh, no.

Visitor: That's a good boy. What would you do with it?

Johnny: I'd spend it.

Finger and Thumb

What did the finger say to the thumb?
People will say we're in glove.

★

Johnny went crying to his mother one day:
'Mum, I shut my fumb in the door.'
'Johnny, it's thumb, not fumb. Let's have a look.'
'All right. I shut my thingers in as well.'

Fingernails

What is a nail?
The place you aim for when you hit your thumb.

★

What should you do with old fingernails?
File them.

★

What nail don't you want to give a hammering to?

Your fingernail.

Fingers

If you lost four fingers in an accident, what would you have?

No more piano lessons.

Fir Trees

What do sad fir trees do?

They pine a lot.

Fire

Mr Able: Last night when I got home my son had a blazing fire going.

Mr Cable: Well, that was a nice welcome, wasn't it?

Mr Able: No! We haven't got a fireplace.

★

Did you know that fire was invented by some bright spark?

★

What lives if you feed it, but dies if you water it?

A fire.

★

Bill: I've just been to a big fire sale.

Ben: What did you buy?

Bill: Two big fires.

★

When does a fire flare up?

★

Scout leader: Right, troop, can anyone tell me what is the best way to start a fire using two sticks?

Silly Billy: Make sure one's a match, sir!

Fire Engine

What would you have if your car's motor was on fire?

A fire engine.

Fire Fly

What did the mother fire fly say to her son?

For a little one you're very bright.

Fire Fuel

Mrs Able was getting very cross one day because she couldn't light her fire. She tried paper, kindling, firelighters and poured on a little paraffin, but the coal would not catch light. She was muttering to herself about how the new coal was no good when her daughter arrived and offered to help. She went to the coal store and filled a bucket with the previous winter's coal, reset the fire and soon had it blazing away.

'You see, Mum,' she said, 'there's no fuel like an old fuel.'

Fireman

A fireman called out, 'Throw the baby down!' to a woman who was trapped at the top of a building on fire.

'I can't!' she screamed back, 'You might drop him!'

'I won't!' shouted the fireman. 'I'm a professional footballer.'

So the woman dropped the baby. The fireman caught him, bounced him three times and kicked him over the fire engine.

★

What did the fireman give his wife on her birthday?

A ladder in her stocking.

★

Who is assured of a warm reception wherever he goes?

A fireman.

Fireplace

Who invented the first fireplace?

Alfred the Grate.

★

Andy: How does the fireplace feel when you've filled it with coal?
Zak: Grate-full, of course!

First Aid
Why is it dangerous to read a first-aid book?
   Because you'll meet with a chapter of accidents.

First Date
A boy and girl were on their first date. They were driving along in the boy's car, and things seemed to be going well. The girl turned to the boy and asked shyly,
'Would you like to see where I was operated on?'
'Why, yes,' stammered the boy.
'OK,' said the girl, 'turn left at the traffic lights and the hospital's on the right.'

Fish
Two fish in a river were enjoying swimming around when it started to rain. 'Quick!' said one, 'Let's swim over and shelter under that bridge.

★

What fish only swims at night?
   A starfish.

★

What fish is famous?
   A starfish.

★

Adam: Did you wash the fish before you cooked it?
Eve: What's the point of washing a fish that's been swimming around in water all its life?

★

Paul: How fast do fish grow?
Saul: Pretty fast, I think – every time my Dad talks about one that got away it's grown another foot.

★

Which fish has the lowest voice?
   A bass.

★

What's the best way to get in touch with a fish?
   Drop it a line.

★

Where do fish wash?
   In a river basin.

★

What's round, leaf-green and smells fishy?
   Brussels sprats.

★

Paul: I heard that fish is good for the brain.
Saul: I eat it all the time.
Paul: Another scientific theory bites the dust.

★

Why are fish well educated?
   Because they travel in schools.

★

Amy: Have you put fresh water in the fish bowl?
Zoe: No, the fish haven't drunk what was in it yet.

★

Which fish can perform operations?
   A sturgeon.

★

How can you stop fish from smelling?
  Cut off their noses.

★

What kind of fish go to heaven when they die?
  Angel fish.

★

What's the difference between a fish and a piano?
  You can't tuna fish.

Fisherman

A very sad-looking man walked in to a fishmonger's one day carrying a fishing rod and bag. He asked the fishmonger to let him have six lovely trout, 'and throw them to me,' he said.
'Why should I throw them to you?' asked the fishmonger.
'I'm a rotten fisherman,' replied the man, 'but I'm not a liar. And I want to be able to say that I caught six trout.'

★

Why are fishermen such good correspondents?
  Because they're always dropping a line!

★

What is essential for deaf fishermen?
  A herring aid.

★

Did you hear about the loony fisherman who baited his hooks with rubber mice because he wanted to catch catfish?

Fishing

Passer-by: Did you catch that great big fish all by yourself?
Little boy: No, a little worm helped me.

★

Forest warden: Hey! There's no fishing allowed here.
Silly Billy: I'm not fishing. I'm just washing my pet maggot.

A little boy sat all alone fishing on the street corner. A lady passing took pity on him and give him 10 pence.
'How many have you caught?' she asked with a smile.
'You're the sixth today!' replied the boy.

★

Andy: How does your dad manage to go fishing right in the middle of the lake?
Zak: Oh, he just takes his robot.

★

Passer-by: Catch any fish?
Fisherman: Did I catch any fish! I got a dozen this morning!
Passer-by: I am the warden, you know.
Fisherman: And I'm the biggest liar in the world.

★

A lady saw a little boy with a fishing-rod and a jar full of tadpoles walking along the river bank one Sunday morning.
'Little boy,' she said, 'don't you know you shouldn't go fishing on a Sunday?'
'I'm not going fishing!' said the little boy. 'I'm going home!'

★

A fisherman sat patiently on a river bank for an hour without getting a single bite. He changed the bait on his hook and recast the line but after another hour without a bite he changed the bait again. He continued to do this all day without getting a single bite. Finally, he packed his fishing gear away in disgust and threw a handful of coins into the river, shouting, 'All right, then! Buy something you like!'

★

Warden: You can't catch fish without a permit.
Fisherman: I'm doing all right with the worms, thank you.

★

Paul: When I was out fishing the other day I spotted a shark.
Saul: That's silly – whoever heard of a spotted shark?

Two friends agreed to go fishing one night. They met at their local pub, got chatting to friends about fishing and the one that got away, and didn't leave until closing time. They staggered out and went to their cars to collect their fishing rods and then went staggering down the road to a bridge. Here they baited their rods and cast them into the darkness and sat down to wait for the fish to take the bait. They sat all night, dozing and hearing the church clock chime away the hours, without a single bite. They were just about to pack up and go home, cold, fed up and sober by now, when the express train went through, pulling the rods right out of their hands!

★

Two old friends went out for a day's fishing. For several hours neither of them moved, but at the end of the morning one became restless. His friend turned to him and said,
'That's the second time you've moved since we sat down. Are you fishing or dancing?'

★

An angler was boasting about his great successes on a recent fishing trip. 'But I have to admit they were biting well. I had to bait my hook behind a tree!'

★

One day Johnny decided to take his kid sister fishing with him. When they got home Johnny told his mother that he'd never take his sister fishing again.
'I didn't catch a thing,' complained.
'Well, I'm sure she could learn to be quiet if you explained to her that the fish go away when there's any noise,' his mother said.
'She didn't make any noise,' said Johnny. 'She ate all the bait!'

★

Why are so many people crazy about fishing?
Because it's easy to get hooked on it.

★

Fisherman: You've been watching me fish all morning. Why don't you try and catch some yourself?

Onlooker: I haven't got the patience.

★

Passer-by: Hello, son. Are you fishing, then?
Silly Billy: No, drowning worms.

★

Novice fisherman: Is this river good for fish?
Old fisherman: I should say so! I've never got any fish to come out.

★

Andy: Did you mark that good fishing spot?
Zak: Yes, I put an X on the side of the boat.
Andy: That's stupid — what happens if we go out in a different boat next time?

Fishmonger
Amy: I bought some fish today and the fishmonger didn't mind filleting it for me one bit.
Zoe: How do you know?
Amy: Because he made no bones about it.

Fishy
How do fish go into business?
They start on a small scale.

Fitted Carpets
Who first laid fitted carpets?
Walter Wall.

Fizzy
What happened to the little boy who drank 8 Cokes?
He burped 7-Up.

Fjord
What is a Fjord?
A Norwegian motorcar.

Flag
What flies without going anywhere?
A flag.

What rises in the morning and waves all day?
A flag.

Flannel
Andy: Why do you call your little brother Flannel?
Zak: Because he shrinks when we wash him.

Flashing By
What goes flashing by without moving?
A telegraph pole seen from inside a moving car.

Flat Feet
Andy: My brother was arrested for flat feet.
Zak: How's that?
Andy: His feet were in the wrong flat.

★

What's the best cure for flat feet?
A foot pump.

Flat Tyres
Rick: I like your new bicycle. But why has it got flat tyres?
Nick: So that I can reach the pedals.

Flea
What do you call a cheerful flea?
A hoptimist.

★

What do you get if you cross a flea with a rabbit?
A bug's bunny.

★

What's a space invader?
A flea that lives in an idiot's ear.

★

How do you start a flea race?
One, two, flea . . . go!

★

Husband: You'll have to keep that dog out of the house. It's full of fleas.
Wife: Spot, don't go in the house, it's full of fleas.

★

1st flea: You're not looking too good.
2nd flea: No, I'm not really up to scratch.

★

What happens when a flea is very angry?
It gets hopping mad.

★

What do you call mad fleas?
Loony ticks.

★

Two fleas were leaving a theatre when they discovered it was raining. 'Shall we walk?' said the first flea.
'No,' said the second, 'let's take a dog.'

★

Adam: Where do all the fleas go in winter?
Eve: Search me.

★

Some say that fleas are black
But I know that is not so,
'Cos Mary had a little lamb
With fleas as white as snow.

★

Why was the mother flea so sad?
Because her children were going to the dogs.

★

How do fleas get from place to place?
By itch-hiking.

Flea Circus
A flea circus in Paris last night was ruined when a dog came along and stole the show.

★

Jack: What does your dad do for a living?
Jill: He works in a flea circus.
Jack: What does your mum do?
Jill: Scratch.

Flea and Fly

What time is it when a flea and a fly pass?
Fly past flea.

Flea-Fly Poem

A flea and a fly in a flue
Were imprisoned, so what could they do?
Said the fly, 'Let us flee!'
Said the flea, 'Let us fly!'
So they flew through a flaw in the flue.

Flies

Two flies were playing football in a saucer.
Said one to the other, 'We'll have to do better than this — we're playing in the Cup next week.'

★

Where do flies go in winter?
To the glassworks to be turned into blue bottles.

★

Tourist: There are an awful lot of flies around here. Don't you ever shoo them?
Native: No, we leave them to go barefoot.

★

How do you keep flies out of the kitchen?
Keep the rubbish bin in the living room.

★

Two flies were sitting on Robinson Crusoe's back as he lay in the sun.
'Bye, bye,' said one, flying off. 'I'll see you on Friday.'

Flood

What causes a flood?
A river that gets too big for its bridges.

Floor

What happens when an idiot sits on the floor?
He falls off.

Florist

What sort of children does a florist have?
Blooming idiots!

★

Did you hear about the florist who got the cards for a funeral wreath and a bride's bouquet mixed up?
She sent the bride a card which said 'With Deepest Sympathy' and the funeral card read 'Hope You'll Be Happy in Your New Home'.

★

Flour

What did the flour say when it fell over?
Don't bother to pick me up, I'm self-raising.

Flower

What flower is common to every country?
The cost-of-living rose.

★

What flower does everyone have?
Tulips.

★

Which flower is silly?
The daftodil.

★

Paul: I used to wear a flower in my lapel, but I had to stop.

Saul: Why's that?
Paul: Because the pot kept hitting me in the stomach.

★

Why were the flowers crying?
Because people were always picking on them.

★

Sign seen outside a monster flower shop:
Say it with flowers: send a triffid.

★

What did the big flower say to the little flower?
How are you, bud?

Flu
How does a flu bug know when it has won?
When it brings a person to his sneeze.

Fly
Customer: Waiter, there's a dead fly in my wine.
Waiter: Well, sir, you did ask for something with a little body in it.

★

What can fly underwater?
A bluebottle in a submarine.

★

Customer: Waiter, there's a fly in my soup.
Waiter: I'm sorry, sir. I didn't realise you wished to eat alone.

★

Customer: There was a fly on the currant bun I bought here yesterday.
Baker: Well, bring me the fly and I'll exchange it for a currant.

★

What is the difference between a fly and a bird?
A bird can fly, but a fly can't bird.

★

Why did the fly fly?
Because the spider spied her.

★

Housefly to bluebottle: I must fly, but I'll give you a buzz later!

Flying
Jenny came back from her holiday abroad and was telling her friends all about it, starting at the very beginning.
'First of all, there was a man outside the terminal shouting "It is against all nature to fly! It is all wrong! If God had meant man to fly he would have given us wings!" '
'Who was he?' asked a friend.
'The pilot,' said Jenny.

★

Instructor: Tomorrow you can fly solo.
Trainee pilot: How low?

★

What happens if the plane you're flying in runs out of fuel?
Everybody gets out to push.

★

Nervous passenger: I've never flown before. You will get us down safely, won't you?
Pilot: Well, madam, I've never left anyone up there yet!

★

At the county show, a pilot was selling flights in his open cockpit bi-plane. One elderly couple stood around and watched him taking off and landing with various passengers but couldn't decide whether to go up or not.
'Come on,' said the pilot. 'I'll take you up for free if you're good passengers and don't make any noise.' So up they went, and the pilot showed off a little, looping-the-loop and dive-bombing the show. When they landed 20 minutes later he congratulated the man on how quiet he'd been.
'Well,' replied the man, 'it wasn't easy. I nearly said something back there when my wife fell out.'

Two friends were discussing their holidays.
'I flew to Germany last year,' said one.
'So did I,' said the other.
'Doesn't it make your arms tired!' they said in unison.

★

During a trans-Atlantic flight, a gentle voice came over the intercom:
Ladies and gentlemen, just sit back, relax, and enjoy your flight. This is an entirely automatic plane. It has automatic handling, automatic food and drinks, automatic landing devices. Nothing can go wrong.... Nothing can go wrong.... Nothing can go....

★

Passenger: Gosh! Don't all those people down there look just like ants!
Her husband: They are ants, you idiot — we haven't taken off yet.

★

When would you be glad to be down, and out?
After a bumpy flight in a plane.

★

Pilot: First one wing came off and then the other wing came off.
Interviewer: What did you do then?
Pilot: I grabbed a drumstick and had a second helping.

★

Pilot's voice: Ladies and gentlemen, we have just crossed the Atlantic in exactly one hour.
Passenger: That must be a record.
Pilot's voice: No, this is the Captain, speaking to you live from the cockpit.

★

Jack: Every night I dream that I'm flying.
Jill: Why don't you sleep on your back?
Jack: I can't fly upside down!

★

Pilot: Do you wanna fly?
Co-pilot: Oh, yes!
Pilot: Well, you'll have to wait until I catch one.

Fly-Fishing
Paul: I went fly-fishing last week.
Saul: Did you catch anything?
Paul: A 2lb bluebottle.

Flypaper
What did the fly say to the flypaper?
I'm stuck on you.

Foam
What do you get if you eat foam?
Soft in the head.

Fog
Bill: Have you heard the story about the fog?
Ben: Yes, it's all over town.

Foil
The Meat Marketing Board announced yesterday that plans to wrap all meat pies in tin had just been foiled.

Food
What's the definition of brain food?
Noodle soup.

★

Paul: I heard that hospital food is really awful.
Saul: Oh really?
Paul: Yes, even the dustbins get indigestion!

★

How can you tell when food is rude?
When it's got sauce.

★

Sister: My boyfriend thinks I look like an Italian dish!
Brother: He's right, too.
Sister: Which one? Gina Lollabrigdia?
Brother: No, spaghetti bolognese!

★

Tramp: I haven't had a single meal all week.
Fat lady: I wish I had your will power.

How can you stop food going bad?
 Eat it?

★

Diner: Waitress, what are these coins doing in my soup?
Waitress: Well, sir, you did say you'd stop eating here unless there was some change in your meals.

★

Diner: Take this steak away! I've been trying to cut it for 10 minutes, but it's so tough I haven't even made a dent in it.
Waiter: I'm sorry, sir, I can't take it back — you've bent it.

★

Amy: What did the fat man say as he sat down to eat dinner?
Zoe: I don't know.
Amy: I'm afraid this food is all going to waist.

★

Waiter: I have cold pressed tongue, fried chopper liver and frogs' legs.
Customer: I don't want to hear your problems! Let me see the menu, please.

Fool
Rick: Do you think I'm a fool?
Nick: No. But what's my opinion against thousands of others?

★

Rick: Only fools are certain. Wise men always hesitate.
Nick: Are you sure?
Rick: Yes, I'm certain.

★

What's worse than being with a fool?
 Fooling with a bee.

★

Rick: Stop acting like a fool.
Nick: I'm not acting.

★

Bill: Are you trying to make a fool out of me?
Ben: No, I never interfere with nature.

★

Paul: Did you hear about the fool who only ever says 'No'?
Saul: No.
Paul: Oh, I didn't know it was you!

★

You can fool some of the people all of the time
and all of the people some of the time
but the rest of the time let them make fools of themselves.

Foot
What does a thirsty foot do?
 Puts on tap shoes.

Football
Why did the football manager have the pitch flooded?
 Because he wanted to bring on his sub.

★

What did the football say to the player?
 I get a kick out of you.

★

Mrs Able: I hear your son has just got in to the football team. What position is he playing?
Mrs Cable: I'm not sure, but I think he's one of the drawbacks.

★

Sam: I tried out for the football team today, Dad!
Father: Good — did you get in the team?
Sam: I think so. At the end of the practice, the coach looked at me and said, 'This is the end.'

★

Bill: Who stands in goal when the monsters play football?
Ben: The Ghoulie, of course.

Why are there fouls in football?
   Because cricket has ducks.

★

Nick: Our local football team's doing really
   badly.
Rick: How badly?
Nick: Well, every time they win a corner they
   do a lap of honour!

★

What do you call the person who carries the
broom in a football team?
   The sweeper.

★

Rick: What's a football made of?
Nick: Pig's hide.
Rick: Why do they hide?
Nick: They don't. The pig's outside.
Rick: Oh, well, you can both come in. Any
   friend of yours is a friend of mine.

Football Boots

What did the left football boot say to the right
football boot?
   Between us we should have a ball.

Football Coach

Tom: Dick's so dumb he thinks a football
   coach has four wheels.
Harry: Why, how many does it have?

Footballers

Why do footballers play so much?
   They do it for kicks.

★

Why do footballers wear shorts?
   Because they'd be arrested if they didn't.

Football Fan

What do you call a noisy soccer fan?
   A foot-bawler.

Football Referee

The football referee blew his whistle and
awarded a free kick.
'Who to?' asked a surprised player.
'Me,' said the referee.

Footprints

What leaves yellow footprints at the bottom of
the ocean?
   A lemon sole.

★

What do you leave more of the more you
take?
   Footprints.

Forebears

Paul: Did I ever tell you about my forebears?
Saul: No, but I've heard about the three
   bears.

Forest

Bill: Did you hear that the Forestry
   Commission has hired a man who can chop
   down 50 trees a day?
Ben: He must be a good feller.

Forfeit

What's a forfeit?
   A quadruped.

Fork

Mother: Poppy, you shouldn't be eating with
   your knife.
Soppy Poppy:
   But my fork leaks.

Forms

Mike Abercrombie had to fill in an application form when he went job-hunting. There were a lot of people in the 'Job Shop' and it was very noisy and crowded. Eventually Mike got to the head of the queue and the harrassed clerk handed him a form, saying, 'Fill this in. Put your last name first and your first name last.' Because of all the noise Mike did not quite hear what the clerk said and asked him to repeat it. The clerk repeated it but still Mike didn't hear. 'Fill it out backwards — the way I told you,' the clerk shouted, when Mike asked him for the third time. Mike thought this was very strange, but shrugged and sat down and wrote, 'eibmorcrebA ekiM.'

Forth Bridge

When was the Forth Bridge Built?
　　After the third one fell down.

Fortunes

What are the very best tunes?
　　Fortunes — made up of bank notes.

Fortune-Telling

A young girl went to consult a fortune-teller. The medium looked into her crystal ball and started laughing. Suddenly the girl leaned across and slapped the woman in the face.
'What did you do that for?' asked the fortune teller.
'Well,' replied the girl, 'my mother always told me to strike a happy medium.'

★

A girl went to a fortune-teller and reluctantly agreed to pay £5 for the fortune-teller to answer two questions.
'But,' she said, as she handed over the money, 'isn't £5 rather a lot for just two questions?'
'Yes, it is,' agreed the fortune-teller, pocketing the money.
'Now what is your *second* question?'

★

One fortune-teller to another: Grand weather we're having. It reminds me of the summer of 1996.

★

Man at employment agency: I used to be a fortune-teller, but I gave it up. There wasn't any future in it.

Forum

What is a forum?
　　Two-um plus two-um.

Fountains

What did the big fountain say to the little fountain?
　　You're too young to drink.

★

What works when it plays, and plays when it works?
　　A fountain.

Fox

Amy: Did you ever see a fox trot?
Zoe: No, but I once saw a goose step.

★

Why did the fox cross the road?
　　Because the chicken was in its mouth.

★

How do foxes feel when they've eaten baby chicks?
　　Down in the mouth.

Fractions

Who invented fractions?
　　Henry the ⅛th.

France

What is French, 30 metres high and wobbles?
　　The Trifle Tower.

★

What's tall, Parisian and wet?
  The Eiffel Shower.

★

When was it always wet in France?
  When the monarchs were reigning (raining).

★

Soppy Poppy: I'm so glad I wasn't born in France.
Mother: Why's that, Poppy?
Soppy Poppy: Because I can't speak a word of French.

Frankenstein

Why was Frankenstein never lonely?
  Because he was good at making friends.

★

How did Frankenstein eat his food?
  He bolted it down.

★

Where does Frankenstein's wife have her hair done?
  At an ugly parlour.

★

What did Frankenstein say when lightning hit him?
  Thanks, just what I needed.

Freckles

Amy: Have you read *Freckles*?
Zoe: No, mine are brown.

Free Speech

Adam: Do you believe in free speech?
Eve: Yes, of course.
Adam: Wonderful – can I use your telephone?

French

Mr and Mrs Able started to take French lessons and a friend asked them why. 'We're adopting a French baby,' they replied, 'and we want to know what she's saying as soon as she starts to talk.'

★

What's French for 'I am an Australian'?
  Moi Aussi.

★

What's French and very, very relaxing?
  A long loaf.

★

What do French children eat for breakfast?
  Huit heures bix.

French Chef

French chef: And how do our French dishes compare with your English ones?
English tourist: Oh, they break just as easily.

★

What does a French chef do if one of his customers faints?
  He gives her the quiche of life.

Frenchman

Did you hear about the Frenchman who jumped into the river in Paris?
  The police declared him to be in Seine.

Friends

Jack: Have you heard the saying, 'A friend in need is a friend indeed'?
Jill: Do I know you, stranger?

★

What do you call a boy known as Lee who has no friends?
  Lone Lee.

★

Who has friends for lunch?
  A cannibal.

Rick: Can you lend me 10p? I want to phone a friend.
Nick: Here's 20p – call all of them.

★

Two old friends bumped in to each other in the street one day, and one exclaimed how much the other had changed:
'Your hair's much more blonde than I remember,' she said.
'And you don't wear glasses any more! What has come over you, Audrey?'
'My name's Beryl, not Audrey,' replied the other.
'And you've even changed your name!' said the first.

Frog

What's a frog spy called?
  A croak and dagger agent.

★

Mother: Johnny, why did you put a frog in your sister's bed?
Johnny: Because I couldn't catch a mouse.

★

What happens if a frog parks his car on a double yellow line?
  It gets toad away.

★

What's a frog's favourite sweet?
  A lollihop.

Which heavyweight African animal leaps around like a frog?
  A hoppy-potamus.

★

Where do frogs leave their hats?
  In the croakroom.

★

Where do frogs sit?
  On toadstools.

★

What's white outside, green inside, and hops?
  A frog sandwich.

★

Where do frogs keep their money?
  In a river bank.

★

What's a frog's favourite drink?
  Croaka Cola.

Frogs' Legs

Customer: Waiter, have you got frogs' legs?
Waiter: No, sir, I always walk this way.

Fruit and Vegetables

What happens to fruit and vegetables in autumn?
  People eat what they can, and can what they can't.

Fruit Cake

What are the best things to put in fruit cake?
  Teeth.

Funeral

As a large funeral passed down the road a man asked a little boy who was watching it intently who had died.
'The person in the coffin,' replied the boy.

★

Have you heard about do-it-yourself funerals?
   They loosen the earth and you sink down by yourself.

Fur
What fur did Adam and Eve wear?
   Bearskins.

★

Said an envious erudite ermine:
'There's one thing I cannot determine;
When a girl wears my coat
She's a person of note,
But when I do I'm only called vermin.'

★

Mrs Able: I'd like a fur coat, please.
Saleslady: Certainly, madam, what fur?
Mrs Able: To keep myself warm, of course.

Sad Sal: I asked my husband for a fur this Christmas. So he scraped some out of the kettle.

Furniture
Mrs Able: I understand you bought some period furniture?
Mrs Cable: Yes, it went to pieces in a very short period.

★

What kind of furniture do people eat?
   Vege-tables.

★

What's the longest piece of furniture in the world?
   A multiplication table.

Galloping
What gallops down the road on its head?
   A nail in a horseshoe.

Gallows
What is the meaning of gallows?
   A place where no noose is good noose.

Gambling
A gambler won £2,000 one night in a casino. When he got home he put the money under his pillow and promised his wife, 'Tomorrow we'll go out and buy you a diamond ring.' He was so excited about his win that he couldn't sleep, so he got up and went back to the casino to try and win some more money. Unfortunately he lost everything. In the morning his wife woke him up and said, 'Let's go and buy that diamond ring.' Her husband slid his hand under the pillow, sighed, and said, 'Go back to sleep. I don't feel two grand.'

★

A father, anxious that his young son should get out of his habit of gambling, approached the boy's headmaster for help. At the end of term the father went to see the headmaster, who reported good news, he thought he had cured the boy:

'One day last week, I caught him staring at my beard, and he said: "Sir, is that a real or false beard? I bet you £5 it's false." I took the bet, let him pull my beard, and then took the £5 from him.'

'Oh, no,' said the boy's father, 'he bet me £10 that he'd pull your beard before the end of term.'

★

What's a Chinese gambler's favourite food?
   Fried dice.

★

Why did the waiter offer the gambler a plate of fish?
   Because he had a chip on his shoulder.

Game

What game can be dangerous to mental health?
   Marbles – if you lose them.

★

Children: Mum, we're going to play a new game. We're going to pretend to be gorillas at the zoo, and we need you to help us.
Mother: What do you want me to do?
Children: Feed us bananas.

★

Which game can be red hot?
   Poker.

★

What game begins with a T, has four letters and is popular all over the world?
   Golf.

★

A mother heard her daughter giggling and whispering with her friends in the bedroom. So she called out to ask what they were doing.
'We're playing at churches,' came the reply.
'Well, you shouldn't giggle and whisper in church,' reminded the mother.
'But we're the choirboys.'

★

Two little boys were walking by a house that had a high wall when the owner suddenly ran up to them. 'Is this your ball?' he asked.
'Has it done any damage?' asked one of the boys.
'No,' said the owner.
'Then it's ours,' said the other boy.

★

What game do you play in water?
Swimming pool.

★

What is a horse's favourite game?
   Stable-tennis.

Gangster

Who's the biggest gangster in the sea?
   Al Caprawn.

Garbage Man

Did you hear about the garbage man whose friends all thought he was very rich?
   He kept telling them he was cleaning up.

Gardener

First gardener: I used to work with thousands under me.
Second gardener: Really? Where?
First gardener: I cut the grass in a cemetery!

★

What makes a gardener angry?
When you plant a foot in his seed bed.

★

What do you call a keen gardener?
Peat.

★

Nosey neighbour: You've been digging your garden all day, what on earth are you growing?
Groaning gardener: Tired!

★

Why did the gardener throw his chrysanthemums on to his burning home?
Because he knew that flowers grow better in hot houses.

Gargoyle

What's a gargoyle?
What ghosts take for a sore throat.

Garlic

Paul: I live on garlic alone.
Saul: I'm not surprised. Anyone who lives on garlic can't help but live alone.

★

Jenny: Oh, quick, run, there's that fierce dog!
Johnny: Oh, he's harmless enough, he eats garlic.
Jenny: So what if he eats garlic?
Johnny: It means his bark is worse than his bite.

Gas

A garage owner in Texas swore that the brand of petrol he sold was superior to all others, and especially to that of his rival across the road. One day, however, when he was having trouble with his Cadillac, his rival managed to persuade him to try *his* brand of petrol, and sure enough, the Cadillac engine roared into life. Its owner grinned wryly and said, 'You're right, your gas is as good as mine.'

Gas Bill

Bill: I had my gas bill in this morning.
Ben: Well, what did you do?
Bill: Exploded!

Gas Meter

What did the gas meter say to the £1 coin?
Glad you dropped in – I was just going out.

Gateposts

Why are gateposts like seeds?
Because they propagate.

Geese

What's the favourite food of geese?
Gooseberries.

Generosity

Andy: I've been really generous to my little sister recently.
Zak: What did you do?
Andy: Gave her the mumps.

Geography

Teacher: Where are the Andes?
Silly Billy: At the end of my armies.

Geometry

What do you call someone who'se good at geometry?
An angler.

German

What's a German's favourite Chinese food?
Sweet and Sourkraut.

German Barber

How do you greet a German barber?
Good morning, Herr Dresser.

German Clock

A German could not get his clock to work properly. No matter what he did with it, it would only *tick*. Finally, completely exasperated, the German held the clock firmly and said to it, 'Ve haf ways of making you tock.'

German Measles

Rick: Have you ever had German measles?
Nick: No, but then I've never been to Germany.

Germs

Biology teacher: Does anyone remember from last week why we said germs are well organised?
Soppy Poppy: Yes, sir. Because they do things in a body.

★

Did you know that deep breathing kills germs?
   Yes, but how do you get them to breathe deeply?

★

Why did the germ cross the microscope?
   To get to the other slide.

Ghost

Did you hear about the young ghost who got very frightened whenever he listened to human stories?

★

Which ghost was once President of France?
   Charles De Ghoul.

★

Why was the ghost arrested?
   Because he hadn't got a haunting licence.

★

Which ghost appears on the front of glossy magazines?
   The cover ghoul.

★

What does a ghost ride on?
   A roller ghoster.

★

Newsflash: A ghost has just been appointed as Spooker of the House of Commons.

★

How does a ghost look when it's worried?
   Very grave.

★

Which ghost made friends with the three bears?
   Ghouldilocks.

★

What do you call a drunken ghost?
   A methylated spirit.

★

What do you call a ghost that's always sleeping?
   Lazy bones.

★

What did the first ghost magician say to the second ghost magician?
   I can see through your tricks, you know.

★

What does a ghost guard say?
   Who ghosts there?

★

What is a ghost boxer called?
   A phantomweight.

★

Where do ghosts like to swim?
  In the Dead Sea.

★

What do you get if you cross a ghost with a packet of crisps?
  Snacks that go crunch in the night.

★

Mother ghost to her son: 'Don't eat with your fingers! I told you to use the shovel.'

★

What do Italian ghosts eat for supper?
  Spook-etti.

★

What do ghosts eat for breakfast?
  Dreaded wheat.

★

Two ghosts were arguing one night about life before death, when one said, 'I don't agree with you at all. I do not believe in people.'

★

What's a ghost's favourite dessert?
  Strawberries and scream!

★

1st ghost: I hear you work for a spiritualist.
2nd ghost: That's right.
1st ghost: Is he any good?
2nd ghost: Oh, medium.

★

When do ghosts haunt skyscrapers?
  When they are in high spirits.

★

Where do ghosts go on holiday?
  To their favourite ghost-house in distant terror-tory.

★

What trees do ghosts like best?
  Ceme-trees.

★

Who said 'Shiver me timbers' on the ghost ship?
  The skeleton crew.

★

Why do ghosts like tall buildings?
  Because of all the scarecases.

★

Why couldn't the ghost get a whisky in the wine bar?
  Because the landlord didn't have a licence to serve spirits.

★

What do ghosts put on their roast beef?
  Grave-y.

★

What is the ghosts' favourite pub?
  The horse and gloom.

★

What do ghosts wear when it's raining?
  Boo-oots and ghoul-oshes.

★

What jewels do ghosts wear?
  Tomb-stones.

★

Greg Ghost: I don't know about you, but I don't seem to frighten people any more.
Gavin Ghost: I know. We might as well be alive for all they care.

★

Why are ghosts very simple things?
  Because you can see through them so easily.

★

What do short-sighted ghosts wear?
  Spooktacles.

★

How do ghosts manage to lie perfectly flat when they sleep?

By using a spirit level.

★

Where do ghosts get their jokes from?

A crypt writer.

★

How do ghosts count?

One, Boo, Three, Four, Five, Six, Seven, Hate, Nine, Frighten!

★

Why was the mother ghost worried about her baby?

Because he was always in such high spirits.

★

Where do ghosts like to go on holiday?

Lake Erie.

★

Have you heard about the ghost who took off from Heathrow?

He was on a night fright.

★

How do ghosts keep fit?

By regular exorcise.

★

Why are ghosts invisible?

Because they wear see-through clothes.

★

What does a ghost read every day?

His horrorscope.

★

Why did the teacher give the ghost bad marks?

Because he always made a ghoul of himself.

★

What name do ghosts give to their Christmas entertainment?

Phantomime.

★

Where do ghosts like to hold their parties?

The morgue the merrier.

What is the correct way to address the King of Ghosts?

Your Ghostliness.

★

Where do ghosts send their laundry?

To the dry screamers.

★

Where does a ghost train stop?

At a manifest-ation.

★

How does a ghost teacher help her class revise?

'Now, we'll just go through that again. . . .'

★

Baby ghost: Please, mum, tell me some more stories about the old haunted house.
Mother ghost: I can't, dear, it's a one-story house.

★

Baby ghost: Mum, what's for supper?
Mother: Ghoulash. Now be quiet, and only spook when you're spoken to.

★

What sort of song does a ghost sing?

A haunting melody.

What kind of mistake did the ghost make?
A boo-boo.

Ghouls

How does a ghoul start a letter?
Tomb it may concern.

★

Ghoul visitor: Hasn't your little ghoul grown!
Ghoul mother: Yes, she's certainly gruesome.

Giant

What's very very tall and goes 'Eef, if, of, muf'?
A backward giant.

Giant Snails

Where do you find giant snails?
On the ends of giants' fingers.

Gifts

Mrs Able: Your husband would seem to be a man of rare gifts.
Mrs Cable: Yes, indeed. It's been years since he gave me anything.

Giraffe

Does a giraffe get a sore throat if it gets wet feet?
Yes, but not until the next week.

★

What's a giraffe's favourite kind of joke?
A tall story.

★

What do you get if you cross a giraffe with a dog?
An animal that barks at low-flying aircraft.

★

What's tall and sweet-smelling?
A giraff-odil.

★

What do you call a giraffe that stands on your toe?
Anything you like – his ears are too high up to hear you.

★

What's worse than a giraffe with a sore throat?
A giraffe with a stiff neck.

★

Is a baby giraffe ever taller than its mother?
Yes, when it sits on its father's shoulders.

★

Why do giraffes have small appetites?
Because a little goes a long way.

★

Why do giraffes have such long necks?
Because their feet smell so terrible.

★

What do you get if you cross a giraffe with a hedgehog?
A very tall toothbrush.

★

Why do giraffes have long necks?
To join their heads to their bodies.

★

Geography teacher: Where are giraffes found?
Soppy Poppy: Giraffes have long necks so they never ever need finding!

Girl

When is a girl not a girl?
When she's a belle.

★

Nick: Sue is really very clever – she has brains for two!
Rick: Then she's just the girl for you!

★

What did the invisible girl want to be when she grew up?
A gone-gone dancer.

Girls and Boys

Jill: Girls are smarter than boys, you know!
Jack: I never knew that.
Jill: See what I mean?

Girl's Name

What girl's name is like a letter?
  Kay.

Give and Take

Mother: How many times have I told you not to fight? You can't always have everything you want. There has to be give and take.
Sam: But there was, Mum! I gave him a black eye and took back my toy!

Glass

Who needs his glass before he can start work?
  A glazier.

Glasses

After a football match the teams were all in the changing room when the trainer came in and asked if anyone had seen his glasses.
'Oh, yes,' said one of the young players. 'I saw them out on the pitch.'
'Did you bring them in with you?' asked the trainer.
'Oh, no. I thought you didn't want them any more, so I trod on them.'

★

Amy: Why do you have three pairs of glasses?
Zoe: One pair is for reading, one pair for distance; and one pair is to help me look for the other two!

★

Optician: You need glasses.
Patient: But I'm already wearing glasses.
Optician: Then I need glasses.

Glass Eye

Mrs Able: Our new neighbour has a glass eye.
Mrs Cable: How do you know?
Mrs Able: It came out in conversation.

Glass of Water

Customer: May I have a glass of water, please?
Waiter: To drink?
Customer: No, I want to rinse out a few things.

★

Silly Billy: Mum! Can I have another glass of water?
Mother: You've had a dozen already!
Silly Billy: I know, but the playroom's on fire!

Glove Compartments

What are most commonly found in glove compartments?
  Fingers and thumbs.

Gloves

Johnny: Why are you wearing only one glove? Did you lose one?
Jenny: No, I found this one!

★

What gloves can you hold but not wear?
  Foxgloves.

Glow-Worm

Why was the glow-worm sad?
  Because she didn't know if she was coming or glowing.

Gnomes

Why don't gnomes like travelling abroad?
  Because they suffer from gnome-sickness.

★

What do you feed under-nourished gnomes?
  Elf-raising flour.

Do gnomes always snore?
  No, only when they're asleep.

Gnus

Paul: I went to the zoo the other day, and the gnus were in two separate pens.
Saul: Why was that?
Paul: Because there were good gnus and bad gnus.

★

Mother Gnu: The baby has been naughty all day. I want you to punish him.
Father Gnu: Not me, you paddle your own gnu.

★

There once was a gnu in the zoo
Who tired of the same daily view.
To seek a new sight
He stole out one night,
And where he went gnobody gnu.

Goalkeeper

Why was the goalkeeper fired?
  Because he was so gentle he wouldn't even catch a fly.

Goat

Why is it difficult to talk when there's a goat around?
  Because he always butts in.

★

A goat was in a rubbish dump looking for food. He discovered a can of film and ate it up very quickly. Along came another goat and asked if the film was any good.
'It was all right,' replied the first goat, 'but I preferred the book.'

★

What would you get if a young goat fell into the food processor?
  A mixed-up kid.

Goblet

What's a goblet?
  A small turkey.

God's Right Hand

Vicar: Who do you think sits at God's right hand, Poppy?
Soppy Poppy: Mrs God?

Goldfish

What is the world's most valuable fish?
  A goldfish.

★

Why are goldfish gold?
  So they won't go rusty.

★

What do you get when you cross a goldfish with an elephant?
  Swimming trunks.

Golf

Bill: I think golf is a rich man's game.
Ben: Nonsense! Look at all the poor players.

★

How did the police know that Juan had been killed with a golf gun?
  Because it made a hole in Juan.

★

A very fat man was advised by his doctor to take up golf.
'That's no good, doctor,' he said. 'I've tried golf before. If I put the ball where I can hit it, I can't see it; and if I put it where I can see it I can't hit it!'

★

'How would you have played that shot?' asked a bad golfer.
'In disguise,' said his partner.

★

Mr Able: My doctor has told me to stop playing golf.

Mrs Cable: Oh – are you in poor health?
Mr Able: Oh, no. He saw my score card.

There was once a terrible golfer who hit a ball on to an ant hill. He walked up to the ant hill and tried to hit the ball, but no matter how many swings he took, he only ever hit the ant hill, killing the ants. Eventually there were only two ants left. One looked at the other and said, 'If we want to stay alive, I suppose we'd better get on the ball.'

There was once a golfer who was such a cheat that the day he got a hole in one he put a zero on his score card.

★

Why does a golfer wear two pairs of trousers?
  In case he gets a hole in one.

Golf Course
Why is a golf-course like Gruyère cheese?
  Because they both have holes in them.

Good Boy!
Did you hear about the very well-behaved little boy? His Dad promised him 5p and a pat on the head every time he was good.
When the lad was eighteen he had £50 in a savings account and a flat head.

Goodbye
Rick: Hasta luego.
Nick: What's that?
Rick: 'Goodbye' in Spanish.
Nick: Poison!
Rick: What's that?
Nick: Goodbye in
    any language.

Good Morning
What says good morning when you put it in your tea?
  Refined sugar.

Good News, Bad News
First, the bad news: we have to amputate both your legs.
Now the good news: the man in the next bed wants to buy your slippers.

First, the good news: Dad bought us an inflatable boat on holiday. Now, the bad news: he forgot to buy any oars.

This is your captain speaking. The good news is that we are flying in perfect weather. We will experience no turbulence and we are making excellent time. The bad news is that we're lost.

Ladies and gentlemen, I have some good news and some bad news.
First, the good news: the dive you just saw in the World Diving Championships was the winning dive!
Now, the bad news: the pool was empty.

Doctor to balding patient: First, the bad news, I can't grow any more hair on your head. Now, the good news: I can shrink your head to fit the hair you have.

First, the bad news: I'm afraid the surgeon cut off the wrong leg. Now the good news: your other leg is getting better.

Message to all soldiers:
First, the good news: everyone will get a change of socks. Now, the bad news: Adams change with Barker, Barker change with Charles, Charles change with Davies. . . .

Slavemaster to galley slaves:
First the good news: you can have 15 minutes rest on your oars. Now the bad news: after that the captain wants to go water-skiing.

★

First, the good news: Paramount loved your novel, absolutely ate it up.
Now, the bad news: Paramount is my dog.

★

First, the good news: I got a goldfish for Christmas!
Now, the bad news: I get the bowl next Christmas.

★

First, the good news: free drinks at the pub!
Now, the bad news: glasses cost £1 each.

★

First, the good news: you can take your hand off the leak in the pipe.
'Why, has the plumber arrived?'
Now, the bad news: no, we need the water because the house is on fire.

Goods Train

What's a goods train loaded with sweets?
  A chew-chew train.

Gooseberry

What's green, hairy, and zooms across the water at 50 mph?
  A gooseberry with an outboard motor.

Gorilla

What do you get if you cross a gorilla with a footballer? I don't know — but when it tries to score a goal nobody tries to stop it!

★

Where does a ton-weight gorilla sleep?
  Anywhere he wants to!

★

A gorilla went in to a cafe and ordered a chocolate milk shake. The waitress was a little surprised that the gorilla could speak, but she gave him a chocolate milk shake and then called the manager.
When the gorilla had finished he went to the desk to pay and handed the manager a £10 note. The manager didn't think the gorilla would know anything about money, so he only gave him £1 in change.
'Thank you for your custom,' he said to the gorilla, 'we don't get many gorillas in here.'
'I'm not surprised,' said the gorilla, 'at £9 for a chocolate milk shake.'

★

Andy: What does it mean when a gorilla beats its chest?
Zak: I don't know.
Andy: It means it's got heartburn.

Gossip

Tom: Dick sure is a gossip!
Harry: Yes, he is. His tongue gets sunburned every time he goes to the beach.

★

What is a gossip?
Someone who knows the details but doesn't know the facts.

★

What are the three best ways of spreading gossip?
Telegraph, telephone – and tell a girl.

★

Mrs Able: Go on, then, tell me some more gossip about Adam and Eve.
Mrs Cable: I can't. I've already told you more than I heard myself.

★

Who gossips?
People who let the chat out of the bag.

Grand Canyon

Mrs Able: My husband's face dropped a mile when he first saw the Grand Canyon.
Mrs Cable: Oh, was he that disappointed with the view?
Mrs Able: No, he fell over the edge.

Grand Central Station

What charges in and out of Grand Central Station balancing a ball on its nose and applauding itself?
A trained seal.

Grandfather

Who is the most musical grandfather you could have?
One who fiddles with his beard.

★

What's pink and grey and old, and belongs to Grandad?
Grandma.

Grandfather Clock

What else do you call a grandfather clock?
An Old-Timer.

Grandmother

My grandmother's wonderful for her age. She's 101 and hasn't a grey hair in her head. She's completely bald.

Grape

Rick: What did the grape say when the elephant trod on its toe?
Nick: Ouch?
Rick: No. It just gave out a little wine.

★

What's purple, round, and floats in space?
The planet of the grapes.

Grapefruit

Jack: There's a lot of juice in this grapefruit.
Jill: Yes, far more than meets the eye.

Grape Nut

What is purple and crazy?
A grape nut.

Grass

Paul: Didn't your dad promise you something if you cut the grass?
Saul: No, but he promised me something if I didn't!

★

What do you get if you put dried grass in your shoes?
Haycorns.

★

Why is grass so dangerous?
Because it's full of blades.

Grasshopper

What's a grasshopper?
An insect on a pogo stick.

Gravestone

Inscription seen on a hypochondriac's gravestone:
I told you I was ill!

Graveyard

Why is a graveyard such a noisy place?
  Because of all the coffin.

★

Why did the vicar put a fence around the graveyard?
  Because so many people were dying to get in.

Great Pyramid

What kind of joke will you find at the top of the Great Pyramid?
  A cone-under-'em.

Grecian Urn

Jack: What's a Grecian urn?
Jill: I'm too embarrassed to ask.

Greece

Which country is used by a chef?
  Greece.

Green

What colour is a grass plot covered with snow?
  Invisible green.

Greengrocer

A man walked into a top-class greengrocers and was amazed: it had every kind of fruit and vegetable available. But he was horrified at being charged over £1 for a few oranges. He paid the girl and left the shop with his oranges. The girl hurried after him, saying, 'You've forgotten your change, sir.'
'Oh, you'd better keep it,' said the customer. 'I trod on a grape on my way in.'

★

A greengrocer was interviewing a young lad for the job of assistant in the shop. He asked if he was any good at figures. 'I think so, sir,' replied the boy.
'Then what would three pounds of apples be at 5p a pound?'
'Bad!' said the boy.
'You've got the job!' said the greengrocer.

Greenhouse

Rick: Dad mended a dozen panes in our greenhouse today.
Nick: Did they break in last night's wind?
Rick: No, but his glasses did.

Green Monster

What do you do with a green monster?
  Wait until he's ripe.

Greensleeves

Customer in record shop: Have you got Greensleeves?
Salesgirl: No, sir. It's the fluorescent lighting.

Grey Hairs

Mother: Oh, look! I've got some grey hairs.
Jenny: Why is that, Mum?
Mother (teasing): Oh, I expect it's because you're such a naughty little girl.
Jenny: Oh, Mum! You must have been really awful to Grandma!

Grouse

Mr Able: I have trouble catching grouse.
Mr Cable: Maybe you're not throwing your dog up high enough.

Growing Up

'Mum, now that I'm sixteen, can I wear lipstick, perm my hair and stay overnight with my girl friends?'
'No, Jack, definitely not.'

Guard

What is a guard with 100 legs called?
  A sentry-pede.

Guerilla Warfare

What is the definition of guerilla warfare?
  Monkeys throwing coconuts at each other.

Guest House

A traveller had made a reservation at a small guest house for the night, but arrived very late. The guest house was all in darkness but as he didn't want to sleep in the car he rang the doorbell. After a while an upstairs light went on, and a woman opened the window.
'Yes?' she shouted.
'My name is Jones,' said the man. 'I'm staying here.'
'All right,' said the woman. 'Stay there then!' And she shut the window and turned out the light.

Guests

A mother said to her son one day, 'Sam, we're having very important dinner guests. Would you go upstairs and have a wash, put on clean clothes and generally make yourself presentable.'
'Why?' said Sam. 'Are they going to eat me for dinner?'

Guidebook

Why is a guidebook like handcuffs?
  Because they're for tourists (two wrists).

Guillotine

Jack: What's a guillotine?
Jill: I'm not sure exactly, but it would sure give you a pain in the neck.

Guilty or Not Guilty?

Judge: How do you plead, guilty or not guilty of begging?
Prisoner: Half-guilty.

Judge: What do you mean, half-guilty?
Prisoner: Well, I asked the gentleman for 50p, but he only gave me 25p.

★

Judge: How do you plead, guilty or not guilty?
Prisoner: I won't know, m'lud, till I've heard the evidence.

Guinea Pig

Johnny: I washed my guinea pig in Freshamatic and it died.
Jenny: I *told* you not to wash it in Freshamatic.
Johnny: The Freshamatic didn't kill it — the tumble dryer did.

Guitars

What do you call small Indian guitars?
  Baby sitars.

★

Amy: How's your new guitar?
Zoe: Oh, I threw it away.
Amy: Why?
Zoe: Because it had a hole in the middle.

★

Jack: I want to learn how to play the guitar.
Jill: Why pick on that?

Gum Arabic

What is Gum Arabic?
The language of toothless Bedouins.

Gun

Why is a gun like a lazy worker?
  Because they're both fired.

Gunpowder

How was gunpowder invented?
  In a flash.

★

Did you know that gunpowder was invented by a woman who wanted guns to look pretty?

145

Gutter

What is the difference between a gutter and a bad fielder?

One catches drops and the other drops catches.

Gypsies

What are gypsies' favourite tunes?
For-tunes.

Ha, Ha, Ha

What goes ha, ha, ha, clonk?
A man laughing his head off.

★

What goes ha, ha, ha, crash?
A man falling apart with laughter.

Hadrian's Wall

Where exactly is Hadrian's Wall?
Around Hadrian's house.

Hail

What is another description of hail?
Hard-boiled rain.

★

Nick: What a day! The hail was coming down in buckets!
Rick: The hail you say?

Hair

Amy: I've decided not to let my hair grow.
Zoe: How can you stop it?

★

Jack: My new girlfriend has beautiful blonde hair all down her back.
Jill: What a pity it's not on her head.

★

Why did the man comb his hair with his toes?
To make ends meet.

★

How can you best avoid falling hair?
By jumping out of the way.

★

Patient: My hair keeps falling out. Can you suggest anything to keep it in?
Doctor: How about a carrier bag?

★

Why do bees have sticky hair?
Because they have honey combs.

★

Amy: Go on, tell me the story about your friend who bleached her hair.
Zoe: No! You know I never tell off-colour stories.

★

Amy: I quite like my hairstyle now.
Zoe: Yes, it grows on you.

146

Hairbrush

Jill: You could get that nail into the wall with a hairbrush.
Jack: Really?
Jill: Yes, use your head.

Haircut

Mother: Did you get a haircut, Billy?
Silly Billy: No, Mum, I got all of them cut.

★

Barber: How would you like your hair cut, sir?
Customer: Off.

★

Barber: How do you want your hair cut, Sam?
Sam: Like Dad's – leave a hole on top.

★

A man went to a barber and explained that he wanted a very special hair cut because he was going on holiday to Italy, and hoped to visit the Vatican and meet the Pope. The barber cut the man's hair and then said,
'Enjoy your holiday. Let me know all about it when you get back.'
A month later the man returned for another hair cut.
'How was the trip?' asked the barber. 'And did you meet the Pope?'
'We had a marvellous time,' said the man. 'I met the Pope, and he even spoke a few words to me.'
'What did he say?' asked the Barber.
'He shook my hand, stared at me, and said "Who the heck cut your hair like that?" '

Hairdresser

Customer: Your hands don't look very clean.
Hairdresser: Yes, I'm sorry, madam. I haven't done a shampoo since I dyed my last customer's hair brown.

Hairpins

Careful shopper: I'd like a packet of invisible hairpins, please.

Shop assistant: Here you are, madam.
Careful shopper: Thank you – and you're sure they invisible?
Shop assistant: Yes, madam. This is the tenth packet I've sold this morning, and we've been out of stock for a week.

Hair Raising

Johnny: Have you ever had a hair-raising experience?
Jenny: Oh, yes – every time I take off my new sweater.

Hair Wash

Why did the man wash his hair without getting it wet?
    Because he was using shampoo for dry hair.

Half

Teacher: What is half of 8?
Smart Alec: Up and down, or across?
Teacher: Whatever do you mean?
Smart Alec: Well, up and down it's 3, and across it's 0.

★

Andy: Can I share your sledge?
Zak: Sure, we can go halves.
Andy: That's really great!
Zak: I'll have it going downhill and you can have it going uphill.

Half-Drowned

Bill: Would you rather be half-drowned or saved?
Ben: Saved, of course!
Bill: But you would be saved if you were half-drowned!

Hallowe'en

Rick: My dad came across a ferocious beast last Hallowe'en and never turned a hair.
Nick: I'm not surprised – your dad's bald.

Ham and Eggs

Waiter: Can I take your order now, please, sir?
Silly Billy: Yes, I'll have MNX, please.

Hamburger

Rick: Why aren't you eating your hamburger?
Nick: I'm waiting for the mustard to cool.

★

What sizzles and lights up?
An electric hamburger.

Hamlet

What did Hamlet say when he found he was putting on weight?
'Tubby or not Tubby ... that is the question?'

Hammer

What's the safest way to use a hammer?
Get someone else to hold the nails.

★

What happened when the hammer was invented?
It was a big hit.

Hamster

How do you fatten a thin hamster?
Throw him over a cliff and he'll come down 'plump'.

Hand

Why is your hand like a DIY shop?
Because they both have nails.

★

Sam: Mum, which hand should I use to stir my cocoa?
Mother: Neither, use the spoon.

★

When can you have four hands?
When you double your fists.

★

Maths teacher: If I had 35 apples in one hand and 55 in the other hand, what would I have?
Soppy Poppy: Big hands.

★

Teacher: Poppy! What would you say if I came to school with hands as dirty as yours?
Soppy Poppy: I'd be too polite to mention it, Miss.

★

What is it that men do standing up, ladies do sitting down, and dogs do on three legs?
Shake hands!

Handwriting

Teacher: Your handwriting seems to be getting worse instead of better, Poppy.
Soppy Poppy: But if you could read my writing you'd see how good my spelling is.

★

Why do we call writing handwriting?
Because if you wrote with your foot it would be footwriting.

★

Teacher: Jenny, I told you to write out this poem a dozen times to try and improve your bad handwriting. But you've only written it six times. Why is that?

Jenny: My arithmetic is bad, too.

Hanging

Andy: In China I saw a woman hanging from a tree.

Zak: Shanghai?

Andy: No, only about five foot off the ground.

★

What do you get if you hang about in pear trees?
  Sore arms.

★

Jack: If you won't marry me, I'm going to put my neck in a noose right in front of your house.

Jill: Please don't – you know my parents don't like you hanging around.

Hangmen

What do hangmen read?
  Noosepapers.

Han Solo

Where was Han Solo when the lights went out?
  In the dark.

Happiness

Nick: Did you say he spreads happiness wherever he goes?

Rick: No! I said *when*ever he goes.

★

What increases the more you share it around?
  Happiness.

Harbourmaster

What did they call the harbourmaster who was a millionaire?
  Paul Jetty.

Hard Work

A man had interviewed many people for a job in his company and was seeing the last applicant.

'Do you like hard work?' he asked.

'No, sir.'

'You're hired – that's the first honest answer I've heard all day.'

Hares

Rick: Did you hear that all the hares escaped from the rabbit farm?

Nick: Oh, what's happening?

Rick: Police are combing the area.

Harp

What is a harp?
  A nude piano.

★

Why do so few people play the harp?
  Because it takes a lot of pluck.

Harvest-Time

What's the best time to gather fruit?
  When the farmer's dog is tied up!

Hat

Sales assistant: That hat fits you nicely, madam.

Customer: Yes, but what happens when my ears get tired?

★

Amy: Oh, what a lovely hat!

Zoe: It's a hunting hat.

Amy: Why is it called a hunting hat?

Zoe: Because my sister will be hunting for it.

★

What sort of hat has fingerprints?
  A felt hat.

★

What did the hat say to the scarf?
  You hang around while I go on ahead.

★

Amy: I've found a wonderful new hat designer
  – he decorates his hats with live birds.
Zoe: I know. And if you don't settle your
  account the hats fly back to the shop.

★

Mrs Able: Whenever I'm down in the dumps
  I get myself a new hat.
Mrs Cable: Oh – so that's where you find
  them!

Hatstand
Why did the hatstand in the hall?
  Because it had nowhere to sit.

Haunted House
Who looks after a haunted house?
  The skeleton staff.

Haute Cuisine
Customer: Waiter, I'd like some greasy chips,
  underdone sausages, and really leathery
  mushrooms, please.
Waiter: I'm sorry, sir, I couldn't possibly serve
  you anything like that.
Customer: Why ever not? You did yesterday.

Hawaii
How does a Hawaiian baritone laugh?
  A low ha!

★

What do Hawaiian policeman say when they
see something suspicious?
  Aloha, aloha, aloha! What have we here?

Headache
Amy: What does your mother do for a
  headache?
Zoe: Sends me to your house to play.

Head Banger
What is a head banger?
  A man with a sausage on his head.

Headstand
Amy: Can you stand on your head?
Zoe: No, it's too high.

Health
Paul: Our next door neighbour's lost his
  health.
Saul: How did that happen?
Paul: He was too busy drinking the health of
  others.

★

What did the health attendant say to his new
assistant?
  Hi, Jean!

Hearing-Aid
Mrs Able: At last I've got my new hearing-aid.
Mrs Cable: Does it work well?
Mrs Able: Nearly three o'clock, dear.

Heart
Why is a heart like a policeman?
  Because it has a regular beat.

★

What sort of bandage do surgeons use after heart surgery?
  Ticker tape.

Heaven

Teacher: What are you drawing, Sam?
Sam: A picture of heaven.
Teacher: That's a little ambitious — no one knows what heaven looks like.
Sam: They will when I've finished, though, won't they?

★

Sunday School teacher: Hands up all those who want to go to heaven! Billy, your hand isn't up. Don't you want to go to heaven?
Silly Billy: Yes, but my Mum told me to go straight home.

Hedgehog

What did the baby hedgehog say when it backed into a cactus?
  Is that you, Mum?

★

What's a hedgehog's favourite food?
  Prickled onions.

★

Why did the hedgehog wear brown boots?
  Because his black ones were at the shoe menders.

★

Why did the hedgehog fight the dog?
  Because he knew he'd win on points.

★

Why did the hedgehog cross the road?
  Because he was tied to the chicken.

★

Why did the hedgehog cross the road?
  To see his flat mate.

★

What do you get when you cross a hedgehog with a worm?
  Barbed wire.

What do you call two hedgehogs in love?
  A prickly pair.

Heifer

What do you call a sleeping heifer?
  A young bulldozer.

Hell

Amy: She looks just like Helen Black.
Zoe: You should see her in red.

Help

If we're here to help others, what are the others here for?

★

What sits in a fruit bowl and shouts for help?
  A damson in distress.

★

A man walking down the road offered to help a delivery man with a large parcel.
'Oh, thank you,' said the delivery man. 'I could use a hand.'
Both men grabbed one end of the parcel and struggled with it for 20 minutes, after which time the delivery man said, 'It's no good, we better give it a rest. Otherwise we'll never get the parcel off the truck.'
'*Off!*' shouted the other man. 'I thought you were trying to get it *on!*'

★

A woman woke her husband one night and whispered,
'Quick, dial emergency. There's a man downstairs eating my home-made apple pie.'
'Who shall I call?' asked her husband sleepily.
'Police or ambulance?'

Henry VIII

Tourist visiting the Tower of London: Why did Henry VIII have so many wives?
Beefeater: Because he liked to chop and change.

Hereafter

Andy: Do you believe in the hereafter?
Zak: Yes, I do.
Andy: Then hereafter leave me alone.

Here or There?

Rick: You're not here, and I can prove it.
Nick: Of course I'm here.
Rick: No, listen. Are you in London?
Nick: No.
Rick: Are you in Washington?
Nick: No.
Rick: Are you in Paris?
Nick: No.
Rick: Right, if you aren't in those places, you must be somewhere else. And if you're somewhere else, you're not here!

Hiawatha

How did Hiawatha?
   With thoap and water.

Hiccups

Buttercups are yellow, so what colour are hiccups?
   Burple.

High Diver

In the national diving competition the first diver announced he would attempt a double backward somersault. The second diver stepped up to the board without making an announcement, so the judge asked him what his dive was going to be. The diver produced a fish and said proudly, 'Forward somersault with pike!'

High Jump

Paul: What animal can jump higher than a house?
Saul: Um, kangaroos?
Paul: All animals can – houses can't jump.

Highwayman

What do you call a highwayman with flu?
   Sick Turpin.

★

What's green and holds up coaches?
   Dick Gherkin.

★

Highwayman: Stick 'em down!
Passenger: What?
Highwayman: I said, stick 'em down!
Passenger: Don't you mean stick 'em up?
Highwayman: Oh! That's why I'm losing money!

Hiking

Scoutmaster: Now, lads, imagine you were off on a hike. You're going north – what's on your right?
Silly Billy: East, sir!
Scoutmaster: Right! What would be on your left?
Silly Billy: West, sir!
Scoutmaster: Right again! And what would be behind you?
Silly Billy: Um, my rucksack, sir!

★

Why was the hiker carrying a Land's End sign on his back?
   Because that's where he was going, and he didn't want to get lost.

Hindu

What's a Hindu?
   Lays eggs.

Hippie

Bill: I heard about a hippie who starved to death.

Ben: Why?
Bill: Because he wouldn't eat a square meal.

★

Bill: What did the hippie say when his cat came indoors from the cold?
Ben: Cool cat!

★

What weighs a ton and goes around with a flower behind his ear?
  A hippie-potamus.

★

Rick: What did the hippie say to the invisible man?
Nick: I don't know.
Rick: You're out of sight, man!

★

What does a hippy call his wife?
  Mississippi.

★

If Flower Garden got married to Jack Power, what would her name be?
  Flower Power.

Hippopotamus
What did the river say when the hippopotamus sat on it?
  Well, I'll be damned.

History
History teacher: Does anyone remember when motor cars first appeared on the streets?
Silly Billy: In King John's time, sir.
History teacher: Why do you say that, Billy?
Silly Billy: Because you told us that King John was always grinding the people down with taxis.

★

Why is history the sweetest lesson?
  Because it's full of dates.

★

Teacher: Billy, your history hasn't been very good this term. Why is that?
Silly Billy: Well, Miss, I think it's best to let bygones be bygones.

★

Father: I see from your school report that you're not doing very well in history.
Soppy Poppy: It's not my fault. The teacher keeps asking me about things that happened before I was born.

★

History teacher: Who can tell me something about Margaret of Anjou?
Soppy Poppy: She was very fat, sir.
History teacher: I didn't know that! Where did you find that out?
Soppy Poppy: Well, it says in the history book that Margaret of Anjou was among Henry's stoutest supporters.

Hobby
Paul: Do you have a hobby?
Saul: Yes – I like sitting in the corner collecting dust.

★

Mrs Able: My husband's at last found a hobby he can stick to.
Mrs Cable: That's nice, what does he do?
Mrs Able: He spends all evening glued to the television.

★

Johnny: Mum, you know you're always saying I should have a hobby?
Mother: Yes. Have you thought of something you'd like to do?
Johnny: Yes, I'm going to collect worms.
Mother: And what are you going to do with them?
Johnny: Press them.

Hogwash
What's hogwash?
  Pigs' laundry.

Holding Hands

Adam: May I hold your hand?
Eve: No thanks, its not heavy

Hole

Where can you find a hold-up man after a hold-up?
   Holed up.

What stays the same weight no matter how big it gets?
   A hole.

★

What grows bigger the more you take from it?
   A hole.

★

When can a trouser pocket be empty and yet have something in it?
   When it has a hole in it.

★

Have you heard the story of the three holes in the ground?
   Well, well, well. . . .

★

A man was putting up knotty pine cupboards in the kitchen when his young son came in and said,
'What are those holes for?'
'They're knotholes,' said his father.
'Then what are they if they're not holes?'

★

What is full of holes but is as strong as iron?
   A chain.

Jack: Do you have holes in your underwear?
Jill: No, of course not. How rude!
Jack: Then how do you get your arms through?

★

Jenny: Mum, I don't like this cheese with holes in it.
Mother: Don't be so fussy. Eat the cheese and leave the holes at the side of your plate.

Holidays

Mrs Able: Did you go to Portugal for your holiday?
Mrs Cable: I don't know, my husband bought the tickets.

★

Bill: My wife and I had a great holiday at the beach this year. We took it in turns to bury each other in the sand.
Ben: Sounds like good fun!
Bill: Yes it was – next year I'll go back and dig her up.

★

A family were setting off on their holiday. For the first time the children had packed their own clothes and toys.
'Well,' said their father, 'have you got everything?'
'Yes!' chorused the three children.
'Did you remember to pack your soaps?' asked their mother.
'Soaps?' said the children. 'We've packed for our holiday!'

★

Mr Able: So you're not going to the Bahamas this year?
Mrs Cable: No, it's Paris we're not going to. It was the Bahamas we didn't go to last year.

★

It was so hot on our holiday last year that we took turns sitting in each other's shadow.

★

Tom: Dick's family are sending him to his pen friend for the summer.
Harry: Does he need a holiday?
Tom: No, but his parents do.

★

Why does Silly Billy always take his holidays in the spring?
  Because he likes clean sheets.

★

The Cable family had a wonderful summer holiday on a farm, and very much wanted to go back. But as they were thinking about it, they remembered how the pigs had smelled. So they decided to write to the farmer to ask if the pigs were still there. Back came the reply, 'Don't worry, we haven't had pigs here on the farm since you were with us last year.'

★

The house we stayed in on holiday last year was only a stone's throw from the beach and very easy to find.
  All the windows were broken.

★

The weather was so bad on my holiday this year that when we went to the zoo the keeper was building an ark.

Hollow
Rick: Hollow!
Nick: What's hollow?
Rick: An empty greeting.

Homesick
Sam: I'm so homesick.
Mother: But this is your home!
Sam: Yes, I know.
  And I'm sick of it.

Homework
Soppy Poppy: Sir, would you punish me for something I haven't done?
Teacher: No, of course not! Why?
Soppy Poppy: Because I haven't done my homework.

★

Soppy Poppy: Dad, will you do my homework for me?
Father: No, it wouldn't be right.
Soppy Poppy: Well, you could at least try!

★

Andy: What did your teacher think of your homework?
Zak: Oh, he took it like a lamb.
Andy: Really? What did he say?
Zak: Baa!

Honesty
Rick: There's only one way of making money honestly.
Nick: How's that?
Rick: Trust you not to know it!

Honey
Why is hunting for honey like a legacy?
  Because it is a bee-quest.

★

Why is honey scarce in Brazil?
  Because there's only one B in Brazil.

Hope
Wife (at the bedside of her sick husband): Is there no hope, Doctor?
Doctor: What are you hoping for?

Horrendous Howlers
An oxygen has eight sides.

★

All people who aren't Jews are reptiles.

★

155

Conservation is when you talk to people.

★

A spatula is the bone behind the shoulder blade.

★

Venison is an Italian city with lots of canals.

★

Vandals are open-toed shoes we wear in the summer.

★

Livid was a famous Roman poet.

★

Margarine is made from imitation cows.

★

Magnets are the little creatures you find in rotten apples.

★

The smallest wind instrument is called the Picadilly.

★

Macaroni invented the radio.

★

Monsoon is a French word meaning Mister.

Horse

A cowboy was boasting about how clever his horse was, 'I was riding the range, all alone, when the horse stumbled over a rabbit hole. I fell off and broke my leg.'
'I suppose you're going to tell us the horse set your leg,' scoffed one listener.
'Oh, no,' said the cowboy. 'But he did take hold of my belt in his mouth to put me in the shade and then gallop to fetch a doctor.'
'Oh, maybe the horse is clever, after all,' said someone.
'Well, not entirely,' said the cowboy. 'The dumb animal brought me a horse doctor.'

★

What's the difference between a sick horse and a dead bee?
One is a seedy beast, the other is a bee deceased.

★

A steeplechase jockey called Ron
A most obstinate mare sat upon.
When half round the course
'That's enough!' said the horse,
And she stopped while the rider went on.

★

What horse can't you ride?
A clothes horse.

★

A man walked into stables near his home one Saturday morning saying, 'I'd like to hire a horse.' The stable owner replied, 'Certainly, sir. How long?' To which the man said, 'The longest you've got – it's for my five children.'

★

What did the horse say when he got to the end of his nosebag?
That's the last straw!

★

What's another word for horse sense?
Stable thinking.

★

An old farmer was showing a group of city children around the countryside one day.
'Well, look here,' he said. 'I've found a horseshoe. Anyone know what that means?'
'Yeah,' said the show-off, 'One of your horses is walking around in his socks.'

★

1st trainer: That was a close finish! Did you think your horse had won?
2nd trainer: Yes, but when I saw the photo finish the answer was in the negative.

★

What do you call a horse with a sore throat?
A hoarse horse.

Why has a horse got six legs?

Because he has forelegs in front and two behind.

★

Friend: Whatever happened to you?
Horse rider (covered in mud): I wanted to go one way and the horse wanted to go the other.
Friend: So, what happened?
Horse rider: We tossed for it.

★

How could a cowboy ride into town on Thursday and, three days later, ride home again to arrive on a Thursday. The name of the cowboy's horse was Thursday.

★

Rick and Nick went to the cinema to see a film about horse racing. To add a little excitement, Rick bet Nick that horse number six would win the final race. Nick agreed to take the bet.
Number six duly won the race but Rick confessed, 'I can't take your money – I've already seen the film.' 'So have I,' said Nick. 'But I didn't think the horse would lose twice in succession.'

★

How do you make a slow horse fast?

Don't feed him for a week.

★

Andy: How have you been getting on with your horse riding?
Zak: I've been taking a running jump.

★

Sam: Dad, the circus was super! There was a man who jumped on a horse's back, slipped underneath, caught hold of its tail and finished up riding backwards on the horse's neck.
Father: That's nothing! I did all that the first time I ever got on a horse.

★

What happens to old horses?

They become nags.

Why are horses badly dressed?

Because they wear shoes but no socks.

★

What's the difference between a horse that's asleep and one that's awake?

With some horses it's difficult to tell.

★

Two friends bought a horse each at a sale and, as the horses looked very similar and were to be kept in the same stables, discussed how to tell them apart.
'I know,' said one friend, 'we'll bob the tail of one horse.'
Unfortunately, both tails were bobbed by mistake, so the friends had to decide again how to tell the horses apart.
'Well, your idea didn't work,' said the second friend, 'but mine will. You keep the black one and I'll have the white one.'

Hospitalisation

1st patient: Does your wife miss you very much?
2nd patient: Not often, she's a very good shot. That's why I'm here.

★

Andy: Did you hear about the man in hospital?
Zak: No, what happened?
Andy: He took a turn for the nurse.

Hot and Cold

What's an example of heat expansion and cold contraction?

Hot summer days are longer than cold winter days.

Hot Dog

Rick: How can you have your hot dog and eat it too?
Nick: I'll bite!

★

Why did the hot dog climb to the top of the roof?

Because he heard that the meal was on the house.

What do you call an extra-long hot dog?
A frankfurter.

★

Why is a hot dog the best of all dogs?
Because it feeds the hand that bites it.

★

What's the connection between hot dogs and outer space?
UFOs – Unidentified Frying Objects!

★

Why do hot dogs always say 'please' and 'thank you'?
Because they're well bread.

Hotel

Hotel guest (on the phone): Is that reception?
Receptionist: Yes, sir. This is the third time you've telephoned. What's eating you?
Hotel guest: That's what I'd like to know.

★

Mrs Able: Our holiday hotel was overbooked last year, and we had to sleep on a door across two trestles.
Mrs Cable: I bet that was uncomfortable.
Mrs Able: Oh no, not really. But it was draughty around the letter box.

★

Hotel manager: I hope you enjoyed your stay with us, sir?
Guest: Yes, I did – but I'm sorry to be leaving the hotel so soon after practically buying it.

★

An overnight guest was leaving after breakfast one morning and he marched up to the reception desk in the hotel to collect his bill. He took one look at it, and shouted, 'This hotel advertised "bed and board". I don't know which was the bed and which was the board!'

★

A hotel manager was giving instructions to a new porter about how to welcome guests. 'It's this hotel's policy to make each guest feel welcome, and at home. One of the best ways to do this is to call them by their names, and you can find out their names by reading their luggage labels.'
The new porter took his first guests up to their room, carefully placed their luggage on the stool and said, 'I hope you will enjoy your stay, Mr and Mrs Cowhide.'

★

Guest: I'd like a room for the night, please.
Receptionist: Single, sir?
Guest: Yes, but I am engaged to be married.

★

Prospective hotel guest: Yes, this is nice, but I would prefer a room with a bath.
Hotel receptionist: This is not your room, sir, this is the lift.

Hot Water

Andy: Did I get into hot water last night!
Zak: How come?
Andy: I had a bath.

★

Paul: Ouch! That water burned my hand.
Saul: Well you should have felt it before you put your hand in.

Hour

Paul: I hear the men are going on strike.
Saul: What for?
Paul: Shorter hours.
Saul: Good for them – I always say 60 minutes is too long for an hour.

★

Interviewer: Are there any questions you'd like to ask me about the job?
Job applicant: Could you tell me about the hours, please?
Interviewer: We have fairly early hours – would that worry you?
Job applicant: Oh, no! I don't mind how early I leave.

158

House

What house weighs the least?
  A lighthouse.

★

Teacher: How far is your house from the school?
Silly Billy: Ten minutes' walk if you run.

★

Mrs Able: Our house is so tumbledown, I'll never know how it keeps standing.
Mrs Cable: The termites must be holding hands.

★

Why did a couple call their new house Simla?
  Because it was similar to all the other houses.

★

Our house is so small we can only use condensed milk in the kitchen.

★

For sale advertisement:
House, 2 bedrooms, lounge, dining-room, kitchen, bathroom, toilet 2 miles Perth.

★

Jack: Do you live in a small house?
Jill: I'll say it's small! Even the mice are round-shouldered.

★

Our house is so damp that we only catch fish in the mousetraps!

★

Newspaper advertisement:
For sale, near Portsmouth, semi-detached house with sea through lounge.

★

Our new house is so small we had to take the wallpaper off in the living room to get the furniture in.

★

Why did the house go to see the doctor?
  Because it had window panes.

Estate agent: This next house hasn't got a flaw.
Customer: What do you walk on then?

★

A little Yorkshireman went to the Council Housing Department one day to complain about his living conditions.
'I've got three older brothers,' he explained. 'We all live in the same room. One of my brothers has a dozen gerbils, one has five cats, and the other one keeps a goat. The smell is terrible and I want you to do something about it.'
'Couldn't you open the windows?' asked the official.
'What – and lose all my pigeons?' said the Yorkshireman.

★

What comes right up to the house but doesn't go in?
  The path.

★

An estate agent was showing a couple around a new house, singing its praises. He finished up by saying, 'And it's only a stone's throw from the bus stop.'
'That decides it,' said the husband to his wife. 'We'd always have something to do in the evening, even if there was nothing on television – we could throw stones at the buses.'

★

If a red house is made from red bricks, and a white house is made of white bricks, what is a green house made of?
  Glass.

Housework

Mrs Able: Does your husband ever help you with the housework?
Mrs Cable: Oh, yes! Yesterday he helped with the windows, and today he's going to help me mop up.

How Do You Do?

Paul: How do you do?
Saul: Do what?
Paul: I mean, how do you find yourself?
Saul: I'm never lost.
Paul: What I mean is, how do you feel?
Saul: With my fingers, of course. Do stop bothering me with all these silly questions!

Human Cannonball

Bill: Hey, did you hear what happened to the human cannonball at the circus?
Ben: No, what?
Bill: He got fired.

Humpty Dumpty

What happened to Humpty Dumpty after he fell off the wall?

He made a great big egg sandwich for all the King's men.

★

Why couldn't Humpty Dumpty be put together again?

Because he wasn't all he was cracked up to be.

★

Jack: What happened when Humpty Dumpty fell off the wall?
Jill: All the king's horses and all the king's men had scrambled egg for breakfast.

Hunch

Bill: I have a hunch.
Ben: And here was I thinking you were round-shouldered.

Hunger

What is the difference between a hungry man and a greedy man?

One longs to eat, the other eats too long.

★

'What a pity you've joined the hunger strike,' said the prisoner's wife one visiting day.

'You believe in the cause, don't you?' he demanded.

'Yes, but today I put a file in your cake.'

★

Jack: Are you hungry?
Jill: Yes, Siam.
Jack: Come on, then, I'll Fiji.

Hunting

Two hunters were marching bravely through the jungle when the biggest lion they'd ever seen stepped out in front of them.

'Let's keep calm,' said the first hunter. 'Remember what we read in the book? If you stand absolutely still and stare the lion out, he'll turn tail and run away, and then we can shoot him.'

'Oh, good,' said the second hunter. 'You've read the book, and I've read the book, but has the lion read the book?

★

1st hunter: I've just seen a huge lion!
2nd hunter: Did you let him have both barrels?
1st hunter: Both barrels? I let him have the whole gun.

★

1st hunter: Hey! You've just shot my wife.
2nd hunter: Oh! I'm so sorry. Here – have a shot at mine.

★

Jack: I shot a 15 foot lion while I was on safari in Africa.
Jill: That's some lyin'.

★

1st hunter: Where are you going with that gun?
2nd hunter: Polar bear hunting.
1st hunter: There aren't any polar bears around here!
2nd hunter: I know that. I wouldn't have to hunt for them if there were, would I?

★

1st hunter: Be careful with that gun. You just missed shooting me.
2nd hunter: Oh, I'm so sorry.

★

A hunter was proudly showing off his trophies to a visitor. He was especially proud of a tiger-skin rug lying in front of a fire and said, 'I shot this one in India. I was sorry to kill him, but it was him or me.'
'Well,' said the visitor, 'he makes a better rug than you ever could.'

★

1st hunter: Let's go home. It's getting very late and we haven't hit a single lion all day.
2nd hunter: Oh, let's just miss a couple more first.

★

Andy: Where did you get that moose's head?
Zak: I went hunting with a club.
Andy: It must have been dangerous, moose-hunting with just a club.
Zak: Oh, no. The club had lots of members and we all had guns.

★

Paul: That's a beautiful stuffed lion.
Saul: Yes, I shot it on an expedition with my uncle.
Paul: What's it stuffed with?
Saul: My uncle.

★

What is the best way to hunt bear?
    With no clothes on.

Hurricane
Mr Able: I was sorry to hear that the hurricane blew away your house – and your wife was still inside!
Mr Cable: Oh, well, she'd been wanting a holiday for ages.

Husband
Jack: Is it true that all women want a husband called Will?

Jill: I suppose so – then they can have a Will of their own.

★

Mrs Able: Isn't that man standing over there dreadful! He's the most unattractive man I think I've ever seen.
Mrs Cable: That man is my husband!
Mrs Able: Oh! My dear, I'm so sorry.
Mrs Cable: You're sorry!

★

Mrs Able: My husband's one in a million.
Mrs Cable: Oh, really? I thought he was won in a raffle.

★

Amy: Have you had any replies to your advertisement for a husband?
Zoe: Yes, and they all say the same thing.
Amy: What's that?
Zoe: 'Take mine!'

Hyena
What happened to the hyena who swallowed an Oxo cube?
    He made a laughing stock of himself.

★

Scientist: I've just crossed a hyena with a snake.
Assistant: What did you get?
Scientist: I don't know. But we better join in when it laughs.

★

What do you get if you cross a laughing hyena with a kitten?
    A gigglepuss.

Hymns
Why are hymns sung in church and not hers?
    Because they finish Amen, not Awomen.

Hypnotism
What's hypnotism?
    Rheumatism in the hip.

How does a hypnotist travel?
    By public transport.

Hypochondria

Inscription seen on the tombstone of a hypochondria:
    See – I *told* you I was ill.

★

My husband is such a hypochondriac that I have to wear lipstick with penicillin in it before he'll agree to kiss me.

Ice

What's Ice?
    Skid stuff.

Ice Cream

One very hot day a little man went into a cafe, put his newspaper on a table and went to the counter for a cold drink. When he turned back to the table he saw a huge man sitting in his place.
'Excuse me,' said the little man, 'I think you're sitting in my seat.'
'Prove it!' snarled the big man nastily.
'Yes, of course,' said the little man. 'You're sitting on my ice cream.'

Icicle

What lives in winter but dies in summer and grows with its roots upward?
    An icicle.

Identification

What's the best way of identifying yourself when a shop wants to check your credit cards?
    Look in a mirror.

Idiot!

What did the idiot do when he was told he had a flea in his ear?
    He shot it.

★

Rick: How do you keep an idiot in suspense?
Nick: I don't know.
Rick: Tell you next week.

Igloo

An Eskimo who had just finished building a new family igloo called his wife and proudly asked her what she thought of it. She replied, 'Ours is an ice house, ours is.'

★

What is an igloo?
   An icicle made for two.

Ignorance

A teacher turned to a pupil one day in exasperation and said, 'Johnny, I've taught you everything I know, and you're *still* ignorant!'

★

What is ignorance?
   When you don't know something and somebody finds out.

Illegal

What's the meaning of illegal?
   A sick bird of prey.

Illness

What is the most common illness in China?
   Kung Flu.

★

Paul: First I had appendicitis, then thrombosis, then tonsilitis. Next came neuralga, and I thought I was finished when they gave me vaccination and innoculation.
Saul: How awful!
Paul: Wasn't it! I thought that spelling test would never end.

Imitation

Mrs Able: Have you told your little girl to stop imitating me?
Mrs Cable: Yes, I have. I told her not to play the fool.

Impeccable

Rick: What's impeccable?

Nick: I don't know, but I bet chickens don't eat it.

Important

What is important today that didn't exist one hundred years ago?
   Me!

Impossible

Busy ant (pulling a blade of grass): Oh! It's so heavy! This is impossible!
Lazy ant (lounging on a blade of grass): Nothing is impossible. I've been doing it for years!

Impressionist

Did you hear about the marvellous farmyard impressionist?
   He did the smells.

★

Did you hear about the little girl who does bird impressions?
   She eats worms.

Imprisoned

A man was boasting to a friend one day that he'd been in prison. 'The police handcuffed my hands behind my back, locked me up, and threw away the key!'
'What did you do?' asked his friend.
'I put my big toe in the keyhole and jerked hard!' replied the boaster.
'And broke the lock?'
'No, I broke my toe.'

Incas

Did you know that the Incas (inkers) were the first people to write with fountain pens?

Income Tax

Why do people never pay their income tax with a smile?
   Because the Revenue insist on money.

Incredible Hulk

What is big and green and sits in the corner all day?

The Incredible Sulk.

India

Geography teacher: Johnny, can you tell me which is further away from the earth — India or the moon?

Johnny: India, miss.

Teacher: Now why do you say that?

Johnny: Because you can see the moon, but you can't see India.

Indigestion

What whirrs in the air and gives you indigestion?

A bellycopter.

Infection

What's the best way to avoid infection from biting insects?

Don't bite any.

Influenza

What's the difference between influenza and photography?

One makes sick families, the other makes facsimiles.

Ink

Visitor: He certainly is a fine pig. But what made you call him Ink?

Farmer: Oh, he's always running out of the pen.

★

Why did the mother take the ink away from the baby?

She knew he was too young to write a book.

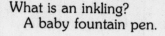

What is an inkling?

A baby fountain pen.

★

When is ink like a sheep?

When it's in a pen.

Insect

Where would you put an injured insect?

In an antbulance.

★

Customer: Waiter, what's this insect in my stew?

Waiter: Don't ask me, sir. I don't know one bug from another.

★

Sam: Dad, what insect has a blue and green spotted body, five jointed legs and pincers?

Dad: I've no idea. Why?

Sam: There's one crawling up your leg!

★

Scientist: I've invented a marvellous insecticide!

Assistant: What does it do?

Scientist: It kills all the crops so that the insects will starve to death.

★

What is a mosquito with an itch?

A jitterbug.

★

Why does the insect kneel before it eats?

Because it's a preying mantis.

★

Patient: Doctor, I have to go to Africa on business soon. What's the best way to prevent diseases caused by biting insects?
Doctor: Don't bite any.

★

Which insect eats the least?
The moth – it just eats holes.

★

Paul: Do you think insects have brains?
Saul: Yes, they soon work out where we're holding our picnic.

Insomnia

Amy: I have terrible trouble getting to sleep at night.
Zoe: Well, you know what they say – count sheep.
Amy: I've tried that – it doesn't work.
Zoe: Why not?
Amy: I can only count up to six.

★

Rick: How's your insomnia?
Nick: Terrible. Now I can't even get to sleep when it's time to get up.

★

Rick: I can't get to sleep at nights. I suffer dreadfully from insomnia. And when I do finally drift off I wake up every hour on the hour and . . .
Nick: Have you ever tried talking to yourself?

Insults

Johnny: I didn't come here to be insulted!
Jenny: Oh, really? Where do you usually go?

★

A hardware shopkeeper was known for miles around as the rudest and meanest man in the town. One day a man walked in to the hardware shop with a chicken under his arm.
'What are you doing with that pig?' said the shopkeeper.
'It's not a pig,' replied the man. 'It's a chicken!'

'Shut up!' said the shopkeeper. 'I wasn't talking to you, I was talking to the chicken!'

Insurance

Mrs Able: Does your husband have life insurance?
Mrs Cable: No, only fire insurance. He says he knows where he's going.

★

A Frenchman decided to swindle his insurance company by getting himself run over. He waited at a bus stop until the bus came along, then stuck out his leg and the bus ran over him. He claimed thousands of francs in insurance, and decided to try the same thing in Italy. He got thousands of lire in compensation. Then he went to England, waited at a bus stop until the bus came along, stuck out his leg, and died of pneumonia.

★

What is insurance?
What you pay for now so that you'll have nothing to worry about when you're dead.

★

An insurance salesman was trying to increase his client's household insurance cover.
'What's in the wall safe?' he asked.
'The wall,' said the client.
'And what if you had a fire?'
'Oh, we'd put that in there too.'

★

An insurance salesman was trying to persuade a housewife that she should take out life insurance.
'Suppose your husband were to die,' he said, 'what would you get?'
The housewife thought for a while, and then said, 'Oh, a parrot, I think. Then the house wouldn't seem so quiet.'

★

An insurance salesman was on the point of selling an expensive life insurance policy, and just needed to make one last sales pitch to convince his client.

'Just imagine,' he said. 'Last week I sold a policy to a man and the next day he was knocked down by a bus. We paid out £50,000. You could be as lucky as that!'

In the Navy
Naval officer: Can you swim?
Recruit: Why, what's happened to all the ships?

Intruder
How does an intruder get in to the house?
Intruder window.

Invention
Andy: Did you hear about the scientist who invented a square bath?
Zak: Why did he do that?
Andy: So it would never leave a ring.

★

Rick: Did you hear about the scientist who invented a fly paper but couldn't discover the right formula?
Nick: Did he give up?
Rick: No, he stuck to it.

★

Paul: Have you heard about Professor Bonkers' latest invention?
Saul: No, what's that?
Paul: A waterproof teabag.

★

What's the most stupid invention of all time?
Non-stick glue.

Invisible
What do invisible babies drink?
Evaporated milk.

★

Why did the invisible woman take her husband to the doctor?
To see why he wasn't all there.

What is even more invisible than the invisible man?
His shadow.

★

Why did the invisible man look in the mirror?
To see if he still wasn't there.

★

Why did the invisible boy upset his mother?
Because he was always appearing.

Invisible Ink
Customer: Do you sell invisible ink?
Sales assistant: Certainly, sir. What colour would you like?

Iodine
Paul: Why are you putting iodine on your pay cheque?
Saul: Because I just got a cut in my salary.

Ireland
What did the Irishwoman sing to her pipe-smoking husband?
'Oh, Danny boy, your pipe — your pipe is smoking.'

★

When does an Irish potato change its nationality?
When it becomes a French fry.

★

What makes Ireland so rich?
The capital — because its always Dublin.

Iron
Amy: I'd say your new boyfriend has an iron deficiency.
Zoe: Why would you say that?
Amy: His shirt needs pressing.

Island

Why is an island like the letter T?
  Because it's in the middle of water.

Italian

Anxious referee to Italian boxer: Are you in a
  daze, Luigi?
Italian boxer: I'ma ina sevena daysa.
Anxious referee: How come?
Italian boxer: Because I'ma weaka.

★

An Italian on holiday in Scotland got lost in
the mist and became known as The Roman in
the Gloamin'.

★

Which Italian secret society beats people up
with table mats?
  The Raffia.

Paul: My Italian penfriend gave me a nick-
  name when I went to stay because I didn't
  like Italian food.
Saul: What's that?
Paul: Antipasta!

★

What's Italian, 182 feet high and tastes
delicious?
  The Leaning Tower of Pizza.

Ivanhoe

Who was Ivanhoe?
  A Russian gardener.

Jack

What did the jack say to the car?
  Let me give you a lift.

Jackal

What did the jackal say when he saw two
hunters in a jeep?
  Ahh, meals on wheels.

Jack and Jill

Jack and Jill went up the hill
To fetch a pail of water.

Jack fell down and broke his crown,
And sued the farmer and his daughter.

★

Why did Jack and Jill roll down the hill?
  It beats walking, doesn't it?

Jackass

Paul: What's the difference between a sigh, a
  Rolls and a jackass?
Saul: I don't know.
Paul: A sigh is 'Oh, dear.' A Rolls is too dear.
Saul: And what's a jackass?
Paul: You, dear!

167

Jacket

Bill: Did you hear about the man who set fire to his jacket?
Ben: No, why did he do that?
Bill: Because it was a blazer.

★

What's the best vegetable to have with jacket potatoes?
   Button mushrooms.

Jack Frost

Bill: How does Jack Frost get to work?
Ben: By icicle, I guess.

Jacques Cousteau

What language does Jacques Cousteau speak?
   Fluid French.

Jazz

Jenny: Does your garden have a swing?
Johnny: No, but it has a beet!

Jeans

A young man walked into a clothes shop and asked for some really tight jeans.
'Certainly, sir. Walk this way, will you?' said the sales assistant.
'I'll probably have to,' said the young man, 'if I get them as tight as yours.'

Jeep

What do you get if you cross a jeep with a sheep dog?
   A land rover.

Jelly

What do you get if you cross a jelly with a sheep dog?
   Collie-wobbles.

★

What sits in a push chair wobbling?
   A jelly baby.

How do you start a jelly race?
   You say, 'Get set!'

Jelly Babies

What do jelly babies wear on their feet?
   Gum boots.

Jellyfish

Where does a jellyfish get its jelly from?
   The ocean currents.

★

Paul: Did you hear about the jellyfish?
Saul: What about it?
Paul: It set.

Je t'adore

Jack: Je t'adore.
Jill: Shut it yourself!

Jeweller

What's the difference between a jeweller and a jailer?
   One sells watches and the other watches cells.

★

Andy: Last year I opened a jeweller's shop.
Zak: Successfully?
Andy: No, he caught me at it.

★

What do jewellers and wrestlers have in common?
    They both know a lot about rings.

Job

Paul: My brother's just started a really good job.
Saul: Oh, what's that?
Paul: Test pilot for Kleenex.

★

Bill: What does your sister do now she's left school?
Ben: She's taking French, German, Italian, Dutch. . . .
Bill: At university?
Ben: Oh, no. She's a hotel receptionist.

★

Sam: Dad, is it right to say that a road sweeper sweeps roads?
Father: Yes, Sam, that's right.
Sam: And does a cake mixer mix cakes?
Father: Yes.
Sam: And a weightlifter lifts weights?
Father: Yes, why all the questions?
Sam: Well, does a shoplifter lift shops?

★

Supermarket manager: Aren't you the same boy who applied for this job a month ago?
Boy: That's right, sir.
Supermarket manager: Didn't I tell you I wanted an older boy?
Boy: Yes, sir. That's why I've come back now.

★

What kind of job is easy to stick to?
    Working in a glue factory.

★

Which job has plenty of openings?
    A doorman's job.

Jockey

Why did the jockey take hay to bed?
    To feed his nightmares.

Did you hear about the short-sighted jockey who couldn't find the weigh-in?

John McEnroe

What film made John McEnroe a star?
    The Umpire Strikes Back.

Joke

Paul: Did you hear the one about the man who heard a good joke and was going to take it home?
Saul: No, what about it?
Paul: He decided that would be carrying a joke too far.

★

Paul: The girl I marry will have to be able to take a joke.
Saul: That's the only kind you'll get.

★

An old man was sitting in his garden enjoying the sunshine and seemingly chatting to himself. Every so often he threw back his head and roared with laughter; occasionally he muttered, 'Rubbish!' in disgust.
A policeman was walking by and asked the old man what was going on. 'I'm telling myself jokes,' replied the old man. 'And some of them are really good.'
'Then why do you keep muttering "Rubbish!" ' asked the policeman.
'Oh,' said the old man, 'that's when I've heard them before.'

★

Jack: Did you hear my last joke?
Jill: I certainly hope so.

★

Andy: I heard a new joke yesterday. Did I tell it to you?
Zak: Is it funny?
Andy: Yes!
Zak: Then you didn't.

★

Sam thought he was a very funny man, and loved telling jokes. He was always on the look-out for new people to whom he could tell his jokes. But the trouble was that Sam's jokes were really awful.

One day Sam got on a train and was delighted when another man got in to the carriage at the next station.

'Want to hear some jokes?' asked Sam.

'All right,' answered the man.

Ten minutes later, as the train drew into the station, the man asked Sam if he made up all his own jokes.

'That's right,' said Sam. 'Out of my head.'

'You must be,' said the man as he got out and slammed the carriage door behind him.

Journalist

Why did the journalist put a torch in his mouth?

Because he wanted to get an inside story.

★

Mrs Able: Why do you take the *Placid Journal?*

Mrs Cable: Because it doesn't have a crossword.

J.R.

Who hit J.R. with a tomahawk?

Sioux Ellen.

Judge

What do you call a judge with no fingers?

Justice Thumbs.

★

How do judges relax?

They play court games

★

The judge was only four feet three inches tall – a small thing sent to try us.

★

Judge: Have you ever stolen before?

Prisoner: Now and then, sir.

Judge: Where have you stolen from?

Prisoner: Oh, here and there.

Judge: Lock him up!

Prisoner: But when do I get out?

Judge: Oh, sooner or later.

★

Judge to dentist: Do you swear to pull out the tooth, the whole tooth, and nothing but the tooth?

★

What did the judge say at the end of a long day's work?

It's been a trying day.

Juggling

What has two eyes like a juggler, two arms like a juggler, two hands like a juggler, but isn't a juggler?

A juggler's photograph.

Jumping

Bill: Jumping off the Forth Bridge is not dangerous.

Ben: How can you say such a thing?

Bill: It's true. Jumping off is not dangerous, but the sudden stop at the other end is.

★

How can you jump over three men sitting down?

Play draughts.

Jumping Beans

It's fun to watch people eating jumping-bean pie – they aim at their mouth, but it lands in their eye!

Jungle

Why did the egg go into the jungle?
　Because it was an eggsplorer.

What grows in the jungle, makes delicious sandwiches and you should avoid at all costs?
　A hambush.

★

Junk

What is junk?
　Things you keep for years and throw out just before you need them.

Kangaroo

Bill: Have you heard about the exhausted kangaroo?
Ben: No, what about him?
Bill: He was out of bounds.

★

What do you get if you cross a kangaroo with a sheep?
　A woolly jumper

★

Why was 1984 a good year for kangaroos?
　Because it was a leap year.

★

What do you do with a sick kangaroo?
　Give him a hoperation.

★

What happened to the two kangaroos that got married?
　They lived hoppily ever after.

What do you get if you cross a kangaroo and a mink?
　A fur jumper with pockets.

★

What do you get if you cross a mink with a kangaroo?
　A fur coat with pockets.

★

Why do mother kangaroos hate rainy days?
　Because their children have to play inside.

★

Biology teacher: Who can tell me what kangaroos have that other animals don't have?
Silly Billy: Baby kangaroos, Miss!

Karate Champion

Bill: Did you hear about the karate champion who joined the army?
Ben: No, what happened?

Bill: The first time he saluted he nearly killed himself.

Keep Off The Grass

Park attendant: What are you doing up that tree, young man?

Silly Billy: Well, your sign says 'keep off the grass'.

Ketchup

Guess what happened when the tap, the dog and the tomato took part in a race?

The tap was running, the dog took the lead, and the tomato tried to ketchup.

Kettle

What disease does a kettle fear?
Boils.

★

Why is a kettle like an animal?
Because it's a water otter.

Key

What is the hardest key to turn?
A donkey.

★

How can you get into a locked cemetery at night?
Use a skeleton key.

Keyhole

What gets in to the house through the keyhole?
A key.

Kidnapping

What is a definition of a kidnapping?
A baby asleep after lunch.

King

Who's the only person a king has to take his hat off to?
His barber.

★

When is a piece of wood like a king?
When it's made into a ruler.

★

Where are English kings usually crowned?
On the head.

★

What was the first thing Henry VIII did when he came to the throne?
He sat down.

King Arthur

Why did King Arthur have a Round Table?
Because he didn't want to get cornered.

★

What was King Arthur's favourite game?
Knights and crosses.

★

Who invented King Arthur's Round Table?
Sir Cumference.

★

Page: Is there anything I can do for you, sire?

King Arthur: Yes, page. Make haste and fetch me a can opener. I have a flea in my knight clothes.

King Kong

What would you get if you crossed King Kong with a bell?
A ding-dong King Kong.

★

Which King was entirely covered with dense, dark hair?
King Kong.

★

When King Kong fell down a well, how did he get out?

Wet.

Kipling
Amy: Do you like Kipling?

Zoe: I don't know, I've never Kippled.

Kippers
A London taxi driver discovered a pair of kippers in the back of his cab. He dutifully took them to the police station, where he was told that if nobody claimed them within six months they would be his.

Kiss
Visitor: Come over here, Jenny, and I'll give you a penny for a kiss on my cheek.

Jenny: Not likely! I get more than that for taking my medicine.

★

What does elliptical mean?

A kiss.

★

A little boy laid in wait for his sister's new boyfriend, jumped out at him and said, 'I saw you kissing my sister last night.'

'All right, all right!' said the boyfriend. 'Keep your voice down. And I'll even give you 50p to keep your mouth shut and not tell anyone.'

'Thanks!' said the brother. 'But just a minute and I'll give you 20p change.'

'What do you mean? You'll give me 20p change?'

'That's what I've always given the others!'

★

Paul: I love Christmas! All that kissing the girls under the mistletoe!

Saul: I prefer to kiss them under the nose.

Kitchen
Customer: You must have a really clean kitchen in this restaurant.

Waiter: We like to think so, sir. But how could you tell?

Customer: Everything I've eaten tastes like soap.

Kitten
Poppy was playing with her kitten in front of the coal fire. The kitten was lying sleepily in the warmth and started to purr.

'Mum!' called Soppy Poppy. 'Come quickly, the kitten's started to boil!'

Kleptomania
Rick: My sister's a maniokleptic.

Nick: I think you mean a kleptomaniac.

Rick: No, I don't – because she walks backwards in to shops and leaves things.

Knickers
Amy: I bought some of those new paper knickers.

Zoe: What are they like?

Amy: Tearable.

Knife and Fork
Paul: What would happen if you swallowed your knife and fork?

Saul: I suppose you'd have to eat with your fingers.

Knife Thrower
Bill and Ben were discussing all the exciting acts they'd seen at their visit to the circus.

'I didn't like the knife thrower very much, did you?' asked Bill.

'Oh, yes! He was great,' said Ben.

'But he kept chucking knives at that stupid girl and he didn't hit her once!'

Knitting
A police patrol car on the motorway overtook a fast car. As they glanced at the car, they were horrified to see the woman at the wheel

173

knitting. 'Pull over!' shouted one of the policeman.
'No!' shouted the woman, 'Socks!'

★

A little old lady went in to a wool shop and asked for enough wool to knit her dog a jacket, without really being able to say how big the dog was.
'Well,' said the sales assistant, 'perhaps you should bring him in and I could measure him. Then we'd know exactly how much wool you'd need.'
'Oh, I can't do that,' said the lady, 'it's supposed to be a surprise.'

★

Mr Able: What are you doing, dear?
Mrs Able: Knitting up a barbed-wire fence.
Mr Able: How?
Mrs Able: I'm using steel wool.

★

Did you hear about the little girl who wanted to give her mother a really expensive birthday present?
   She knitted her a string of pearls.

★

Who makes up jokes about knitting?
   A nitwit.

Knobs

What has knobs on and wobbles?
   Jellyvision.

Knock Knock

Knock Knock.
   Who's there?
Abyssinia.
Abyssinia who?
Abyssinia soon.

— *Oh, heard it before, have you?*

— *Alex.*
Alex who?
Alexplain later.

— *Aladdin.*
Aladdin who?
Aladdin the street is waiting for you.

— *Accordion.*
Accordion who?
Accordion to the paper, it's going to snow today.

— *Alison.*
Alison who?
Alison on my headphones on the way to school.

— *Alison.*
Alison who?
Alison to pop music.

— *Amos.*
Amos who?
A mosquito bit me.

— *Andy.*
Andy who?
And he bit me again!

— *Ammonia.*
Ammonia who?
Ammonia little girl and I can't reach the doorbell.

— *Arthur.*
Arthur who?
Arthur any more biscuits in the tin?

— *Arthur.*
Arthur who?
Arthur any more at home like you?

— *An author.*
An author who?
An author joke like that and I'm off.

— *Annie.*
Annie who?
Annie thing you can do I can do better.

— *Bernardette.*
Bernardette who?
Bernardette all of my dinner.

— Ben.
Ben who?
Ben Dover and touch the floor.

— Cargo.
Cargo who?
Cargo 'beep, beep'.

— Cantaloupe.
Cantaloupe who?
We cantaloupe tonight. My parents are watching me.

— Canoe.
Canoe who?
Canoe come out and play with me?

— Cindy.
Cindy who?
Cindy next one in, please.

— Cereal.
Cereal who?
Cereal pleasure to meet you.

— Carol.
Carol who?
Carol go if you put oil in it.

— Cook.
Cook who?
Goodness me.
Is it one o'clock already?

— Cows.
Cows who?
Cows go 'moo', not 'who'.

— Dishwasher.
Dishwasher who?
Dishwasher the way I spoke before I had false teeth.

— Dishes.
Dishes who?
Dishes the FBI – open up.

— Don.
Don who?
Don mess about, open the door.

— Distress.
Distress who?
Distress hardly covers my knees!

— Dismay.
Dismay who?
Dismay be a joke, but I'm not laughing.

— Dr Livingstone.
Dr Livingstone who?
Dr Livingstone I. Presume.

— Doughnut.
Doughnut who?
Doughnut ask me silly questions.

— Doris.
Doris who?
Doris is closed, that's why I knocked!

— Dwayne.
Dwayne who?
Dwayne the bathtub – I'm dwowning.

— Dummy.
Dummy who?
Dummy a favour and get lost.

— Eileen.
Eileen who?
Eileen'd over the fence too far and it broke.

— Euripides.
Euripides who?
Euripides trousers, you buy me some more.

— Europe.
Europe who?
Europe early this morning.

— Elsie.
Elsie who?
Elsie you later, alligator.

— Four eggs.
Four eggs who?
Four eggsample.

— Felix.
Felix who?
*Felixcited about the
party tonight.*

— Felix.
Felix who?
Felix my ice cream again I'll hit him.

— Freddie.
Freddie who?
Freddie or not, here I come.

— Fred.
Fred who?
*Fred this needle for me,
will you?*

— Francis.
Francis who?
Francisn't the capital of Paris!

— Godfrey.
Godfrey who?
Godfrey tickets for the football match.

— Hawaii.
Hawaii who?
Hawaii today?

— Harvey.
Harvey who?
Harvey going to have lunch yet?

— Hurd my.
Hurd my who?
Hurd my hand knocking on the door.

— Hugh.
Hugh who?
Yoo hoo yourself.

— Howard.
Howard who?
Howard I know?

— Howie.
Howie who?
I'm okay. How are you?

— Iowa.
Iowa who?
Iowa lot of money to the income tax people.

— Ida.
Ida who?
Ida terrible time getting here.

— I.B.
I.B. who?
I. B. waiting here a long time.

— Isadora.
Isadora who?
Isadoran exit?

— Irish stew.
Irish stew who?
Irish stew in the name of the law.

— Java.
Java who?
Java telephone I can use?

— Juno.
Juno who?
Juno what time it is?

— Joan.
Joan who?
Joan call us, we'll call you.

— Jimmy.
Jimmy who?
Jimmy a little kiss, will ya?

— Justin.
Justin who?
Justin time for tea.

— Kent.
Kent who?
Kent you tell?

— Lee.
Lee who?
*Lee me alone,
I have a headache.*

176

— Luke.
Luke who?
Luke through the keyhole and see.

— Little old lady.
Little old lady who?
I didn't know you could yodel.

— Marcella.
Marcella who?
Marcella's full of water.

— Major.
Major who?
Major open the door, didn't I?

— Madam.
Madam who?
Madam finger's caught in the door.

— Matthew.
Matthew who?
Matthew laces are undone.

— Matt.
Matt who?
Matter of fact it's me.

— Matilda.
Matilda who?
Matilda not to do it, but she would insist.

— Max.
Max who?
Max no difference –
just open the door.

— Minerva.
Minerva who?
Minerva's wreck from
all these questions.

— Mia.
Mia who?
Miand my shadow.

— Minnie.
Minnie who?
No, not Minnie who –
Minnie ha ha.

— Mister.
Mister who?
Mister last bus home.

— N.E.
N.E. who?
N. E. body you like so
long as you let me in.

— One.
One who?
One-der why you keep
asking that?

— Olive.
Olive who?
Olive here. What's your excuse?

— Nicholas.
Nicholas who?
Nicholas girls shouldn't climb trees.

— Owen.
Owen who?
Owen are you going to let me come in!

— Oswald.
Oswald who?
Oswald my bubble gum.

— Orange.
Orange who?
Orange you glad I called?

— Philip.
Philip who?
Philip my cup, please, I'm thirsty.

— Percy.
Percy who?
Persevere and you may find out.

— Paul.
Paul who?
Paul harder and maybe the door will open.

— Police.
Police who?
Police let me in – I've lost my key.

— Romeo.
Romeo who?
Romeover to the other side of the lake and I'll tell you.

— Queenie.
Queenie who?
Queenie's gwasses for me, pwease.

— Sarah.
Sarah who?
Sarah doctor in the house?

— Sam.
Sam who?
Sam Bridges and cake for tea.

— Sally.
Sally who?
Salleluyah, at last you've answered the door!

— Snow.
Snow who?
Snow use, I've forgotten my name again.

— Shirley.
Shirley who?
Shirley you know me by now.

— Scot.
Scot who?
Scot nothing to do with you.

— Teresa.
Teresa who?
Teresa Green.

— Stu.
Stu who?
Stu late to be asking questions.

— Soup.
Soup who?
Soup-erman!

— Tick.
Tick who?
Tick 'em up! I'm a tongue-tied towboy.

— Thistle.
Thistle who?
I suppose thistle have to do.

— Thesis.
Thesis who?
Thesis a recording.

— Tuba.
Tuba who?
Tuba toothpaste, please.

— Toby.
Toby who?
Toby or not Toby – that is the question.

— Tina.
Tina who?
Tina baked beans.

— Una.
Una who?
Una who I mean?

— Victor.
Victor who?
Victor his trousers on the slide.

— Waiter.
Waiter who?
Waiter minute while I tie my shoelaces.

— Wendy.
Wendy who?
Wendy red, red robin comes bob, bob, bobbin' along.

— Wayne.
Wayne who?
Wayne is pouring out here!

— Warner.
Warner who?
Warner lift? My car's outside.

— Wood.
Wood who?
Wood you believe I've forgotten.

178

— *William.*
William who?
Williamind your own business.

— *Wendy.*
Wendy who?
Wendy joke is over, you'd better laugh or else!

— *York.*
York who?
York coming over to my house.

— *X.*
X who?
Xtremely nice to see you again.

— *Wooden Shoe.*
Wooden Shoe who?
Wooden Shoe like to know!

— *Zoom.*
Zoom who?
Zoom are you expecting?

— *Zeno.*
Zeno who?
Zeno very well who's knocking.

— *Yvonne.*
Yvonne who?
Yvonne to be alone.

Knots
What's a forget-me-knot?
  The tie you make in your handkerchief so you won't forget.

Knowledge
What is full of knowledge but knows nothing at all?
  A bookcase.

Koala
What would you call a bald koala?
  Fred bear.

Ladder
Notice in school lobby:
Will the person who borrowed the ladder from the caretaker please return it immediately or further steps will be taken.

★

Silly Billy: Mum, come quickly! I've just knocked over the ladder at the back of the house.
Mother: Run and tell your father, then, I'm busy right now.
Silly Billy: Dad already knows – he's hanging from the roof.

179

Ladybird

Why was the ladybird kicked out of the forest?
  Because she was a litter bug.

★

What is a baby ladybird called?
  A little humbug.

Lady Pilots

Why are there so few lady pilots?
  Well, would you choose to be a plane woman?

Lamb

What does lamb become when it's one year old?
  Two years old.

★

What do people who live in the Soviet Union call little black lambs?
  Little black lambs.

Landing

1st pilot: I made a first-class three-point landing today!
2nd pilot: Oh, I did better than that! I made a perfect one-point landing.
1st pilot: How's that?
2nd pilot: Nose first!

Landlord

Tenant: When I left my last address my landlord wept!
New landlord: Not me – I ask for rent in advance.

Languages

Visitor: Well, Jenny, what are you learning at school these days?
Jenny: This term we started geometry, and I'm doing French and Spanish too.
Visitor: Which country speaks Geometry?

★

First cow: Moo-ooo-ooo.
Second cow: Cock-a-doodle-doo-ooo.
First cow: What's with the 'Cock-a-doodle-doo-oo'?
Second cow: I'm learning foreign languages.

★

When is it stupid to learn a language?
  When you begin Finnish.

★

Paul: I can speak any language in the world except Greek.
Saul: OK – speak some Russian.
Paul: That's Greek to me.

Lap

What do you lose each time you stand up?
  Your lap.

Lapland

Geography teacher: Lapland is very thinly populated.
Soppy Poppy: Please, sir, how many Lapps are there to the mile?

Laryngitis

Jack: Why do you call your boyfriend 'Laryngitis'?
Jill: Because he's a pain in the neck.

Laser

How can you tell a laser from a telephone?
  The laser is the one without the dial.

★

What is a laser?
  It's what a Chinaman shaves with.

★

Notice in Job Centre:
Wanted: Man to operate Cyclotronic Hyperbolic Sub-atomic Phaser-reactive laser.
No experience necessary.

Lassie

What made Lassie so famous in films?
   She always took the lead.

Last Day

What will a wise man say on the Last Day?
   Armageddon out of here.

Last Words

What were Tarzan's last words?
   'Who greased the vine?'

Late For School

Teacher: Sam, you're late for school.
Sam: I sprained my ankle, sir.
Teacher: What a lame excuse!

★

Teacher: Sam, why are you always late for school?
Sam: Because you always ring the bell before I get in.

★

Why was the little boy late for school?
   Because he was dreaming about a football match and it went into extra time.

★

Silly Billy raced into the class room, late for school, saying, 'I'm sorry, Miss. I hurt two fingers banging in a nail before I left home.'
'I don't see any bandages, Billy,' said his teacher.
'Oh,' said Silly Billy, 'they weren't my fingers.'

★

Teacher: Sam, why are you late for school?
Sam: Sorry, Miss. I must have over-washed.

★

Teacher: What's your excuse for being late today, Poppy?
Soppy Poppy: There was a notice on the bus saying 'Dogs must be carried' and I spent ages looking for one.

Late For Work

Boss: Why are you late again this morning?
Secretary: I'm afraid I overslept.
Boss: You mean you sleep at home as well?

★

Workman: Sorry I'm late, boss, the bus is always late these days.
Foreman: Well, if it's late again tomorrow, you'll have to catch an earlier one.

★

Boss: Why are you late for work this morning?
Workman: I got married, sir.
Boss: Well, see it doesn't happen again.

Latin

Latin is a dead language,
As dead as dead can be.
It killed the ancient Romans,
And now it's killing me!

Laughter

What kind of cattle laugh?
   Laughing stock.

★

Andy: Why are you laughing so much?
Zak: My dentist just took out one of my teeth.
Andy: That's no laughing matter!
Zak: He took out the wrong one!

★

Why do we say people 'laugh up their sleeves'?
   Because that's where they keep their funny bones.

★

Laugh and the class
   laughs with you,
but you stay after school
   alone.

Laugh and the world laughs with you;
cry and you get your temperature taken.

Law
Why is the law like an ocean?
  Because trouble comes from breakers.

Law of Gravity
Did people fall off the earth
  before the law of gravity was passed?

Lawyer
Why did the lawyer carry a ladder to work?
  So that he could take his case to a higher court.

★

Client: Right, we have a bargain. I'll give you £500 and you do the worrying for me.
Lawyer: Fine. Where's the £500?
Client: That's your first worry.

★

What is a lawyer's favourite pudding?
  Suet.

★

What do lawyers wear in court?
  Law suits.

Laziness
Two lazy Boy Scouts were lounging by their tent at the camp site instead of going swimming. One said to the other,
'Watch it, there's a snake by your foot.'
'Which foot?' asked the other without looking up.

★

Adam: Why does Tom always go around with his mouth wide open?
Eve: Because he's so lazy. It saves him having to open it when he wants to yawn.

★

A site foreman had ten very lazy men working for him, so one day he decided to trick them into doing some work for a change.
'I've got a really easy job today for the laziest one among you,' he announced. 'Will the laziest man please put his hand up.'
Nine hands went up.
'Why didn't you put your hand up?' he asked the tenth man.
'Too much trouble,' came the reply.

★

What's the definition of a really lazy person?
  Someone who calls the dog in to see if it's raining outside.

★

Why is a lazy dog like a hill?
  Because it's a slow pup.

Lazy Bones
What is the definition of lazy bones?
  A skeleton that doesn't like work.

Leaf
What promise did Adam and Eve make after being thrown out of the Garden of Eden?
  To turn over a new leaf.

Leaning Tower of Pisa
What did the leaning tower of Pisa say to Big Ben?
  If you've got the time, I've got the inclination.

Learning
Mother: Did you learn anything at school today, Johnny?
Johnny: Yes – how to get out of class early by sticking pens in my ears.

★

Father: How is your arithmetic coming along, Poppy?
Soppy Poppy: Well, I can add up all the zeros, but I'm still having trouble with the numbers.

Learner Driver

Rick: My driving instructor says my test is going to be a close thing.
Nick: Why's that?
Rick: Because I've got three more lessons and they've only got two more cars.

★

Bill was learning to drive, and explained to his younger brother Ben that was why he had a big red 'L' on the car. Bill passed his test and was packing his car ready to go on holiday on the continent.
'Bill,' said Ben, 'does the big 'GB' sticker mean that you're getting better?'

★

One hot summer afternoon a particularly boring teacher was rambling on and on when he saw a boy's head under his desk lid.
'What are you doing?' he called. 'Learning something?'
'Oh, no, sir,' said the boy, 'I'm listening to you.'

Leather

Paul: What kind of leather makes the best shoes?
Saul: I don't know, but banana peel makes the best slippers.

Leaves

Paul: My stupid cousin hurt himself raking up leaves.
Saul: How did he do that?
Paul: He fell out of the tree.

Leaving

Amy: Wasn't your boss furious when you said you'd be leaving next month?
Zoe: Yes! He thought it was this month!

Lecturing

Lecturer: Would anyone like to ask any questions?
Member of the audience: Yes – when are you going?

Leg

What is it that is alive and has only one foot?
  A leg.

★

What has a bottom at its top?
  A leg.

★

What has fifty legs but can't walk?
  Half a centipede.

★

What has no legs but always walks?
  A pair of shoes.

Lemon

What's the best way to make a lemon drop?
  Shake the tree hard.

★

What is yellow and flickers?
  A lemon with a loose connection.

★

What's lemonade?
  When you help an old lemon across the road.

★

Have you heard about the lady who uses lemon juice for her complexion and always looks sour?

★

Nick: What's the difference between a lemon, a hippo and a pot of glue?
Rick: Um, well, you can squeeze a lemon, but you can't squeeze a hippo. But what about the pot of glue?
Nick: I knew that's where you'd get stuck.

Letter

Amy: What are you doing?
Zoe: Writing a letter to myself.
Amy: What does it say?
Zoe: I won't know until I get it tomorrow.

★

Boss: Why is this letter damp?
Secretary: Maybe there's postage dew.

★

Why did the little girl write in huge handwriting to her grandmother?
    Because her grandmother was deaf and she thought she had better write loudly.

★

What do you call a letter when it's dropped down the chimney?
    Blackmail.

★

Extract from a letter written by a mother to her son at camp:
Your Aunt Adeline's just had all her teeth out and a new fireplace put in. Well, I must write quickly now because my pen's running out. . . .

★

Johnny was writing his thank you letters to uncles and aunts for their Christmas presents, when suddenly he stopped.
'What's the matter?' asked his mother.
'It was on the tip of my tongue and now it's gone,' said Johnny.
'Well, if you concentrate hard, it'll come back,' said his mother.
'No, concentrating won't bring it back,' said Johnny. 'I swallowed the stamp!'

★

Where do you post letters to boys?
    In a male box.

Letters of the Alphabet

Why does a young lady need the letter Y?
    Because without it she'd be a young lad.

How do you get rid of varnish?
    Take away the letter R.

★

Why should you never put the letter M in the fridge?
    Because it turns ice into mice.

★

What is the centre of gravity?
    The letter V.

★

Which letter is never found in the alphabet?
    The one you post!

★

Why is the letter S scary?
    Because it makes cream scream.

★

Why is the letter A like noon?
    Because it comes in the middle of the day.

★

Why is a bull like the letter V?
    Because he comes after U.

★

What stands in the middle of Paris?
    The letter R.

★

Teacher: Poppy, say something beginning with 'I'.
Soppy Poppy: I is . . .
Teacher: No, Poppy, you must say 'I am'.
Soppy Poppy: All right, then – I am the ninth letter of the alphabet.

184

How can we tell that the letter Y is nine inches long?
　　Because it's a quarter of a yard.

★

Why is gossip like the letter W?
　　Because it makes ill will.

★

How does the letter A help a deaf lady?
　　It makes her hear.

★

Why should we avoid the letter A?
　　Because it makes men mean.

★

Why is the letter A like a flower?
　　Because a B comes after it.

★

What letter stands for the ocean?
　　The letter C.

★

Why is B hot?
　　Because it makes oil boil.

★

What comes after the letter A?
　　The rest of the alphabet.

★

What is in fashion, but always out of date?
　　The letter F.

★

Why is the letter E lazy?
　　Because it's always in bed.

★

What letters are bad for your teeth?
　　D-K.

★

How do you spell 'dried grass' in three letters?
　　H-A-Y.

★

Why is the letter G like the sun?
　　Because it is the centre of light.

Why is the letter F like a cow's tail?
　　Because it's always at the end of beef.

★

Why are the letters N and O important?
　　Because you can't get 'on' without them.

★

What occurs once in every minute, twice in every moment, but never in one hundred thousand years?
　　The letter M.

★

Why does Lucy like the letter K?
　　Because it makes Lucy lucky.

★

What's the blackest letter in the alphabet?
　　'O' – because it's put twice in soot.

★

Did you hear about the man who wanted his typewriter fixed because the 'O' kept coming out upside down?

★

What three letters of the alphabet do athletes need?
　　N-R-G.

★

Why is the letter T important to a stick insect?
　　Because without it he would be a sick insect.

★

What letter is a vegetable?
　　A P.

★

What four letters end a game of hide-and-seek?
　　O-I-C-U.

★

How many letters are there in the alphabet?
　　Twenty-four – ET's gone home.

★

How can you spell Indian tent with just two letters?

TP.

Teacher: What comes after G?
Silly Billy: Whizz!
Teacher: No, try again. What comes after T?
Silly Billy: V?
Teacher: Billy, you're not trying! What comes after O?
Silly Billy: Boy! Am I ever in trouble!

Which two letters of the alphabet have nothing between them?

N and P – O is between them.

How do you spell 'hungry horse' in four letters?

M T G G.

Lettuce

Mother: This lettuce doesn't taste very nice. Are you sure you washed it as I asked you?
Soppy Poppy: Yes. Look, you can still see the soap on it.

What makes a good lettuce generous?

Its big heart.

What's the difference between a mouldy lettuce and a dismal song?

Easy – one's a bad salad and the other's a sad ballad.

Level-Crossing

What's shut when it's open and open when it's shut?

A level-crossing.

Liars

What do liars do after they die?

They lie still.

What's the best way to find a liar out?

Visit his home when he's not in.

Librarian

Librarian: Poppy, your library book is overdue.
Soppy Poppy: Fine.

What did the book say to the librarian?

Can I take you out?

Library

Librarian: Sh-hh-hh! The other people in here can't read.
Soppy Poppy: Oh, what a shame. I could read when I was six.

Lice

What happened when the two lice moved to a new address?

They decided to give a louse-warming party.

Lies

Mr Able came across a gathering of boys and in the middle was a puppy. 'What are you all up to?' he asked. His son Sam answered, 'We're swapping lies. Whoever tells the biggest lie gets to keep the puppy.'
'Why, that's terrible! When I was a young lad I never dreamt of telling lies.'
'You win, Mr Able. You get to keep the puppy,' said one of the boys.

What kind of animal tells little white lies?
    An amphibian.

★

Andy: I can't stop telling lies.
Zak: I don't believe you.

Life
Who never starts at the bottom in life and works his way up?
    A swimmer.

★

Don't worry if your life's a joke
And your successes few.
Remember that the mighty oak
Was once a nut like you.

Lifejacket
Why did the man wear a lifejacket at night?
    Because he was sleeping on a water-bed.

Lift
What did one lift say to the other life as they passed?
    I think I'm coming down with something.

Lift Operator
Did you hear about the man who lost his job as a lift operator because he couldn't learn the route?

Light
What always stays in the house even when you put it out?
    A light.

★

Science teacher: The light from the sun travels towards us at a speed of approximately 186,000 miles per second.
Mary: Yes, but it's all downhill.

Light Bulb
What did the little light bulb say to its mother?
    I wuv you watts and watts.

★

What would you use if you swallowed a light bulb?
    A candle.

★

What did the boy light bulb say to the girl light bulb?
    You really turn me on.

Lightning
Why is lightning a shocking thing?
    Because it doesn't know how to behave.

★

Paul: What's the difference between lightning and electricity?
Saul: I don't know.
Paul: Have you ever had a lightning bill?

Limbs
What has lots of limbs but still can't move?
    A tree.

Limericks
There once was a chief of the Sioux,
Who into a gun-barrel blioux
To see if 'twas loaded;
The rifle exploded –
As he should have known it would dioux!

★

There was a young man from Leeds,
Who swallowed a packet of seeds;
Within just an hour
His nose was a flower
And his head was a riot of weeds!

★

There was a young man from Bengal
Who was asked to a fancy-dress ball.
He said he would risk it
And went as a biscuit,
But a dog ate him up in the hall!

There once was a writer named Wright,
Who instructed his son to write right;
He said, 'Son, write Wright right.
It is not right to write
Wright as 'rite' – try to write Wright aright!'

★

There was a young man from Quebec
Who wrapped both his legs round his neck!
But then he forgot
How to untie the knot,
And now he's an absolute wreck!

★

There was a young lady from Riga,
Who rode with a smile on a tiger.
They returned from the ride
With the lady inside,
And the smile on the face of the tiger.

★

An earnest young fisher named Fisher
Once fished from the edge of a fissure.
A fish with a grin
Pulled the fisherman in –
Now they're fishing the fissure for Fisher!

Lion

Did you hear about the scientist who crossed
a parrot with a lion?
It bit off his arm and then said, 'Who's a pretty
boy then!'

★

Did you know a mane is a lion's principal part?

★

What is long-haired and has purple feet?
  A lion that makes its own wine.

★

What lion never attacks?
  A dandelion.

★

What do you get if you cross a lion with a
mouse?
  MIGHTY MOUSE!

Jack: If you were walking through the woods,
  would you rather be eaten by a lion or a
  bear?
Jill: I'd rather the lion ate the bear.

★

A lion who was the star of the circus show was
walking among the other animals' cages when
he came across a monkey. 'Who's the greatest
animal in this circus?' he roared.
The monkey was very frightened, and said,
'You are, O mighty lion!' This pleased the
lion, of course, so he walked on, and met a
performing seal.
'Who is the greatest animal in this circus?' he
roared again, taking away the seal's ball. 'You
are, O mighty lion!' squeaked the seal, so the
lion gave him his ball back. Then the lion met
an elephant and repeated his question. Instead
of answering, the elephant picked the lion up
in his trunk, twirled him around a few times
and threw him into the air. The lion picked
himself up off the ground, dusted himself off
and said,
'There's no need to get rough just because
you don't know the answer.'

★

Bill: I used to be a lion hunter in the Arctic.
Ben: There aren't any lions in the Arctic.
Bill: I know, I shot them all.

★

Jack: I was surrounded by lions this morning.
Jill: Lions! How frightening!
Jack: Yes, dandelions.

★

Why do lions eat raw meat?
  Because they've
never been to
cookery classes.

A man in the jungle saw a lion and promptly fainted. When he came to he saw that the lion was praying, and he said: 'Thank you for not eating me.'

'Quiet,' said the lion, 'I'm saying grace.'

★

What did the lion do when the man put his head into the lion's mouth to see how many teeth it had?

The lion closed its mouth to see how many heads the man had.

Lion Tamer

Paul: I saw that circus man the other day – the one who used to put his right arm down the lion's throat. What was his name?

Saul: I don't remember, but I heard they're calling him Lefty now!

Liquid

What liquid can you never freeze?

Hot water.

Lisp

After years of speaking with a lisp, Mrs Able decided to take elocution lessons in an attempt to cure it. A friend met her after a few weeks of lessons and asked how everything was going. 'Fine,' said Mrs Able. 'Today I learned to thay, "This is Sooty sitting on a cushion".'

'Well done,' said the friend.

'Thank you,' replied Mrs Able. 'But it'th *tho* difficult to bring into the converthation.'

★

Paul: Did you hear about the rabbit with a lisp who went to the dentist to have a tooth out?

Saul: No, tell me.

Paul: Well, the dentist asked him if he wanted gas, and the rabbit said, 'No, I'm an ether bunny'.

Little Bo Peep

Why do Little Bo Peep lose her sheep?

Because she had a crook with her.

Little Jack Horner

Little Jack Horner sat in a corner
Eating his Christmas pie.
He put in his thumb, but instead of a plum
He squirted fruit juice in his eye.

Little Miss Muffet

Little Miss Muffet sat on her tuffet,
Eating her curds and whey,
When along came a spider
Who sat down beside her
And said, 'Too much cholesterol, I'd say!'

Live Wire

Interviewer: Your references are very good. You seem to be a real live-wire salesman. What were you selling?

Job applicant: Live wires.

Living Room

What did the living room say to the lamp?

You light up my life.

Loaf

What's half a loaf?

Better than no free time at all.

Lobster

Why did the lobster blush?

Because the sea weed.

Locked Out!

What do you do if you are locked out of your house and want to get in?

Sing until you get the right key.

Log

A log in the jungle woke up one morning and announced to all the trees and animals: 'I feel wonderful! I slept like a human being last night.'

Lollipop

How do you stop a lollypop slipping out of your mouth?

Grit your teeth.

★

Why are lollipops like racehorses?

Because the more you lick them the faster they go.

London Palladium

A visitor stopped a man carrying a cello case and asked, 'How do I get to the London Palladium?'

'Practice,' came the reply.

Lonely Hearts Club

Did you hear about the man who sent his photograph to a Lonely Hearts Club?

He got it back with a note saying they weren't that lonely.

Lone Ranger

Why is the Lone Ranger rich?

Because he always rides on Silver.

Longest Night

Which is the longest night of the year?

A fortnight.

Long Face

My husband has such a long face that his barber charges him double for shaving it.

Long John Silver

Did you hear about the actor who was so keen to get the part of Long John Silver that he had his leg cut off?

He still didn't get the part, though – it was the wrong leg.

★

Who wears thermal and lurex underwear?

Long John Silver.

Loom

What did one loom say to the other?

Let's spin a good yarn.

Losing Hair

Andy: My dad has lost all his hair.
Zak: Why's that?
Andy: He worried so much about losing it.

Lost

Tom: Dick cheats. I'm not playing golf with him again.
Harry: Why not?
Tom: He said he found his lost ball and it was in my pocket all along.

★

Mother: Why are you crying, Bill?
Bill: Ben's lost his best white socks.
Mother: But why are you crying about it?
Bill: Because I was wearing them when he lost them.

★

Advertisement in the newspaper:
Lost – a white kitten by an old lady who answers when you call Snow White.

★

Advertisement: Lost – a wristwatch by a man with a cracked faced.

★

What's the best way to find a lost rabbit?

Make a noise like a juicy carrot.

Lot's Wife

What did Lot do with his wife when she turned into a pillar of salt?

He put her in the cellar.

Love

It is better to have loved a short person than never to have loved a tall.

★

190

What's the difference between an accepted lover and a rejected lover?

One kisses his miss, the other misses his kiss..

★

Adam: Since I met you I can't sleep, I can't eat, I can't drink. . . .
Eve: Why?
Adam: I'm broke.

★

Adam: Do you love me?
Eve: Who else?

★

Eve: Do you love me?
Adam: Oh, yes, I do. I'd die for you.
Eve: You're always saying that, but you never do it.

★

Boy piece of coal: I'm burning with love for you.
Girl piece of coal: Oh, don't make a fuel of yourself!

★

Did the rooster really fall in love with the hen at first sight?

Not really – she egged him on a bit.

★

Amy: I thought you were going to marry Sam? You said it was love at first sight.
Zoe: The second and third sights put me off completely.

★

Who were the world's smallest lovers?

Gnomeo and Juliet.

★

A vicar came across two little boys fighting one afternoon.

'You shouldn't be fighting,' he said to the bigger boy.

'Remember, you should love your enemy.'

'But he's not my enemy,' said the boy, 'he's my brother.'

Lucky Charms

Two men met by chance for the first time in many years. The first man asked, 'How's life been treating you?'

'Not so well,' replied his friend. 'My wife left me, my son was arrested for breaking and entering, my daughter is in hospital with a broken arm. I'm going bald, all my teeth are being taken out tomorrow and my dog died yesterday.' 'Oh, that is terrible, I'm so sorry to hear all that. You still have a job, though. What line of business are you in?' 'I sell lucky charms.'

★

Gypsy at the door: Buy a lucky charm, lady. Take away the curse I've just put on your house.

Luke Skywalker

How does Luke Skywalker shave?

With a laser blade.

Lumberjack

What did the lumberjack do just before Christmas?

He went on a chopping spree.

★

What's the difference between a lame bull and a lumberjack?

One hops and chews, the other chops and hews.

Lunatics

Three lunatics were at work on a building site, supposedly digging a trench. Along came the foreman, and he was very surprised to see two of the men standing stock still with their picks in the air while the third was digging.

'What do you think you're doing?' he asked.

'We're lamp posts,' said the two men.

'You're fired.' shouted the foreman. They left the building site but the third man stopped digging and climbed out of the trench.

'You carry on,' said the foreman 'I haven't fired you.'

'Don't be stupid,' said the third lunatic. 'How do you *expect* me to work in the dark?'

Lunch

How does Batman's mother call him in for lunch?

Batman, din-ner, din-ner, din-ner, din-ner, d-i-n-n-e-r!

Mother: Now you've finished your lunch, you may say grace.
Jenny: OK – 'Thanks a bunch for lunch, Lord'.
Mother: That wasn't much of a grace, Jenny.
Jenny: Well, it wasn't much of a lunch.

★

Machines

Farmer: This machine I've just bought does the work of a dozen men. It's so fantastic it almost has a brain.
Farmhand: Not if it does all that work it hasn't.

★

Interviewer: Have you any experience with machines?
Job applicant: Oh, yes! I'm an ace on space invaders!

Mad

Why is the letter D like a naughty boy?
Because it makes Ma Mad.

★

What's black, crazy and sits in trees?
A raven lunatic.

★

How do you stop a mad doctor following you?
Carry an apple.

Where do mad squirrels go?
To the nut house.

★

What do you call mad fleas?
Loony ticks.

★

Rick: I've been talking to myself – do you think I'm mad?
Nick: Only if you answer yourself too!

Magic

Sam: Will you pull a rabbit out of your hat, mister?
Magician: I'm sorry, son, but I've just washed my hare, and I can't do a thing with it.

★

Andy: My dad has a magic slipper.
Zak: Oh really?
Andy: Yes, when he waves it I disappear!

Magician

Proud mother: Ever since Johnny was little he's wanted to be a magician and saw people in half.
Visitor: Is he your only child?
Proud mother: Oh, no, he has several half brothers and sisters.

★

City visitor: That farmer's a magician.
Country boy: What makes you say that?
City visitor: He just told me that he was going to turn his sheep into a field.

★

Mary: What happened to the girl you used to saw in half?
Magician: She's now living in San Francisco and New York.

★

What do you call a space magician?
A flying saucerer.

★

A magician walked in to an agent's office and announced that he had a totally original act to offer.
'What is it?' asked the agent.
'I saw a woman in half,' said the magician.
'That's one of the oldest tricks in the business,' said the agent. 'Every magician on my books can do that.'
'Yes,' said the magician, 'but I do it lengthways.'

★

What did the magician's greensward say?
I want to be a-lawn.

★

Once upon a time there was a little boy called Merlin. He was a truly amazing magician. He went around the corner and turned into a sweetshop!

★

How does one magician greet another?
'Hello, Merlin. How's tricks?'

Why do magicians drink tea?
Because sorcerers need cuppas.

Magna Carta

History teacher: Who signed the Magna Carta, Billy?
Silly Billy: I don't know, Miss, but it wasn't me!

Magnets

What did the boy magnet say to the girl magnet?
I find you really attractive.

Maid

Lady Snob: We'll have breakfast tomorrow morning at *exactly* 8 o'clock.
Maid: All right, madam. But if I'm not downstairs on time, do start without me.

Mail

When it comes to spreading news, the female is much better than the mail.

Making Faces

Who makes faces at Luke Skywalker and Han Solo?
Princess Leer.

Man

Why does a tall man eat less than a short man?
Because he makes a little go a long way.

★

When is a man not a man?
When he's abed.

★

Are you a man or a mouse?
Squeak up!

What was the name of the first mechanical man to be invented?

Frank N. Stein.

Manhole Cover

Why did the drunk lift up the manhole cover and take it home?

Because he wanted to listen to it on his stereo.

Manners

Mrs Able: My husband's manners have really improved recently!

Mrs Cable: Why's that?

Mrs Able: His new job is in a refinery.

★

Mrs Able: My husband has such bad table manners I'm embarrassed to go out with him. He will hold his cup of tea with his little finger sticking straight out.

Mrs Cable: But in some circles it's considered very polite to hold out your little finger when you're drinking tea.

Mrs Able: With the tea bag hanging from it?

★

Mrs Cable: My husband's really very polite. He always takes his shoes off before putting his feet on the table.

★

Mrs Cable: When our visitors come to tea, you will be on your best behaviour, won't you?

Mr Cable: What do you mean, my best behaviour?

Mrs Cable: Well, perhaps you wouldn't drink your tea from your saucer the way you usually do.

Mr Cable: What do you want me to drink it from?

Mrs Cable: Out of the cup, of course.

Mr Cable: But if I drink it out of the cup I'll get the teaspoon in my eye!

★

Mother: Billy, don't reach across the table. Haven't you got a tongue?

Silly Billy: Yes, but my arm is longer.

★

What is the keynote of good manners?

B natural.

★

A very fat woman turned to the man sitting next to her on the bus and said in a loud voice: 'If you were a gentleman, you'd stand up and let one of those women sit down.'

'And if you were a lady,' replied the man, 'you'd stand up and let all four of them sit down.'

Marbles

Amy: What is the matter with your brother today? I've just seen him running down the road, shouting and tearing out his hair!

Zoe: Oh, he's just lost his marbles.

★

A mother was trying to persuade her young son to let his younger sister play with his marbles.

'But she wants to keep them,' complained the little boy.

'Oh, I'm sure she doesn't,' replied his mother.

'Then why does she keep swallowing them?' the little boy asked.

March

What is in the middle of March?

The letter R.

Marines

Why was the sergeant kicked out of the Marines?

Because he was rotten to the Corps.

Marriage

1st sailor: Have you heard that the captain's new wife has run away?

2nd sailor: Yes, shame, isn't it? He took her for a mate but she turned out to be a skipper.

★

An elderly spinster astounded her friends by announcing that she was going to be married. 'But you always said men were stupid,' said one friend, 'and you told us you'd never marry!'
'Yes, I did,' said the spinster, 'but I found one who asked me.'

★

Johnny was unmarried at the age of 30, and his father took him aside one evening and said, 'It really is time you settled down with a wife and home of your own, you know. Why, at your age I'd been married for years!'
'But you were married to Mum,' said Johnny. 'You wouldn't want me to marry a stranger, would you?'

★

Suitor: Sir, I would like your daughter for my wife.
Father: Why can't she get one of her own?

★

Jack: Why aren't you going to marry Dick after all?
Jill: Because he said he'd just die if I didn't, and I just wanted to see. . . .

★

Amy: I can marry anyone I please, so there!
Zoe: But you don't please anyone, my dear!

★

Boss: Why do you want time off next week?
Workman: To get married, sir.
Boss: What idiot woman would want to marry you?
Workman: Your daughter, sir.

★

Mrs New: Darling, today we've been married exactly 12 months!
Mr New: Seems more like a year to me.

Wife: I've given you the best years of my life!
Husband: So? Do you want a receipt?

★

Wife: One more word out of you and I'm going back to mother.
Husband: Taxi!

★

Jack and Jill wanted to get married but couldn't find anywhere to live. One of Jack's friends was listening to them talking over their problem one evening and thought he had the solution.
'Why don't you live with Jill's parents?'
'We can't do that,' said Jack and Jill in horror. 'They're still living with *their* parents!'

★

Mrs Cable: Don't you think our daughter's too young to get married?
Mr Cable: Not if I think of it this way – I'm not losing a daughter, I'm gaining a telephone.

★

Rick: I know a man who married his sister.
Nick: He can't do that – it's against the law!
Rick: Not if he's a parson, it isn't.

★

Why did the teacher marry the caretaker?
Because he swept her off her feet.

★

Why is marriage like hot water?
Because it's not so hot once you get used to it.

★

Visitor to newly-weds: Your bride worships you, doesn't she!
Husband: She must do – she puts burnt offerings in front of me three times a day.

★

Jack: Will you marry me, darling?
Jill: I don't know. You have been married five times already and there are terrible stories going around about you.
Jack: Don't listen to them, my dearest. They're just old wives' tales.

Johnny: Mummy, who's that man you just said hello to?
Mother: That's the man who married me.
Johnny: If that's the man who married you, who's Daddy?

★

Andy: Why aren't you married?
Zak: I was born that way.

★

Bill: Have you noticed how many girls don't want to get married these days?
Ben: No. How do you know?
Bill: I've asked them all.

Marshmallow
Andy: Last night I dreamed that I was eating an enormous marshmallow.
Zak: So? It was only a dream!
Andy: Yes, but when I woke up this morning I couldn't find my pillow!

Mask
Amy: Oh, I was so embarrassed when they asked me to take off my mask at the New Year's Eve fancy dress party.
Zoe: Why?
Amy: I wasn't wearing one.

★

Why do doctors and nurses wear masks?
So that if they make a mistake no one will know who it was.

Massage
Amy: Why do you enjoy a massage so much?
Zoe: Because I like to feel kneaded.

Match
Jack: This match won't light.
Jill: What's the matter with it?
Jack: I don't know, it worked a moment ago.

★

Paul: Which is the heavier, a match or a lighter?
Saul: A match?
Paul: No, because they're both lighters!

★

What is long, has a black hat and lies in a box?
A match.

★

What did the match say to the man who lit it?
How dare you strike me!

Mathematics
What animals are mathematical?
Rabbits – because they multiply so well.

★

Son: Dad, will you help me with my homework, please? I have to find the least common denominator.
Father: Hasn't anyone found it yet? Everyone was looking for that when *I* was a child.

★

If two's company and three's a crowd, what is four and five?
Nine.

★

Maths teacher: Sam, tell me – if you washed cars for 20 people in your road and they each paid you 50p, what would you get?
Sam: A BMX.

★

What happened to the plant in the maths class?
It grew square roots.

If your maths teacher faints, what number does she need? You must try to bring her 2.

Matterhorn

What would you shout as you fell off the Matterhorn?
Aaa-alp!

Mattress Factory

Why did the man lose his job in the mattress factory?
Because he fell awake on the job.

Mayflowers

If April showers bring May flowers, what do May flowers bring?
Pilgrims.

Mayonnaise

What did the mayonnaise say to the fridge?
Close the door, please, I'm dressing.

Meanness

Have you heard about the meanest man in the world? On Christmas Eve he goes outside, fires off his shot gun, goes back inside and says to his children, 'Sorry, no Christmas presents this year. Father Christmas just shot himself.'

★

Did you hear about the lady of the manor who was so mean she kept a fork in her sugar-bowl?

★

Who's the meanest man in the world?
The man who finds a crutch, and then breaks his leg so that he can use it.

Measles

Grandmother: What are you going to give your baby brother for Christmas, Johnny?
Johnny: I don't know. Last Christmas I gave him measles.

Meat

Waiter: And how did you find the meat, sir?
Customer: Oh, I just lifted up a chip and there it was.

★

Why did the family eat all the white meat off the turkey?
To make a clean breast of it.

★

How can you save meatballs from drowning?
Put them in gravy boats.

Medals

What did the banana republic general get all his medals for?
About £5.

★

Amy: What did you get that little medal for?
Zoe: For singing.
Amy: And what did you get the big medal for?
Zoe: For stopping.

Medicine

Mother: What are you going to take your medicine with today?
Soppy Poppy: A fork, please.

★

Mother: Jenny, the doctor says you should take one of these pills four times a day.
Jenny: But, Mum, how can I take it more than once?

★

Doctor: Did you drink the medicine after your bath?
Patient: After drinking the bath I didn't have too much room for the medicine.

★

Mother: Sam, come and take your medicine.
Sam: I'll just run the bath.
Mother: Why?
Sam: Because the medicine has to be taken in water.

Doctor: I hope that medicine I gave your old aunt last week sorted her out?
Mrs Able: I don't know, doctor, we buried her yesterday.

★

Visitor: Why are you jumping up and down like that, Billy?
Silly Billy: I've just taken some medicine and I forgot to shake the bottle.

★

What is the first mention of medicine in the Bible?
When the Lord gave Moses two tablets.

★

Mother: How did you manage to get Sam to take his medicine? I haven't heard the usual fuss.
Father: I shot it into him with a water pistol.

★

What is the difference between a bottle of medicine and a door mat?
One is shaken up and taken, the other is taken up and shaken.

Medium

What happened when Silly Billy went to a mind reader?
She gave him his money back.

Meeting

Two stupid friends were arranging to meet:
'If I get there first, I'll put a chalk mark up,' said the first.
'Right,' said the second. 'And if I get there first, I'll rub it off.'

★

Mrs Able: Did you meet your son at the airport?
Mrs Cable: Oh, no! I've known him for years!

Melancholy

What does melancholy mean?
It's a dog that likes watermelons.

Member of Parliament

Nathaniel Nathan, recently elected to serve as the Member of Parliament for Puddledock, took his seat in the House of Commons yesterday. Today he was forced to put it back.

Memory

Amy: My brother's got a memory like an elephant's.
Zoe: And the shape to go with it.

★

Amy: My Mum's memory is the worst in the world.
Zoe: Do you mean she forgets everything?
Amy: No, she remembers everything.

★

Teacher: Who can tell me what happened in 1066?
Silly Billy: I can't even remember what happened last night!

★

Paul: I went to the doctor today about my bad memory.
Saul: What did he do?
Paul: He made me pay in advance.

★

Paul: Did you ever hear the memory joke?
Saul: No.
Paul: Oops, sorry, I've forgotten it.

Menu

Rick: Have you seen the unique menu outside the new restaurant?
Nick: No, what do they have?
Rick: Soup in the basket.

Meringues

What kind of meringues repeat on you?
Boo-meringues.

★

What's white, sweet and fluffy, has whiskers, and floats?
A catameringue.

What's white, fluffy and hangs from a baker's ceiling?
A meringue-outang.

★

Mermaid
What is a mermaid?
A deep-she fish.

★

What do mermaids eat for breakfast?
Toast and merma-lade.

Merry-Go-Round
Nick: There I was – with wild horses prancing all around me, and a tiger right in front –
Rick: What happened then?
Nick: The merry-go-round stopped.

Messenger
The large store's managing director was doing a round of inspection one day when he came across a young man lounging about in the post room. 'How much do you get a week?' he asked angrily, to which the young man replied, 'Ten pounds.' The managing director gave him £10 from his wallet, shouted, 'Now go!' and turned to the post room manager. 'Who on earth employed that lazy so-and-so?' 'Nobody,' came the reply, 'he was a messenger.'

Metal
Bill: Did you hear about the man who ate little bits of metal all day?
Ben: No . . .
Bill: It was his staple diet.

Metronome
What is a metronome?
A dwarf in the Paris underground.

Mexican Chilli
How do you make a Mexican chilli?
Take him to the North Pole.

Mexico
Who was Mexico's most famous fat man?
Pauncho Villa.

Mice
Hickory, dickory, dock,
Two mice ran up the clock,
The clock struck one,
But the other one got away.

★

Did you hear about the young bride who thought the patter of tiny feet meant mice?

★

1st mouse: I've finally trained that scientist.
2nd mouse: How?
1st mouse: Well, every time I run through the maze and ring the bell, he puts some cheese underneath it.

★

What do angry rodents send to each other at Yuletide?
Cross-mouse cards.

★

What has 12 legs, three tails and can't see?
Three blind mice.

Mickey Mouse
Who has large antlers and wears white gloves?
Mickey Moose.

★

Why did Mickey Mouse want to have a flight on the space shuttle?
Because he wanted to find Pluto.

Midnight
Two young boys decided to spend the night in a tent in the garden. It was of course very dark and they were getting a little frightened when they heard the town hall clock strike twelve. After a while one said, 'How much after midnight is it now?' To which the other replied, 'I don't know, my watch only goes as high as twelve.'

Milk

Customer: Waiter, this milk is very weak.
Waiter: Well, the cow must have got caught in the rain.

★

What happens if you make milk out of wool?
 The cow feels a little sheepish.

★

City boy: And do these cows really give milk?
Farmer: Not quite – you have to squeeze it out of them.

★

When is it socially correct to serve milk in a saucer?
 When you give it to a cat.

★

Mrs Able: Two gallons of milk tomorrow, please, milkman. I want to have a milk bath.
Milkman: Pasteurised?
Mrs Able: I'll be happy if it comes up to my waist.

★

Teacher: I asked you to write an essay on milk, and you've only written half a page when I expected much more. Why?
Soppy Poppy: I wrote about condensed milk.

★

What has only one horn and gives lots of milk?
 A milk lorry.

★

Paul: Did you hear about the lady who got hurt taking a milk bath?
Saul: How did she get hurt taking a milk bath?
Paul: The cow fell on her.

★

Customer: May I have my milk bill, please?
Milkman: My name's not Bill!

★

Some city boys went for a day out in the country, and one of them discovered a pile of empty milk bottles in a hedge. 'Quick!' he shouted to the others. 'Come over here! I've found a cow's nest.'

★

Mrs Goodey-Twoshoes was walking home from shopping one morning when she saw a driverless milk float slowly rolling towards her. She dropped her shopping, jumped into the float and put the brake on. A very cross-looking milkman poked his head in to the cab, and Mrs Goodey-Twoshoes said,
'If this is your van, you should take more care. It was rolling down the street and I stopped it.'
'I know that,' said the milkman, 'the battery is flat and I was pushing it.'

★

What's the most difficult thing about milking a mouse?
 Getting the bucket under it.

★

Andy: Did you hear what happened at the milking competition?
Zak: No, what?
Andy: There was udder chaos.

Milkmaid

Why does a milkmaid sit on a stool?
 Because she can't stand milking.

Million

If twenty make a score, how many make a million?
 Very few.

200

Millionaire

What's another name for a millionaire's son?
  A million heir.

★

Why did the millionaire have no bathrooms in his house?
  Because he was filthy rich.

★

How did the Japanese millionaire make all his money?
  He just had a yen for that sort of thing.

★

Mrs Verity Rich made her husband a millionaire.
  Before she married him he was a multi-millionaire.

★

Paul: I feel like a million dollars!
Saul: You look like a million dollars — counterfeit!

Mind

Adam: I've changed my mind.
Eve: Oh, good. Does the new one work any better?

★

What is mind?
  No matter.

★

What is matter?
  Never mind.

Mind-Reader

Paul: What makes you say I'm stupid?
Saul: Well, that mind-reader only charged you half price.

Ming

Why did Mrs Able buy a Ming vase?
  To go with her ming coat.

Miniatures

What are miniatures?
  Dwarfs when they eat toffees.

Minimum

What's the definition of minimum?
  A very small mother.

Mink

What do you get when you cross a mink with a gorilla?
  A very, very long-sleeved mink coat.

Miracle

A man returning home from a pilgrimage to Lourdes had to go through Customs at the airport. He said he had nothing to declare, but the customs officer asked him to open up his suitcase just the same.
'What's in this bottle?' asked the customs officer.
'That, sir, is holy water,' replied the man. But the suspicious customs officer opened the bottle, dipped his finger in it and licked it.
'This is brandy!' he said.
'Oh, God be praised!' said the man. 'Another miracle!'

★

Did you hear about the secretary who was a miracle?
  It was a miracle if she turned up to work on time.

Mirror

Customer: I'd like a mirror, please.
Sales assistant: Certainly, madam. A hand mirror?
Customer: No, one I can see my face in.

★

What turns everything back to front but doesn't move?
  A mirror.

Amy: Do you look in the mirror when you've washed your face?
Zoe: No, I look in the towel!

★

Mrs Able: Why have you put a mirror on your television set, dear?
Mrs Cable: Because I wanted to see what my family looked like!

Misers

What do misers do in cold weather?
Sit around a candle.

★

What do misers do in very cold weather?
Light it.

Missionaries

Rick: What's a cannibal's favourite food?
Nick: Missionaries – because they go down so well.

★

Advertisement:
Become a missionary – give cannibals a taste of Christianity!

Mississippi

What has four eyes but still cannot see?
The Mississippi.

Mistake

A man who had finished his lunch and paid his bill got up and took a coat from the coathooks. Another man approached him and said, 'Excuse me, are you Charlie Cable?'
'No,' replied the first man.
'Well I am,' said the second. 'And that's my coat you're putting on.'

★

Teacher: I don't understand how one person can make so many mistakes in one day!
Soppy Poppy: I get up early.

Why is it always a mistake to put on your shoe?
Because you're putting your foot in it.

★

Teacher: Why should we learn from the mistakes of others?
Smart Alec: Because we won't be around to make them all by ourselves.

Modesty

My sister's so modest, she was born in a nappy!

★

My auntie's so modest, she blindfolds herself in the shower.

Moles

How can you stop moles digging up your garden?
Hide the spade.

★

A man was tired of the mole holes in his otherwise beautiful lawn, and went to a garden centre to seek advice. The sales assistant recommended the four-day cure.
'What's that?' asked the gardener.
'Well,' said the assistant. 'At six o'clock every morning for three mornings you drop an apple and a biscuit down the mole hole. But on the fourth morning you only drop an apple down the hole. Then you sit down to wait – five or ten minutes should do it. All of a sudden the mole comes up to ask where the biscuit is and you hit him on the head.'

Momentous Misprints

The new bride over the river is approximately twenty feet wide from buttress to buttress.

★

Foreign ministers declared today that their summit meeting had been a hug success.

★

Ice cream sellers in London say they have ordered huge socks because of the unusual hot weather spell.

★

Husbands and children were included in last night's Women's Institute pot luck supper.

★

Weather forecast: A depression will mope across the country.

★

Before Miss Amy Able concluded her concert with 'Abide With Me', she was prevented with a bouquet of flowers by the orchestra leader.

★

No responsibility is accepted for typographical errors – advertisers are expected to check their own smalls to ensure accuracy.

★

The new hospital extension will enable patients to be prepared and served in a way that has previously been impossible.

★

There were scenes of disorder in the House of Commons last night, with one member of the Opposition shaking a clenched fish at the Prime Minister.

★

As the Prince and Princess of Wales entered the dining hall, the state trumpeters played a funfair.

★

Mrs Cable recently invested in a cow, and she is now supplying the neighbourhood with fresh dairy produce.

Brigadier Bollsover, the bottle-scarred veteran, died at his home last week, aged 85.

Mona Lisa

The reason she smiled (Mona Lisa)
Was seeing the Tower of Pisa.
They didn't quite mean
To make the thing lean,
But they built it that way just to please 'er.

★

Mr Able: My wife's just like the Mona Lisa.
Mr Cable: As beautiful as that, and with the mysterious smile?
Mr Able: No, she ought to be in a museum.

Money

Paul: How much money do you have in your wallet?
Saul: I'm not sure, between £45 and £50.
Paul: Isn't that a lot to be carrying around?
Saul: No, £5 isn't that much.

★

Mrs Able: I hear your son is a writer. Does he write for money?
Mrs Cable: That's right – in every letter we get.

★

What's the easiest way to get close to money?
Lean against the bank wall.

★

Employee: You should be ashamed to give me such a poultry pay cheque.
Employer: You mean paltry.
Employee: No, I mean poultry. This is chicken feed.

★

Did you hear about the country which needed more money, and opened its Mint from 6 pm until midnight?
It's the world's largest after-dinner mint.

★

Mother: Sam, why did you swallow the money I gave you?

Sam: Because you said it was my lunch money.

★

Why is money sometimes called dough?
    Because we all knead it.

★

How can you make more of your money?
    Screw up a note and you will find it in creases.

★

How did all the rich people get their money?
    They were calm and collected.

★

Johnny: I know a horse worth £100,000.

Jenny: Goodness! How could a horse save so much?

★

Maths teacher: Billy, if you found 10p in one pocket and 10p in another pocket, what would you have?

Silly Billy: Someone else's trousers.

★

What goes farther the slower it goes?
    Money.

★

How can you double your money instantly?
    Fold it.

★

A beat policeman was walking down the High Street late one evening when he saw a man on his hands and knees.

'Looking for something, sir?' asked the policeman.

'Yes, I dropped a pound coin in Church Street,' replied the man.

'But if you dropped the coin in Church Street, why are you looking for it here?' asked the policeman.

'Because,' answered the man, 'there are no street lights in Church Street.'

Workers in the Mints throughout the world are threatening to go on strike – unless they make less money.

★

Jack: My teacher said I'd make a very good moneylender.

Jill: Why's that?

Jack: Because I take such an interest in my work.

★

Why are money and a secret so alike?
    Because they're both hard to keep.

Monk

A man got caught in a torrential thunderstorm one night and all the electrics on his car went dead. He pushed the car to one side and started to walk on through the rain. Eventually he came to a sign which read, 'St Francis's Monastery' and, soaked to the skin, he walked up the driveway to knock on the monastery door. The monk who answered let him in and showed him to a cell, apologising for the fact that he would have to share it with a monk. Inside the cell was a box, and the man asked what was in it, thinking it might be extra blankets.

'Sorry, I can't tell you,' replied the monk, 'you have to be a monk.'

All night the man lay wondering what might be in the box and by the next morning he had decided he just had to know what was in the box, even if it meant becoming a monk. So for five years he trained as a monk and was eventually sent back to the original monastery. He went straight to the cell and was relieved to see the box still there. Slowly he lifted the lid of the box and looked inside. Inside the box was a notice which read, 'Sorry, I can't tell you, you have to be a monk.'

★

One day while riding through a thunderstorm, a cyclist got a puncture outside a monastery. A monk came out and invited him inside to have dinner and spend the night. The cyclist accepted because he had got very wet and the nearest town was a long way away. He had a splendid meal of fish and chips and decided to compliment the chef, so he went in to the kitchen and asked the cook:

'Are you the fish friar?'

'No,' the man replied, 'I'm the chip monk.'

Monkey

Why is a monkey like a flower?
  Because it's a chimp-pansy.

★

What can a monkey hold in his right hand that he can't hold in his left?
  His left elbow.

★

How do monkeys toast bread?
  They put it under the g'riller.

★

Why do monkeys swing in the trees?
  Because there aren't any swings in the jungle.

Monologue

A monologue is a conversation between a woman who has just had a baby and one who has yet to give birth.

Monster

What's a vampire's son called?
  Bat Boy.

★

Why did the monster visit the psychiatrist?
  Because he thought everyone was beginning to love him.

★

Baby monster: Mummy, mummy, why do I keep going round in circles?
Mother: Be quiet, or I'll nail your other foot to the floor.

★

What is a monster's last drink.
  His bier.

★

What would you do if a monster broke in through your front door?
  Run out through the back door.

★

What's a monster's favourite way to travel?
  By blood vessel.

★

Where do vampires collect their post from?
  The Dead Letter Office.

★

What happened when the boy monster met the girl monster?
  They fell in love at first fright!

★

Amy: Yesterday I took my boyfriend to see 'Monster's Revenge' at the cinema.
Zoe: What was he like?
Amy: Oh, about ten foot tall, with two heads and a bolt through each neck. Really, really awful.
Zoe: I didn't mean your boyfriend – what was the monster in the film like?

★

What goes out only at night and goes, 'Chomp, suck . . . ouch!'
  A vampire with a rotten fang.

★

Why did the monster stop playing with his brother?
  He got tired of kicking him around.

★

Did you hear about the girl monster who wasn't pretty and wasn't ugly?
  She was pretty ugly.

★

What do monsters have every day at mid-morning?
  A coffin break.

205

How do you greet a two-headed monster?
Hello, hello; how are you? how are you?

★

Mother monster to a visitor: Don't set in that chair, it's for Rigor Mortis to set in.

★

What do you call a stupid monster?
A dummy mummy.

★

How does a monster count to 19?
On its fingers.

★

What does a monster do when he loses his head?
He calls a head hunter.

★

What does a monster do if he loses his hand?
He goes to a second hand shop.

★

What do monsters do with old cannon balls?
Play marbles.

★

Why did the monster give up boxing?
Because he didn't want to spoil his looks.

★

What kind of monster has the best hearing?
The eeriest.

★

What do you call a pretty, tidy, kind and considerate lady monster?
A failure.

Who won the Monster Beauty Competition?
Nobody.

★

1st monster: Would you like to play vampires?
2nd monster: How do you play that?
1st monster: Oh, for very high stakes.

★

What do monsters sing at Christmas?
Deck the halls with poison ivy. . . .

★

1st monster: That girl over there rolled her eyes at me.
2nd monster: Well, roll them back again.

★

What would you do if you saw six space monsters walking down the road?
Hope they were going to a fancy dress party.

★

What is the monsters' favourite ballet?
Swamp Lake.

★

Why did the monster want to buy a sea-horse?
So he could play water-polo.

★

How do monster snowmen feel when they melt?
Abominable.

★

What's a monster's favourite song?
'A pretty ghoul is like a malady'.

Months
Jack: Which month has 28 days?
Jill: Easy — they all have!

Moon
Why did the moon turn pale?
At-mos-fear.

★

A man went to the rocket station and asked for a ticket to the moon
'Sorry, sir,' the attendant said, 'the moon is full just now.'

★

What holds the moon up?
   Moon beams.

★

Why do girls look at the moon?
   Because there's a man in it.

★

Which is heavier, a full moon or a half moon?
   A half moon, because a full moon is lighter.

★

What's big, bright and stupid?
   A fool moon.

★

Two astronauts went in to a pub on the moon, but they didn't stay long. They said it had no atmosphere.

Moose
What do you get if you cross a cocoa bean with an elk?
   A chocolate moose.

Mop
Mother: Why are you carrying that mop, Billy? I thought you were going to football.
Silly Billy: I am. But the coach said there'd be a lot of dribbling this week.

Morning Time
Mother: Sam! Time to get up! It's 7.15.
Sam: Who's winning?

★

Andy: Did you hear that big noise this morning?
Zak: Yes. Was it the crack of dawn?
Andy: No, it was the break of day.

Morons
Rick: There were once eight morons, Do, Re, Fa, So, La, Ti, Do, . . .
Nick: What about Mi?
Rick: Oh, sorry — I forgot about you!

Morris Dancing
We were going to have some Morris Dancing, but Morris couldn't come.

Moses
Why was Moses hidden quickly?
   It was a rush job.

★

How do we know that Moses wore a wig?
   Because sometimes he was seen with Aaron and sometimes without.

★

Rick: What was Moses doing at the Red Sea?
Silly Billy: The splits!

Mosquito
What's the difference between someone who's just been bitten by a mosquito and a 100-metre athlete about to start a race? One is going to itch, the other is itching to go.

★

A much-travelled man was giving a lecture on his latest visit to Africa.
'There were huge mosquitoes . . .'
'Oh!' said a listener. 'Were they vicious?'
'Not at all,' said the explorer. 'They'd eat right out of your hand.'

★

Paul: Aren't the mosquitoes thick around here!
Saul: Do you like them thin, then?

★

Why are mosquitos annoying?
   Because they get under your skin.

★

Two little boys decided to sleep in a tent in the garden one night. There were a lot of mosquitoes and the boys got way down in their sleeping bags to avoid being bitten. One of the boys came up for some air and saw some fireflies. He nudged his friend and said, 'It's no good, we'll have to go indoors. They're coming after us with torches now.'

Motel

What is the definition of motel?
  William Tell's sister.

Moth

The baby moth had been very naughty, and his mother spanked him very hard, but he said nothing at all. Which only goes to prove that it's very difficult to make a moth bawl.

★

What's the biggest moth the world has ever known?
  The mam-moth.

Mothballs

A lady bought a dozen boxes of mothballs one day and was back in the shop the very next day to buy another dozen boxes.
'You must have a lot of moths,' said the salesgirl.
'Yes, we do,' replied the lady. 'I spent all day yesterday throwing these things at them but I only hit one.'

Motherhood

A very proud mother phoned up a national newspaper and reported that she had given birth to 15 children. The girl on the news desk didn't quite hear the message and asked: 'Would you repeat that?'
'Not if I can help it,' replied the mother.

Mother-In-Law

My mother-in-law makes her own yoghurt. She has a pint of milk delivered and sits and stares at it.

Mother Nature

Mrs Able: I think Mother Nature is wonderful.
Mrs Cable: Yes, but why?
Mrs Able: Well, millions of years ago she didn't know man was going to invent glasses, but look where she put our ears!

Motorbike

What's a comedian's favourite motorbike?
  A Yama-ha-ha.

What kind of motorbike can cook eggs?
  A scrambler.

A man ran out of a supermarket, jumped in the air and fell into the gutter. Another man, somewhat startled, went over to him and said, 'Are you all right?'
'Yes,' replied the first, 'but whoever moved my motorbike won't be!'

Motorist

A motorist who had been arrested for speeding came home in the afternoon after his court appearance.
'How did you get on in court?' asked his anxious wife.
'Oh, fine,' replied the man.

Where can a motorist stop for a drink?
  At a T-junction.

Motto
Always be nice to your mother about her cooking and she may help you with the dishes.

Mountain
Amy: What's flat at the bottom, pointed at the top, with ears?
Zoe: I don't know. What?
Amy: A mountain.
Zoe: What about the ears?
Amy: What's the matter with you – haven't you ever heard of mountaineers?

Mountain Climbers
Why are mountain climbers curious?
  They always want to take another peak (peek).

★

Nick and Rick went mountain-climbing one day when Nick suddenly slipped and fell down a deep crevasse. Rick lowered a rope and called for his friend to grab hold of it.
'I can't,' shouted back Nick, 'I think both my arms are broken.'
'Put the rope in your mouth, then,' shouted Rick, 'and I'll pull you up.' Slowly, Rick began to pull Nick up the crevasse and when he was very near the top Rick called out,
'Are you all right, Nick?'
'Yeh-h-h . . . h . . .'

★

Two mountaineers finally reached the top of the mountain. Exhausted by exhilaration they collapsed in the snow and one said to the other,
'Well, it took a lot of effort, but it was worth every step to be able to plant our flag at the top. Pass it to me, will you, please?'
The second mountaineer stared at him open-mouthed and finally stammered out, 'But you were supposed to pack the flag!'

What happened to the idiots' mountaineering team when they tried to scale Mount Everest?
  They ran out of scaffolding 100 feet from the summit.

Mountains
Did you hear about the guide who told his visitors:
'These are the highest mountains in the world, apart from those in other countries.'

★

What do South Americans call the mountains in their countries?
  Handy Andes.

★

A tourist walking in the mountains looked with horror at the steep slope down the side of the mountain and said to his guide, 'That looks really dangerous. There ought to be a sign warning of the danger.'
'We had a warning side up there for a couple of years,' replied the guide, 'but nobody fell over the side so we took it down.'

Mouse
What did the mouse say when it broke two of its front teeth?
  Hard cheese.

★

What did the giant mouse say when it walked into the alley?
  Here, kitty, kitty, kitty.

★

Teacher: Who wrote 'To a Field Mouse'?
Soppy Poppy: Whoever it was, I bet he didn't get a reply.

★

How do you save a drowning mouse?
  By mouse to mouse resuscitation.

★

Amy: What would you do if you heard a mouse squeak in the night?

Zoe: I'm not sure, but I wouldn't get up to oil it!

★

Paul: I had a narrow squeak yesterday.
Saul: What happened?
Paul: I trod on a mouse.

★

What do you get if you cross a mouse with an elephant?
　Great big holes in the skirting board.

★

What's grey, has four legs and a trunk?
　A mouse going on holiday.

★

What's grey, has four legs and a great big trunk?
　A mouse emigrating.

★

What's the largest species of mouse in the world?
　A hippopotamouse.

Mousetrap

Sam: I want a mousetrap, please. And can you be quick, I have to catch a bus.
Salesman: Here's the biggest trap in the shop — but it still won't catch a bus.

★

A man bought a mousetrap to stop his garage being overrun by mice. When he got home, he discovered he had no cheese with which to bait it, so he drew a beautiful picture of a piece of cheese, coloured it a creamy golden colour, and put the picture in the trap. The next morning when he looked at the mouse-trap the picture of the cheese was gone and in its place was a picture of a mouse.

Mouth Organ

A mouse went in to a music shop and asked the owner for a mouse-organ. The owner was very surprised, but managed to stammer out,

'I've been serving customers since I opened this shop in 1947, and no one has ever asked for a mouse-organ before today. And you're the second!'
'Oh,' said the mouse, 'that'll have been 'Armonica.'

Movies

Sales assistant: Haven't I seen you some-where before?
Movie star: Perhaps in the movies?
Sales assistant: Could be. Where do you usually sit?

Moving

As the removal man was struggling with a large cupboard, the lady who was moving house asked him, 'Why don't you get the man who came with you to help you with that?'
'He's inside carrying the clothes,' was the reply.

★

Father: Do you like moving pictures?
Sam: Oh, yes, Dad.
Father: Good. Help me carry some down-stairs, will you?

Mud

Mother: Sam! Scrape some of that mud off your shoes before you come indoors.
Sam: What shoes?

★

What did the dirt say to the rain?
　If this keeps up my name will be mud!

Mud Pack

Soppy Poppy was watching her sister put a mud pack on her face. 'What's that for?' she asked.
'It's to make me beautiful. Now go away and let me have a rest.' When Soppy Poppy heard her sister going into the bathroom a little while later, she went in too, and watched her sister

washing off the mud pack and patting her face dry.

'Well,' she said slowly, 'it didn't work, did it?'

Mud Pies

Jenny: I like making mud pies, Mum.
Mother: Just make sure you wash your hands before you eat them, dear.

Multiplication Tables

Two friends were discussing their arithmetic lessons.

'I wonder why we stop learning multiplication tables at 12?' said one.

'I expect it's because it's unlucky to have 13 at a table,' replied the other seriously.

Mumbo Jumbo

What's big, grey and mutters?
    A mumbo jumbo.

Mummified

Two small children stood in front of a mummy case in the natural history museum.

'1000 BC,' read one, looking at the label on the case.

'What does that mean?'

'I guess it's the number of the car that ran him down,' said the other.

★

Why do mummies tell no secrets?
    Because they keep everything under wraps.

★

A young girl mummy was excitedly getting ready to go to her first dance with her mother mummy's help.

'Mummy,' asked the girl, 'did you go to dances when you were alive?'

★

Why did the mummy leave his tomb after 3,000 years?
    He thought he was old enough to leave home.

How can you tell when a mummy is angry?
    He flips his lid.

Mushroom

What is a mushroom?
    The place where Eskimos keep their dogs.

★

Which room can you never go in?
    A mushroom.

★

Why are mushrooms like umbrellas?
    Because they increase where it's wet.

Music

What's the proper name for musical insects?
    Humbugs.

★

Music teacher: Poppy, 'f' means forte, so what do you think 'ff' means?
Soppy Poppy: Eighty!

★

Jack: I'm told I have music in my feet.
Jill: Yes, two flats!

★

Teacher: Have you managed to pick up music yet?
Twins: Yes, sir!
Teacher: Good. You two move the piano then.

★

Teacher: Why do you always play the same piece of music?
Pupil: Because it haunts me.
Teacher: I'm not surprised, you murdered it months ago.

What has eight feet and sings?
A quartet.

★

Customer: Will the band play any request?
Waiter: Yes, sir.
Customer: Ask them to play cards, then.

★

What is musical and handy in a supermarket?
A Chopin Liszt.

★

Mother: Do you think Jenny should take up
the piano as a career?
Music teacher: No, I think she should put
down the lid as a favour.

★

A country boy went in to market one day and
saw a most beautiful music stool in a shop
window. He bought the stool and took it
home. On his next visit to market he stormed
in to the shop, shouting,
'I bought this stool from you two weeks ago!
I've been sitting on it for two weeks and it
hasn't played a note yet!'

★

Dance hall owner: Can you stretch the music
out a bit?
Conductor: Sorry, this is a dance band, not a
rubber band.

Musical Instrument

What musical instrument never tells the truth?
A lyre.

What musical instrument do you have in your
ears?
Drums.

★

What musical instrument could be used for
fishing?
A cast-a-net.

Musician

Rick: Why did they arrest the musician?
Nick: He got into treble.

★

Did you hear about the musician who spent
all his time in bed?
Yes, he wrote sheet music.

Mussels

What food should you eat if you want to be
big and strong?
Mussels and brawn.

★

What's black and comes out of the sea at 500
miles an hour?
A jet-propelled mussel.

Mustard

What can you keep hot in the refrigerator?
Mustard.

Myth

Teacher: What's a myth?
Soppy Poppy: A lady with a lisp but no
husband, miss!

212

Nailbiting

What's the best thing for people who bite their nails?

Sharp teeth.

★

Father: I've finally cured my son of biting his nails.
Friend: Really? How did you manage that?
Father: I knocked all his teeth out.

★

Mrs Able: My husband bites his nails.
Mrs Cable: Yes, I know lots of people who do.
Mrs Able: These are six-inch nails – my husband's a carpenter.

★

Mrs Able: I finally stopped Sam biting his nails.
Mrs Cable: How did you do that?
Mrs Able: Bought him some shoes.

Nails

What's the difference between a nail and a bad boxer?

One's knocked in, the other's knocked out.

★

Customer: I'd like some nails, please.
Sales assistant: Certainly, sir. How long would you like them?
Customer: Well, actually, I'd like to keep them.

★

Silly Billy got a job nailing the planks on a timber-frame house. His friend Simple Simon came to see how he was getting along and noticed he was throwing half the nails away.
'Why are you doing that?' he asked.
'Because the heads are on the wrong way,' said Silly Billy.
'Oh, you idiot!' said Simple Simon, 'They're for the other side of the house.'

Name

A little girl was asked her name, 'Jenny,' she replied.
'I know that. What's your last name?'
'I don't know,' said Jenny. 'I'm not married yet.'

★

What did Big Chief Running Water call his baby?

Little Drip.

★

Sam: I'm really glad you named me Sam.
Mother: Oh good, why?
Sam: Because that's what all the kids at school call me.

★

'So you want to come and work with this company,' said the company manager.
'Yes, sir!' replied the boy.
'What's your name?'
'David Gower, sir,' said the boy.
'David Gower! That's a well-known name, isn't it!' said the company manager, laughing.

'It should be,' said the boy. 'I've been delivering the newspapers around here for years!'

★

What did Ferdinand and Liza call their baby?
  Ferdilizer.

★

Headmaster: What's your name, boy?
Boy: Harold.
Headmaster: Say sir when you speak to me!
Boy: All right, then, Sir Harold.

★

Postman: Is this parcel for you? The name is obliterated.
Customer: No, it can't be mine. My name is O'Brien.

★

What belongs only to you but is used more by other people?
  Your name.

★

1st five-year-old: What's your name?
2nd five-year-old: Um, let me see. (Singing quietly.) Happy birthday to you, happy birthday to you, happy birthday dear Johnny. Oh yes! It's Johnny!

★

Lady of the manor: What's your name, my man?
Chauffeur: Charles, madam.
Lady of the manor: I always call my chauffeurs by their surname. Kindly tell me what yours is.
Chauffeur: Darling, madam.
Lady of the manor: Drive on, Charles.

★

A little boy whose name was James Mickey Brown came from home school one day in a furious temper.
'What's the matter, James?' asked his mother.
'It's the new teacher. She won't call me by my proper name.'
'What do you mean?'
'She calls me James Brown,' said the boy.

'Well, most people aren't called by their full names.'
'Maybe,' said the boy. 'But *I* don't like having the Mickey taken out of me.'

★

What did the simple man call his pet tiger?
  Spot.

★

New neighbour: And what might your name be, little boy?
Little boy: It might be Bartholomew, but it isn't.

★

On the first day of a new term a small boy was being seen by the school secretary.
'What's your father's name?' she asked.
'Same as mine,' replied the boy.
'No, no,' said the secretary, 'I mean his first name.'
'Oh, I don't know,' said the boy.
'Well, what name does your mother call him?' asked the secretary.
'She doesn't call him names – she likes him.'

Napoleon Bonaparte

Teacher: Alec, can you tell me which nationality Napoleon Bonaparte was?
Smart Alec: Corsican!

★

Where did Napoleon keep his armies?
  Up his sleevies.

National Anthem

Why do all international football matches start with the national anthem?
  So the coaches can count that all the players turned up.

National Sport

Bill: It says here that the national sport in Spain is bull fighting and in England it's fishing.
Ben: I'd rather live in England then.
Bill: Why?
Ben: It must be easier to fight fish.

214

Nativity

A little girl decided to make her own Christmas cards one year. She assembled crayons and paper and tinsel, sat down, and at the end of half an hour took her first picture to show her parents. They duly admired the nativity scene, noticing the manger, shepherds and Wise Men and the Holy Family.

'What's in the corner of the picture?' asked her father.

'Oh,' replied the little girl. 'That's their television!'

Neatness

A girl we all know as Beat
Is so unusually neat
She washes all day
To keep microbes away,
And wears rubber gloves just to eat.

Nelson

In which battle was Nelson killed?
   His last one.

★

Why did Nelson wear a three-cornered hat?
   To keep his three-cornered head warm.

★

What was the name of Nelson's little brother?
   Half-Nelson.

Neptune

What did Neptune say when the sea dried up?
   I haven't a notion.

Nerves

What is a nervous sorceress?
   A twitch.

Net

A net is a set of holes tied together with string.

Netball

Why did the netball team coach give her players a lighter?
   Because they kept losing their matches.

New Car

Soppy Poppy went out one day to buy a new sports car, and especially liked one in the showroom. 'Does it really go fast?' she asked the salesman.

'Fast! replied the salesman, 'why if you got in that car now, you'd be at Land's End by midnight.

Soppy Poppy went home to think about it and returned the following morning. 'I'm not going to buy that car', she told the salesman. 'I've been thinking about what you said, and I can't think of a single reason to be in Land's End at midnight.'

★

Two days after buying a new car a man walked into the dealer's sales office and said, 'You gave me a year's guarantee with my new car.'

'That's right,' said the salesman.

'And you'll replace anything that breaks?'

'That's right, too,' said the salesman.

'Good. I need a new set of gates.'

Newsagent

Have you heard about the man who bought a paper shop?
   It blew away.

★

Customer: Do you keep stationery?
Sales assistant: No, madam. I usually go home for lunch.

Newsflash

Local man takes first prize in dog show.

★

Newsflash: Thousands of mattresses have been stolen from a local factory. Police are springing into action.

Newspaper

'Excuse me, sir,' said the very polite tramp. 'Are you reading that newspaper you're sitting on?'

★

Rick: What do you do when all the world is grey and gloomy?
Nick: I deliver newspapers.

★

Why do you get a charge out of reading a newspaper?
Because it's full of current events.

★

Why is a newspaper like an army?
Because it has leaders, columns and reviews.

★

I heard that newspapers are going up tomorrow, so I bought all the copies I could find today.

★

Paper boy: Do you know, there's a man on my paper round who has *all* the daily papers. I stagger with them to his place every morning.

Friend: He must spend all day reading!
Paper boy: Oh, he doesn't read them – he owns a pet shop.

★

Rick: I was a newspaper man once.
Nick: What happened?
Rick: Someone stole my stand.

★

Adam: My uncle owns a newspaper.
Eve: So what? A newspaper only costs 25p.

New Year's Resolution

What has the shortest life-span in the world? A New Year's Resolution – because it's born before midnight and is dead and forgotten the next day.

New Zealand

Why is New Zealand a cold place?
Because they always export frozen meat.

Nightingale

What's a nightingale?
A very windy evening.

Night School

Enrolling teacher: And why are you enrolling for night school?
Silly Billy: To learn to read in the dark.

Night Train

Customer: Does the night train to Aberdeen have a sleeping car?
Railway clerk: Yes, sir.
Customer: Well, wake it up then!

Night Watchman

What's the difference between a night watchman and a butcher?
One stays awake and the other weighs a steak.

What man never worked a single day in his life?

A night watchman.

Nile River

Andy: A man sold me the Nile River yesterday.

Zak: Egypt you.

Nitrates

Science teacher: What can you tell me about nitrates?

Silly Billy: They're cheaper than day rates, Miss.

Noah's Ark

Where did Noah keep his bees?

In the Ark hives.

★

Noah saw his sons fishing from the Ark one day and called out,

'Go easy on the maggots, lads. I've only got two.'

★

What was Noah's profession?

He was an ark-itect.

★

How did Noah manage in the dark?

He used ark-lights or flood-lights.

★

Why didn't the two worms go into Noah's Ark in an apple?

Because everyone had to go in pairs.

★

Two kangaroos were going into the Ark. 'It better had rain,' said one to the other, 'it's been a long hop getting here.'

★

Johnny: Were you in Noah's Ark, sir?

Elderly visitor: No, Johnny, I wasn't.

Johnny: Then how come you weren't drowned?

After the Great Flood, Noah started to set all the animals free. He lined them up two by two, let down the gangplank and said, 'Go forth and multiply.' Off went the apes, the bears, and the camels, followed by the eagles and the frogs and all the other animals, until Noah looked around his almost empty Ark. In the corner were two snakes, intertwined and crying softly. 'Didn't you hear me tell you all to go forth and multiply?' he asked them.

'Yes, but we can't,' said the snakes sadly. 'We're adders.'

Noise

Amy: What's the definition of noise?

Zoe: A skeleton dancing on a tin roof.

★

What can you make that nobody can see?

A noise.

Noodles

What's watery, very frightened and full of noodles?

Chicken soup.

Norway

What's Norway like?

Sweden with no matches.

Nose

Did you hear about the little boy whose nose was eleven inches long? He was worried that if it grew any longer it would turn into a foot.

★

Why did the little boy take his nose apart?

To see how it ran.

★

If your nose runs and your feet smell, what's wrong with you?

You're built upside-down.

★

Amy: How's your nose?
Zoe: Shut up!
Amy: Mine, too, it must be the weather.

★

Why is your nose in the middle of your face?
Because it is the scenter (centre).

★

What happens if you always keep your nose to the grindstone?
You end up with a flat face.

Notice

Notice noticed on a notice board:
Notice:
Please notice this notice.
And when you have noticed this notice you will notice that it is worth noticing and worth noticing well.

★

Interviewer: We need someone who is clever and quick to take notice.
Job applicant: Oh, that's me, all right. I had notice twice last month!

Nougat

Amy: Have a piece of nougat.
Zoe: It's nougaR. The t is silent.
Amy: Not the way you eat yours.

Nouns

English teacher: Name three collective nouns, please Billy.
Silly Billy: The dustbin, the rubbish bin and the vacuum cleaner.

Novel

Who wrote Great Eggspectations?
Charles Chickens.

Nuclear Shelter

Paul: Are you going to buy one of those fall-out shelters in case the bomb drops?
Saul: No, I'll wait for the sales.

Nudists

What illness worries nudists the most?
Clothestrophobia.

Nuns

If a nun rolling down a hill goes black-and-white-and-black-and-white-ouch, what is black-and-white and goes ha-ha?
The nun that pushed her.

Nuts

Customer in greengrocer's: I'd like a pound of mixed nuts, please – and not too many coconuts.

★

Jenny: Will you pass the nuts, Miss?
Teacher: No, I think I'll fail them, Jenny.

★

Which nut is like a sneeze?
A cashoo!

★

Greengrocer: What kind of nuts would you like, madam?
Customer: Cashew.
Greengrocer: Bless you! What kind of nuts would you like?

★

Noisy boy at the fair: Who's in charge of the nuts?
Stall holder: Just a minute, sonny, and I'll take care of you.

Oak Tree

What is the differences between an oak tree and a tight shoe?

One makes acorns and the other makes corns ache.

Ocean

Why is the ocean angry?

Because it's been crossed so many times.

★

When is the ocean like a piece of string?

When a ship makes knots in it.

★

Why did the ocean roar?

Because it had lobsters in its bed.

October

What do you call an Indian who hitchhikes in October?

An Indian thumber.

Octopus

Who snatched away the baby octopus and held its parents to ransom?

Squidnappers.

★

How does an octopus go in to battle?

Well armed!

★

What did the boy octopus say to the girl octopus?

Please let me hold your hand, hand, hand, hand, hand, hand, hand, hand.

★

What do you call a neurotic octopus?

A crazy, mixed-up squid.

Off!

'Off!' shouted the referee, blowing his whistle and pointing to the dressing room.
'Off?' cried the player. 'What for?'
'For the rest of the afternoon!'

Oil

What did the Arab say when he left his friends?

Oil see you again.

★

What's black, floats on water and shouts, 'I beg your pardon'?

Refined oil.

★

What's black, floats on water and shouts, 'Knickers'?

Crude oil.

★

What has oily feathers and flies very, very fast?

A Kestrel GTX.

★

What is oil before it is pumped out of the ground?
    A well-kept secret.

★

An oil rig diver had just reached the sea bed when he received an urgent message from the surface:
'Come up quickly – the rig is sinking.'

★

Which animals do you have to oil?
    Mice – because they squeak.

Old Car

Andy: Why is an old car like a classroom?
Zak: Because it has a lot of nuts with a crank up front.

★

Jill: Why did you bury your old car?
Jack: Well, the battery was dead, the pistons were shot, and then the engine failed.

Olden Times

Soppy Poppy: I wish I'd been alive in olden times.
Mother: Why?
Soppy Poppy: There wouldn't be so much history to learn.

Olive Oil

What would happen if the world ran out of olive oil?
    There'd be rusty olives.

Olympic Games

Why did all the opticians go to the Olympic Games?
Because it was such a spectacle.

Omelette

What's yellow, soft, and goes round and round?
    A long-playing omelette.

One-Eyed

Lady in the street: Little boy, will you help me look for my cat with one eye?
Silly Billy: Wouldn't it be quicker if I used both eyes?

One Good Turn

What does one good turn give you?
    All the blankets.

One Leg

What is a one-legged woman called?
    Eileen.

One Man and a Dog

A man waiting at a bus stop was eating a hamburger and chips. A lady with a dog came up and stood beside him, also waiting for a bus. The dog got very excited at the smell of the man's hamburger and whined and started to jump up on the man.
'Do you mind if I throw him a bit?' asked the man.
'No, that's very kind,' replied the lady.
So the man picked up the dog and threw him across the road.

One-Man Bus

Mrs Able: I went on a one-man bus for the first time today.
Mrs Cable: How was it?
Mrs Able: I spent the whole journey wondering who was driving the bus when the fares were being collected upstairs.

Onions

City slicker to farmer: Why do you plant onions alongside potatoes?

Farmer: The onions will make the potatoes' eyes water, and then I won't have to worry about the dry weather.

★

Adam: Why have you got onions in your ears?

Eve: Could you speak up, please? I have onions in my ears.

Open Sesame!

What did the cave reply when Ali Baba shouted 'Open Sesame!'

'Says who?'

Opera

A godmother took her goddaughter to the opera for the first time as a birthday treat. The conductor waved his baton and the soprano began her aria. The little girl loved everything and sat listening and watching with shining eyes. But soon she turned to her godmother and said, 'Why is he hitting her with his stick?'

'He's not,' replied the godmother.

'Well, if he's not hitting her, why is she screaming?'

★

Jack: Do you like going to the opera?

Jill: Apart from the singing, yes!

★

What does operetta mean?

She's the girl who works on the telephone switchboard.

Operation

Famous surgeon: Doctor, this is the umteenth operating table you've ruined this week. You really must learn not to cut so deeply.

★

Adam: When is an operation funny?

Eve: I don't know.

Adam: When it leaves the patient in stitches.

Wife: They can't do my operation yet, there aren't any beds available.

Husband: Looks like you'll just have to carry on talking about the old one.

Opinion

Rick: Would you look at my painting and tell me what you think of it? I'd really value your opinion.

Nick: Frankly, it's worthless.

Rick: I know, but I'd like to hear it just the same.

Opinion Poll

What happened to the lady who collected information for an opinion poll?

She got the sack because her vital statistics were wrong.

Opposites

If Sadness is the opposite of Happiness, is Woe! the opposite of Gee-up!?

Optician

Did you hear about the optician who fell into the lens-grinding machine and made a spectacle of himself?

★

A man went to the opticians and said: 'I'm having terrible trouble with these contact lenses. I just can't get them over my glasses.'

Oranges

An orange telephoned a friend, but the other orange didn't give her the message. Why?

Because the pips went.

★

Can an orange box?

No, but a tomato can.

★

What's round, orange and can't sit down?

A seatless satsuma.

Orchestra

Paul: What's that book the orchestra keeps looking at?
Saul: That's the score.
Paul: Oh, really? Who's winning?

Orders

What are everyone's favourite orders?
    Postal orders.

★

Judge: Order, order in court!
Prisoner: A ham and salad sandwich, please.

Orson Welles

Young mother with pram: I'm going to call my baby Orson, after Orson Welles.
Another young mother with another pram: What's your surname?
First mother: Cart.

Ostrich

What do you get if you cross an ostrich with a centipede?
    You'll find out when you catch it!

Otter

Which animal is it best to be in a snowstorm with?
    A little otter.

Out

Rick: Can you help me out?
Nick: Certainly, which way did you come in?

Overboard

On a school trip by ferry to Calais, the teachers were reminding the children to behave properly. 'And,' said the Headmaster, 'what do you do if one of the children falls overboard?'
'Shout, "boy overboard!", sir,' said Silly Billy.
'Good. And what do you do if one of the teachers falls overboard?
'Which one, sir?'

Overnight Guest

Mr Able had been visiting Mr Cable one evening. When it was time to leave they realised it had been snowing for hours and driving would be very difficult.
'You'd better stay the night,' said Mr Cable.
'Thank you very much,' said Mr Able. 'I will. I'll just pop home for my toothbrush.'

Overpowering

What overpowers you without hurting you?
    Sleep.

Owl

A man was walking down the street with an owl on a leash. Another man walked up to him and said, 'Where did you get him?'
The owl replied, 'I won him at the fair.'

★

What animal always forgets?
    An owl – because it keeps saying, 'Who? Who?'

★

Why does the owl make everyone laugh?
    Because he's such a hoot.

★

What do owls sing when it's raining?
    Too-wet-to-woo.

What did the owl and goat do at the square dance?

The hootenanny.

★

What do you get if you cross an owl with a skunk?

A bird that smells but doesn't give a hoot.

Oxen

What happens if two oxen bump in to each other?

There's an oxident.

Oxygen

Teacher: If we breathe oxygen in the daytime, what do we breathe at night?

Silly Billy: Nitrogen?

Oysters

A man walked in to a pub one hot day and ordered a pint of best bitter. He savoured every mouthful and, when he had finished it, said to the barman, 'That was the best pint of bitter I think I've ever drunk. And to show you how much I enjoyed it, I'm going to leave you these as a present.' And he took a dozen oysters out of his pocket and put them on the bar. The barman didn't know quite what to do, but eventually he said, 'Thank you very much. I'll take them home for dinner.' 'Oh no,' said the customer, 'they've already had dinner. Take them to the pictures.'

★

Paul: What is an oyster?

Saul: Um, what you shout when you want some to lift up your grandmother.

Pack of Cards

Jack: I've got a new pack of cards.

Jill: That's not such a big deal.

★

What is brought to the table and cut but never eaten?

A pack of cards.

Paddington and Winnie the Pooh

What did Paddington and Winnie the Pooh take on holiday?

Only the bear essentials.

Paddling

Two little girls were paddling in the sea when one said to the other, 'Ooh, aren't your feet dirty!'

'Yes,' said the second little girl, 'we didn't come last year.'

★

Little old lady: My goodness, little boy! Why are you paddling in your socks?

Little boy: Because the water's always cold in February.

Pain

Patient: Doctor, I have a terrible pain in my left foot. What should I do?
Doctor: I suggest you walk on the right one.

★

Sam came in from school groaning and holding his arm.
'What's the matter, Sam?' asked his mother. 'Are you in pain?'
'No,' said Sam, 'the pain's in me!'

Paint

What is the best way to get paint of a chair?
Sit on the chair before the paint's dry.

★

Patient: Doctor, I have this tremendous urge to paint myself all over with gold paint.
Doctor: I'd say you were suffering from a gilt complex.

★

Did you hear about the man who wore all his clothes to paint his house because the tin said, 'Put on three coats'?

Painter

Andy: What did the painter say to the wall?
Zak: One more crack like that and I'll plaster you.

Painting

What did the oil painting say to the wall?
First they framed me, then they hung me.

★

What colours would you paint the sun and the wind?
The sun rose, and the wind blue.

Pair of Socks

How do you make a pair of socks?
Take two socks . . .

★

Rick: What a strange pair of socks – one with blue spots and the other with green stripes.
Nick: Yes, aren't they good! And I've another pair at home just like it.

Palmist

Paul: I can't decide whether to go to a palmist or a mind-reader.
Saul: Better go to a palmist – at least you know you've got a palm.

★

A man at a fair was asked if he'd like his palm read.
'No, thank you,' was his reply, 'I like it the colour it is.'

Pancake Day

Sam: Mum, what's the best day of all to make pancakes?
Mother: Fry-day.

★

Customer: Waiter, will the pancakes be long?
Waiter: No, sir, round.

Panther

What do you call a cat that strolls around the jungle wearing chains and leather?
The Punk Panther.

Pantomime

Which Pantomime is about a cat in a chemist's shop?
Puss in Boots.

Paper

What did the paper say to the pencil?
Write on!

Paper Bag

What lives in a paper bag and hangs around in French cathedrals?
The lunch-pack of Notre Dame.

Parachuting

Mr Able: What made you decide to take up parachuting?
Mr Cable: A plane with three dead engines.

★

Bill: Have you heard the latest down-to-earth story?
Ben: Do you mean the one about the parachute jumper?

Parade

What did Mrs Stupid say when she saw her son Stanley in the cadet parade?
Oh look! Our Stanley's the only one in step!

★

Jack: Did you see the parade go by?
Jill: No, I was waving my hair.
Jack: How odd. I was waving my flag.

Paralyse

What is the definition of paralyse?
Two fibs.

Paratrooper

What is a paratrooper?
An Army dropout.

Pardon?

What's big, floats in space, and keeps saying pardon?
A Deaf Star.

Parenthood

Father: Don't you think our son got his intelligence from me?
Mother: Must have — I've still got mine!

Park

Paul: Where's the park?
Saul: There isn't a park around here.
Paul: But that sign says 'Park Here'!

Parking

Judge: Why did you park your car where you did?
Motorist: Well, there was a sign saying, 'Fine for Parking'.

Parrot

What's a parrot?
A wordy birdy.

★

Why wouldn't the parrot talk to the Dutchman?
Because he only spoke pigeon English.

★

What do you call parrots' food?
Pollyfilla.

★

A man went in to a pet shop to buy a parrot. He was very taken with one the sales assistant showed him, but didn't understand why the parrot had a string attached to each foot. 'Oh,' said the assistant, 'this is a highly-trained parrot. You don't need to say anything to make him speak to you — if you just pull the string on his left foot he'll say "Good morning" and pull the string on his right foot for "Goodbye."'
'What happens if I pull both strings at the same time?'
'I fall off the perch, you idiot!' squawked the parrot.

★

Whose parrot sits on his shoulder shouting, 'Pieces of four!'
Short John Silver.

★

A magician who used a parrot in his act worked for years in nightclubs, with the occasional spot on television. But the parrot became very bored watching the same act over and over again, so the magician decided to get a job abroad. The parrot was still bored watching rabbits come and go out of top hats and silk scarves multiply. But one evening there was an enormous explosion as the gas pipe leading to the night club blew up, and the parrot and the magician found themselves sprawled on the pavement, the night club razed to the ground behind them.

'All right,' said the bemused parrot. 'I'll buy this one. What did you do with it?'

★

A man who wanted to buy a parrot went to an animal auction. He found just what he wanted – a beautiful African bird – and decided to bid for it. The bidding went higher and higher, but finally the man was the winning bidder. He went excitedly to collect his bird, and suddenly remembered that he had forgotten to ask the most important question about the parrot.

'Does the parrot talk,' he asked the auctioneer anxiously.

'Of course he talks,' replied the auctioneer. 'Who do you think was bidding against you all the time?'

★

Explorer: Once when I was stranded on an island and on the verge of starvation I ate my pet parrot.
Interviewer: What did it taste like?
Explorer: Chicken, duck, goose, turkey – you name it. That bird could imitate anything!

★

A lady bought a pair of parrots to keep her company, one of which the pet shop owner warned her was very aggressive. The next morning she uncovered the cage to discover that the aggressive parrot had killed the other, so she decided to teach it a lesson and bought a kestrel. The next morning when she uncovered the cage the kestrel was dead! Not to be outdone by a parrot, the lady went back to the pet shop and bought an eagle. The next morning when she uncovered the cage – the eagle was dead and the parrot had not a single feather on its body. As it stood shivering on its perch it looked at the lady and said,
'I really had to take my coat off to that one!'

Partridges in a Pear Tree

How many partridges would be left in a pear tree if a farmer shot one and missed the other five?

None – the other five flew away.

Party

Angry neighbour: Didn't you hear me banging on your ceiling last night?
Hungover neighbour: Oh, that's all right. We had a party last night and were making a lot of noise ourselves.

★

Rick: Do you want to come to an Adam and Eve party?
Nick: Oh, yes!
Rick: Right, leaves off at eleven.

★

Where's the best place to hold a ship-board party?

Where the funnel be.

★

Mother: Did you thank Mrs Able for Jenny's lovely birthday party?
Soppy Poppy: No, I was going to, but the little girl in front of me said 'Thank you,' and Mrs Able said, 'Don't mention it.'

★

Tom: Did you go to Dick's party?
Harry: No, the invitation said 'from five to nine', and I'm ten.

★

How would you describe a party at a camping site?

Intense excitement.

Pas de Deux

What does 'pas de deux' mean?
Father of twins.

Passer-by

Jack: Did you see me just now when I went by?

Jill: Yes.

Jack: But you'd never seen me before, had you?

Jill: No, I don't think so.

Jack: Then how did you know it was me?

Patient

When is a sick person a contradiction?
  When he's an impatient patient.

Pawnbroker

A burglar on his first robbery held up a pawnbroker.

'Hands up or I'll shoot!' he said.

'I'll give you £10 for the gun,' said the pawnbroker.

Peach

What's yellow, fuzzy, and goes at 180 miles per hour?
  A fuel-injected peach.

★

Customer: Barman, do you know how to make a fresh peach punch?

Barman: Certainly, sir — give her boxing lessons.

★

Paul: I call my girlfriend Peach.

Saul: Because she's so pretty?

Paul: No, because she has a heart of stone.

Peaches and Cream

Sister: My boyfriend thinks I have a peaches and cream complexion!

Brother: You do — a 19-year-old peach and sour cream!

Peacock

If your neighbour's peacock lays an egg in your garden, who does the egg belong to?
  No one — only peahens lay eggs.

★

Did you hear the story about the peacock?
  It's a beautiful tail.

Peanuts

What happens if you pay people peanuts?
  You get monkey workers!

★

Why did the peanut go to the police?
  He claimed he'd been assaulted.

★

A woman on a bus sat eating peanuts and, to be friendly, she offered some to the woman sitting beside her.

'No, thank you!' said the second woman. 'They're fattening.'

'Why do you think that?' said the first woman, worriedly.

'Well, haven't you ever seen an elephant?'

Pear Tree

Farmer: What are you doing up my pear tree, sonny?

Sonny: One of your pears fell down and I'm putting it back.

Peas

I eat my peas with honey,
I've done it all my life;
It does make them taste funny,
But they do stay on the knife.

★

How many peas in a pint?
  Only one!

227

Pebble

What did the shy pebble on the beach say?
  I wish I was a little bolder.

Pedestrian

Andy: What's a pedestrian?
Zak: Someone who can be easily reached by car.

★

Rick: Did you hear about the monster with pedestrian eyes?
Nick: What on earth does that mean?
Rick: They look both ways before they cross.

Pedigree

Mrs Able: Our new puppy has a pedigree.
Mrs Cable: You mean you have papers for it?
Mrs Able: Oh, yes — all over the house.

★

Andy: Has your dog got a pedigree?
Zak: Well, he has on his mother's side, but his father comes from the wrong side of the tracks.

Peephole

What's a peephole?
  A group of human beings.

Pelicans

What's a pelicans favourite fish?
  Anything that fits the bill.

★

Why did the pelican put his leg in his mouth when he ate out?
  Because he wanted to foot the bill.

Pen and Paper

What did the pen say to the paper?
  I dot an 'i' on you.

Pen and Pencil

You can drive a pen, but a pencil works best when it's lead.

Pencil

Why does a pencil seem heavy if you write with it for a long time?
  Because it's full of lead.

★

What did the pencil say to the rubber?
  Take me to your ruler.

★

Shall I tell you the joke about the pencil?
  No, there's no point in it.

★

Why did the man take a pencil to bed with him?
  To draw the curtains.

★

What did one pencil say to the other?
  I've got a leadache.

Penguin

What do you get if you cross a penguin with a lamb?
  A sheepskin dinner jacket.

Pensioner

An old man went to the Post Office to collect his pension. As he hadn't got a pen with him, he signed for his money in pencil, but the clerk wouldn't accept this, and said, 'Would you mind inking it over, sir?'
The old man went away for a while and, returning to the counter, said, 'I've thought it over, and I still want my pension.'

Peppermint

What's wet, round, and tastes of peppermint?
  Water Polo.

Pepper Pot

Mother: Poppy, have you put the pepper in its pot?
Soppy Poppy: No, it's really difficult getting it in all the little holes.

Perfume

What is a popular perfume called?
  A best smeller.

★

Adam: What's your new perfume?
Eve: 'High Heaven'.
Adam: It certainly smells to it!

★

What makes perfume so obedient?
  Because it is scent wherever it goes.

★

What smells good and rides a horse?
  The Cologne Ranger.

★

Jack: Is that perfume I smell?
Jill: It is – and you do.

Periscope

Newsflash: The Chairman of the British Periscope Manufacturers' Association said yesterday that business was looking up. . . .

Permanent Waving

Have you heard that hairdressers aren't doing any more permanent waving?
  It makes their arms too tired.

Pet Food

Rick: I heard a great idea for saving money on pet food.
Nick: What's that?
Rick: Buy a polar bear – he lives on ice.

Petrol

Sam: Mum! Dad says to tell you he's going out.
Mother: Well, pour some more petrol on him, then.

Pets

Aunt Annabelle went to a pet shop to buy a dog as a birthday present for her niece. 'Are you quite sure this one will make a good pet?' she asked the owner.
'Of course, madam,' he replied. 'He's really gentle. He'll eat anything, and he's especially fond of children.

Phantom

There once was a phantom named Pete
Who never would play, drink or eat.
He said, 'I don't care
For Coke or éclair,
Can't you see that I'm dead on my feet?'

Philatelist

What's a philatelist?
  A person of the right stamp.

Phone Book

Teacher: Poppy, will you tell us about the book you chose?

Soppy Poppy: Well, I chose the phone book. It hasn't got much of a plot, but it's got a cast of thousands!

Photographer

What is a press photographer?
  A flash guy.

★

Why was the photographer arrested?
  Because he shot people and blew them up.

Photographs

Amy: I don't like this photo of me, it doesn't do me justice.
Zoe: It's mercy you want, not justice.

★

Amy: Do you think this is a good photograph of me?
Zoe: Well, it makes you look older.
Amy: That's all right. It'll save me having another one done next year.

★

What did Cinderella say when her pictures didn't arrive?
  'Some day my prints will come. . . .'

★

Soppy Poppy: Now come on, everybody, get into focus, please!

Photographic Memory

Amy: My sister has a photographic memory.
Zoe: How useful!
Amy: No, not really. Nothing ever seems to develop.

Pianist

A famous concert pianist used to practise the piano for an hour every morning. He gave his butler orders that under no circumstances whatsoever was he to be disturbed.
One morning a visitor arrived at the door and insisted on seeing the pianist.

'I'm sorry, sir,' said the butler, 'but he's out.'
'He's not out!' said the visitor, 'I could hear him playing the piano as I drove up.'
'I think you're mistaken, sir,' said the butler. 'I was simply dusting the piano keys.'

Piano

Piano tuner: Would you open the piano for me, please?
Soppy Poppy: I can't – the keys are on the inside.

★

Pupil: Did you say you learned to play the piano in six easy lessons?
Music teacher: Yes, that's right. It was the 600 that came afterwards that were the hard ones.

★

A pianist walked in to an agent's office to try to get a job. The agent agreed to listen to him play and, at the end of a very bad performance, the pianist proudly said that he played everything by ear.
'That explains it,' said the agent. 'I didn't think that noise could have been made by human hands.'

★

Visitor: Where is your little brother, Billy?
Silly Billy: He's in the living room playing a piano duet. I finished first.

★

Bill: What do you get if you drop a grand piano down a pit shaft?
Ben: I don't know – what do you get?
Bill: A flat minor.

★

Paul: Why do you have a piano in your bathroom?
Saul: Because I'm practising Handel's Water Music.

★

Proud Mother: Jenny learned to play the piano in no time at all.

Visitor: Yes, I heard her playing like that as I came in.

★

Have you heard about the man who stopped playing the piano after five years?
    His fingers were tired.

★

Amy: I've played the piano for 20 years on and off.
Zoe: Slippery stool?

★

Why are pianos noble?
    Some are upright, the rest are grand.

★

Piano tuner: Good morning, madam – I've come to tune your piano.
Householder: But I didn't send for you.
Piano tuner: I know, but your neighbours did.

★

Bill: I can play the piano with both hands tied behind my back.
Ben: How do you play, then?
Bill: By ear.

Picket
A famous trade union leader broke his nose and went to the doctor. The doctor's advice was, 'Don't picket for a few weeks.'

Pickpocket
What did one pickpocket say to another?
    Every crowd has a silver lining.

Picnic
A group of neighbours got together to organise a picnic but unfortunately forgot to invite an eccentric old lady who lived in their road. On the very morning of the picnic the neighbours all realised their mistake and sent one of the children to invite the old lady. The little girl knocked on the old lady's door and delivered her message, to which the old lady replied, 'It's too late now! I've already prayed for rain.'

Picture
Andy: Have you heard the story about the picture window?
Zak: No.
Andy: Oh, never mind, you'd see through it anyway.

Teacher: And what are you drawing, Jenny?
Jenny: A picture of a cow eating grass.
Teacher: Where's the grass?
Jenny: The cow ate it.
Teacher: And where's the cow?
Jenny: Gone home. It didn't want to stay in the field when there wasn't any grass.

Pie
Customer: Waiter, is this pie chicken or ham?
Waiter: What did you order, sir?

Which is the left side of a pie?
    The piece that is left over.

★

Jack: You remind me of a pie.
Jill: You mean I'm sweetness and light?
Jack: No, you've got some crust.

Piece of Cake
Visitor: Now, Billy, as there are only two pieces of cake left, a big one and a little one, which will you give to your brother?
Silly Billy: Do you mean my big brother or my little brother?

Mother: Why is your little sister so upset?
Son: Because I wouldn't give her a piece of my cake.
Mother: Is hers all gone?
Son: Yes. And she was upset when I ate that, too.

Pier
Sam: Johnny and I were playing on the pier when one of the planks broke and he fell in.

Mother: That's terrible! Is he all right?
Sam: Oh, yes. It was only a drop in the ocean.

Pigs

What do you call the story of the three little pigs?
  A pigtail.

★

What do you get when you cross a hog with a penguin?
  Wet and dirty.

★

Why are baby pigs so greedy?
  Because they want to make hogs of themselves.

★

What do you call a stupid pig thief?
  A hamburglar.

★

What did one pig say to the other pig?
  Let's be pen pals.

★

Why didn't the piglets listen to their father?
  Because he was such a boar.

★

What is it called when pigs do their laundry?
  Hogwash.

★

Where do pigs go when they die?
  To the sty in the sky.

★

What are high-rise flats for pigs called?
  Styscrapers.

★

Why did the pig swill?
  Because he saw the barn dance.

★

City visitor: What's your pig's name?
Farmer: Ballpoint.
City visitor: Is that his real name?
Farmer: No, it's his pen name.

★

Customer: Do you have pigs' feet?
Butcher: Yes, indeed, sir.
Customer: Well, if you wear shoes nobody will notice.

★

Father: Sam, you're a pig! Do you know what a pig is?
Sam: Yes, Dad. A pig is a hog's little boy.

★

What would happen if pigs could fly?
  Bacon would go up.

★

Paul: What squeals more loudly than a pig caught under a fence?
Saul: Two pigs caught under a fence.

★

Andy: I've just bought a pig.
Zak: Where on earth are you going to keep it?
Andy: Under my bed.
Zak: But what about the smell?
Andy: Oh, I reckon he'll soon get used to it.

★

Rick: The man who stole my uncle's pig is in gaol.
Nick: How was he caught?
Rick: The pig squealed.

Pigeons

Jack: What did one pigeon say to another when a strange pigeon came into their loft?'

Jill: Look at that odd pigeon – he's people-toed!

★

All but one of the baby pigeons had learned to fly and left the mother's nest. She said to the last one, 'If you don't learn to fly soon, I'll have to tow you along behind me.' 'No! No!' said the little pigeon. 'I'll learn! I don't want to be pigeon-toed!'

★

Two pigeons were flying over a garage selling second-hand cars when one said to the other, 'Let's put a deposit on that Rolls.'

★

What do you get if you cross a carrier pigeon with a woodpecker?

A bird that knocks when it delivers a message.

★

A lady on a Venetian waterbus was very surprised to see a man standing opposite her with a pigeon on each shoulder. He was reading a magazine and paid no attention to the comings and goings of the passengers. Just before the lady got off, her curiosity got the better of her, and she said,

'Excuse me, could you please tell me what those pigeons are doing on your shoulders?'

'I haven't the faintest idea,' replied the man. 'They got on at St Mark's Square.'

Pillow

What is a pillow?

Headquarters.

★

Mrs Able: Have you any idea how much feather pillows cost these days?

Mrs Cable: Can't say I have.

Mrs Able: Honestly, even down is up.

★

Did you hear about the man who slept with his head under the pillow?

When he woke up in the morning the fairies had taken all his teeth out.

Pillowcase

Silly Billy went in to a shop to buy a pillowcase and the saleslady asked what size he wanted. 'I don't really know,' said Silly Billy, 'but I wear a size six hat.'

Pills

Jack: How come you're so clever?

Jill: I take clever pills.

Jack: Let me have some!

Jill: Take two of these.

Jack: They aren't pills – they're sweets!

Jill: See! They're working already.

Pilot

What did the pilot say as he left home to go to work?

Must fly now!

★

A pilot was flying a small plane one day when the engine failed. Quickly he ejected and para-chuted down to safety in the jungle. Unfortu-nately, he landed in a cannibal's cooking pot. The cannibal fished him out, inspected him and said,

'What's this flier doing in my soup?'

Pin

What's the easiest way to find a pin in a carpet?

Walk around in your bare feet.

★

What is pointed in one direction and headed in another?

A pin.

Ping-Pong Ball

What's small, white, round, and smells awful?

A ping-pong ball.

Piranhas

How do piranhas win the football pools?
  With eight score jaws.

Pirates

Rick: Do you know what pirates used to eat?
Nick: Sure, pieces of ate.

★

What is a pirate's favourite musical instrument?
  The loot.

Pixie

How does a pixie eat?
  By goblin.

Place of Birth

Andy: Where were you born?
Zak: America.
Andy: Which part?
Zak: All of me, of course!

Place Setting

Mother: Why didn't you put a knife and fork for Mrs Pushkin when you laid the table, Poppy?
Soppy Poppy: Because Daddy always says she eats like a horse.

Plane Crash

If a plane crashed on the American-Canadian border, where would the survivors be buried?
  Nowhere – you don't bury survivors!

Plants

Why are plants like naughty children?
  They grow up better with a stick.

★

Which is the poorest plant?
  A vine – because it can't support itself.

Plasterers

Why should you never believe plasterers?
  Because they lay it on thick.

Plastic Surgeon

Rick: Have you heard what happened to the famous plastic surgeon?
Nick: No, what?
Rick: He sat by the fire and melted.

★

An Englishman was sitting in his garden one day when a flying saucer came in to land. He watched calmly as a creature emerged that had three eyes – one red, one purple and one green – and thin pointed ears. It walked on its elbows and its nose lit up like a light bulb.
'Take me to your leader,' it commanded.
'Nonsense,' said the Englishman, 'what you need is a plastic surgeon.'

Play Time

Soppy Poppy: Mum, can I go out and play?
Mother: What? With those holes in your woolly tights?
Soppy Poppy: No, with Jenny next door.

★

A little boy knocked on his neighbour's front door and asked whether the little boy who lived there could come out to play.
'No, it's too wet,' replied his mother.
'Well, then, could his football come out to play?'

★

A mother rushed in to the garden when she heard a tremendous noise. Johnny was playing the drums on an upturned tin bath with the garden tools.
'What are you doing?' she asked him.
'I'm playing to the baby,' said Johnny.
'Where's the baby?' asked his mother.
'Under the bath.'

Plug

If a plug doesn't fit, do you socket?

Plumber

What do you call a highly educated and skilled plumber?

A drain surgeon.

Plums

If you wanted to calculate the exact colour of plums, what would you use?

A green gauge.

Plurals

Teacher: Who can tell me what the plural of baby is?

Soppy Poppy: Twins?

★

Teacher: There's no 'a' before a plural, Jenny. We don't say 'a horses', we say 'horses'.

Jenny: Then why does the vicar always say 'a-men'?

Pocket Calculator

Salesman: Would you like to buy a pocket calculator, sir?

Customer: No, thanks, I know how many pockets I've got.

★

Poems

Mary had a parrot,
She killed it in a rage,
For every time her boyfriend came,
The darn thing told her age.

★

She stood on the bridge at midnight,
Her lips were all a-quiver;
She gave a cough, her leg fell off
And floated down the river!

★

Mary had a little lamb,
Her father shot it dead.
And now it goes to school with her
Between two chunks of bread.

Poetry

Teacher: Who would like to read their poem to the class?

Soppy Poppy: I will!

Teacher: Go ahead, Poppy.

Soppy Poppy: A silly little girl whose name was Nellie
Fell into the water right up to her knees.

Teacher: That's hardly poetry! It doesn't rhyme at all.

Soppy Poppy: I know, Miss, but the water wasn't deep enough.

★

What's another name for a lady poet?

A meter maid.

Pogo Stick

How do you keep a pogo stick in good working order?

Spring-clean it!

Poison

What happened to the scientist who crossed poison ivy with a four-leaf clover?

He had a rash of good luck.

★

Science teacher: Can anyone give me the name of a deadly poison?

Silly Billy: Yes, Miss. Parachuting.

Science teacher: Parachuting isn't a poison, Billy.

Silly Billy: One drop and you're dead, though, miss.

Polar Bear

Baby polar bear: Mum, am I a real polar bear?

Mother polar bear: Yes, of course you are.

Baby polar bear: Mum, are you sure?

Mother polar bear: Yes, I'm sure. Why do you ask?

Baby polar bear: Because the cold is killing me!

★

What did the polar bear have for lunch?

Iceburgers.

Pole

Johnny: My father was a Pole.
Jenny: North or South?

★

How can you tell a Pole?
By his wooden expression.

Police

Policeman: I'm sorry, but I'm going to have to lock you up for the night.
Man: What's the charge?
Policeman: Oh, there's no charge. It's all part of the service.

★

What happens when you dial 666?
A policeman comes up walking on his hands.

★

A man woke one night to hear loud knocking at his front door.
'Who's there?' he called.
'Police!' was the reply.
The man put the chain on the door, opened it a crack and peered out. 'But you're not in uniform!'
'I'm CID.'
'Oh, why didn't you say so? Come on in, Sid.'

★

Rick: The police are looking for a man with a deaf-aid.
Nick: Why aren't they using glasses?

★

How do police give chase under water?
In a squid car.

★

What did the policeman say to the naughty frog?
Hop it.

★

Andy: What kind of dog is that?
Zak: A police dog.
Andy: It doesn't look much like a police dog to me!

Zak: Well, he wouldn't – he's a plain clothes police dog.

★

What sort of gun does a police dog use?
A dogmatic.

★

Why do policemen like their jobs so much?
Because their customers are never right.

★

What kind of policeman is a poor dresser?
A plain clothes policeman.

★

What made the policeman sad?
Not being able to take his panda to bed with him.

★

A police sergeant was radioing for help while the new recruit chased a thief, but the thief got away.
'How could you lose him?' shouted the sergeant. 'It's broad daylight and you'd nearly caught him.'
'I couldn't help it,' said the recruit. 'He ran into the cinema.'
'Then why didn't you run in after him?' asked the sergeant.
'Because I'd already seen the film.'

★

What did the policewoman use to tie up her hair?
Red tape.

★

What did the policeman say to his stomach?
I've got you under a vest.

Politician

Which politician has the biggest head?
The one with the biggest hat.

★

Canvassing politician: Good evening, young man. Do you happen to know which party your mother is in?

236

Silly Billy: She hasn't gone to the party yet. She's still in the bath.

★

Rick: What's the definition of politics?
Nick: Politics is a parrot that has swallowed a watch.

Polygon
What's a polygon?
　A dead parrot.

Pond
Grandmother: Be careful! Don't fall into that pond – it's very deep.
Soppy Poppy: It can't be that deep – it only reaches up to the middle of those ducks.

Pony
What medicine do you give a pony with a cold?
　Cough stirrup.

★

Where would you take sick ponies?
　To horsepital.

★

Art teacher: Poppy, you were all asked to draw a pony and trap, but you've only drawn the pony!
Soppy Poppy: Well, I thought the pony could draw the trap.

Poodle
What would you get if you crossed a chicken with a poodle?
　Pooched eggs.

★

How can you tell if a toy poodle is French?
　By the way it says, 'Boux-woux'.

Poor
Silly Billy: Dad, are the people who live across the road very poor?

Father: I don't think so, Billy.
Silly Billy: Then why did they make such a fuss when their baby swallowed a 20p piece?

Popeye
What happened when Popeye tried to cook a pizza?
　There was Olive Oyl over the place.

Pop Music
What would happen if pop music went metric?
　You'd have Mick Jagger singing with the Rolling Kilos.

★

Did you hear about the pop singer whose shoelaces got tangled up in his hair?
　When he stood up he broke his neck.

Pop Up!
Amy: I've found the perfect way to get up in the morning.
Zoe: What's that?
Amy: Last thing at night I put the toaster under my bed, and in the morning I just pop up!

Porcupine
What do you get if you cross a porcupine with a mole?
　A tunnel that leaks.

What did the near-sighted porcupine say when he bumped in to a cactus?

Sorry, friend.

Pork

Why is roast pork like an old radio?

Because they both have a lot of crackling.

Porridge

What's grey and comes at you from all sides?

Quadrophonic porridge.

Portable

Craft teacher: What are you making, Poppy?

Soppy Poppy: A portable.

Craft teacher: Very interesting – a portable what?

Soppy Poppy: I haven't decided – I've only made the handles so far.

Porthole

Cruise passenger: Steward, I've put all my clothes in that little cupboard with the window.

Steward: Oh dear, madam – that's the porthole!

Portrait Paintings

Why are portraits like a tin of sardines?

Because they're usually in oil.

Post

What's the cheapest way to post somebody?

Stamp on their foot.

Postage Stamp

What's the difference between a postage stamp and a girl?

One is a mail fee, the other is a female.

Postman

You can take away my first letter; you can take away my second letter; in fact you can take away all my letters and I remain the same. What am I?

A postman.

★

Why do postmen carry letters in sacks?

Because letters can't go anywhere on their own.

★

A lady telephoned the Police Station one day in a great state of excitement. 'You'll have to get over here straight away.' 'What's the matter, madam?' asked the desk sergeant. 'There's a new postman, and he's sitting in a tree in my front garden teasing my Alsatian.'

Post Office

A man went in to the Post Office one day to collect his post because he had lost the key to his post box. He marched up to one of the windows where the clerk was busy working, head down.

'Any letters for Mike Howe?' he asked.

Without looking up, the clerk said, 'No, not for your cow or your calf either.'

Potato

Andy: Have you heard about the new group, Instant Potato?

Zak: No.

Andy: They've had a Smash Hit!

★

What do you call a King Edward with chicken pox?

A specked-tater.

★

What peels and chips but never cracks?

A potato.

★

What do you call a rude King Edward who shouts?

A common-tater.

New farmer: Do you have a potato patch?
Old farmer: Why, is your potato leaking?

★

Customer: The potatoes I bought from you yesterday are full of eyes.
Shopkeeper: Well, you did say you wanted enough to see you through the week.

★

What did the potato say when it was wrapped in aluminium foil and placed in the oven?
'Foiled again!'

★

Maths teacher: If a mother had six children but only five potatoes, how could she give each child a fair share?
Soppy Poppy: By mashing the potatoes.

★

Jack: Did you hear about the two potatoes?
Jill: What about them?
Jack: They didn't see eye to eye.

★

Where were potatoes first found?
In the ground.

Pottery
Mother: How did you get on at school today, Jenny?
Jenny: My teacher didn't like what I made in pottery.
Mother: Oh, what did you make?
Jenny: Mistakes.

Poverty
A little girl from a very poor family went to the baker's for a loaf of bread.
'Mum says would you slice it, please – with a jammy knife.'

★

Rick: My family was so poor that I was ten years old before I realised that shoes weren't made of paper and string.
Nick: That's nothing. My family was so poor

that when we were ill we were only allowed one measle at a time.

★

I was so poor as a child that I only ever had one letter in my alphabet soup.

POW Camp
The detainees in a prisoner-of-war camp were given official permission to start playing football. In fact, the Camp Commandant thought it was a very good idea and announced a series of practices. 'My men will practise in the field; my officers will practise in the compound; and the prisoners will practise in the minefield.'

Power
How do you save power?
Kill a watt today.

Prayers
Father: Johnny, I can't hear your prayers.
Johnny: Well, I wasn't talking to you.

★

Do you know how a CB enthusiast's child finishes his prayers?
'God bless Daddy and Mummy and me. Over and out.'

★

A little boy was finishing his prayers:
'Goodbye, God. I won't be talking to you tomorrow, we're moving.'

Prescription
A famous pop star went to his doctor because he had a swelling on his leg. 'If it gets any bigger,' said the pop star, 'I won't be able to get my trousers on.'
'Don't worry,' said the doctor, 'I'll give you a prescription.'
'What for?' said the pop star.
'A prescription for a skirt.'

Present

Jack: Say you like the dictionary I bought you for your birthday.
Jill: Yes, I do. I just can't find the words to thank you enough.

★

Did you hear about the little girl who wanted to buy her Grandma hankies for her birthday but couldn't remember the size of her Grandma's nose?

★

Nick: You've just written a cheque for a £100!
Rick: I know — it's a birthday present for my sister.
Nick: You forgot to sign it.
Rick: No, I didn't. I'm sending it anonymously.

★

What's the ideal present for people who play it cool?
A combined stereo and air conditioner.

Price

Smart-alec customer: How much are your £5 shoes?
Smarter salesman: £2.50 a foot, sir.

Prince Charles

What's the difference between the Prince of Wales and a tennis ball?
One is heir to the throne and the other is thrown in the air.

★

Why is Prince Charles like a cloudy day?
Because he is likely to reign.

★

Why is Prince Charles the Prince of Wales?
Because he was such a cry-baby.

Prince William

Why is Prince William like part of the Postal Service?
Because he's a royal male.

Printer

What is a printer?
A man of letters.

★

Paul: Why did you become a printer?
Saul: I guess I was the right type.

Prison

Prisoner: The judge sent me here for the rest of my life.
Prison governor: Have you any complaints?
Prisoner: Do you call breaking rocks with a hammer rest?

★

'I understand that it took six policemen to lock you up last night,' said the magistrate in court one morning.
'That's right, sir,' said the prisoner, 'but it would only take one to let me out!'

★

Did you hear about the man who was sent to prison for something he didn't do?
He didn't jump into the get-away car fast enough!

★

What's the longest sentence in the world?
Life imprisonment.

★

Escaped prisoner: I'm free! I'm free!
Little boy: So what? I'm four!

Prisoners

1st prisoner: Why did they put you in prison if you were making big money?
2nd prisoner: Because I was making it three centimetres too big.

Newsflash: Two prisoners escaped from custody today. One is seven feet tall and the other four feet three. Police are looking high and low for them.

★

A warden was escorting a prisoner to court for an appeal when his hat blew off.
'Oh,' said the prisoner, 'let me run and get it for you.'
'I'm not stupid!' said the warden. 'You stay here and I'll get it.'

★

What kind of party do prisoners like most of all?
  A going-away party.

Prize
Father: Whoever marries my daughter will get a real prize.
Suitor: Can I see the prize?

Professional
Which man in the professions works with a will?
  A solicitor.

Professor
How do you become a professor?
  By degrees.

Promises
Father: You promised to be good, didn't you?
Son: Yes, Dad.
Father: And I promised to punish you if you weren't good?
Son: Yes, Dad. But I won't mind if you break your promise too!

★

What can you break without hitting it or dropping it?
  A promise.

Proposal
Adam (on the telephone): Will you marry me?
Eve: Yes, of course! Who's calling?

★

Jack: Will you be my wife one day?
Jill: Not for a minute, you creep.

★

Jack: Will you marry me?
Jill: No, but I shall always admire your good taste.

★

When accepting a young man at Kew,
A maiden said, 'Yes, I'll be true.
But you must understand,
As you've asked for my hand,
That the rest of me goes with it too.'

Psychiatry
Psychiatrist: Don't be sad, Mr Able. We've finally cured you of your madness.
Mr Able: Wouldn't you be sad if you'd been Nelson all your life and now you were a nobody?

★

What did the psychiatrist say at the end of a busy day?
  It was like a madhouse!

★

How much did the psychiatrist charge the hippopotamus?
  £10 for the appointment and £100 for the couch.

★

Rick: Fancy meeting you here at the psychiatrist's office. Are you coming or going?
Nick: I don't know. That's why I'm here.

★

Why pay to visit a psychiatrist . . .
  when you can stay at home and talk to the ceiling for nothing?

★

'Next!' called the psychiatrist, and looked up with surprise when a tortoise walked in to the surgery. Recovering, he said, 'What can I do for you?'

'Oh, doctor,' said the tortoise. 'Please help me, I'm so shy.'

'Never mind,' said the psychiatrist, 'we'll soon have you out of your shell.'

★

Patient: Doctor, you've got to help me to stop talking to myself.
Doctor: Why is that?
Patient: I'm a door-to-door salesman and I keep selling myself things I don't want.

★

Psychiatrists say that one out of every five people is mentally ill.
Think about your friends! If four of them are all right, then it's you!

Pudding

How do you start a milk pudding race?
  Sago.

★

What is one of the hardest things to do?
  Milk puddings.

Puddle

What did the puddle say to the rain?
  Drop in and see me some time.

Puffin

What bird is always out of breath?
  A puffin.

Pulse

Nurse: May I take your pulse, please?
Patient: Haven't you got one of your own?

★

A little girl went on her first visit to the school clinic. The doctor said, 'I'm going to take your pulse,' and she burst into tears.

'What's the matter?' asked the doctor. 'I haven't done anything!'

'No,' said the little girl. 'But you said you were going to take my pulse, and I think I might need it!'

Punctuality

Teacher: You should have been here at nine o'clock.
Soppy Poppy: Why, what happened?

Punctuation

Interviewer: And, finally, Miss Bird, you do understand the importance of punctuation in a secretarial job?
Miss Bird: Oh, yes. I always get to work on time.

Puncture

Paul: I had a puncture yesterday.
Saul: What bad luck. Was it a nail?
Paul: No, a milk bottle.
Saul: Didn't you see it in the road?
Paul: No. The stupid woman had hidden it under her coat.

★

What's the best way to mend a puncture in the rear tyre of your bike?
  Raise the seat.

★

A country policeman came across a lady trying to change a punctured tyre. His offer of help was gratefully accepted and the lady said, 'The jack seems to have stuck and I can't winch the wheel down.'

'Well, I'll have a look,' said the policeman.

'Oh, Thank you,' said the lady, 'and could you lower the car quietly, please. My husband is asleep inside.'

★

Jack: I think we've had a puncture.
Jill: What makes you say that?
Jack: I saw a fork in the road.

Punishment

Mother: Why are you spanking Sam?
Father: Because his school report is due tomorrow and I won't be here.

★

A little boy whose father had punished him one morning was watching television when his father came home in the evening.
'Mum,' he shouted, 'your husband's home!'

Punk

What do you call a six-foot tall, 15-stone punk with his portable radio on full blast?

Anything you like, because he won't hear you.

Puppetry

How can you best get in to the puppetry business?

Pull a few strings.

Puppies

What's the best way of keeping a noisy young dog quiet?

With Hush-Puppies.

Mrs Able: You'll have to control that puppy, my dear, he's just bitten my ankle!
Mrs Cable: Well, he's not big enough to bite you in the neck!

★

Soppy Poppy: I'd like to buy a puppy, please. How much do they cost?
Pet shop owner: £10 apiece.
Soppy Poppy: Oh! That's a lot. How much does a whole one cost?

★

Johnny: How's your new puppy?
Jenny: Oh, he's a howling success.

Pushchairs

What's it called when two French pushchairs collide?

A crèche.

Putt

What goes putt-putt-putt-putt?

A bad golfer.

Pyramids

Rick: My teacher really shouted at me today because I didn't know where the Pyramids were.
Nick: Well, you should remember where you put your things.

Python

What did the python say to its victim?

I've got a crush on you.

Q

Rick: What's five Q and five Q?
Nick: Ten Q.
Rick: You're welcome!

Quadruplets

What does a mother say when she has quadruplets?

Four crying out loud!

Queen

What did the Queen say to Prince Charles when he was naughty?

If you don't stop it, I'll crown you.

★

What does the Queen do if she burps?

She issues a royal pardon.

★

What do you call a half-eaten apple thrown away by the Queen?

The Royal Flying Corps.

Questions and Answers

What asks no questions but demands an answer?

A telephone that's ringing.

Queue

There's always a long queue of people at this theatre — waiting to get out.

Quick Draw

A tomboy rushed out of nursery school one afternoon, ran up to her mother and insisted on going to the toy shop straight away.

'What do you want to buy in such a hurry?' asked the mother.

'I need a gun belt and a gun for school tomorrow morning,' said the tomboy. 'The teacher says she's going to teach us how to draw.'

Rabbit

What do you call a rabbit with a lot of money?
 A million-hare.

★

Why is a rabbit's nose always shiny?
 Because its powder puff is on the wrong end.

★

What did the baby rabbit want to do when he grew up?
 He wanted to join the hare force.

★

Why did the rabbit cross the road?
 To prove to his girlfriend that he had guts.

★

What do you call a rabbit that has fleas?
 Bugs bunny.

★

What do you get if you pour boiling water down a rabbit hole?
 Hot Cross Bunnies.

★

Paul: Have you ever seen a dog make a rabbit hutch?
Saul: No, but I've seen a fox make a chicken run.

★

What's a twip?
 It's what a wabbit takes when he wides in a twain.

Who's in charge of rabbits' money?
 The Burrow Treasurer.

★

What's the best way to catch rabbits?
 Hide in the woods and make a noise like a lettuce.

★

What's the best way to get back runaway rabbits?
 Hare restorer.

★

Did you hear about the two rabbits that got married?
 They went to Majorca on a bunnymoon.

★

What would you get if you crossed a rabbit with a leek?
 A bunion.

★

How do rabbits keep their fur so neat and tidy?
 They use a hare-brush.

Rabbit Stew

A magician went in to a restaurant and ordered rabbit stew. When he had finished eating it he got up from the table and rushed out of the restaurant, calling to the waiter, 'That rabbit stew has made me sick!'

'Well, I never,' said the waiter. 'That must be the first time a rabbit has ever made a magician disappear.'

Rabies

The doctor walked up to his seriously ill patient in the hospital ward and said, 'I'm sorry to have to tell you that you may have rabies as a result of that dog bite. You may die.' The patient thought for a moment, and then said, 'Bring me a pen and some paper, please.'

'You're going to make your will, then?' asked the doctor.

'Never!' said the patient. 'I want to make a list of all the people I'm going to bite.'

Race

What is the greatest race on earth?
The human race.

★

Two fat men ran in a race. One ran in short bursts, the other in burst shorts.

Racehorses

Two racehorses met in the paddock. One said to the other, 'Your pace is familiar, but I don't remember your mane.'

Racing

Paul: The police finally caught up with my uncle.
Saul: Your uncle's never a crook!
Paul: No, he's a racing driver.

Racing Cars

Why do racing cars get stiff joints?
They have vroomatism.

Racing Pigeons

Mr Able: What is your hobby?
Mr Cable: I race pigeons.
Mr Able: Oh, do you ever beat them?

Radio

Why is a radio never complete?
Because it is always a wireless.

Radio Announcer

How are radio announcers paid?
So much announce.

Radishes

Doctor, doctor, I've got radishes growing out of my ears.
My goodness, how did that happen?
I don't know – I planted carrots.

Rag and Bone Man

Sam: Mum! The rag and bone man's here.
Mother: Say no, thank you, Sam. We've got enough rags and bones today.

Railway Crossing

A man was being interviewed for the job of attendant at a railway crossing. The first question he was asked was, 'What would you do if you saw two trains going towards each other on the same line?'

'I'd change the points so that one train was switched to another track.'

'Good,' said the interviewer. 'What would you do if the points were jammed?'

'I'd run out on to the line with a red flag.'

'And suppose the train driver didn't see you?'

'Oh, then I'd call my little boy.'

'Why would you call your little boy?'

'He just loves train crashes.'

Railway Station

Why was the railway station called Fish Hook?
Because it was the end of the line.

Rain

Paul: Is it raining outside?
Saul: Well, it doesn't often rain inside!

★

Rick: Why does it rain?
Nick: To make things grow, silly. The flowers, the grass, the trees, the crops.
Rick: So why does it rain on the pavement?

★

Amy: It looks like rain.
Zoe: I know it does, but it says chicken soup on the packet.

★

Sidney and Sally Forth were on holiday in Russia. They had a guide called Rudolph, and Sidney and Rudolph argued all the time. As they arrived in Red Square Sidney said, 'Look, it's snowing.' The guide disagreed. 'No, sir, it's raining.'
'It's definitely snowing,' grumbled Sidney.
His wife interrupted, 'Rudolph the Red knows rain, dear.'

★

Johnny: Do you think it's going to rain?
Jenny: That depends on the weather, doesn't it.

★

What often falls but never gets hurt?
    Rain.

★

Amy: It's raining cats and dogs.
Zoe: I know – I just stepped into a poodle.

★

What happens when it rains beer?
    There's an ale storm.

★

What is worse than raining cats and dogs?
    Hailing taxis.

Rainbow

What bow can't be tied?
    A rainbow.

Raincoat

What is the difference between a raincoat and a baby?
    One I wear, the other I was.

Rainhat

Mr Drip: My rainhat has a waterproof label.
Mr Drop: Pity the whole hat isn't waterproof.

Raisin

What is a raisin?
    A grape that's wrinkled from too much worry.

★

1st farmer: Do you like raisin bread?
2nd farmer: Don't know. Never raised any.

Ranch Brand

1st rancher: What's the name of your ranch?
2nd rancher: The Lazy Double-O Diamond Crossed Forks.
1st rancher: And how many head of sheep do you have?
2nd rancher: Not many – few survive the branding.

★

Who designed the first raincoat?
    Anna Rack.

Raspberry

What's red, bumpy, and rides alone in the desert?
    The Lone Raspberry.

Rat

What would you get if you crossed a rat with a woodpecker?
    A rat-a-tat-tat.

★

Andy: Why did the rat gnaw a hole in the carpet?
Zak: Why?

Andy: Because he wanted to see the floor show.

★

Monster: I'd like some rat poison, please.
Sales assistant: Certainly, sir. To drink here or take away?

Ray

What happened to Ray when an elephant stepped on him?
He became an X-ray.

Razor Blades

A nosey neighbour watched with interest as Mr Next Door planted rows of razor blades in his potato bed.
'What are you hoping to grow?' he asked.
'Chips,' said Mr Next Door.

Reading

Train passenger: Do you know that you're reading your newspaper upside down?
  Commuter: Of course I do – do you think it's easy?

★

Andy: What are you reading?
Zak: I'm reading about electricity.
Andy: Current events?
Zak: No, light reading.

★

Optician: Right, you're all set. With these glasses you'll be able to read everything.
Silly Billy: Oh, Great! No more school!

★

What kind of book does Frankenstein like to read?
  One with a cemetery plot.

★

A nursery school teacher was finding out about her new pupils' abilities, and asked Billy if he could read and write.
'I can write,' said Silly Billy, 'but I can't read.'

'Well, then,' said the teacher, 'write your name here for me.'
Silly Billy wrote something on a piece of paper and gave it to the teacher, who looked at the scribbling and said, 'What's this?'
'I told you,' said Silly Billy, 'I can't read.'

Rebate

Jenny: What does rebate mean?
Mother: It's what Dad does when he's out fishing and a fish gets his worm.

Records

A young policeman brought a suspected thief into the station.
'Well done, lad,' said the sergeant. 'Any record?'
'Oh, yes,' said the policeman. 'I searched his room and found three by Wham! and several chart singles.'

★

Andy: I've got over 2,000 LPs.
Zak: 2,000 LPs! You must like music very much.
Andy: Oh, no. I collect the holes in the middle.

Red Arrows

Definition of the word Information:
How the Red Arrows fly.

★

What's blue, V-shaped and flies?
  The Red Arrows in disguise.

Red China

Paul: What's your opinion of Red China?
Saul: That depends on the colour of the tablecloth.

Red Cross

During one winter's heavy snowstorms a village in the Swiss Alps was totally cut off from the rest of the world. A Red Cross rescue team went by helicopter to within a mile of the village, and trudged the rest of the way through enormous snow drifts. They shovelled a path to the door of the first house in the village and banged on the door. Eventually the door was opened, and one of the rescuers said,

'We're from the Red Cross.'

'Oh, my,' said the man in the house, 'it's been a really hard winter and I don't think we can give to your collection this year.'

Red Face

Mother: Sam, why is your face so red?

Sam: I ran up the street to try and stop a fight.

Mother: Well, that's good of you. Who was fighting?

Sam: Me and another boy.

Redhead

Why is a redheaded idiot like a biscuit?
  Because he's a ginger nut.

Red Indian

What is a small laugh in Red Indian language?
  A minnehaha.

★

A tourist came across a Red Indian lying with his ear to the ground in America's mid west.

'What are you listening for?' asked the tourist.

'Stage coach went through some time ago,' said the Red Indian.

'Oh, how do you know?' asked the tourist, fascinated.

'It broke my neck.'

Amy: I spent ages with an Indian tribe once. I learned all their dances and they gave me an Indian name.

Zoe: What name did they give you?

Amy: Clumsy.

★

If a Red Indian's wife is called a squaw, does that mean their babies are called squawkers?

★

Where does an Indian ghost live?
  In a creepy tepee.

★

Why does an Indian wear feathers in his hair?
  To keep his wigwam.

★

How come the Red Indians occupied America before the white settlers?
  The Red Indians had reservations.

★

Which Red Indian tribe had the most lawyers?
  The Sioux.

★

If a cowboy's gun was a six-shooter, does that make an Indian's bow a stick-shooter?

Red Sea

How do you part the Red Sea?
  With a sea-saw.

Referee

Did you hear about the referee who used to work at a rocket launching site? He'd count a boxer out, 'Ten, nine, eight, seven, . . .'

★

Andy: I went to see a film about referees in a space-war.

Zak: What was it called?

Andy: The Umpires Strike Back.

Reference

Did you hear about the stupid man who was proud of his previous employers's reference? It said he was the best employee they'd ever turned out!

Refrigerators

Old refrigerators never die.
  They just lose their cool.

Regatta

What's a regatta?
  A sails meeting.

Regret

Sam announced that he was leaving school with regret.
  He was sorry he'd ever had to go.

Reincarnation

Did you hear about the man who believed so completely in reincarnation that in his will he left everything to himself?

Reindeer

What do reindeer say before they tell a joke?
  This one will sleigh you!

★

Adam: What's the use of reindeer?
Eve: It makes the flowers grow, darling.

Relations

A couple's happily married life was nearly ruined by old Aunt Adeline's living with them. She stayed with them for ten years, always bad tempered and very difficult to please. Eventually she died and on the way back from the funeral, the husband confessed to his wife, 'You know, darling, if I didn't love you so much, I don't think I could have put up with having your Aunt Adeline living with us all those years.'

'*My* Aunt Adeline!' cried his wife. 'I always thought she was *your* Aunt Adeline!'

★

Sally: Mum, is it true that we're descended from apes?
Mother: I don't know, dear. I never met your father's relatives.

★

What relation is your uncle's sister to you if she's not your aunt?
  Your mother.

★

What is kindred?
  When you're terrified of relatives coming to visit.

Religion

What's green, curly and religious?
  Lettuce pray.

Remark

What can you catch, but never see?
  A remark.

Removals

What's the difference between the business of a removal firm and an office supplies shop?
One's moving, the other's stationery.

Reptile

What do you call a sick reptile?
  An illigator.

Restaurant

Jack: How did you like the new restaurant?
Jill: It wasn't a restaurant – more like a Bureau of Missing Portions.

★

First customer: This is a wonderful restaurant – I ordered a fresh egg, and they gave me the freshest egg in the world. And then I

250

ordered coffee, and they gave me the freshest coffee in the world.

Second customer: I know — I ordered a small steak and got a calf.

Retirement

Did you hear about the Headmaster whose retirement present was an Illuminated Address?

His pupils burnt his house down.

Retreads

When is it time to get your tyres retreaded?

When you drive over a penny and can tell whether it's heads or tails.

★

Why is a reviewer like an illness?

Because his best work is always critical.

Revolving Door

The absent-minded professor was spotted going round and round in a revolving door by a friend. 'How are you?' he called.

'Oh, I'm in trouble here,' said the professor, 'I can't remember whether I'm coming or going.'

★

Rick: Have you heard that Adam and Eve are still going around together?

Nick: That doesn't surprise me. They met in a revolving door.

Reward

Father: If you're good and help with all the chores, I'll give you a shiny new 10p piece.

Son: Oh, Dad. I wouldn't mind if it was a dirty old 20p piece!

Rheumatism

Silly Billy: Doctor, do you remember that last year when I came to see you about my rheumatism you told me to stay away from dampness?

Doctor: Yes, I remember.

Silly Billy: Well, as it's much better can I take a bath now?

Rhubarb

What is rhubarb?

Celery with high blood pressure.

★

What happened to the man who stole some rhubarb?

He was put into custody.

Ribbon

What kind of ribbon do policemen use?

Red tape.

Rice Krispie

How can you tell an orphan Rice Krispie?

It goes snap, crackle, and no pop.

Rich

Patient: Doctor, I have a huge problem. I live in an old stately home, I have three brand-new cars, my children are all at boarding school, and my wife has the finest furs and jewellery. . . .

Doctor: So exactly what is your problem?

Patient: I only earn £50 a week.

★

Amy: My family are very, very rich.

Zoe: How rich?

Amy: Well, we've got three swimming pools.

Zoe: Why three?

Amy: One hot, one cold and one empty.

Zoe: What's the empty one for?

Amy: For people who can't swim.

★

Why can you get rich by keeping your mouth shut?

Because silence is golden.

★

A very rich businessman was stranded one night at a small country hotel. No one knew who he was and therefore didn't know how wealthy he was, and the hotel staff treated him exactly the same as they treated the other guests. In the morning he decided he would show them just how rich he was, so at breakfast he asked the waiter to bring him £10 worth of scrambled egg and bacon.

'I'm sorry, sir,' said the waiter. 'We don't serve half-portions.'

Rich Putt, Putt

What's rich and goes putt-putt?

A sun golf professional.

Riddle

A doctor and a boy were fishing. The boy was the doctor's son, but the doctor was not the boy's father. Who was the doctor?

His mother.

Riding

Jack: I went riding this afternoon.

Jill: Horseback?

Jack: Yes, we came back together.

Rifle

What's a rifle with three barrels called?

A trifle.

Right Hand

Jack: May I sit on your right hand at school today?

Jill: Yes, all right, until I have to write my essay.

★

A labourer who injured his hand at work went to the casualty department to have it seen to. The doctor who examined it shook his head at the sight and said, 'I'm afraid it will never be right.'

'Why ever not?' asked the man.

'Because it's your left hand,' said the doctor.

Ringleader

What is a ringleader?

The first one in the bathtub.

Rings

Amy: What's a ring on your finger worth?

Zoe: Two on the phone.

River

Andy: A cow wanted to cross a river to get to the lush green meadow on the other side. There was no bridge and the river was too deep for the cow to wade. How did the cow cross?

Zak: I give up.

Andy: So did the cow.

★

What river never begins and never ends?

S-ever-N.

★

What has a big mouth but never says a word?

A river.

★

Why does a river have lots of money?

Because it's got two banks.

★

What do you call small rivers that flow into the Nile?

Juveniles.

Road

A motorist stopped in a country village and asked a passer-by if he could tell him where the road went.

'It don't go nowhere,' replied the local man. 'It stays right where it is.'

★

What do you call a road that has cats-eyes made of diamonds?

A jewel-carriageway.

★

What goes all the way from John O'Groats to Land's End without moving an inch?

The road.

Road Sweeper

Why did the road sweeper lose his job?

Because he couldn't keep his mind in the gutter.

Roast Beef

When is roast beef highest in price?

When it's rarest.

Roast Boar

Rick: We had roast boar for dinner yesterday.
Nick: Wild?
Rick: Well, he wasn't too pleased.

Robbery

Did you hear about the man who robbed the Bank of England? He rushed home to cut the legs off his bed.

'What are you doing that for?' asked his wife.

'I have to lie low for a while,' he explained.

★

Why do robbers wear braces?

Because they're hold-up men.

★

A jeweller was standing in his shop when a man came crashing through the plate-glass window.

'What do you think you're doing?' he asked.

'I'm very sorry,' said the man, 'I forgot to let go of the brick.'

★

Two men jumped on a pedestrian in a lonely street one night. The pedestrian put up a fight but eventually the robbers managed to empty his pockets. All the man had was a pound coin. The robbers were amazed, and one said, 'You fought all this time for the sake of one pound?'

'Well,' said the pedestrian in a frightened voice, 'I thought you were after the savings I keep in my shoe.'

★

Thief: Quickly! The police are on their way. Jump out of the window!
Accomplice: But we're on the thirteenth floor!
Thief: This is no time to get superstitious!

★

What sort of robbery is the easiest?

A safe robbery.

★

Rick: Last week a man stole a trolley full of goods and a pair of trousers from my uncle's supermarket.
Nick: Did your uncle chase him?
Rick: No, they were his trousers.

★

Two small-time thieves were told to steal a lorry load of bathroom supplies for the boss man who was redecorating his huge house. One of the thieves went in to the store while the other kept watch. Several hours went by and the look-out was getting very worried, so he went inside the store and met his companion.

'What's the matter?' he asked. 'Why haven't you brought anything out yet?'

'The boss said to take a bath,' replied his friend. 'But there's no soap and towel anywhere.'

Robin

What is the definition of a robin?

A bird that steals.

Robin Hood

Why did Robin Hood only take from the rich?

Because the poor didn't have anything to take.

★

What did Little John say when Robin Hood fired at him?

That was an arrow escape.

Robinson Crusoe

What did Robinson Crusoe say when he found out who the footprints belonged to?
  Thank goodness it's Friday.

Robot

Why was the robot being silly?
  Because he had a screw loose.

What do you call a robot who always goes the long way round?
  Artoo Detour.

What is 'sitting comfortably' to a robot?
  Bolt upright.

What did the robot say to the petrol pump?
  Take-your-finger-out-of-your-ear.

★

Do robots have brothers?
  No, they only have tran-sisters.

Rock Eater

What's big and red and eats rocks?
  A big, red rock-eater.

Rock 'N' Roll

How can you learn to play rock 'n' roll guitar in one day?
  Put on your roller skates, stand on a rocking chair and start playing your guitar!

Why did the little old lady put wheels on her rocking chair?
  Because she wanted to rock and roll.

Rock Pool

The tide had gone out when one rock pool said to the other:
  'Go on, show us your mussels.'

Rocket

What do you get if you cross a round black hat with a rocket?
  A very fast bowler.

Rocket Pilot

Space traffic control: Please relay your height and position.
Daft rocket pilot: I'm 1.6 metres tall, and I'm sitting at the control panel.

Roller Skates

Why is a pair of roller skates like an apple?
  Because both are responsible for the fall of man.

Rolls

Adoring fan: What are your favourite roles?
Actor: Hamlet, Othello, cheese and onion.

Rolls Royce

A little boy was going home from playing football in the park when he saw a beautiful new Rolls Royce in the car park. He was bouncing the football on and off the bumpers and bonnet when the ball bounced on to the windscreen and smashed it to smithereens. The boy's father, who was walking up to collect him, shouted angrily,
'I've told you! If you burst that ball I'm not buying another one!'

Romance

Adam: Do you really love me, darling?
Eve: Oh, yes, I do.
Adam: Then whisper something soft and sweet in my ear, darling.
Eve: Marshmallows.

★

Jill: The man that I marry must be as brave as Hercules, as wise as Solomon, as noble as King Arthur and as handsome as Apollo.
Jack: Aren't you lucky you met me!

Romans

Why did the Romans build straight roads?
  So that the Britons couldn't hide round corners.

★

What's the difference between a Roman barber and an excited circus-owner?
  One is a shaving Roman and the other is a raving showman.

★

Why did the Romans build such straight roads?
  Because they didn't want their soldiers to go round the bend.

★

Teacher: What was the Romans' most remarkable achievement?
Silly Billy: Learning Latin!

Rome

History teacher: When was Rome built?
Silly Billy: At night-time.
History teacher: Why do you say that?
Silly Billy: Because my Mum always says Rome wasn't built in a day.

Romeo and Juliet

What did Juliet say when she met Romeo on the balcony?
  Couldn't you get seats in the stalls?

Room

What room has no floor, ceiling, windows or doors?
  A mushroom.

★

Hotel guest: Can you give me a room and a bath, please?
Receptionist: I can give you a room, sir, but you'll have to take your own bath.

Ruler

Jack: Have you heard about the new electric ruler?
Jill: No, what about it?
Jack: Switch it on and it rules the world.

Running Away

What happened to the little boy who ran away with the circus?
  The police made him bring it back.

★

A policeman was nearly knocked down by a little boy who was running down the street and disappeared around the corner. A few minutes later the little boy charged by again, and again, and then again. The policeman stopped him and said, 'What's going on? Why are you running around like this?'
'I'm running away from home,' said the little boy.
'But why are you running up and down and round the corner?'
'Because my mother won't let me cross the road.'

Russian

What cow can speak Russian?
  Ma's cow (Moscow).

Rooster

Why is a rooster fussy?
  Because he never lends his comb.

★

Why did the rooster refuse to fight?
Because he was a chicken.

Rope Joke

Paul: Have you heard the rope joke?
Saul: No, tell me.
Paul: No, skip it.

Rose-Coloured Glasses

What happens to people who wear rose-coloured glasses?
They end up seeing red.

Roses

Amy (writing): Roses are red, violets are blue . . .
Zoe (giggling): And mine are white!

Rough Crossing

A man on a cross-Channel ferry was feeling increasingly sea sick as the crossing was very rough and the ferry pitched and rolled. He went up on deck for some fresh air and a steward asked him if he would like lunch.
'Oh, no,' said the green-faced man. 'Throw me overboard and save me the trouble.'

Roundabout

Paul: I just had ten rides on the Roundabout.
Saul: You really get around, don't you!

Rower

What does a rower drink at bed time?
Oar-licks.

Rubber Band

Paul: Is work hard in the rubber band factory?
Saul: No, it's a snap.

Rubber Gloves

How can you wash your hands without getting them wet?
Wear rubber gloves.

Rubbish Collector

Sam: Is there any special training for my new job as rubbish collector?
Employer: No, you can just pick it up as you go along.

Runner Bean

Where had the runner bean?
To see the celery stalk.

Russian Tarzan

What did the Russian Tarzan say when he met a crane?
Me Tarzan, Ukraine.

Russian Roulette

How do you play Russian Roulette in India?
Play the flute with six cobras in six separate baskets and try not to get the cobra that's deaf.

Rust

Motorist: When I bought this car you said it was totally rust-free. But look at all this rust underneath!
Secondhand car dealer: I did sell you the car, sir — but the rust was free.

Sacked
Who gets the sack as soon as he starts work?
  A postman.

Sacks of Corn
Bill: If one man had two sacks of corn and another man had three sacks, which of them would be carrying the heaviest load?
Ben: The man with three sacks, of course.
Bill: No, the man with two sacks because the other man had empty sacks.

Saddler
A very mean man went to his local saddler and asked if he could buy just one spur.
'Why do you only want one?' asked the saddler.
'Because if I can get one side of the horse to go, the other side is sure to come with it.'

Safari
A famous surgeon was asked on his return from safari in Africa how everything had gone.
'Most disappointing,' was his reply. 'I didn't kill a thing. I'd have been better off staying at the hospital!'

★

Andy: My uncle was a big game hunter in Africa, but he disappeared on one safari.
Zak: What happened?
Andy: My Dad says something he disagreed with ate him.

Sahara Desert
What do you send people out in the Sahara Desert who are dying of thirst?
A 'get well' card.

Sailing
An incompetent sailor named Scott
Tried crossing the Channel by yacht.
A storm blew him off course,
So he tapped out in Morse:

Sailor
Andy: Did you hear about the smallest sailor in the world?
Zak: No, what about him?
Andy: He used to sleep on his watch.

★

Captain: Well, sailor have you swabbed the decks and emptied the bilges?
Sailor: Aye, aye, sir! And I've swept the horizon with your telescope, sir.

★

What do you call a sailor who is married and has five children?
  Daddy.

★

Why did the sailor grab a sack of rains before he jumped off the sinking ship?
  Because he hoped the currants would carry him to the shore.

257

Do sailors go on safaris?
  Not safaris I know.

★

Why do sailors know the Top Ten?
  Because they always study the charts.

Salad Bowl

Jack: Did you ever see a salad bowl?
Jill: No, but I once saw a horse box.

Sales

Woman in crowd at the sales: Hey! Just who
  do you think you're pushing?
2nd woman: I don't know. What's your
  name?

Salesman

A young man got a job selling encyclopaedias
door-to-door. He had very bad luck his first
week, going from house to house without
making one sale. He went to the last house in
the street one evening and rang the doorbell.
As soon as a woman opened it, he began his
sales spiel:
'Everything you ever wanted to know from A
to Z – animals, botany, cookery, deserts, etc.
There are twenty-six leather-bound volumes
with 2,600 pages and each volume is two
inches thick.' 'Just a minute,' said the woman
at the door, and she closed the door. She
reappeared a few moments later and said,
'I'll take Volumes I and II.'
'Why only Volumes I and II?' asked the
puzzled salesman. 'Why not have all twenty-
six?'
'Because my son's broken bed leg is only four
inches long.'

★

A salesman called at a house and when the
lady opened the door he said,
'Want any brushes today, madam?'
'No thank you,' she replied.
'Any dusters?'
'No, thank you.'
'Any window cleaner? Furniture polish? Floor
polish?'

'No, thank you. Nothing at all.'
'The lady next door said it would be a waste
of my time because you never clean the house!

Salmon

Mrs Able (in fishmonger): Doesn't that salmon
  look good.
Mrs Cable: That's not salmon – that's
  haddock blushing at the asking price.

Salt

Two men met at a sales conference of a large
food manufacturers.
'What do you sell?' said one.
'Salt,' replied the other.
'I'm a salt-seller, too,' said the first.
'Shake,' said the second.

★

Mother: Jenny, these cookies don't taste too
good. Are you sure you added a pinch of salt?
Jenny: A pinch! I thought you said an inch!

Sandman

Where does the Sandman keep his sleeping
sand?
  In a knapsack.

Sandpaper

What is sandpaper?
  A map of the desert.

Sandwich

Why did the little boy call his dog Sandwich?
  Because it was half-bred.

★

What kind of sandwich speaks for itself?
  A tongue sandwich.

★

What's a sandwich man?
  A cannibal's quick lunch.

★

258

What are a traffic warden's favourite sandwiches?

Traffic jam sandwiches.

★

What happens if you wrap up your sandwiches in your favourite comic?

You get crumby jokes.

Santa Claus

Jack: Santa Claus has another job, you know.
Jill: How do you know?
Jack: He must be a farmer because he's always saying 'Hoe, hoe, hoe.'

★

Who takes Christmas presents to police stations?

Santa Clues.

★

Amy: Why does Santa Claus always go down the chimney?
Zoe: Because it soots (suits) him.

★

Who is Santa Claus's wife?

Mary Christmas.

Sardine

What happened to the sardine who was late for work?

It was canned.

★

What did one sardine say to the other?

Move over, can't you? You're squashing me.

★

Why are sardines the stupidest fish in the sea?

Because they crawl into cans, lock themselves in, and leave the key on the outside.

Satanic

A man walked in to a shop selling dress material and said, 'I'd like three yards of satan for my wife.'

'You mean *satin*, sir,' said the shop assistant politely. '*Satan* is something that looks like the devil.'

'Oh, you've seen my wife, then?'

Satisfaction

How can you get satisfaction?

From a satisfactory.

Saucer

What did the saucer say to the cup?

That's enough of your lip.

Sausage

Why did the little boy have a sausage stuck behind his ear?

Because he'd eaten his pencil at lunch time.

★

How do you make a sausage roll?

Push it.

★

How do you know a sausage doesn't like being fried?

Because it splits.

★

Patient: Doctor, my family all think I'm mad.
Doctor: Why do they think that?
Patient: Because I like sausages.
Doctor: That's silly – I like sausages too.
Patient: Really? You must come round and see my collection. I have hundreds!

★

What do you get if you cross a zebra with a pig?

Striped sausages.

Saver Stamps

Rick: Did you hear about the man found guilty of sticking Saver Stamps on his National Insurance card?
Nick: No, what happened to him?
Rick: He got three months' imprisonment and a toaster.

Saving

Jenny: Dad, I've got a way for you to save some money.
Father: Really, how?
Jenny: Remember you said you'd give me £5 for passing my exams?
Father: Yes.
Jenny: Well, you don't have to pay me.

Savoir Faire

What happened to the man who thought he had *savoir faire*?
   It turned out he didn't even have bus fare!

Scaffolding

Two little boys were watching some men working on top of high scaffolding, repairing a church. 'What would you do,' said Sam, 'if you were right up at the top and that all fell down?'
'Well,' said Johnny, 'I'd wait until it was almost touching the ground and then I'd jump.'

Scales

Shopper: I sent my son to get 2lbs of butter cookies, and you only sent me 1½ lbs. Is there something wrong with your scales?
Grocer: There's nothing wrong with my scales, madam. Have you weighed your son?

★

A man stepped on to the scales on a station platform while waiting for the train, and got the shock of his life when the scales said, 'Go weigh!'

Scandinavia

What's the cheapest way to get to Scandinavia?
   Be born there.

Scarecrow

Two farmers were trying to outdo each other on the efficiency of their scarecrows. 'My scarecrow is so lifelike it frightens off every crow for miles,' said one.
'That's nothing,' said the other, 'mine scared the crows into bringing back all the grain they stole last year.'

★

Why don't scarecrows have any fun?
   Because they're stuffed shirts.

Scenery

Mrs Able: Did you enjoy the scenery in Switzerland on your holiday?
Mrs Cable: We didn't see very much. There were too many mountains in the way.

Scholarships

On what kind of ships do students study?
   On scholarships.

School

Headmistress: I hear you missed school yesterday.
Soppy Poppy: Not one bit.

★

Teacher: When do you like school best?
Jenny: At weekends, when I'm not here.

★

'Mum, don't make me go to school. I don't want to go to school!'
'But you must go to school, dear, and for two very good reasons. First, they'll be expecting you and second, you're the headmaster!'

★

Mother: How was your first day at school?

Silly Billy: All right, really. Except for some man called Sir who kept wanting us to do as he said.

★

Visitor: How do you like going to school, Sam?

Sam: Going's all right and so is coming home. It's the in-between that I don't like.

★

Headmaster: I've had complaints about you, Johnny, from all your teachers. What have you been doing?

Johnny: Nothing, sir.

Headmaster: Exactly!

★

Teacher: Sam, name me two pronouns.

Sam: Who, me?

Teacher: Right!

★

Andy: I think our school must be haunted.

Zak: Why?

Andy: Well, our headmaster's always talking about the school spirit.

★

Mrs Able: How is your son getting on at school?

Mrs Cable: Well, I wouldn't say he's hopeless, but he has to cheat to come last.

★

What's everyone's favourite expression at school?

I don't know!

★

Sam: I'm not going back to school again.

Mother: Why's that?

Sam: Last week the teacher said five and five make ten. On Monday she said six and four make ten. Today she said seven and three make ten – I'm not going back until she makes up her mind.

★

Sam came home from his first day at school, threw his bag on the floor and stomped upstairs, shouting,

'I'm not going back tomorrow.'

'Why ever not, Sam?' asked his mother.

'Well, I can't read or write, and they won't let me talk, so what's the use?'

★

A little boy came home from his first day at school and his mother anxiously asked him how the day had gone.

'Nothing much happened,' he said. 'Except some lady didn't know how to spell mat. I told her.'

★

Mother: Did you enjoy your first day at school?

Sam: First day? Do you mean I have to go back tomorrow?

★

A school inspector asked the class to call out a number. 'Twenty-three,' said someone, and the inspector wrote 32 on the blackboard. 'Give me another number, please,' he said, 'Thirteen,' said another child. And the inspector wrote 31 on the blackboard. As none of the children pointed out his error, the inspector carried on, 'Another number, please.' 'Thirty-three,' shouted someone from the back, followed by 'let's see how he messes that one up!'

★

Jack: I only got 25 in arithmetic and 45 in English, but I was a knock-out in history.

Jill: What did you get?

Jack: Zero.

★

Sam: I got 100 at school today.

Mother: Well, done, Sam! Wht did you get 100 in?

Sam: Two things, actually. I got 50 in sums and 50 in spelling.

★

Father: Well, Sam, how are your marks at
   school?
Sam: Under water.
Father: What on earth do you mean?
Sam: They're below 'C' level.

★

Sam was away from school one day and when
he returned the teacher asked him if he had
brought a note from one of his parents
explaining his absence. But Sam had no note.
'Well,' said the teacher, I shall expect to
receive a note tomorrow morning from your
mother and father telling me why you were
away.'
The following morning Sam left the following
note on the teacher's desk:
'Dear Teacher, Sam was away from skool
becos he had a temprecher. Yours sinseereley,
My Mother.'

School Report

Father: Why is your school report so bad,
   Billy? The teacher seems to be saying you're
   positively stupid.
Silly Billy: Well, she would think I'm stupid —
   she's a graduate.

★

Father: Sam! Your school report is terrible!
   You've come last in *every* subject of the
   thirty boys in your class.
Sam: It could be worse, though, Dad! There
   could be more boys in the class.

★

Amy: I got a zero in one subject at school.
Zoe: Which subject was it?
Amy: Attendance.

★

What is a school report?
   A poison pen letter from your teacher.

★

Father: Sam, your school report isn't as good
   as last term. Why's that?
Sam: It's the teacher's fault, Dad.

Father: What do you mean? You've still got
   the same teacher, haven't you?
Sam: Yes. But she moved Smart Alec to the
   front row — he used to sit next to me!

School Swot

Jenny: Mum, you'll be really pleased to know
   that I won a prize at school for being the
   best swot!
Mother: Well done, Jenny!
Jenny: I killed more flies than anybody else
   in school.

School Test

Silly Billy: What did I get for my history test?
Teacher: Well, first the good news — you
   spelled your name correctly. . . .

★

A very irate mother went to see her daughter's
teacher at school one day.
'Why did you give Poppy minus one in her
test?' she asked.
'Well,' replied the teacher, 'the only thing she
wrote on the paper was her name, and she
spelled that wrong.'

School Trip

An enthusiastic music teacher was trying to
get her class to enjoy classical music, so she
arranged an outing to a famous concert hall.
To make the occasion even more special, she
treated the whole class to a soft drink, ice
cream, and a small bag of sweets each. At the

end of the concert the children were climbing into the coach to go home, all saying their thank yous.

'I'm very pleased to hear you all enjoyed yourselves,' said the teacher.

'Oh, it was lovely!' said Jenny. 'Everything except the music was great.'

Schoolwork

Sam: Mum, I'm not going to do any studying tonight. I'm just too tired.
Mother: Come along, Sam. Hard work never killed anyone.
Sam: No, and I'm not going to be the first!

Science

Science teacher: What does HN03 stand for?
Silly Billy: Um, let me think – it's on the tip of my tongue.
Science teacher: Well, spit it out at once – it's Nitric Acid!

★

Why do scientists always look into everything twice?

Because they are re-searchers.

Science Fiction

Rick: How was the science fiction film you saw?
Nick: Oh, the same old story – boy meets girl, boy loses girl, boy builds new girl.

Scientist

Why did the scientist take a ruler to bed?

Because he wanted to see how long he slept.

★

Why did the scientist have his phone disconnected?

Because he wanted to win the Nobel prize.

Scotsman

Visitor: 'You're a Scotsman, aren't you?'
Scotsman: Aye.
Visitor: What does 'I dinna ken' mean?
Scotsman: I don't know.
Visitor: I thought you said you were a Scotsman!

★

News from the Scottish Office: Angus McTavish from Inverness washed his kilt yesterday and now he can't do a fling with it.

Scrambled Egg

Why is a scrambled egg like a losing football team?

Because both are beaten.

Scratch

Aunt Adeline: Johnny, why are you scratching yourself?
Johnny: No one else knows where I itch!

Screw

Why is a cautious man like a screw?

His head stops him going too far.

Sculptor

What is a sculptor's favourite cake?

Marble.

Sea

Eve: You remind me of the sea.
Adam: Because I'm so wild, reckless and romantic?
Eve: No, because you make me sick.

★

Why is the sea like glass?

Because the waves keep breaking on the shore.

★

Why doesn't the sea ever fall over the horizon?

It's tide.

Sea Monsters

What's the favourite food of sea monsters?
  Fish and ships.

Seance

Mrs Cable, recently widowed, went to a seance to see if she could get in touch with her late husband. The medium said that would be possible, and a delighted Mrs Cable settled down to start straight away.
'What's your hurry?' asked the medium.
'I've just locked myself out of the house,' said Mrs Cable, 'and my husband's the only one that knows where the spare key is hidden.'

Sea Shells

What do you fire from underwater guns?
  Sea shells.

Seasickness

What's the best cure for seasickness?
  Bolt your food down.

★

What is seasickness?
  What a doctor does all day.

★

What's the difference between seasickness and an auction?
  One's the effects of a sail, the other is a sale of effects.

Seasons

Soppy Poppy thinks that the four seasons are: salt, mustard, vinegar, pepper.

Sea View

Hotel manager: Rooms overlooking the sea are £10 extra.
Mean guest: How much if I promise not to look?

Seconds

Paul: There are 52 weeks in the year, right?
Saul: Right.
Paul: So how many seconds are there in a year?
Saul: I don't know.
Paul: Twelve: 2nd January, 2nd February, ...

★

What do you call a Scotsman who lives in Switzerland?
  MacAlpine.

★

Jock was telling his friends all about his trip to London. 'It's a lovely place,' he said, 'but they have some really strange customs. Every night the people in the rooms around mine knocked on the walls, on the ceiling, sometimes even on the floor. I could hardly hear my bagpipes.'

Secret

A secret is something you only tell one person at a time.

★

What's too much for one, enough for two, but nothing for three?
  A secret.

★

Why did the secret agent talk into the hairdryer?
  Because it was a short-wave radio.

★

What are secret agents' favourite animals?
  Spy-ders.

★

Why is it difficult to keep a secret in the North Pole?
  Because your teeth tend to chatter.

Secretary

Why did the secretary cut her fingers off?
  Because she wanted to write shorthand.

Security Guard

Jack: I lost my job as a security guard today.
Jill: What happened?
Jack: A man held up the van. I drew my gun and told him that if he took another step towards me I'd let him have it.
Jill: What happened then?
Jack: He took another step towards me, so I let him have it. I never wanted the gun anyway.

Seeds

Customer: Are these seeds quick-growing?
Shop assistant: Certainly, sir. After planting them, stand aside!

★

What grows if you plant seeds in a pile of rubble?
  Wallflowers.

Seeing

What gadget do we use to see through a wall?
  A window.

★

Optician: What can you see out of that window?
Patient: Only the sun.
Optician: How far do you want to see, then?

Seven Seas

Who sailed the Seven Seas searching for rubbish and blubber?
  Binbag the Whaler.

Seven-Year Itch

How long does treatment last for the seven-year itch?
  Eighty-four months.

Sex Lesson

Sam came home from school one day and his parents anxiously asked how his first sex lesson had gone.
'Oh,' said Sam, 'it was useless – we only did the theory today.'

Shakespeare

What is Shakespeare's most popular play in the East?
  Asia Like It.

★

Shakespeare (very excitedly): I've written a new play today! I'm going to call it *Julius, Grab the Girl Quickly Before She Gets Away.*
Ann Hathaway: That's a long title, isn't it? Why don't you just call it *Julius Seize Her?*

★

Which Shakespearean play was written for baby pigs?
  Hamlet.

★

Teacher: Why was Shakespeare such a good writer?
Silly Billy: Because where there's a Will, there's a way.

★

Tourist: Is this the right road for Shakespeare's birthplace?
Local: Yes, go straight on. But you needn't hurry. He's been dead for years.

Sharing

A visitor gave Jack a large apple and a small apple, and told him to share them with his sister. So Jack gave Jill the small apple.
'Well!' said Jill. 'If I'd been given these apples I'd have given you the large one and eaten the small one.'
'That's what you've got,' said Jack, 'what are you complaining about?'

265

Shark

What kind of shark is the most cunning?
  The loan shark.

★

Amy: I saw a man-eating shark at the marine show.
Zoe: So what? I saw a man eating herring in the restaurant.

★

What's another name for a giant legal shark?
  The Lord Chief Jawstice.

★

Who eats its victims two by two?
  Noah's shark.

★

Why did the shark not attack the woman who fell overboard?
  Because it was a man-eating shark.

Sheep

What would you get if you crossed a sheep with an octopus?
  A sweater with eight sleeves.

★

What keeps sheep warm in winter?
  Central bleating.

★

What do lady sheep call their coats?
  Ewe-niforms.

★

A man went in to a butcher's shop and said, 'Have you got a sheep's head?'
'No,' replied the butcher, 'That's just the way I part my hair.'

★

Why do white sheep eat more than black ones?
  Because there are more white sheep in the world.

★

Paul: Do you know it takes three sheep to make one jumper?
Saul: I didn't even know sheep could knit.

★

Patient: Doctor, I've just swallowed a sheep.
Doctor: How do you feel?
Patient: Very ba-a-a-ad.

★

What would you get if you crossed a sheep with a rainstorm?
  A wet blanket.

★

Where do sheep go on holiday?
  The Baahaamas.

Sherlock Holmes

Sherlock Holmes, the amazing solver of mysterious crimes, took his companion Dr Watson completely by surprise one day by saying, 'Ah, Watson, wearing your red thermals again today!'
'Why, Holmes, however did you deduce that?' asked Watson.
'Elementary, my dear Watson,' came Holmes's reply. 'You forgot to put your trousers on.'

★

What did Sherlock Holmes say to Dr Watson about The Case of the Grass-stained Carpet?
  I haven't a clue.

Ship

How does a ship hear?
  Through its engineers.

★

What is the most untidy place on board ship?
  The Officers' Mess.

★

Where do sick ships go?
  To the dock.

★

What do you call a ship's diary written on 25 December?

A Yule log.

Shipwreck

Two sailors who were shipwrecked clambered to safety on an iceberg. 'Do you think we'll be here for ages?' asked the first.

'Oh, no,' said the second, 'look, here comes the Titanic.'

★

What did they call prehistoric ship disasters?

Tyrannosaurus wrecks.

Shirt

What did the boy do when his grandmother sent him a shirt for his birthday that was too small?

He wrote a short thank you letter, finishing, 'I would write more, but I'm all choked up.'

★

Bill: Have you heard the story about the dirty shirt?

Ben: No.

Bill: That's one on you.

★

Andy: You're just like a shirt button.

Zak: Why's that?

Andy: You keep popping off.

★

Mr Able: The laundry must have sent us back someone else's shirt. The collar is so tight I can hardly breathe.

Mrs Able: Don't be silly, you've put your head through a button-hole.

★

What do you get if you cross a shirt with a piece of jewellery?

A ring around the collar.

★

Shish Kabob

What is the correct name for a shish kabob?

A shish ka-Robert.

Shoemaking

A little boy was watching a shoemaker at work.

'What do you fix the shoes with?' he asked.

'Hide,' said the shoemaker.

'What?' asked the boy.

'Hide, I said,' said the shoemaker, getting cross.

'What for?' asked the boy.

'Hide! The cow's out at the back.'

'But I'm not afraid of cows,' said the little boy.

Shoes

What runs around all day and lies at night with its tongue hanging out?

A training shoe.

★

Bill: I wish I was in your shoes.

Ben: Why's that?

Bill: Because mine have holes in them.

★

Mother: Poppy, have you put your shoes on yet?

Soppy Poppy: Yes, Mum, all but one!

★

Why do people always put their right shoe on first?

Well, it would be silly to put the wrong shoe on, wouldn't it!

★

Why is a tight shoe like good summer weather?

Because they both make corn grow.

★

Did you hear about the man who threw away his shoes because he thought they were sticking their tongues out at him?

★

267

Blacksmith: So you want to work here. Can you shoe horses?
Silly Billy: No, but I can shoo flies.

Shoot!

Mr and Mrs Cable were on safari in the African jungle. They were on their way back to camp, picking their way carefully, when suddenly a lion sprang out in front of them, grabbed Mrs Cable in its mouth and started dragging her back to his lair.

'Shoot! Shoot!' she screamed.

'I can't!' shouted back Mr Cable. 'I've run out of film!'

★

Gunman: Your time's up, I'm going to shoot you.
Man: Why?
Gunman: I've always said I'd shoot anyone who looked like me.
Man: And I look like you?
Gunman: Yes.
Man: Shoot, please!

★

Bill: I went shooting with my Dad yesterday! We got four pheasant and a potfer.
Ben: What's a potfer?
Bill: Cooking the pheasant.

★

Butcher: I'm sorry, sir, we don't have any pheasant in today. How about a nice chicken?
Customer: Don't be ridiculous! How can I go home and tell my wife I shot a chicken?

Shop

When is a shop like a boat?
  When it has sales.

Shopkeeper

Why did the shopkeeper put bells on his scales?
  So that they would jingle all the weigh.

Shoplifter

Where would you find a stupid shoplifter?
  Squashed under the shop.

★

Did you hear about the dopey shoplifter who stole a free sample?

Shopping

Husband: Were the shops crowded because of the sales?
Wife: So crowded I saw two women trying on the same dress.

★

Mrs Able: I never know what to cook for dinner these days.
Mrs Cable: Why don't you kick the supermarket shelf and see what falls off?

★

What is the study of shopping called?
  Buy-ology.

★

Amy: I got this dress for an absurd price.
Zoe: You mean for a ridiculous figure.

★

A fairly large lady went shopping one day but, despite the efforts of the salesgirl, could find nothing she liked.

'I should like to see just one dress that fits me,' said the customer.

'So would I,' said the salesgirl.

★

A woman had spent half an hour in a shop opening and closing every suitcase in the luggage department. When there was only one remaining, she said to the sales assistant, 'I'm not buying anything, you know – I'm only looking for a friend.'

To which the bored assistant replied, 'Do go ahead and look in that one if you think she's in it.'

★

Customer: I'm looking for something cheap and nasty to give my mother-in-law as a birthday present.

Sales girl: I've got just the thing, sir. My father-in-law.

Short Circuit

How do you fix a short circuit?

Lengthen it.

Short-Sighted

Did you hear about the man who was so short-sighted he couldn't get to sleep unless he counted elephants?

Shotgun

A city man asked a farmer why there were two barrels on his shotgun.

'So that if I miss with the first I can get the creature with the second,' said the farmer.

'Oh. Why don't you fire with the other first, then?'

Shower

A man telephoned the Meteorological Office one evening and said, 'How about a shower tonight?' and got the reply,

'That's fine by us. You have one if you want one.'

Show Jumper

How did the champion show jumper break his nose?

He jumped against the clock.

Show-Off

Interviewer: And when you had your big success in Paris, did you manage to see some sights? The Venus de Milo, for instance?

Silly celebrity: See her! I shook hands with her!

★

Tom: That Dick is such a show-off.

Harry: Well, tell him he should be on the stage – sweeping it!

★

Why did the circus show-off throw a bucketful of water in to the ring?

Because he wanted to make a big splash.

Shy

What makes people shy?

Coconuts.

★

Did you hear about the girl who was so shy she went into a cupboard to change her mind?

Sick

Jenny: Mum, I'm not going to school today.

Mother: Why not?

Jenny: I feel sick.

Mother: Where do you feel sick?

Jenny: In school.

Sideburns

What are sideburns?

What you get when your electric blanket is too hot.

Side-Splitting

What do you do if you split your sides laughing?

Run until you get a stitch.

Signature

Amy: What's a signature?

Zoe: I don't know.

Amy: A baby swan's autograph.

Signs

Sign seen on a causeway:
   When this sign is under water, the road is closed to traffic.

★

Sign seen outside a cinema:
Showing now: 'The Strongmen', featuring Samson, Hercules, Goliath. ALL WEAK.

★

A fishmonger was painted a sign saying 'Fresh Fish Sold Here Today' above his shop. A well-meaning passer-by stopped to watch him and said, 'You don't need to put up "Today" do you? I mean, whenever you're selling the fish it will always be today!'
'That's true,' said the fishmonger, 'thank you.'
'And you don't need "Here" either – you're not selling it anywhere else, are you?'
'No, I'm not,' said the fishmonger.
'And unless you're giving the fish away, you don't need to put up "Sold" either, do you?'
'No, I don't,' replied the fishmonger.
'And you don't need "Fresh" – you wouldn't sell stale fish, would you?'
'No, certainly not! said the fishmonger. 'You really have saved me a lot of time and trouble.'
'Oh, one last thing,' said the man. 'I wouldn't bother to put up "Fish" at all – I could smell it as I turned the corner.'

★

Sign seen outside a shoe shop:
   Boots and shoes polished inside.

★

Sign seen outside a newly-opened shop:
   Don't go elsewhere to be robbed – try us first!

★

Sign seen outside a composer's studio:
   Out Chopin, Bach in a minuet.

★

Sign seen outside photographer's studio:
For sale: Camera stand for photographer with three legs.

★

Sign seen outside a country village:
We welcome careful drivers.
One person is knocked down in this village every 30 minutes and he's getting very tired of it.

★

Sign seen outside a butcher's:
William White butchers pigs like his father.

★

Sign seen in wrecker's yard:
   Rust in Peace.

★

Outside a dry cleaner's specialising in gloves:
   We clean your dirty kids.

★

Sign seen outside a barber's:
Hair cut for 50p. Children for 25p.

★

Sign seen outside a hotel:
Workers wanted – only the inn-experienced need apply.

★

Sign seen outside a music shop:
Violins for sale.
Cheap.
No strings attached.

★

Sign seen on newly seeded lawn:
Dogs beware, Vicious man.

★

Sign seen outside gas board office:
Wanted: boy to trace gas leaks by candlelight. Must be willing to travel.

★

Sign seen outside a stationer's:
Calendars and Diaries For Sale – One Year Guarantee.

★

Sign seen outside a health farm:
The world is in terrible shape –
but you needn't be!

House for sale:
Within striking distance of local engineering works.

★

Sign on house: Trumpet for sale.
Sign on neighbouring house: HOORAY!

★

Sign seen outside a chemist's:
Cough and cold? Try our cough medicine.
You'll never be better!

★

Sign seen at a cemetery:
Due to a strike, grave-digging will be done by a skeleton crew.

★

Sign seen in a restaurant window:
Eat now – pay waiter.

★

Sign seen at a wig-maker's shop:
If your hair isn't becoming to you,
it should be coming to us!

★

Sign seen in the underworld:
Earn cash in your spare time: blackmail your friends!

★

Sign seen outside a funeral parlour:
Satisfaction guaranteed or your mummy back.

★

Sign seen outside a butcher's shop:
Honest scales – no two weighs about it.

★

Sign in the window of a health food store:
Closed on account of sickness.

★

Sign seen outside a butcher's shop:
Pleased to meet you and meat to please you.

★

Sign seen outside a tyre shop:
We skid you not.

Sign seen outside an estate agent's:
Lots for little.

★

Sign seen at a golf club:
Back soon. Gone to tee.

★

Sign seen outside a hairdresser's:
We curl up and dye for you.

★

For sale: delicate Victorian porcelain statuette, belonging to elderly lady only slightly cracked.

Silence

The proud parents brought home their new baby and boasted to everyone that he was as good as gold and as quiet a mouse. He never woke them up as a baby but as he grew older the parents began to worry a little because he never made a sound. One day, when the boy was ten years old, he suddenly said,
'May I have some sugar, please.'
His father was very shocked and asked, 'Why have you never spoken a word in ten years?'
'Well,' said the ten-year-old, 'up until now everything was just fine!'

Silver

King Midas sat on gold – so who sat on silver?
  The Lone Ranger.

Singer

There was once a singer who gave an open-air concert. He was so bad that a dozen litter bins got up and walked away.

★

When is a pop singer not a pop singer?
  When he's a little hoarse.

★

Two singers were about to go on stage when one of them had a terrible coughing fit.
'Are you all right?' asked the other.
'I think I've got a frog in my throat,' choked the first.

'Well I think you should let the frog sing – it's got a much better voice than you.'

Singing

Why is a girl learning to sing like a man opening a tin of sardines?

Because they both have trouble with the key.

★

Why did Soppy Poppy stand on a ladder when she sang a song?

So she could reach the high notes.

★

Amy: Didn't the voice teacher say your singing was heavenly?

Zoe: We-ell-ll – she did say it was like nothing on earth.

★

There was once a man who could not stop singing. He was such a nuisance to everyone that eventually he was told that if he did not stop singing he would be shot at dawn by a firing squad. Still he would not stop, and so the firing squad got ready. As is the custom, he was offered one final wish before his execution and of course the man asked if he could sing a last song. His wish was granted and he started to sing: 'There were 100,000 green bottles hanging on a wall . . .'.

★

Johnny: What does your father sing in the bath?

Jenny: Pop music.

★

Rick: I can sing the 'Star Spangled Banner' for hours.

Nick: That's nothing! I can sing 'Stars and Stripes Forever'.

★

Singer: Did you notice how my voice filled the hall?

Critic: Oh, yes. And did you notice how the people left the hall to make room for it?

Adam: Can you sing top C?

Eve: No, I sing low-sy!

★

Rick: Don't you think I sing with feeling?

Nick: No. You wouldn't sing if you had any feeling.

★

Amy: The last time I sang, my voice fell on hundreds of ears.

Zoe: Were you singing in a cornfield then?

Sinking Ship

Andy: Have you heard about the ship loaded with red paint that crashed in to a brown buoy?

Zak: What happened?

Andy: The crew were marooned.

★

Why is a sinking ship like a prisoner?

Because they both need bailing out.

Sisters

Bill: My three sisters all work in the same restaurant.

Ben: What do they do?

Bill: One washes up, one dries up, and the third one picks up the pieces.

★

Sister Suzie sitting on a thistle – how many S's in that?

There aren't any S's in THAT!

Sistine Chapel

Where did Michelangelo paint the Sistine Chapel?

On his back.

Skating

Paul: How long have you been learning to skate?

Saul: Oh, about a dozen sittings.

272

Skeleton

What's a skeleton?
A person with their outsides off and insides out.

★

Why didn't the skeleton want to go to school?
Because his heart wasn't in it.

★

What is a skeleton?
Someone who went on a diet and forgot to say 'when'.

★

Why didn't the skeletons cross the road?
Because he didn't have the guts.

★

What would you do if you saw a skeleton having a good time?
Jump out of your skin and join him.

★

What do you call a skeleton in a kilt?
Bony Prince Charlie.

★

Why didn't the skeleton go to the disco?
Because he had nobody to dance with.

★

What did the angry skeleton say to his friend?
I've got a bone to pick with you.

★

What do skeletons have at their balls?
A rattling good time!

★

Why do skeletons drink so much milk?
Because it's good for the bones.

Skewered

What did the meat say just before it was put on a skewer?
Oh! Spear me! Spear me!

★

Skier

What do people sing when it's a skier's birthday?
Ski's a Jolly Good Fellow.

Skin-Diving

Which animal goes skin-diving?
A mosquito.

Skirts

How short can girls' skirts get?
They'll always be above two feet.

Skunk

Did you hear about the blind skunk who fell in love with a sewerage pipe?

★

What fur do you get from a skunk?
As fur as possible.

★

How do you stop a skunk smelling?
Put a clothes peg on its nose.

★

What did the skunk say when the wind changed direction?
Ah, it's all coming back to me now.

★

Why did the skunk take an aspirin?
Because he had a stinking headache.

★

Why is a skunk like a chauffeur?
Because they both drive you away.

★

Why is a skunk in the house like a fire?
The sooner you put it out the better.

★

What's the difference between a skunk and a rabbit?
The skunk uses cheaper deodorant.

★

What did one skunk say to the other?
  And so do you?

★

Paul: Why do skunks argue?
Saul: I give up.
Paul: Because they like raising a stink.

★

What did one skunk say to the other when they were cornered?
  Let us spray.

★

How many skunks does it take to make a big stinker?
  A phew.

★

What is a skunk's best defence against enemies?
  Instinct.

Sky High

Why is the sky so high?
  So the birds won't bang their heads.

Sledge

A mother was dressing her son warmly against the winter weather. He was making a fuss about having to wait while she put on layers of clothes so she told him a little story. 'Once upon a time, there was a little boy who wanted to go outside and play in the snow with his sledge. He wouldn't put on a coat or his gloves and he caught a chill, the chill turned into flu, and the little boy died.'
'Oh, Mum,' said the mother's little boy, 'whatever happened to the sledge?'

★

Andy: Can I share your sledge?
Zak: Sure, we can go halves.
Andy: That's really great!
Zak: I'll have it going downhill and you can have it going uphill.

Sleep

How do you know when someone's sleeping like a log?
  When you hear them sawing.

★

Bill: Which side do you sleep on, left or right?
Ben: I sleep on both sides. All of me goes to sleep at the same time.

★

Andy: I woke up this morning feeling terrible. My head was spinning and the room was going round and round.
Zak: You must have slept like a top.

★

Amy: Are you a light sleeper?
Zoe: No, I sleep in the dark.

★

Paul: Why do you sleep under your old car?
Saul: Because I want to wake up oily in the morning.

★

What knocks you out every night but doesn't harm you?
  Sleep.

★

Rick: I haven't slept for days!
Nick: Why ever not?
Rick: Because I sleep at night.

★

Why couldn't the boy sleep in class?
  Because the teacher talked too loudly.

★

To which question can you never answer, 'Yes.'?
  'Are you asleep?'

★

Amy: I bet I know where you're going tonight!
Zoe: All right, where am I going tonight?
Amy: To sleep.

Sleep-Walking

Patient: Doctor, have you got a cure for sleep-walking?

Doctor: Have you tried putting thumb tacks on your bedroom carpet?

★

Paul: Do you still walk in your sleep?

Saul: Not any more. I take my bus fare with me when I go to bed.

Sliding

Mother: Jenny! I wouldn't slide down the banisters like that if I was you.

Jenny: All right, Mum. How would you slide down them?

Sling

Andy: Why is your arm in a sling?

Zak: Oh, I get all the breaks.

Slippers

What kind of shoes are made out of banana skins?

Slippers.

Smashing!

Paul: Mum thinks Dad's a real smasher.

Saul: That's nice.

Paul: That's why she never lets him do the washing up.

Smile!

What do people like the more you crack it?

A smile.

Smog

Paul: There's one good thing about smog.

Saul: Oh, what's that?

Paul: You can at least see what you're breathing.

Smoke Signals

A settler came across a lone Indian on the prairie sending up smoke signals.

'What's the matter?' asked the settler.

'We have no water,' said the Indian.

'Are you praying for rain?' asked the settler.

'No,' replied the Indian, 'I'm sending for the plumber.'

★

An Indian chief was travelling home to his reservation from the town when his car broke down. So he resorted to old Indian customs and climbed up a hill, lit a fire and sent a smoke signal to his tribe asking for money.

The tribe signalled back asking why he needed money. Before the chief could reply, nuclear scientists exploded an atom bomb in the valley below him. A huge column of smoke climbed into the sky and filled out into a mushroom shape. Back came hurried signals from the reservation: 'All right, we only asked! The money's on its way!'

Smoking

Mother: Why are you home so early from school?

Johnny: The teacher sent me home because the boy sitting next to me was smoking.

Mother: But why were you sent home if he was smoking?

Johnny: Because I set light to him.

★

Two men were discussing cigarette brands, and as they lit their cigarettes discovered that they smoked the same brand. 'Oh,' said the first smoker, 'do you save the coupons? I never bother.'

'Of course I do,' said the second smoker. 'How do you think I could afford my artificial lung?'

Why is a chocolate bar no substitute for cigarette smoking?
  Because a chocolate bar won't light up.

Snails
What do you do about two fighting snails?
  Let them slug it out.

★

Waiter: Yes, we're famous for snails here, sir.
Diner: I know. I'm being served by one.

★

One day towards the end of winter a snail started to climb an apple tree, much to the amusement of some sparrows who were playing in a nearby tree. After much laughter they took pity on him and one flew over and said,
'Don't you know there aren't any apples on the tree yet?'
'Yes,' said the snail, 'but there will be by the time I get up there.'

Snake
What's green and slimy and goes hith?
  A snake with a lisp.

★

What happened to the snake with a cold?
  She adder viper nose.

★

A little boy was out playing when he saw a grass snake for the first time. He ran inside, calling, 'Mother! Mother! Here's a tail without a body.'

★

A man who kept pet snakes had to go to hospital when one of them bit him on the leg. 'Did you put anything on it?' asked the doctor. 'No, replied the man, 'he liked it just the way it was.'

★

Amy: A snake just snapped at me.
Zoe: Snakes don't snap!
Amy: This one did – it was a garter snake.

Why can you never play jokes on snakes?
  Because you can't pull their legs.

★

Said one snake to another: Are we supposed to be poisonous?
Second snake: Why?
First snake: I just bit my lip.

Sneezing
Jack: Why do you put your hands up to your mouth when you sneeze?
Jill: To catch my teeth.

Sniffing
A man on a crowded bus was becoming increasingly irritated by the little boy next to him who was sniffing. Eventually he couldn't stand it any more and asked,
'Haven't you got a handkerchief?'
'Yes,' he replied. 'But I'm not allowed to lend it to strangers.'

Snooker
Bill: Did you hear about the snooker-playing thief?
Ben: How did the police find out he played snooker?
Bill: Because he pocketed the ball.

★

What has six legs, is green and can kill you if it jumps at you.
  An angry snooker table.

Snoring
Bill: I used to snore so loudly that I woke myself up every night.
Ben: Have you cured your snoring now?
Bill: Yes. I sleep in the next room.

★

Paul: Do you always snore?
Saul: Only when I'm asleep.

Snow

What is Indian snow?
Apache here, Apache there.

★

What is heavy Indian snow?
  Apache everywhere.

★

Three men got stuck in a snow drift. Only two got their hair wet. Why?
  The other one was bald!

Snowdrop

Why did the snow-drop?
  Because it heard the cro-cuss.

Snowflake

What's white and goes up?
  A silly snowflake.

Snowman

What do you get if you cross a snowman and a man-eating shark?
  Frostbite.

Snow White

Who was Snow White's brother?
  Egg white. Get the yoke?

Snuff

Mr Able: I'm closing up my snuff shop at the end of the month.
Mr Cable: Why's that?
Mr Able: I'm tired of sticking my business up other people's noses.

Soap

Customer: I'd like a bar of soap, please.
Salesgirl: Scented or unscented?
Customer: Oh no, I'll take it with me.

Soapflakes

Paul: Mum made a terrible mistake at breakfast time this morning. She gave Dad soapflakes instead of cornflakes!
Saul: Was he very angry?
Paul: Just foaming at the mouth.

Soccer

Captain: Why didn't you stop the ball?
Goalie: What do you think the net is for?

Socks

Silly Billy: You sold me socks with holes in them!
Sales assistant: Yes, sir. How else would you get your feet in them?

★

How can you tell a pair of golf socks from an ordinary pair?
  They usually have a hole in one.

★

Mother: Why have you got your socks inside out, Johnny?
Johnny: Because there are holes on the other side.

★

Mr Able: These socks have holes. Will you mend them for me?
Mrs Able: Have you bought the mink wrap for me yet?
Mr Able: No, I haven't.
Mrs Able: Well, if you don't give a wrap, I don't give a darn.

Soft and Sweet

Keep your words soft and sweet –
you never know when you might have to eat them!

Soldiers

Where do you find baby soldiers?
In the infant-ry.

★

Why is a cowardly soldier like butter?
Because they both run when exposed to fire.

★

Why didn't the soldier go to the end of the line as he was told?
Because there was someone standing there already.

Son Day

Andy: Have you noticed that there's a Mother's Day, a Father's Day, but no Son Day?
Zak: That's because there's a Sunday in every week.

Song

What's the song of the world's most conceited man?
The best things in life are me.

★

What kind of song do you sing in a car?
A cartoon!

★

What kind of song is 'Soap, soap, soap, soap, soap'?
Five bars.

Son-In-Law

Sam went to ask for his girlfriend's hand in marriage and was very carefully questioned by the girl's father. At the end of half an hour the old man said,

'So, you want to be my son-in-law!'
'Not really,' said Sam, 'but if I want to marry your daughter, what choice have I got?'

Sons

How can two boys be born on the same day, to the same parents, and look, talk, think and behave alike yet not be twins?
They're two of a set of triplets.

Soup

Customer: Waiter, this soup tastes funny.
Waiter: So laugh, sir.

★

How do you make gold soup?
Put 14 carrots in it.

★

Customer: Waiter, what soup is this?
Waiter: It's bean soup, sir.
Customer: I don't care what it was, I want to know what it is now.

★

Jack: Will you join me in a bowl of soup?
Jill: Do you really think there's room for both of us?

★

At Brownie camp, the strict Brown Owl insisted on really good food for everybody. One day she stopped two Brownies who were carrying a large soup bowl, saying, 'Just a minute, I want to taste that.' The Brownies started to say something, but Brown Owl butted in saying, 'No arguments, please. Get me a spoon.' One of the Brownies got a spoon and Brown Owl took a mouthful which she spat out shouting, 'This isn't soup!'
'That's what we were trying to tell you, Brown Owl,' said one of the Brownies, 'it's washing-up water!'

★

Daddy Bear staring into empty bowl: Somebody ate my soup.
Baby Bear: And somebody ate my soup!

278

Mummy Bear: Stop complaining – I haven't even made the soup yet.

★

Jill: How do you manage to eat soup through your moustache?
Jack: Well, it is a bit of a strain.

South Pacific
What do fish sing in the South Pacific?
  Salmon Chanted Evening.

Soviet Agents
Why do Soviet agents always work fast?
  Because they are rush'n'.

Spaceman
What do you call a crazy spaceman?
  An astronut.

★

What's a spaceman's favourite game?
  Astronaughts and crosses.

★

Experienced astronaut to novice: Let me give you a tip about travelling in space: don't look down.

★

Why did the spaceman walk?
  Because he missed the bus.

Spaceship
What do you get if you cross a miserable man with a spaceship?
  A moan rocket.

★

Man: How does it feel to hurtle through space?
  Astronaut: It hurtles!

Spade
Did you hear about the man who believed in calling a spade a spade, until he tripped over one in the dark?

Spaghetti
What is fake spaghetti?
  Mockoroni.

★

Where would you find exploding spaghetti?
  At the Minestrone of Defence.

★

How do Italians eat spaghetti?
  Like everyone else – they put it in their mouths.

★

What did the spaghetti say to the bolognaise?
  That's enough of your sauce.

★

How long do you cook spaghetti?
  Oh, about 20 centimetres.

★

Who invented spaghetti?
  Someone who used his noodle.

Spanish Farmer
What did the Spanish farmer say to his chickens?
  Olé!

Spectacles
Patient: Doctor, will I be able to read with these new spectacles?
Doctor: Yes, you will.
Patient: That's wonderful news! I never knew how to read before, you see.

★

World traveller: There are some spectacles in the world one can never forget.
Mrs Silly: Would you get me some, please? I'm always forgetting mine.

Optician: Here are your new glasses, sir. But only wear them when you're working.
Patient: Oh, that could be tricky.
Optician: Why's that?
Patient: I'm a boxer.

★

Soppy Poppy: Mum, Grandma ought to get glasses.
Mother: What makes you say that?
Soppy Poppy: She's in the kitchen watching Grandad's long john's in the washing machine.
Mother: Well, that's all right, isn't it?
Soppy Poppy: I suppose so, except she thinks she's watching the wrestling on television!

★

Doctor: You need glasses.
Patient: How do you know?
Doctor: I could tell as soon as you walked through the window.

Speed

When can you move as fast as a train?
  When you're inside it.

★

What's white on top, has sleek lines and leaves others standing at traffic lights?
  A turbo-charged grannie.

★

Captain: This boat can make 20 knots an hour.

Passenger: If it does, how long does it take the crew to untie them?

Speeding

Judge: The charges are that you ran over this man and you were speeding.
Motorist: Yes, your Honour. I was hurrying to get over him.

★

Policeman: I'm going to have to arrest you for speeding, sir. You were doing over 70 miles an hour.
Motorist: Rubbish! I've only been in the car for 10 minutes.

★

Traffic policeman: Did you not see the speed limit sign?
Motorist: No, officer. I was driving too fast to see it.

★

A man driving at over 100 miles per hour on the motorway was given the signal to pull over by the traffic police.
'Sorry,' he said, 'was I driving too fast?'
'Oh, no, sir,' said the policeman. 'Just flying too low.'

★

Policeman (to speeding motorist he had flagged down): You were exceeding the speed limit, sir. Why is that?
Motorist: Well, officer, my brakes are bad and I wanted to get home before I had an accident.

Spelling

Teacher: Sam, your spelling test was very poor. For instance, r-a-i-n-d-e-a-r does not spell 'reindeer'.
Sam: What does it spell then?

★

How do you spell 'hungry horse' in just four letters?
  M-T-G-G.

English teacher: Spell 'needle', please Sam.
Sam: N-e-i-.
Teacher: No, Sam, there's no 'i' in needle.
Sam: What a rotten needle!

★

Teacher: Billy, will you spell 'pole', please?
Silly Billy: P-O-L.
Teacher: That's not all. What comes at the end?
Silly Billy: Telephone wires. But I can't spell that yet.

★

Teacher: Poppy, how do you spell 'rain'?
Soppy Poppy: R-A-N-E.
Teacher: That's the worst spell of rain we've had for ages!

★

Teacher: Poppy, you've put two Ts in 'rabbit', and there should only be one.
Soppy Poppy: Sorry, miss – which one should I have left out?

★

Andy: Can you spell blind bird?
Zak: Yes. B-l-i-n-d b-i-r-d.
Andy: Wrong. It's b-l-n-d b-r-d. It it had two I's it wouldn't be blind!

★

Which is easier to spell – here or elsewhere?
  Elsewhere – because it has more ease (E's).

★

How can you spell contentment in four letters?
  A-P-N-S.

★

Teacher: How do you spell 'Crocodile', Billy?
Silly Billy: K-r-o-k-o-d-i-a-l.
Teacher: That's not how the dictionary spells it.
Silly Billy: But you didn't ask me how the dictionary spells it!

★

Spell 'mousetrap' in three letters.
C-a-t.

Johnny: Mum, how do you spell 'arry?
Mother: Do you mean Harry?
Johnny: No, I've written the H already.

★

Teacher: What does n-e-w spell, Billy?
Silly Billy: New.
Teacher: Good, that's right. Now if I put a 'k' in front of it, what does that spell?
Silly Billy: Canoe?

★

Teacher: Poppy, can you spell banana?
Soppy Poppy: I'm not sure. I can start, but I don't know when to stop.

★

New neighbour: You say your son is only four, and he can spell his name backwards and forwards? What's his name?
Proud mother: Otto.

Spending

Maths teacher: Billy, if apples were 35p a pound, how many pounds would you get for £1.40?
Silly Billy: None, sir.
Maths teacher: What do you mean, none?
Silly Billy: I'd go to the cinema with £1.40, sir.

Spiders

A very young girl – call her Emma –
Was seized with a terrible tremor.
  She had swallowed a spider
  Which stung her inside her –
Gadzooks, what an awful dilemma!

★

Sarah Spider: I don't know what to get my husband for Christmas.
Samantha Spider: Do what I did – get him four pairs of socks.

★

What do you call two spiders who have just got married?
  Newly-webs.

Spinning Top

Have you heard about the new spinning top that's also a whistle?

Now you can blow your top. . . .

Spirits

Who serves the spirits on an aeroplane?

The air ghostess.

Splinters

Which book can you get splinters from?

A log-book.

Sponge

What is full of holes but still holds water?

A sponge.

Sponge Cake

Mrs Able: Have a piece of sponge cake, dear?

Mr Able: Thank you. It's a bit hard (chewing).

Mrs Able: I wonder why? I bought the sponge at the chemist's only this morning.

Spooks

How do spooks get to work each night?

On ghost trains.

Spoon

What happened to the boy who swallowed a spoon?

He couldn't stir.

Sport

Amy: I love playing golf – I could go on playing like this forever.

Zoe: Goodness! Don't you ever want to improve?

★

Son: Were you good at sport at school, Dad?

Father: I shall never forget the time I ran fifteen hundred metres in ten seconds. And if I ever find out who put those wasps in my shorts, I'll kill them!

★

Which is the quietest sport?

Bowling – because you can hear a pin drop.

★

Sports teacher: Poppy, you really are useless at sports. You'll never be first at anything!

Soppy Poppy: Oh, sir! I'm first to get changed after sports!

★

Sportsmaster: Now, who can tell me – if you have an umpire in cricket, and a referee in football, what do you have in bowls?

Silly Billy: Goldfish, sir.

Sports Fan

A sports fan went to an away match and stopped to have a drink at the local pub before he went home. As he stepped outside he saw that someone had painted his car in the away team's colours. He marched back in to the pub, and shouted, 'All right then? Who painted my car?' As he looked around, a very tall man stood up and said,

'I did. What about it?'

'Oh,' stammered the visitor. 'I just wanted to tell you that it's dried beautifully!'

Sports Kit

A little boy was sent home from school for not bringing his sports kit. He came back in the afternoon soaking wet. 'What's the meaning of this?' asked the football trainer.

'Well,' said the little boy. 'You told me I had to do football in my sports kit, but it was all in the wash.'

Sports Stadium

Paul: How many people would fit into the world's biggest empty sports stadium?

Saul: One. After that it wouldn't be empty any more.

Spring Song

Adam: Have you heard the spring song?

Eve: Is that the one that goes 'Boinnngg! Boinnngg!?

Sprinting

Rick: I'm champion at school of the 100 metres.

Nick: What do you do it in?

Rick: Vest, shorts, socks and training shoes.

Nick: Ha, ha! I still bet I could beat you with a yard start.

Rick: Oh yes? Where?

Nick: Up a ladder!

Spy

Why does a spy prefer to work on a sunny day rather than on a rainy day?

Because he can then see where his shadow is.

★

Where do spies shop?

At the snoopermarket.

★

Who was the world's first underwater spy?

James Pond.

★

Where would a spy deliver a message in his sleep?

In a pillow box.

★

What do you call a frog spy?

A croak and dagger agent.

★

What spy hangs around department stores?

A counter spy.

★

Jack: Did you hear about the dancer who became a spy?

Jill: No – how?

Jack: His phone was tapped.

★

What's the most common illness among spies?

A code in the nose.

★

Why did the bald spy throw away his keys?

Because he didn't have any locks.

Squash

Andy: My doctor says I can't play squash.

Zak: Oh – he's played with you too, has he?

★

Paul: Squash is my favourite game.

Saul: Why's that?

Paul: My two brothers are in that racket.

★

Mr Able: Are you going to be putting up your garage shelves this afternoon?

Mr Cable: Yes, that's right.

Mr Able: Good. Can I borrow your squash racket, then? You won't be needing it!

Squid

A whale came across a squid in the ocean one day.

'I feel terrible,' said the squid. 'I've got such a headache.'

'Well,' said the whale, 'when I have a headache I swim further down.'

'That sounds like a good idea,' said the squid, and they both swam to the depths of the ocean, where they came across a shark.

'Hello, shark,' said the whale. 'Here's the sick squid I owe you.'

Squirrel

What's the best way to catch a squirrel?

Climb up a tree and act like a nut.

★

Where do squirrels go when they have a nervous breakdown?

The nuthouse.

★

Which animals use nutcrackers?

Squirrels with no teeth.

Stag

What did the stag say to his children?
  Hurry up, deer.

Stagecoach

Paul: I once knew a man who drove a stage-coach that didn't have any wheels.
Saul: What held it up?
Paul: Bandits.

Stamp

What did the stamp say to the envelope?
  I've become attached to you.

★

What can travel around the world while staying in the same corner?
  A stamp.

★

Why are stamps such weaklings?
  Because they always take a licking.

★

Post Office clerk: Here's the last of your stamps, sir.
Customer (laden with parcels): Do I have to stick it on myself?
Post Office clerk: Oh, no, sir. On the envelope.

★

Post office clerk: Madam, you've put too many stamps on this letter.
Customer: Oh dear, it won't go too far, will it?

Star

When is a window like a star?
  When it's a skylight.

★

Paul: That star over there is Mars.
Saul: Which one's Pa's, then?

★

Johnny was caught cheating in astronomy class. When the teacher asked him to describe the stars he started to hit himself on the head.

★

What do you get if you cross a group of stars with a silver cup?
  A constellation prize.

★

What stars go to gaol?
  Shooting stars.

Statue of Liberty

Tourist: Why are the fingers of the Statue of Liberty 11 inches long?
Exhausted guide: Because, madam, if they were 12 inches they would be a foot.

★

Why does the Statue of Liberty stand in New York harbour?
  Because she can't sit down.

Stealing

I'm learning to steal – a cat burglar is teaching miaow.

★

Judge: William Barrett, you were arrested for stealing a hippopotamus. Why did you steal a hippopotamus?
Silly Billy: My father once told me, 'Willy, if you're going to steal, then steal big.'

284

Sam: Dad, what would happen if I stole a lamb?
Father: You'd go to prison, Sam.
Sam: But you would feed him while I was away, wouldn't you?

★

Judge: You are charged with stealing a car.
Prisoner: I only took it for a joke, sir.
Judge: Where did you take it?
Prisoner: Over to France, sir.
Judge: That's taking a joke too far. Fined!

Steeplejack
Have you heard about the man on a steeple who was told the joke about the missing ladder?
   He fell for it.

Steps
Paul: If a lion were stalking you, what steps would you take?
Saul: The longest steps I could.

Stew
What do you get if you cross a plateful of stew with a cowboy?
   Hopalong Casserole.

St George and the Dragon
A wet, cold and tired tramp came across a pub called the George and Dragon and decided to see if he could get some food and shelter. He knocked on the door and when a woman opened it he said,
'Could you spare me something to eat?'
'No!' shouted the woman, and slammed the door.
The tramp decided to try again.
'Could you give me shelter for the night?' he asked.
'Go away, you dreadful little man!' shouted the woman, and again she slammed the door.
After a while the tramp knocked again on the door and when the woman opened it he said,
'Excuse me, could I speak to George this time, please?'

Stirling Moss
What comes out of a wardrobe at 200 kilometres per hour?
   Stirling Moth.

St Ives
As I was going to St Ives,
I met a man with seven wives.
Every wife had seven sacks,
Every sack had seven cats.
Every cat had seven kits —
Kits, cats, sacks, wives,
How many were going to St Ives?

Just me — all the rest were coming *from* St Ives.

Stockings
Mother: Poppy, pull up your stockings, they're all wrinkled.
Soppy Poppy: Mother, I'm not wearing any stockings.

★

What did the stocking say to the shoe?
   Well, I'll be darned!

★

What do all women look for but hope never to find?
   Holes in their stockings.

Stomach Ache
Johnny went home from school complaining of stomach ache.
'I expect that's because it's empty,' said his mother.
'You'll feel a lot better when you've got something inside it.'
A few hours later Johnny's father came home from work complaining that he had a headache.
'I expect that's because it's empty,' said Johnny. 'You'll feel a lot better with something inside it.'

Stones

Angry neighbour: I'll teach you to throw stones at my greenhouse!

Little horror: I wish you would – I keep missing.

Stopwatch

How can you make a stopwatch?
  Don't wind it.

Stork

Poppy's parents took her to the zoo for the first time, and she insisted on going to see the stork. She stood outside the fence for ages watching the stork wading up and down and then suddenly burst into tears.

'Whatever's the matter?' asked her father.

'He never even recognised me!' howled Poppy.

★

Why does a stork stand on one leg?
  Because if it lifted the other one it would fall over.

Storms and Anchors

Teacher: Alec, if you were in a sailing boat when an unexpected storm blew up, what would you do?

Smart Alec: Throw out the anchor!

Teacher: And what would you do if another storm blew up?

Smart Alec: Throw out another anchor.

Teacher: Yes, but suppose yet another storm blew up?

Smart Alec: I'd throw out yet another anchor.

Teacher: Tell me, where are you getting all these anchors?

Smart Alec: Same place you're getting all your storms!

Story

How can you make a long story short?
  If a very tall girl called Anna Story married Robert Short.

Storytellers

Why are storytellers such weird creatures?
  Because tales come out of their heads.

Straight Line

Teacher: If a straight line is the shortest distance between two points, what is a bee line, Poppy?

Soppy Poppy: The shortest distance between two buzz stops.

Straight Man

Andy: Who was the straightest man in the Bible?

Zak: Joseph, because King Pharaoh made a ruler out of him.

Strawberries

What's the best way to raise strawberries?
  With a spoon.

Strawberry Jam

Why was the little strawberry worried?
  Because his father and mother were in a jam.

Streaky Bacon

What is streaky bacon?
  A pig running around with no clothes on.

String Quartet

What is a string quartet?
  Four people playing tennis.

Strong Man

What did the strong man say on his way to the beach?
  I'm mussel-bound!

What man can hold up a car with one hand?
  A policeman.

Student

Rick: Did you hear about the strange student in school?
Nick: How, strange?
Rick: He remembered to take in his holiday project at the beginning of term.

★

Rick: I spent eight hours over my chemistry books last night.
Nick: That's a lot of studying!
Rick: I never said anything about studying! The books were under my bed.

Stunt Man

What happened when the stupid stunt man tried to drive a double-decker bus over a column of motor cycles?
Someone rang the bell.

Stupid

A little boy had the reputation for not being very smart, and school friends often used to play silly tricks on him to make him look a fool. One of their favourites was to put a coin in each hand — a £1 coin and a 50p piece — and tell him to close his hand over the one he wanted. The boy always took the 50p piece.
One day a kindly lady saw this trick being played on him and as he put the 50p piece in his pocket and the others walked away sniggering, she asked him if he didn't realise that the £1 coin was worth twice as much as the 50p piece, even though it was smaller.
'Yes, I know that,' replied the boy. 'But if I took the £1 coin, they wouldn't play the trick on me any more, would they?'

Sty

What do you call pigs who live together?
Pen friends.

Submarines

Jill: Why was your brother thrown out of the submarine service?
Jack: He liked to sleep with the windows open.

Substitute

What did the football player say when the substitute changed places with him?
What a relief!

Subtraction

How many times can you subtract 16 from 160?
Once — because after that you wouldn't be subtracting from 160.

Success

Jack: I've been successful in business by reversing the usual rule.
Jill: How's that?
Jack: I started at the top and worked down — I'm a wallpaper hanger!

★

The secret of success is getting ahead — but not a big one.

Sugar

What happened to the man who ate a lot of sugar?
He got a lump in his throat.

★

Amy: I put a lump of sugar under my pillow every night.
Zoe: Why?
Amy: So that I can have sweet dreams.

Sugar Daddy

What's another name for a sugar daddy?
A lolly-pop.

Suicide

A man who decided to commit suicide wanted to do the job properly so he bought poison, a rope, a gun, some paraffin and a box of matches.
He poured the paraffin over himself, climbed a tree and crawled out on to a branch overhanging a river. He put the rope round his

neck and jumped, drank the poison, lit the matches and then shot himself.

But he missed his head and the bullet hit the rope, he fell into the water and the water doused the flames. He swallowed so much water that it neutralised the poison and then he had to swim as fast as he could to the shore in order not to drown.

Suit

I've just bought a suit that fits me like a glove – four trouser legs and one sleeve!

★

What makes suits and eats spinach?
 Popeye the Tailorman.

★

Bill: What do you think of my new suit? I had it made in Hong Kong.
Ben: It's nice except for the hump on the back. What's that?
Bill: The tailor – he's still working on it.

Suitor

Why did the Princess's suitor not win her hand?
 Because he didn't suit her.

Sums

When does 3 plus 3 equal 7?
 When you're no good at maths.

★

Why should you never do sums in the jungle.
 Because if you add 4 and 4 you get 8.

★

Smart Alec: Do you say 'nine and five is thirteen', or 'nine and five are thirteen'?
Teacher: Nine and five are thirteen.
Smart Alec: Wrong! Nine and five are fourteen!

Sun

Did you hear about the man who stayed up all night trying to work out what happened to the sun when it went down?
 It finally dawned on him.

★

Sam was out playing in the garden one hot summer's day. His mother went out and saw him squinting in the sunlight.
'Why don't you move out of the sun?' she asked.
'Why should I?' asked Sam. 'I was here first!'

Sunbathing

Amy: I just love sunbathing.
Zoe: So do I. I could lie in the sun all day and all night.

Sunburn

A little girl looked at her peeling sunburn in the mirror and said, 'I'm only five years old and I'm wearing out already.'

★

Amy: I got terribly sunburned on holiday.
Zoe: Well, I guess you basked for it.

Sunday Lunch

Mother: We're going to Grandma's for Sunday lunch.
Johnny: Oh, no! Enthusiasm Stew again!
Mother: What do you mean?
Johnny: She puts everything she's got into it.

Sunday School

Vicar: I heard you played football last week, Sam, instead of coming to Sunday School.
Sam: That's not true, sir. And I've got the fish to prove it.

★

Sunday School teacher: Why do you think we pray for grace, Poppy?
Soppy Poppy: Because she's been a very naughty girl!

Sundial

Why did the idiot floodlight his sundial?
  So that he could tell the time at night.

Sunglasses

Have you heard about the man who wore sunglasses all the time and always took a dim view of everything?

Sunrise

Mrs Able: Our new house is wonderful! I can lie in bed and watch the sun rise.
Mrs Cable: That's nothing. I've always been able to sit at my breakfast table and watch the kitchen sink.

Sunset

Bill: Isn't that sunset beautiful on the horizon?
Ben: Yes, but I'm going indoors before it touches the water and explodes.

Superman

Where does Superman shop for the food he needs to make him so big and strong?
  At the supermarket.

Supermarket

What's romantic, tuneful and necessary in a supermarket?
  A Chopin Liszt.

★

Rick: A terrible thing happened today at the supermarket!
Nick: What?
Rick: A customer was strangled by five fish fingers.

★

Why did the supermarket keep bandages in the refrigerator?
  For cold cuts.

Superstitious

Have you heard about the borrower who went around asking people if they were superstitious?
  And then asked for £13?

Surf-Riding

Did you hear about the man who wanted to go surf-riding – his horse wouldn't go near the water!

Surgeon

What do you call a thirsty physician?
  A dry doc.

Survival

Suppose you were locked in a room with only a bed and a calendar – how would you survive?
  You could drink water from the bed springs and eat dates from the calendar.

Suspicious

Tom: Dick's really suspicious. . . .
Harry: I'll say. Both his eyes watch each other all the time!

Swallow

Where does a swallow live?
  In a stomach.

★

A flock of swallows set off on their annual migration and one at the back said to another, 'Why do we always follow the same leader?' 'He's the one with the map,' said the other.

Swap

Passer-by: What's the matter? Why are you crying?
Sam: I swapped my puppy for a bottle of squash because I was thirsty.
Passer-by: And now you wish you hadn't?
Sam: Yes!
Passer-by: Because you realise how much you love and miss him?
Sam: No! Because I'm thirsty again!

289

Sweden

Why doesn't Sweden export cattle?
    Because she wants to keep her Stockholm.

Sweets

Jack: Here you are, sweets to the sweet.
Jill: Oh, thank you. Have a nut.

★

Three little boys went in to a sweetshop to spend their pocket money. The first asked for five pence worth of licorice chews, and pointed to the jar on the top shelf. The shopkeeper went to the back of the shop to get his ladder, climbed up, got down the jar, and gave the boy five pence worth of licorice chews. Then he took the ladder to the back of the shop again.
'What would you like?' he said to the second little boy.
'Five pence worth of licorice chews, please.'
So the shopkeeper went to the back of the shop to get his ladder, climbed up, got down the jar, and gave the boy five pence worth of licorice chews.
Then he turned to the third little boy and said, 'Do you want five pence worth of licorice chews too?'
'No, thank you,' came the reply.
So the shopkeeper took the ladder to the back of the shop, came back, and said to the third little boy,
'What would you like?'
'Ten pence worth of licorice chews, please.'

★

What happens to people who eat too many sweets?
    They take up two seats.

★

Eve: Say something sweet to me!
Adam: Black Forest Gateaux.

Swimmer

Did you hear about the slow swimmer who could only crawl?

A man went swimming and while he was gone all his clothes were stolen. Guess what he came home in.
    The dark!

★

What goes in pink and comes out blue?
    A swimmer in winter.

★

What swims along the sea bed and gets trodden on?
    A wall-to-wall carp.

★

A boy who had grown up beside the sea and learned to swim in the sea went to a swimming pool for the first time. After he had been swimming for a little while he got out and went up to the attendant, 'I'm very sorry,' he said. 'I swallowed some of your water.'

★

Mrs Able: I'm taking up swimming. I heard that it's one of the best ways to slim and keep in trim.
Mrs Cable: Oh, I don't agree.
Mrs Able: Why not?
Mrs Cable: Have you ever seen a whale?

★

Johnny: Why can't I go in swimming? Daddy's in swimming!
Mother: He's insured.

★

Bill and Ben went exploring in the woods one day and Ben fell into the river. Bill stood on the bank and shouted, 'Hey, Ben! If you don't come up again can I have your Swiss Army knife?'

★

Jack: Where do you swim?
Jill: In the spring.
Jack: I said where, not when!

★

Is it dangerous to swim on a full stomach?
    Yes, it's much safer to swim in water!

How do you swim a 100 metres in two seconds?
Over a waterfall.

★

Forest warden: Miss, I'm going to have to arrest you for swimming in the lake.
Young lady: Well! You might have told me before I changed into my swimsuit.
Forest warden: There's no law against *that*, miss.

★

Why couldn't the man who went swimming in the river on Sunday get out of the water?
Because the banks were all closed.

★

Where do ghouls most like to swim?
Off the South Ghost.

Swimming Pool
Sam: Dad, there's a man at the door collecting for a new swimming pool.
Father: Give him a bucket of water.

Swimming the Channel
Paul: Did you hear about the latest attempt to swim the Channel?
Saul: Did they make it?
Paul: No, two miles from the French coast he was so tired he turned back.

Swimming Trunks
When do swimming trunks go ding, dong?
When you wring them out.

Swiss Roll
How do you make a Swiss roll?
Push him off the top of an Alp.

Switzerland
What would Switzerland be without all its mountains?
Alpless.

Swordfight
Where's the perfect place for two motorists to have a swordfight?
On a duel carriageway.

Sword Swallower
Did you hear about the sword swallower who went on a diet?
He had pins and needles for months.

★

There was once a sword swallower who swallowed an umbrella.
He was putting something away for a rainy day.

★

Rick: Have you heard the sword-swallower from the circus has been arrested and put in jail?
Nick: Why, what did he do?
Rick: He hiccoughed and stabbed two people.

★

Bill: I saw the most amazing sword-swallower at the circus last night. He swallowed a sword two metres long!
Ben: What's so amazing about that?
Bill: He's only a metre and a half tall.

Sylvester Stallone
'Name?' asked the policeman, charging the drunk at the police station.
'John Brown,' said the drunk.
'Oh, come now, sir,' said the policeman. 'Everyone says that!'
'All right, then,' said the drunk, 'Sylvester Stallone.'
'That's better,' said the policeman, and wrote it down. 'You can't fool the police that easily, you know!'

Synonym
A synonym is a word you use in the place of another word you can't spell.

Table

Customer: How can I hire a table?

Shop assistant: How about a book under each leg, sir?

★

Poppy was asked to read out her tables in class:

'Bed-side table, dining table, kitchen table, television table. . . .'

Tablecloth

What did the tablecloth say to the table?

Don't move – I've got you covered.

Tadpoles

Where do tadpoles change into frogs?

In the croakroom.

Tailor

What's the difference between a tailor and a horse trainer?

One mends tears and the other tends mares.

★

A man went in to a tailor's shop for a new suit. The shop was very busy and all the assistants were looking after customers. The manager was getting very flustered and when eventually one of the assistants became free he turned to the man and said,

'Right, sir, go over there, will you, and have a fit?'

What's a tailor's dummy?

It's what a tailor's baby sucks.

★

What is a tailor's son called?

The son of a sew-and-sew.

Talk

The local vicar was visiting a school in his parish and visiting each of the classrooms. As he went into the youngest class and greeted the teacher, he smiled at the children and asked, 'What shall I talk to you little ones about?'

From the back of the classroom came a little voice, 'About five minutes.'

★

Paul: Do you think that women talk more than men?

Saul: No, they just use more words.

Tap Dancing

Adam: Why did you give up your tap dancing classes?
Eve: Because I kept falling in the sink.

Taps

What did the big tap say to the small tap?
  Little squirt!

★

And what did the small tap reply?
  Big drip!

★

What can run but has no legs?
  A tap.

Tarzan

What's blue and swings through the trees?
  Tarzan in a boiler suit.

★

What did Tarzan say when he saw the elephants coming?
  Here come the elephants.

★

What did Tarzan say when he saw the elephants coming with sunglasses on?
  Nothing – he didn't recognise them.

Tax

What would a tax on hitchhikers be called?
  A thumb tax.

Taxi

How can you travel around quickly at the bottom of the sea?
  By taxi-crab.

★

Fat hotel guest: Please call me a taxi.
Hotel porter: OK, you're a taxi. But you look more like a bus to me.

★

Andy: My uncle used to be a taxi driver.
Zak: Why did he give it up?
Andy: He drove all his customers away.

Tea

What kind of tea do they drink at Women's Lib meetings?
  Libber tea.
      ★

What kind of tea makes you feel fearless?
  Safety.

★

Apprentice: What kind of clothes are you going to make with all these tea bags?
Fashion designer: Baggy tea shirts!

Teacher

Mother: Why don't you like your new teacher?
Soppy Poppy: Because she told me to sit at the front for the present and she didn't give me a present.

★

Why did the teacher give the boy a B?
  Because he had hives.

★

Teacher: Are you good at arithmetic?
Silly Billy: Yes and no.
Teacher: What on earth do you mean?
Silly Billy: Yes, I'm no good at arithmetic.

★

Why is a teacher like a bird of prey?
  Because he watches you like a hawk!

★

Did you hear about the cross-eyed teacher?
  She couldn't control her pupils.

★

Teacher: How can you prove that the world is round?
Silly Billy: But I never said it was, sir!

★

Teacher: Did your father help with your homework?
Sam: No, I got it wrong all by myself this time.

★

Teacher: Where was the Magna Carta signed?
Soppy Poppy: At the bottom, miss.

★

Teacher: What is the Order of the Bath, Ben?
Ben: Mum, Dad, then me.

★

What's the difference between a schoolteacher and a train?
A teacher says, 'Spit the toffee out,' a train says, 'Choo, choo.'

★

What makes teachers special?
Being in a class of their own.

★

Amy: I was teacher's pet at my last school.
Zoe: Was that nice?
Amy: It was only because she couldn't afford a dog.

★

Amy: Our teacher likes me more than she likes you.
Zoe: Why do you say that?
Amy: She puts more kisses in my book than she does in yours.

★

Headmaster: Has anyone any idea how we can raise the level of our students?
Teacher: Why don't we use the upstairs classrooms?

★

Headmaster to new teacher: Your teaching and class control are excellent. How do you manage to keep on your toes?
Teacher: The children put drawing-pins on my chair.

Teapot
What is the teapot's favourite song?
'Home, Home on the Range.'

Tears
What are tears?
Glum drops.

Teaspoonsfuls
Doctor: Take four teaspoonfuls of this medicine before *every* meal.
Patient: But we've only got three teaspoons at home.

Teddy Bear
A teddy bear who had a job on a building site arrived at work one morning to find that his pick had been stolen. He reported the theft to the foreman, who said,
'That's because today's the day the teddy bears have their picks nicked.'

★

How do you start a teddy bear race?
Ready, Teddy, go.

Teenager
Father: You're usually on the phone for hours. How come that last conversation only lasted 30 minutes?
Teenage daughter: Wrong number, Dad.

Teeth
A man who had broken his false teeth went out one morning to get some more. As he was standing in front of the shop window choosing his dentures a policeman arrested him, saying, 'It's against the law to pick your teeth in public.'

★

What did one tooth say to the other?
Get your cap on, the dentist is taking us out tonight.

★

What has teeth but never bites?
A comb.

★

Why do you forget a tooth as soon as the dentist pulls it?
Because it goes right out of your head.

★

Bill: What are those little white things in your head that bite?
Ben: Teeth, stupid.

★

'Your teeth are like the stars,' he said.
And pressed her hand so white.
He spoke the truth, for like the stars
Her teeth came out at night.

Telegram

Lady in post office: I'd like to send a telegram to Washington, please.
Post office clerk: You can't do that, madam – he's dead.

Telephone

When is the cheapest time to ring your friends?
When they're out.

★

A little old lady called the operator almost as soon as her phone had been installed.
'I'm sorry to bother you,' she said, 'but my telephone cord is too long. Could you pull it back a bit from your end, please?'

★

Caller: Could you connect me with Lenny the Lion, please?
Operator: Sorry, lion's busy.

★

Mr Able's telephone rang in the middle of the night and a voice said, 'Is that 1212?'
'No, he replied, 'this is 1211.'
'Sorry to have troubled you,' said the caller.
'Oh, that's all right,' said Mr Able, 'I had to get up to answer the telephone anyway.'

Johnny: Can you telephone from a Space Shuttle?
Jenny: Of course I can tell a phone from a Space Shuttle – the Shuttle's got a rocket booster.

★

What did the big telephone say to the little telephone?
You're too young to be engaged. Why don't you give the ring back?

★

Why doesn't a telephone work under water?
Because it's wringing wet.

★

The new company clerk had to answer the telephone one day because everyone else was out of the office. He buzzed the managing director's number and said,
'I think this call is for you, sir.'
'What do you mean you *think*?' asked the managing director.
'Well, when I answered the phone a voice said, "Is that you, you silly old fool?" '

★

How can you tell how old a telephone is?
Count its rings.

★

Amy: Yesterday I was talking to my friend in a telephone booth.
Zoe: So?
Amy: Someone wanted to make a call so we had to get out.

★

Adam: Who was that on the phone?
Eve: No one special. Just a man who said it's a long distance from Australia. But I knew that already.

★

Amy (answering the telephone): Hello.
Zoe: Hello, Amy.
Amy: Oh, Zoe. Can you call back later when I've finished my tantrum?

Operator: Number, please.
Caller: Interpol, quick.
Operator: You'll have to dial the overseas operator.
Caller: Oh, all right. (Dials again.)
Overseas operator: Number, please.
Caller: Interpol, quick. It's urgent.
Overseas operator: Number, please.
Caller: I don't have the number. Can you get it for me?
Overseas operator: I'll put you through to Directory Enquiries in Paris. Hold on, please.
Paris operator: 'Ello?
Caller: Can you give me the Interpol number, please. It's very urgent.
Paris operator: Oui, monsieur. The number is Paris 12345.
Caller: Thank you! (Dials desperately.)
Interpol operator: 'Ello?
Caller: Interpol?
Interpol operator: Oui, monsieur.
Caller: Oh, thank goodness! Listen — can you take an order to send some flowers to my mother. . . .

★

Operator: Is that the mental institution?
Voice on the line: Yes, but we're not on the phone.

★

Andy: Hello, can I speak to Zak?
Zak: This is Zak.
Andy: Are you sure it's Zak?
Zak: Of course I'm sure it's Zak.
Andy: Well, listen, Zak. Can I borrow £10 from you tonight?
Zak: I'll ask Zak when he comes in.

★

Mrs Able: Who was that on the phone?
Mr Able: Wrong number — they were after the Met. Office, wanted to know if the coast was clear.

★

Jill (on the telephone): You don't say. No! You don't say!
Jack: Who was that on the phone?
Jill: He didn't say.

Strongman: I'm so strong I can tear up a telephone directory.
Little boy: That's nothing — yesterday morning my brother ran out of the house and tore up the street.

★

Why is a telephone useful in a laundry room? Because it is a good ringer.

★

What do you get if you dial 876493211897543?
A sore finger.

★

Hans: What is your telephone number?
Gerda: 999–9999.
Hans: All right, don't tell me.

★

Why aren't there many telephones in China?
Because there are so many Wings and Wongs there that people are afraid they might wing the wong number.

★

When is a telephone like a trapeze act?
When you're left hanging on.

★

Why are telephone wires so high up?
So that they can keep up the conversation.

Television

Andy: What's the best thing you've seen on television this year?
Zak: The 'off' switch.

★

Rick: It's true, you know, that television causes violence.
Nick: Why do you say that?
Rick: Because every time I switch the television on my Dad hits me.

★

Son: What's on television tonight, Mum?
Mother: Same as always, dear — a vase of flowers and a bowl of fruit.

Rick: Television will never replace newspapers.
Nick: Why ever not?
Rick: Well, have you ever tried to swat a fly with a television set?

★

Actor: Have you ever seen me on television?
Acquaintance: Yes, on and off.
Actor: How did you like me?
Acquaintance: Off.

Television Licence

Magistrate: Now, madam, why do you think you should get a television licence for half price?
Little old lady: Because I've only got one eye.

★

Rick: I heard the Queen's going to do a telly-cost at our school.
Nick: What's a tellycost?
Rick: About £100.

Temper

What kind of apple has a short temper?
    A crab apple.

★

When is it a good thing to lose your temper?
    When it's a bad one.

Temperature

When you're ill, what is taken but never missed?
    Your temperature.

Tennessee

What did Tennessee?
    The same as Arkansas.

★

Teacher: Can anyone spell Tennessee?
Silly Billy: One-a-see, two-a-see. . . .

Tennis

Why is tennis such a noisy game?
    Because every player raises a racket.

★

Paul: What can you serve, but never eat?
Saul: I don't know. What?
Paul: A tennis ball.

★

Why do people who string tennis rackets have to be brave?
    Because it takes guts.

Terrorist

Did you hear about the stupid terrorist who tried to blow up a bus?
    He burnt his lips on the exhaust pipe.

Test

Paul: Wonderful news! Our English teacher said we would have a test today come rain or shine.
Saul: What's so wonderful about that?
Paul: It's snowing!

★

Roses are red, violets are blue
I copied your test and I failed too.

Thames

What do you get if you jump in the Thames?
    Wet.

Thank You

A little boy was having tea with his grandmother.

'Would you like some bread and butter?' she asked.

'Yes, thank you,' said the little boy.

'What nice manners,' said his grandmother. 'I do like to hear you say thank you.'

'I'll say it again if you put some jam on for me,' said the little boy.

That's Entertainment!

An entertainer went to see his psychiatrist. 'The problem is,' he said, 'I can't sing or dance, I'm useless at telling jokes, I can't act or do any of the variety turns. I can't actually do anything!'

'Then give up show business,' suggested the psychiatrist.

'Never!' said the entertainer. 'I'm a *star*!'

Theatre

Why did the horses go to the theatre?
    Because they wanted stalls for Saturday night.

★

Adam: I went to see a play last night.
Eve: Did it have a happy ending?
Adam: Oh, yes. I was glad when the curtain came down.

★

Why is the theatre such a sad place?
    The seats are always in tiers.

★

Man in darkened theatre: Excuse me, madam, did I tread on your toes a few minutes ago?
Lady: Yes, you did.
Man: Oh, good. That means I'm in the right row.

The Other Side

Paul: Is this the other side of the street?
Saul: No, the other side of the street is over there.
Paul: Well! The policeman over there said it was over here.

The Sack

Rick: I got the sack today.
Nick: What for?
Rick: For good!

The Thinker

Art teacher: Now, class, we've been studying Rodin's life and works. What do you think Rodin's 'Thinker' might have been thinking of:
Soppy Poppy: I should guess he's thinking about where he left his clothes.

Thief

Why is a thief strong?
    Because he holds up people.

★

Did you hear about the thief who robbed a music shop and ran off with the lute?

★

What do thieves have for lunch?
    Beefburglars.

Thin

My mother must think I'm thin – she says she can see right through me.

Thor The Thunder God

Thor the thunder god went for a ride on his favourite horse, crying out, 'I'm Thor! I'm Thor!'

'That's becauth you forgot the thaddle, thilly,' replied the horse.

Three-Legged Race

What always starts with a tie?
    A three-legged race.

Throwing Stones

Mother: Johnny, when that little boy threw stones at you, you should have come

298

straight to me instead of throwing stones back.

Johnny: What for? You can't throw straight.

Thunderstorm

What's the difference between a thunderstorm and a lion with toothache?

One pours with rain, the other roars with pain.

★

During a thunderstorm a mother went up to her little girl's room to make sure the thunder and lightning weren't frightening her. 'Are you all right?' she asked quietly.

'Yes, Mum,' replied the little girl. 'But why is Dad messing about with the television at this time of night?'

★

Father: What a thunderstorm last night. Did you hear it, Sam?

Sam: Yes, it was loud.

Mother: Why didn't you wake me up? You know I can't sleep when there's thunder and lightning!

Thursday

Paul: I know somewhere where Thursday comes before Wednesday.

Saul: Where?

Paul: In the dictionary.

Tickle

What kind of tickle doesn't make you laugh?
A tickle in the throat.

★

What is a ticklish subject?
The study of feathers.

Ticks

What ticks on the wall?
Ticky paper.

★

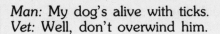

Man: My dog's alive with ticks.

Vet: Well, don't overwind him.

Tidy

What's the best way of keeping your country tidy?
Export all your rubbish.

Tie

What kind of tie does a pig wear?
A pig-sty.

★

Andy: That's a nice Easter tie.

Zak: Why do you call it an Easter tie?

Andy: Because it's got egg all over it.

Tiger

Who went into the tiger's den and came out alive?
The tiger.

★

Mother tiger: What are you cubs doing?

Oldest tiger cub: We're chasing a hunter round a tree.

Mother tiger: How many times have I told you not to play with your food?

★

Why should you never grab a tiger by his tail?
Well, it may only be his tail, but it could be the end of you!

Tightrope Walker

Why did the tightrope walker always carry his bank book?
To check his balance.

★

Why are tightrope walkers like book keepers?
Because they know how to balance.

★

Paul: I've discovered the tightrope walker's secret.

Saul: How did you do that?
Paul: I tapped his wire.

Tiles
Lady of the house: Are there any tiles that won't stick on the wall?
Decorator: Reptiles, madam.

Time
Andy: Is it true that you can't stop time?
Zak: I don't know. My mother went next door this morning and stopped hours.

★

How can you tell the time at any hour of the night?
  Look at the bedroom clock.

★

Two little boys camping out in their back garden wanted to know what the time was, so they began to sing as loudly as they could. Soon their father opened his bedroom window and shouted down to them,
'Hey, you two! Cut it out! Don't you know it's two o'clock in the morning?'

★

Bill: Time hangs so heavily on my hands these days.
Ben: If I were you I'd wear a wristwatch, then, instead of that grandfather clock.

★

A man walked in to an office block one day and saw a clock on the wall. He checked the time against his own watch and then said to the security guard,
'That clock is fast, isn't it?'
'It certainly is, sir,' replied the guard, 'it would fall down otherwise.'

★

How do you tell the time by candles?
  By the candles-tick.

★

Paul: What time is it?
Saul: I've no idea.
Paul: I know that, but what time is it?

★

1st Roman: What's the time?
2nd Roman: XII.XXX.

★

What time is it when the clock strikes thirteen?
  Time to get a new clock.

★

How can you check the time without looking at your watch?
  Eat an apple and count the pips.

★

What's the slickest thing in the world?
  Time – because you can never hold it.

★

What can't you see but is always in front of you?
  The future.

★

What is always behind time?
  The back of a clock.

Time and Motion
After spending a month observing in an office the time and motion inspector went over to a pretty office clerk and said, 'I'm sorry to have to tell you this, but I've had to note in my report that you waste too much time checking your appearance.' 'That's all right,' replied the clerk. 'But I don't think I've wasted the time. I started here the month before you came, and the managing director and I have just announced our engagement.'

Timetable
Traveller: The train timetable is useless! The trains never run on time.
Guard: But you wouldn't know that, sir, if it wasn't for the timetable.

Tin

Which floats the best, tin or stainless steel?
  Tin. Stainless steel sinks.

★

What is a happy tin in the USA?
  A merry can.

Tin Openers

What dance do tin openers do?
  The Can-Can.

Tipping

Customer: Are the waiters tipped here?
Waiter: Yes, sir!
Customer: Then tip me, will you? I've been
  waiting here for hours.

Toad

Did you hear about the beautiful maiden who
kissed a prince at a New Year's Eve Party?
  He turned into a toad.

Toadstool

How would you know your dustbin was full
of toadstools?
  Because there wouldn't be mushroom
inside.

Toaster

Amy: We've just got a new toaster.
Zoe: Is it a pop-up model?
Amy: No, a Red Indian model.
Zoe: What's that?
Amy: It sends up smoke signals.

★

What did the toaster say to the bread?
  Pop up and see me some time.

Toes

Jill: Are you a toe dancer?
Jack: No, why?
Jill: Then just get off my toes, will you?

★

Amy: When I was on holiday at the seaside a
  crab bit off one of my toes.
Zoe: Which one?
Amy: I don't know. They all look alike to me.

★

What did the big toe say to the little toe?
  There's a big heel following us.

★

Said the toe to the sock:
  'Let me through, let me through.'
Said the sock to the toe:
  'I'll be darned if I do!'

Toffee

Why did a man spend his time in the cinema
hunting for a toffee?
  Because his teeth were in it.

★

Sister: I made a lovely batch of toffee and the
  dog's eaten it!
Brother: Don't worry, we'll get another dog.

Tomatoes

Bill: What gave you that lump on your head?
Ben: A tomato hit me.
Bill: But tomatoes are soft.
Ben: Not when they're in a tin.

What did one tomato say to the other tomato?
   If you'd kept your big mouth shut we wouldn't be in this pickle.

★

What floats on the ocean, weighs 200,000 tons and tastes of tomatoes?
   A soupertanker.

Tomorrow
What is always coming, but never actually arrives?
   Tomorrow, because as soon as it comes it's today.

★

A traveller once, to his sorrow,
Requested a ticket to Morrow.
Said the agent, 'It's plain
That there isn't a train
To Morrow today, but tomorrow!

Tongue
Paul: I'm so thirsty my tongue's hanging out.
Saul: Oh – I thought it was your tie.

Tongue Twisters
If Harry hurries, will hairy Henry hand him a hundred hammers?

★

Six skyscrapers stood side by side, shimmering by the seashore.

★

Meek Morgan Matthews made weak
   Matty Morgan many milkshakes.

★

Esther Elephant eats eighty-eight Easter eggs eagerly every Easter.

★

Ninety-nine naughty nick-nacks were nicked by ninety-nine naughty knitted nick-nack nickers.

Sammy Smilie smelt a smell of small-coal
Did Sammy Smilie smell a smell of small-coal?
If Sammy Smilie smelt a smell of small-coal,
Where's the smell of small-coal Sammy Smilie smelt?

★

Slim Sam shaved six slippery chins in sixty-six seconds.

★

Our black bull bled black blood on our black-thorn flower.

★

Pitter-patter pitter-patter, rather than patter-pitter patter-pitter.

★

Quixote Quicksight quizzed a queerish quidbox.

★

Am I and Amy aiming anaemic anemones on my many enemies?

★

She sells sea-shells on the sea-shore.

Tonsils
What's the cause of inflamed tonsils?
   Tonsil-lighters.

★

First tonsil: Why are you getting all dressed up?
Second tonsil: The doctor is taking me out tonight.

★

A mother marched in to the Casualty Department of the local hospital, dragging her six-year-old son behind her. She angrily demanded to see the doctor on duty and when he appeared she asked:
'Can a boy of six perform an operation to remove tonsils?'
'No, of course not,' replied the doctor.
'I told you,' said the boy's mother.
'You put them back at once!'

Tools

Which tools are useful in arithmetic?
  Multi-pliers.

Tooth

Teacher: Jenny, why weren't you here yesterday?
Jenny: I had a bad tooth, miss.
Teacher: Oh, I'm sorry to hear that. Is it better now?
Jenny: I don't know – I left it at the dentist's.

What's the best way to get through life with only one tooth?
  Grin and bear it.

What did one tooth say to the other tooth?
  There's gold in them there fills.

Toothless

Andy: I wish sharks were born without teeth.
Zak: They usually are!

Toothpaste

What did the toothpaste say to the toothbrush?
Give us a squeeze and I'll meet you outside the Tube.

Jenny was learning to clean her teeth. Her mother showed her how to squeeze the toothpaste 'about the size of a bean' on to the toothbrush and then left her to answer the phone. Jenny came downstairs with toothpaste spread from ear to ear and her mother said,
'I told you the size of a bean!'
'Oh, I thought you meant a runner bean,' said Jenny.

★

Andy: Did you hear about the man who didn't know toothpaste from putty?
Zak: What happened?
Andy: All his windows fell out.

Torch

Andy: I swallowed a torch last night.
Zak: Are you all right?
Andy: Oh, yes. I spat it out this morning and now I'm delighted.

Tornado

Two explorers came across a third sitting by a huge canyon.
'You can't go across,' he said to them. 'A tornado just passed by and swept the rope bridge away.'
'How did your rucksack get across, then?' asked the two explorers.
'Well,' said the third, 'I just sat down here and thought it over.'

Torpedo

What is a torpedo?
  A sea shell.

Tortoise

Bill: What's a tortoise?
Ben: What the teacher did in school today.

Tortoises

Once upon a time, two big tortoises and a little tortoise went into a café and ordered three chocolate sundaes. As they were waiting to be served it started to rain, and they realised that they hadn't taken an umbrella with them. The two big tortoises decided that the little one should go home to get an umbrella. But the little tortoise didn't want to go as he thought the big ones would eat his sundae while he was gone. They promised not to and so the little tortoise agreed to get the umbrella.
The two big tortoises waited all that day and all the next day; and at the end of the third day one of the big tortoises said,
'Let's eat his sundae.'
'Yes, let's,' agreed the other.
'Caught you, caught you! I knew you wouldn't keep your promise,' shouted the little tortoise, sticking his head out of his shell as he crawled out from underneath a table by the café door.

Touch

Why does your sense of touch suffer if you're sick?

Because you don't feel well.

Tough!

Grandad: That meat we had for dinner last night was terribly tough. I hope you've given me something tonight I can get my teeth into.

Grandma: Yes, I have – here's a glass of water.

★

Mr Cable: I'm sorry to have to say it, dear, but this toast is tough.

Mrs Cable: You're eating the plate, dear.

Toupee

Mr Able: Do you like my new toupee, then?

Mr Cable: Yes, indeed! You can't even tell it's a wig.

Touring

Did you hear about the tour guide who took visitors 'where the hand of man has never set foot'?

★

An Australian was proudly showing an American tourist the Sydney Bridge. 'Isn't that beautiful?' he asked.

'Well, sure,' said the American, 'but we have bigger bridges than that at home.'

'What about the park,' said the Australian, 'have you seen anything like this before?'

'Sure have,' answered the American. 'Our parks at home are much bigger.' And then they saw a kangaroo. 'Well, now,' said the American, 'I'll have to admit your grasshoppers sure are bigger than ours.'

★

Tourist: Whose skull is that over there?

Guide: That, madam, is the skull of Julius Caesar.

Tourist: And whose is the little one beside it?

Guide: That, madam, is the skull of Julius Caesar when he was a little boy.

★

American tourist in Italy: Waiter, I'd like some of what's written on the menu here.

Waiter: The orchestra is playing it now, sir.

Towel

What gets wetter the more it dries?

A towel.

Tow Truck

Paul: What was that tow truck doing at the races?

Saul: Trying to pull a fast one, I guess.

Toy

A very angry mother stormed in to a toy shop two days after Christmas. 'I want my money back,' she said. This unbreakable toy robot is useless!'

'I don't believe any child could have broken it already,' said the sales assistant.

'My child hasn't broken it. He's broken all his other toys with it!'

Traffic Jam

Did you hear about the little boy who went to the corner of his road to see the traffic jam? A truck came along and gave him a jar.

★

What is heavier in warm weather than in winter?

Traffic to the seaside.

Traffic Light

Two creatures from outer space landed by a traffic light.

'I saw her first,' said one.

'Maybe,' said the other, 'but I'm the one she winked at.'

★

A man and his friend were driving through the centre of a town while on holiday and the driver's car handling was deteriorating at every crossroads. 'Bill,' said his friend, 'why are you shutting your eyes at every red light?'
'Oh,' said Bill, 'if you've seen one red traffic light, you've seen them all, no matter which city it is.'

★

What did the traffic lights say to the lorry?
Don't look now, I'm changing.

★

A set of traffic lights was stolen from a main road junction in a country town. Police said, 'Some thieves will stop at nothing.'

Train

Passenger: Does this train stop at the Gare du Nord?
Guard: Well, if it doesn't there'll be an enormous crash.

★

Which is the hardest train to catch?
The 12.50, because it's ten to one if you catch it.

★

How can you tell when a train has gone?
It leaves tracks behind.

★

Platform guard: Pass right along inside the cars, please. Pass right down inside the cars!
Little boy: That's not Pa, it's Grandpa, and he's not inside yet!

★

Commuter: Is the train on time?
Guard: We're happy if it's on the track, sir.

★

Why is it not safe to sleep on a train?
Because trains always run over sleepers.

★

Traveller: Stop the train! An old lady's just fallen off!
Guard: It's all right, sir, she'd paid for her ticket.

★

A girl was standing on a train platform holding the carriage door open when the guard wanted to blow his whistle.
'Come along, there,' he called. 'Shut that door, please!
'Oh!' cried the girl, 'I wanted to kiss my sister goodbye!'
'As I said, miss,' said the guard. 'Shut that door. I'll do the rest!'

★

Passenger: Is this my train?
Guard: No, sir, it belongs to British Rail.
Passenger: Don't make jokes with me! Can I take this train to Liverpool?
Guard: Oh, no, sir. It's too heavy.

★

Traveller: How long will the next train be?
Guard: Four carriages if it's the local, twelve if it's the express.

★

Andy: Did you hear about the fight on the train?
Zak: No, what happened?
Andy: The inspector punched a ticket.

★

As the train crawled across the Indian plains, a very hot and tired English tourist decided he couldn't stand the slow pace any longer. When the train stopped at one of the many stations, he got out and marched up to the driver's cab. 'Can't you go any faster?' he asked.

'Yes, I can,' replied the driver. 'But I'm not allowed to leave the train!'

★

Guard: Madam, I'm sorry, but your ticket is for Paris and this train is going to Amsterdam.

Traveller: Well tell the driver to turn the train round.

★

Why are people who read on train journeys very clever?

Because they can read between the lines.

★

A lady put her elderly mother on the train asking the ticket-collector to let her know when the train reached Norwich. The ticket-collector promised to do so, but he was very busy and forgot until the train was pulling out of Norwich station. He hurried to the guard who pulled the communication cord, and the driver slowly backed the train into the station. The guard picked up the old lady's luggage, shouting, 'Quickly, madam, this is Norwich!'

'But I don't want to get off at Norwich,' said the old lady. 'I only wanted to know because I haven't got a watch and my daughter said that when we got to Norwich it would be time to take my pills.'

★

On her first train ride, Mad May was having a wonderful time running up and down the carriage, knocking over cups of tea and sending sandwiches tumbling to the floor. Her parents were highly embarrassed and eventually her father said, 'I'll smack you if you don't come and sit still.'

Mad May stopped her crashing and banging at the far end of the corridor and shouted, 'If you do, I'll tell the ticket-collector how old I *really* am!'

Paul: My new house is right by a railway station.

Saul: Won't the trains disturb you at night?

Paul: They say I'll get used to it in a few nights, so for the first week or so I'm going to sleep in a hotel.

★

What's yellow and white and travels at over 70 mph?

A train driver's egg sandwich.

★

Passenger: How can I be sure the trains are running on time?

Guard: Just before the train comes in, put your watch on the railway line.

★

What's the difference between a train in its shed and a tree?

One leaves its shed, the other sheds its leaves.

Train Station

Johnny: Mum, what was that station called we just stopped at?

Mother: I didn't notice. Can't you see I'm reading?

Johnny: Yes, but I thought you'd like to know where Jenny got off.

Tramp

The lady of the manor opened her door and discovered a tramp on the doorstep.

'Can you give me a bite to eat?' asked the tramp.

'No, I never feed tramps,' came the frosty reply.

'Oh, that's all right,' said the tramp, 'I'll feed myself.'

★

A tramp knocked on a house door and asked the lady of the house for food.

'Didn't I give you some cake last week?' she asked.

'Yes, ma'am,' the tramp said. 'But I've recovered now.'

306

Did you hear about the tramp who stole a bottle of perfume and was convicted of fragrancy?

Trampled
Did you hear about the man whose herd of sheep trampled him to death?
He sort of dyed-in-the-wool.

Trampoline
What's a trampolinist's favourite time of year?
Spring time.

★

What's business like in the trampoline trade?
Up and down!

Travel
What people travel the most?
Romans.

★

Fatty: They say that travel is broadening.
Skinny: Have you been around the world, then?

★

Passenger on plane: Does this plane travel faster than sound?
Air hostess: No, madam.
Passenger: That's a relief. My friend and I want to talk.

★

Bill: My wife's gone on holiday abroad.
Ben: Jamaica?
Bill: No, she went of her own free will.

★

Paul: But if you're going to hitch-hike round Greece, how are you going to get round the islands?
Saul: There are ferries at the bottom of my garden.

★

Mr and Mrs Cable were off on holiday! They got to the airport with only a few minutes to spare and suddenly Mr Cable said, 'I do wish I'd brought the television.'
'What on earth for?' asked Mrs Cable.
'The tickets are on top of it.'

★

Did you hear about the man who was so afraid of flying he took a train all the way to Spain?
It crashed – a plane fell on it.

★

A lady who planned to travel from Rome to Istanbul telephoned her travel agent to see how long the flight would be.
'Just a minute,' said the clerk.
'Thank you,' said the woman, and hung up.

Travel Agent
Sign seen in a travel agent's window:
Please go away!

Treason
Paul: I learned the definition of treason today.
Saul: What is it?
Paul: Treason is the male offspring of a tree.

Tree
What tree are deck chairs made from?
A beech tree.

★

Farmer: This is a dogwood tree.
City man: How can you tell?
Farmer: By its bark.

★

Which is the warmest tree?
A fir tree.

★

What kind of tree do you find in a kitchen?
A pantry.

★

What swings from a tree in a suit and tie?
A Branch Manager.

What tree can't you climb?
A laboratory!

★

What is everyone's favourite tree?
A popular tree.

★

What makes a tree noisy?
Its bark.

★

What tree does everyone carry around with them?
A palm.

★

What tree can you see after a fire?
An ash.

★

Jill: Do you think I look like a slender young birch?
Jack: Not really, more like a knotty pine!

★

What trees do hands grow on?
Palm trees.

★

What's white and climbs trees?
A fridge (I lied about it climbing trees).

★

What's blue and white and climbs trees?
A fridge in jeans (I lied again about it climbing trees).

★

What trees grow near the seaside?
Beech trees.

★

Why do trees get petrified?
Because the wind makes them rock.

★

Did you hear about the tree surgeon who fell out of his patient?

Why is a tree surgeon like an actor?
Because he's always taking boughs.

Trespass
A farmer was chasing two small boys across his field and finally caught up with them.
'Don't you know you're trespassing?' he roared. 'Didn't you see the notice?'
'Yes,' said one little boy quickly. 'But it said "Private", so we didn't like to read any more.'

★

A couple of city slickers were out in the country for the day and were walking across a field. Suddenly they saw a bull and called out to the farmer, 'Is that bull safe?'
Replied the farmer, 'He's a lot safer than you are!'

Tricycle
Jack: What's a fast tricycle?
Jill: I don't know. What?
Jack: A tot rod.

Trifle
What did the man who had jelly in one ear and custard in the other say?
'You'll have to speak up a bit, I'm a trifle deaf.'

★

Who was the trifle's favourite artist?
Bottijelli.

Trigonometry
What is trigonometry?
Learning to shoot a gun.

Trio
What has six feet and sings?
A trio.

Trip
Andy: I had a trip to Paris yesterday!

Zak: Oh, what a shame. Did you hurt yourself?

Trojan Horse
What was the Trojan Horse?
  A phony pony.

Trouble
What is easy to get into but hard to get out of?
  Trouble.

★

A lady named her cat 'Trouble'. One night it sneaked out of the house and the lady was so worried that she went out searching for it in her dressing-gown. She was stopped by a police car and an officer got out and asked her what she was doing outdoors in the middle of the night dressed only in her nightwear.
'I'm looking for Trouble,' she said.

Troubles
Rick: My car wouldn't start this morning – the battery was flat *and* I had a puncture.
Nick: You think you've got troubles – my sundial is slow.

Trousers
What is the best way to make a pair of trousers last?
  Make the jacket first.

★

Why wasn't the man arrested for going around without any trousers?
  Because he was wearing a kilt.

★

What has 100 legs but still cannot walk?
  50 pairs of trousers.

★

What does a boy do when he wears his trousers out?
  Wears them in again!

Truant
A little boy playing truant from school was discovered hiding in a tree.
'When are you going to come down?' asked his teacher.
'As soon as you go away,' he said.

True Words
Have you heard the expression, 'Many a true word is spoken through false teeth'?

Trumpet
Jenny: Mum, there's a man at the door with a trumpet.
Mother: Tell him to blow, will you?

★

Where could you get a job if you were a rubber trumpet player?
  In an elastic band.

★

Father: If you don't stop blasting away on that trumpet, I'll go crazy.
Son: But, Dad, I stopped an hour ago.

Truth
What is the naked truth?
  The bare facts.

★

Scientist: Try some of my new invention -- it's a truth drink.
Assistant: All right. Yuk! It's turpentine!
Scientist: Ain't that the truth!

Tsar's Children
What did the Tsar of Russia call his children?
  Tsardines.

Tuba
What tuba can't be played?
  A tube a toothpaste.

Tudor Monarchs

History teacher: The Tudor monarchs were Henry VII, Henry VIII, Edward VI, Mary . . . who came after Mary?
Soppy Poppy: The little lamb?

Tug-Of-War

The planned tug-of-war between England and France has had to be cancelled.

No one can find a rope long enough to stretch over the Channel.

Turkey

Why is a turkey like an evil little imp?
Because it's always a-goblin'.

★

The mother turkey was scolding her children for being naughty.
'You bad children,' she said, 'if your father could hear you now he'd turn in his gravy.'

★

Why did the turkey cross the road?
To prove he wasn't a chicken.

★

What happens if you cross a turkey with an octopus?
Everyone gets a leg at Christmas.

Turtledove

Adam: What kind of bird never leaves its shell?
Eve: Birds don't have shells!
Adam: A turtledove does!

Turtle Soup

Customer: Waiter, I've found a hair in my turtle soup.
Waiter: So, the hare and the turtle finally got together.

Twig

Customer: Waiter, there's a twig in my soup.
Waiter: Just a minute, sir, I'll get the branch manager.

Twins

Johnny: I used to be twins.
Jenny: How do you know?
Johnny: My mother has a picture of me when I was two.

★

Why are twin doctors like a puzzle?
Because they're a paradox.

★

Paul: My girlfriend's a twin.
Saul: How do you tell them apart?
Paul: Her brother's got a beard.

★

What language do twins speak in Holland?
Double Dutch.

★

Did you hear about the witch who had identical twins and couldn't tell which from which?

Typing

Job interviewer: Can you type?
Soppy Poppy: Not very well. But I can rub out at 65 words a minute.

Tyres

Why wouldn't the cyclist put more air in his tyres?
Because he couldn't stand the pressure.

★

Policeman: One of your car tyres is bald, sir.
Motorist: OK, officer, I'll see it gets some 'air.

Ugly

1st brontosaurus: What's that creature over there?
2nd brontosaurus: That's a stegosaurus.
1st brontosaurus: I wouldn't like to have to live with such an ugly face!

★

Jack: You're really ugly!
Jill: You're drunk!
Jack: Maybe, but I'll be sober in the morning.

★

Rick: My baby sister's so ugly Mum doesn't push the pram.
Nick: What does she do then?
Rick: She pulls it!

Umbrella

Soppy Poppy cut a hole in her umbrella so that she could see when it had stopped raining.

★

Did you hear about the umbrella who got arrested?
It was a put-up job.

★

Amy: Why do you call your umbrella Adam?
Zoe: Because one of its ribs is missing.

★

What kind of umbrella do politicians from all different parties carry on rainy days?
A wet one.

What goes up a chimney down, but won't go down a chimney up?
An umbrella.

★

A man going into a museum was stopped by an attendant who said, 'Please leave your umbrella in the cloakroom, madam.'
'But I haven't got an umbrella,' replied the lady.
'Then I'm afraid you can't come in, madam. I am under strict instructions not to allow anyone in unless they leave their umbrellas in the cloakroom.'

★

Did you hear about the umbrella-maker?
He was saving money for a sunny day.

★

Why do City businessmen carry umbrellas?
Because umbrellas can't walk.

Unabridged

Teacher: What is the meaning of unabridged, Poppy?
Soppy Poppy: A river you have to wade through, miss!

Undertakers

How do undertakers speak?
Gravely.

311

Underwater

What can fly under water?
    A fly in a submarine.

★

What was the name of the underwater cowboy?
    Billy the Cod.

Unit

What is the meaning of unit?
    It's a term of abuse.

United Nations

What worried the United Nations about the waiter dropping his tray?
    It meant the fall of Turkey, the break-up of China and the overthrow of Greece.

University

What key attended university?
    A Yale.

★

Father: What do you mean, you've been expelled from university?
Son: I've become a fugitive from the brain gang.

Unlucky

Tom: I'm so unlucky, my plastic fruit went bad.
Dick: I'm more unlucky than that — my stuffed bird flew away.

Harry: That's nothing. When I went ice skating the rink caught fire.

★

Andy: I met the unluckiest man in the world today.
Zak: Who?
Andy: Someone who broke his arm in an ear, nose and throat hospital.

Unpopular

Amy: I'm so unpopular at school, no one will talk to me.
Zoe: That's nothing. I'm so unpopular my phone doesn't even ring when I'm in the bath.

Up

Amy: My Dad beats me up every morning.
Zoe: How awful!
Amy: Yes, he gets up at 6, and I get up at 7.

Up and Down

What goes up and down but never moves?
    A flight of stairs.

Upbringing

Passenger: Sixth floor, please.
Lift operator: Here we are, sonny.
Passenger: Don't call me sonny! You're not my father!
Lift operator: I brought you up, didn't I?

USA

Why is a healthy boy like the USA?
    Because he has a good constitution.

Useful?

What is made by someone who does not need it, bought by someone who does not use it, and used by someone unknowingly?
    A coffin.

Vaccination

A doctor gave a little boy a vaccination, and as he was putting a plaster over it the little boy said,

'Would you put the plaster on the other arm, please?'

'Why?' said the doctor. 'I've covered the vaccination so that the boys at school won't bang into it.'

'You don't know the boys at school', said the little boy sadly.

Vacuum Cleaner

A salesman telling vacuum cleaners knocked at the door of an isolated farmhouse. The farmer's wife opened the door, and the salesman started his patter: 'Madam, I'm going to show you something amazing, something you'll never forget.' And so saying, he threw a bag of dirt on to the hall floor and continued his sales pitch: 'Now, I'm going to make a bargain with you, madam. If this marvellous new cleaner doesn't pick up *every* last bit of that dirt, I'll eat it.'

'Here's a spoon,' said the farmer's wife. 'We don't have electricity here.'

Valentine Cards

Amy: I got 30 Valentine cards last year!
Zoe: What a lot!
Amy: But I couldn't afford the stamps for them.

★

Salesgirl: This card has lovely words – 'To the only boy I've ever loved'.
Young girl: That'll do. I'll have a dozen, please!

Vampire

Vinny the Vampire: Mum, what's a vampire?
Mother: Shut up and drink your soup before it clots.

★

What did the polite vampire say to his dentist after having treatment?
 Fangs very much.

★

Who did the vampire marry?
 The girl necks door.

★

Can a toothless vampire bite you?
 No, but he can give you a nasty suck.

★

1st vampire: How's things?
2nd vampire: Terrible! Today I had a letter from my manager, saying I'm overdrawn 50 pints at the blood bank.

★

Why do vampires brush their teeth?
 To stop bat breath.

★

Where do vampires keep their money?
  In a blood bank.

★

What dance do vampires do?
  The Fangdango.

★

Why are vampires crazy?
  Because they are often bats.

★

Why do vampires go to Earls Court?
  To see the Bat Show, of course!

★

First vampire: A tramp stopped me in the street and said he hadn't had a bite for days.
Second vampire: What did you do?
First vampire: I bit him.

★

What kind of boat does a vampire sail in?
  A blood vessel.

Vanity

Jill: Do you think I'm vain?
Jack: No, why do you ask?
Jill: Well, because other girls as beautiful as me usually are.

★

Amy: Dad says I'll grow up to be a raving beauty.
Zoe: Why? Is he going to put you in a mad house?
Amy: No! He says I'll always have men at my feet.
Zoe: Oh, I'm sure you will – all chiropodists!

Varnish

Paul: How awful that your uncle drowned in a tub of varnish.
Saul: Yes, but what a finish.

Vegetable

How would you feel if you crossed a vegetable with a fruit?
  Melon-cauli.

★

What's a fresh vegetable?
  One that insults a farmer.

★

What vegetable needs a plumber?
  A leek.

Vegetarian

Did you hear about the vegetarian cannibal who only ate Swedes?

★

What does a vegetarian earn?
  Celery.

★

Vegetarian: I've lived on vegetables for years.
Bored friend: So what? I've lived on earth all my life.

★

Rick: Why did the cannibal become a vegetarian?
Nick: I don't know.
Rick: He was fed up with people.

Venetian Blind

How do you make a Venetian blind?
  Poke a finger in his eye.

★

What did the window pane say to the window sill?
  If it wasn't for venetian blinds it would be curtains for all of us.

Venison

Customer: What sort of meat is this?
Butcher: Venison, madam.
Customer: Is it very expensive?
Butcher: Yes, madam – it is deer.

Verb

English teacher: Sam, what is the imperative of the verb, to leave?
Sam: I don't know.
English teacher: Leave, Sam, LEAVE!
Sam: Oh, thank you, sir!

Vet

Anxious owner: My canary has just swallowed a roll of film.
Vet: Don't worry, nothing serious will develop.

Vicars

How do vicars make telephone calls?
Parson to parson.

★

One afternoon a vicar was playing a round of golf with one of his parishioners. The layman wasn't playing at all well and kept saying 'Oh darn' every time he missed the ball. The vicar decided he could not let the parishioner continue to swear and said, 'You really should not use such language, or the good Lord may well strike you.'
At that precise moment, there was a huge flash of lightning and the vicar was consumed in flames. Above the noise of the thunder could be heard a deep voice saying, 'Oh, darn, I've missed.'

★

Where would you go to look for a lost vicar?
The Bureau of Missing Parsons.

Video

Billy asked his father if they could buy a video but his father had to say no because they couldn't afford one. The next day Billy came staggering home with the latest video machine.

'Billy! Where did you get the money for that?' asked his father.
'No problem,' said Silly Billy. 'I sold the television.'

View

Where do you get the longest view in the world?
At the roadside where there are telegraph poles – because there you can see from pole to pole.

Vikings

What did Vikings use for secret messages?
The Norse Code.

Vineyard

How do you think you'd feel after a big lunch in a vineyard?
Grapeful!

★

Who swings through the vineyards?
Tarzan of the grapes.

Violin

Mother: Sam, come inside for your violin lesson!
Sam: Oh, fiddle!

★

Why did the girl keep her violin in a deep-freeze?
Because she liked to play it cool.

★

Why is a violin like a car?
They are both at their best when they're tuned up.

Viper

Why couldn't the viper wipe her nose?
Because the adder 'ad 'er 'andkerchief.

Vitamin

What does vitamin mean?

It's what you do when someone comes to your house.

★

Patient: I still feel terrible, doctor, in spite of all the vitamin pills I'm taking.

Doctor: Well, perhaps you should think about changing your diet.

Patient: Oh! Do I have to eat as well as take the vitamins?

Volkswagens

Where do Volkswagens go when they get old?

The Old Volks Home.

Vowels

When did the first two vowels appear?

Before U and I were born.

Wages

A young man was being interviewed for a clerk's job.

'You'll get £20 a week to start off with,' said the employer, 'and after six months you'll get £40 a week.'

'Oh, right,' said the young man. 'I'll come back in six months.'

Wagging Tail

A wagging tail is something with a happy ending.

Wagon Train

Why did the wagon train stop in the middle of the prairie?

Because it had injun trouble.

Waiter! Waiter!

— *Waiter, you've got your sleeve in my soup!*

There's no arm in it sir!

— *Waiter, would you say were an independent sort of person?*

Yes, sir! I never take orders from anyone.

— *Waiter, do you play badminton?*

Yes, sir! You should see my service action.

A waiter is someone who thinks money grows on trays.

— *Waiter, there's a fly in my soup.*

They don't seem to care what they eat, do they sir?

— *Waiter, there's a fly in my soup.*

Yes, sir, the chef used to be a tailor.

— *Waiter, I wish to complain to the chef. Ask him to come to my table.*

I can't do that, sir. He's just gone out for dinner.

— *Waiter, there's a bug in my soup.*

That's strange, it's usually a fly.

— *Waiter, there's a frog in my soup.*
That's right, sir. The fly's on holiday.

— *Waiter, this plate is dirty.*
Well, it's not my fingerprint, sir.

— *Waiter, you've brought me the wrong order.*
Well, sir, you did say you wanted something different.

— *Waiter, is the water healthy here?*
Of course, sir, we only serve well water.

— *Waiter, there's only one piece of meat here.*
All right, I'll cut it in two for you.

— *Waiter, what is this fly doing in my soup?*
Looks as if he's trying to get out, sir.

— *Waiter, how long will my sausages be?*
About four inches.

— *Waiter, there's a film on my soup.*
Oh, have you seen it before, then?

— *Waiter, is there rice pudding on the menu?*
There was, sir, but I've wiped it off.

— *Waiter, I'd like a glass of water and a piece of fish, please.*
Fillet, sir?
— *Of course – to the top of the glass!*

— *Waiter, there's a dead fly in my soup.*
Yes, sir, it's the heat that kills them.

— *Waiter, have you smoked salmon?*
No, madam, I've only ever smoked a pipe.

— *Waiter, why is this piece of toast all broken?*
Well, you said, 'Toast, coffee, and step on it,' so I did.

— *Have you ever visited the zoo?*
No, sir.

— *Well, you'd get real pleasure from watching the snails speed by.*

— *Waiter, this coffee is very weak.*
What do you expect me to do, sir? Give it weight training?

— *Waiter, I can't eat this soup.*
I'm sorry, sir. I'll get the manager.
— *Manager, I can't eat this soup.*
I'm sorry, sir. I'll call the chef.
— *I can't eat this soup, chef.*
Why not, sir?
— *I haven't got a spoon.*

— *I'll have a hamburger, please.*
With pleasure.
— *No, just the usual relish, please.*

— *Waiter, this stew isn't fit for a pig.*
I'll take it away, sir, and bring you some that is.

— *Waiter, there's a fly in my soup.*
Throw him this doughnut, sir. It'll make a good lifebelt!

— *Waiter, what is that fly doing on my sorbet?*
Learning to ski, sir.

— *Waiter, there's a button in my potato.*
Well, you did ask for a jacket potato, sir.

— *There's something wrong with these eggs.*
Don't blame me, sir. I only laid the table.

— *Hey, waiter, hey!*
Very good, sir. But that's a special order and we'll have to send out for it.

— *This goulash is terrible!*
The chef here has been making goulash since before you were born.
— *Maybe, but why did he save it for me?*

— *Waiter, the crust on that steak and kidney pie was tough.*
That wasn't the crust, sir. You've eaten the paper plate.

— *Waiter, it's been an hour since I ordered turtle soup.*
Yes, sir, but you know how slow turtles are.

— *Waiter, didn't you hear me say 'Well done'?*
(Not looking at the rare steak): Yes, sir. And I'd like to thank you for the compliment, we don't get many around here.

A waiter who had worked in the same restaurant for many years finally died. His wife was very upset and decided that she would like to contact him. She went to a fortune-teller, who could not help, and then to a medium, who suggested that they should try to contact her husband's ghost at the restaurant where he used to work.
They went to the restaurant and the medium and widow sat down to try to summon the husband's ghost. Very soon the widow heard her husband's voice, quietly saying, 'Hello.'
'Oh, John, is that you?' she asked.
'Yes,' he whispered.
'Speak up, please,' she said, 'I can hardly hear you.'
'I can't speak any louder.' replied her husband.
'Then come a little closer,' said the widow.
'I can't do that,' said John. 'That's not my table.'

— *Oh, sir, I am sorry I spilled water on you.*
Oh, don't worry. My suit was too big, anyhow.

— *Waiter, there's a fly in my soup.*
That's all right, sir. The spider on your bread will soon take care of it.

— *Waiter, there's a fly in my soup.*
Well, now, sir, how much can one little fly drink?

— *Waiter, that meal has given me heartburn.*
What were you expecting, sir? Sunburn?

— *What dishes shall I have to eat today?*
You eat dishes?

— *Waiter, this plate is wet.*
That's your soup, sir.

— *Waiter, what is this fly doing in my soup?*
It looks like the crawl to me, sir.

— *Waiter, your thumb is in my soup!*
Don't worry, sir, it's not hot.

— *I'm really hungry, waiter. I'd like a mashed potato sandwich on brown bread.*
You can't eat mashed potatoes on brown bread!
— *Maybe you're right. Make the sandwich on white toast.*

Now don't complain about the coffee, sir. You too may be old and weak some day.

— *Waiter, this lemonade is cloudy.*
No, sir, it's the glass that's dirty.

— *Waiter, there's no chicken in this chicken pie.*
Now, sir, are you the kind of person who expects dogs in dog biscuits?

— *Waiter, waiter, there's a dead fly in my soup.*
What do you expect for 50p, a live one?

— *Waiter, waiter, there's a fly in my soup.*
Oh, dear, it must have committed insecticide.

— *Waiter, waiter, this lobster's only got one claw.*

I'm sorry sir, it must have been in a fight.
— *Well, bring me the winner then.*

— *Waiter, waiter, there's soap in this pie.*
That's to wash it down with, sir.

Why are waiters good at mathematics?
  Because they know their tables.

★

Paul: Do you know what a representative of
  the Waiters' Union is called?
Saul: No, what is he called?
Paul: A chop steward.

★

Why did the waiter get on the head waiter's
nerves?
  Because he couldn't stand the sound of
breaking crockery.

Waitress
A new waitress was very nervous on her first
day at work, and dropped a pile of dishes in
the morning. In the afternoon she dropped a
second pile, and the manager called out, 'More
dishes?'
'No, sir,' said the waitress, picking up the
pieces, 'less!'

Wales
Amy: I hear Wales is sinking slowly into the
  sea.
Zoe: Because of all the leeks, I suppose.

Walk
Why did the beetle walk over the hill?
  Because it couldn't walk under it.

★

Isn't it amazing how a person can walk a mile
without moving more than two feet?

★

Bill: I couldn't walk for a whole year.
Ben: How awful! Why was that?
Bill: I wasn't old enough.

Father: When I was your age I thought
  nothing of walking to school.
Silly Billy: I don't think much of it either.

★

Mother: Billy, pick up your feet when you
  walk!
Silly Billy: Why, Mum? I've only got to put
  them down again.

★

Father: Take the dog out for some air, will
  you, Billy?
Silly Billy: Yes, Dad. Where's the nearest
  garage?

Wallet
Why is an empty wallet always the same?
  Because there's never any change in it.

Wallpaper
Customer: Have you any
  flowered wallpaper?
Sales assistant:
  Yes, madam.
Customer: Can I put
  it on myself?
Sales assistant:
  Yes, madam —
  but it might
  look better
  on the wall.

Walls
Amy: Have you heard the joke about the wall.
Zoe: No, tell me.
Amy: No, you'd never get over it.

★

Telephone caller: Is Adam Walls there?
Voice on phone: No.
Telephone caller: Is Basil Walls there?
Voice on phone: No.
Telephone caller: Then what's holding up the
  roof?

Walnuts

What nuts do you need to build a house?
  Walnuts.

Waltz

Bill: What's waltz?
Ben: Walt's what?

War

Bill: If I had an army of a thousand men, and you had an army of a thousand men and we had a war, who do you think would win?
Ben: Um, . . . I give up, who?
Bill: I would – you just gave up!

Warts

Andy: The doctor says my brother has warts.
Zak: What are they?
Andy: I'm not sure, but they have a way of growing on you.

Washable

Washable is a bull you can put in the tumble dryer.

Washing

Why wouldn't the little boy wash his face?
  Because it meant getting his hands wet – and they weren't dirty!

★

Sam: I hate having my face washed.
Mother: Well, you'll always have to do it – even when you're grown up.
Sam: No, I won't. I'll grow a beard.

Washing Machine

What animal can you find in your washing machine?
  The wash-and-were-wolf.

Wasps

Where do you take a sick wasp?
  To waspital.

Where do wasps come from?
  Stingapore.

★

One wasp came across another having a high old time dancing on top of a jar of jam.
'Why are you dancing like that on top of a jar of jam?'
'Because the jar says, "Twist to Open",' replied the dancing wasp.

Wasted Energy

Teacher: In this year of energy conservation, who can give me an example of wasted energy?
Soppy Poppy: Well, miss, it would be wasting energy to tell a hair-raising story to a bald man.

Watch

Bill: My mother should have been in the watch business.
Ben: Why's that?
Bill: Whatever I do, she watches.

★

Paul: I've got a wonder watch. It only cost me £1.
Saul: What's a wonder watch?
Paul: Every time I look at it I wonder if it's still going.

★

Did you hear about the clown who bought a wristwatch and arranged to pay for it later?
  He got it on tick.

★

Bill: I woke up last night convinced that my watch had gone.
Ben: Had it gone?
Bill: No, but it was going.

★

Bill: Did your watch stop when you dropped it?
Ben: Well, you didn't expect it to go through the floor, did you?

What sort of watch suits people who don't like to have time on their hands?

A pocket watch.

★

Jack: I once ate a watch.
Jill: Wasn't that time-consuming?

★

Amy: Is your watch going?
Zoe: It's brand-new – of course it's going.
Amy: Then when will it be back?

★

Paul: How do you like your new watch?
Saul: It's wonderful! If I wind it up fully it does an hour in 55 minutes.

★

What did the girl watch say to the boy watch?

Keep your hands to yourself.

Watchdog

Paul: Is your new dog any good as a watch dog?
Saul: He certainly is! The other day he stopped a burglar eating a pie my Mum had left on the kitchen table.
Paul: He didn't!
Saul: He did! He ate it himself.

★

Bill: This dog is a good watchdog.
Ben: How do you know?
Bill: He's full of ticks.

★

Saul: Why does your dog keep running round in circles?
Paul: Because he's a watchdog.

Watchmaker

What's the difference between a watchmaker and a sailor?

One sees over watches, the other watches over seas.

Water

How can you stop water coming in to your house?

Don't pay the water bill.

★

Why is life like a shower?

One wrong turn and you're in hot water.

★

What falls on water but never gets wet?

A shadow.

★

Silly Billy: Mum! There's something running across the bathroom floor that hasn't got any legs!'
Mother: Don't be silly, Billy! What are you talking about?
Silly Billy: Water!

★

Silly Billy had to write a sentence for science homework on water. He wrote: 'Water is a colourless liquid that is hot or cold and turns black when I put my hands in it.'

★

Paul: I once lived on water for eight months.
Saul: When was that?
Paul: When I was in the Navy.

★

Customer: Is your water healthy?
Waiter: Yes, sir, we only use well water.

★

A young lad started work in a garage. When he was asked to put water in all the cars he put buckets on all the passenger seats.

★

When is water musical?

When it's piping hot.

★

Soppy Poppy: Mum, do you water a horse when it's thirsty?
Mother: Yes, dear.
Soppy Poppy: Then I'm going to milk the cat.

Water Bed

How do you make a water bed more comfortable?
    Use a water softener.

Waterfall

How do you make a waterfall?
    Throw a bucket of water out of the window.

Water on the Brain

Andy: A scientist has just invented a cure for water on the brain.
Zak: What's that?
Andy: A tap on the head.

Water on the Knee

Did you hear about the man who had water on the knee?
    When the test results came back they showed the water was polluted.

What's the best thing for water on the knee?
    Drainpipe trousers.

A sports trainer went to see his doctor:
'And what's the matter with you?' asked the doctor.
'Water on the knee,' replied the trainer.
'How do you know?' asked the doctor.
'I dropped a bucketful on it!'

Water Polo

What happened to the stupid water polo player?
    His horse drowned.

Water Skiing

Silly Billy went out one day to water ski, but he gave up and went home when he couldn't find a sloping lake.

Waves

What's the best way to cut through giant waves?
    Use a sea saw.

Wavy Hair

Bill: What happened to your wavy hair?
Ben: It waved goodbye.

Weapon

What weapon do knights fear most?
    A tin-opener.

Weasel

How can you tell a weasel and a stoat apart?
    A stoat's stoatally different.

Weather

Mrs Able: Does this hot weather trouble you?
Mrs Cable: Oh, no. I throw the thermometer out of the window and watch the temperature drop.

Owing to a strike at the Meteorological Office, there will be no weather tomorrow.

★

Adam: How did you find the weather when you were on holiday?
Eve: Oh, I just went outside and there it was.

Lady (on the telephone): What's the weather like with you?
Friend (also on the telephone): It's so hot the cows are giving evaporated milk.

Johnny: What's the weather like?
Jenny: I don't know, it's too foggy to see.

★

Jack: Did you hear about the lady who walked around with her purse open all the time?
Jill: No, why did she do that?
Jack: She had heard that there was to be some change in the weather.

Weather Forecast

Amy: Have you heard the weather forecast for tomorrow?
Zoe: Yes, they said it's going to be dry and sunny and . . .
Amy: Oh, good!
Zoe: There's a 75 per cent chance that they're wrong.

★

Silly Billy and a friend were playing one day when the friend noticed a piece of rope hanging from Silly Billy's bedroom window.
'Why is that rope hanging there?' he asked.
'Oh, that's my new weather forecaster,' said Silly Billy.
'When the rope's swinging, I know it's windy, and if it hangs very still I know it's freezing outside.'

★

There was an old countryman with a considerable reputation as a weather forecaster. Farmers and gardeners for miles around sought his advice. But one day there was great concern because the old man stopped giving his forecasts. A deputation of farmers went to see him, and the spokesman asked, 'We're all very sorry that you've stopped giving us your weather forecasts. May we ask why?'
'Radio's bust,' replied the old man.

Web

What did Mrs Spider say when she broke her new web?
   Darn it!

Wedding

Jenny and her mother stopped outside a church to watch the bride arrive then went on to do some shopping. On their way back home, the bride and groom were coming out of church and Jenny said,
'Why did the bride change her mind?'
'What do you mean?' asked her mother.
'Well,' said Jenny, 'she went in to church with one man and came out with another!'

Wedding Presents

What wedding presents do you give when a snake-charmer and an undertaker marry?
'Hiss' and 'Hearse' pillow cases.

Weeds

Why do gardeners hate weeds?
   Because if you give them an inch they'll take a yard.

Week

Who invented the five-day-week?
   Robinson Crusoe – he had all his work done by Friday.

Weight

Johnny: I only weighed one kilo at birth.
Jenny: That's amazing – did you live?
Johnny: Live! You should see me now.

★

Doctor: What's your average weight?
Patient: I don't know!
Doctor: Well, what's the heaviest you've ever weighed?
Patient: Thirteen stone.
Doctor: Right, and what's the least you've ever weighed?
Patient: Seven pounds eleven ounces.

★

Tom: I see much more of Dick than I used to.
Harry: Yes, he has put on some weight recently.

If you have half an egg and half a chicken, what weight is a pound of butter?

A pound of butter always weighs a pound.

★

What's a good way to put on weight?

Eat a mango, swallow the centre, and you've gained a stone.

Well

A country doctor went out on his rounds and at a new patient's house he saw a deep well in the garden. He walked over to it to have a closer look, but unfortunately tripped just as he reached it. He fell down the well and was killed instantly.

Moral: Doctors should tend the sick and leave the well alone!

Werewolf

What did the werewolf write on his Christmas card?

Best vicious of the season.

★

Sam: Mum, I don't want to go to school. All the children say I look like a werewolf.

Mother: Shut up and comb your face.

Western Settler

Who settled in the West before anyone else?

The sun.

Wet

What never gets any wetter no matter how much it rains?

The sea.

Whale

What do you get if you cross a whale with a duckling?

Moby Duck.

Why did the whale set Jonah free?

Because he couldn't stomach him.

★

Andy: What do you call a baby whale that's crying?

Zak: I don't know.

Andy: A little blubber!

★

If a whale had boy and girl twins what would they be?

Blubber and sister.

★

Where do you weigh whales?

At the whale weigh station.

Wheel

What happened when the wheel was invented?

It caused a revolution.

Whisky

What do you get if you pour whisky on to shallots?

Pickled onions.

★

What is the difference between a whisky and a glass of water?

Have you ever paid for a glass of water?

Whistle

A railway guard ran out of the country station and dashed in to the local greengrocer's.

'Quick!' he said. 'The pea's dropped out of my whistle. Give me one of yours!'

But the greengrocer only had split peas. The next time the guard blew his whistle only half the train left the station.

★

Foreman: Please don't whistle while you work.

Workman: Who's working, boss?

What whistles when it gets hot?
  A kettle.

★

Rick: I know someone who whistles while he works.
Nick: He must be happy in his work.
Rick: No, he's a traffic policeman.

Whistler's Mother
What did the artist, Whistler, say when he found his mother wasn't sitting in her rocking chair?
  Mother, you're off your rocker!

White Elephant
How do you get rid of a white elephant?
  Put it in a jumbo sale.

White Lines
What puts the white lines on the sea?
  An ocean liner.

White Stick
Rick: Do you know that there's a jungle belief that a lioness will not harm you if you carry a white stick?
Nick: Maybe – but how fast do you have to carry the white stick?

Wholesome
Wholesome is the only thing from which you can take the whole and still have some left.

Wicket-Keeper
Paul: I think the wicket-keeper has the hardest job in the cricket team.
Saul: Why's that?
Paul: Well, there are so many catches in it.

Wife
Visitor (walking up driveway): Is your wife home?
Aggrieved husband: Well, I'm certainly not washing the car because I want to.

★

Did you hear about the man who keeps his wife under the bed?
  He thinks she's a little potty.

★

Foreign business visitor: And is this your most charming wife?
English host: No, she's the only one I've got.

Wig
Silly Billy went into a wig shop and asked for a wig that had a hole in the top.
'But, sir,' said the salesman, 'if the wig has a hole in the top people will see that you're bald.'
'I know,' said Silly Billy. 'But if people see that I'm bald they won't think that I'm wearing a wig.'

★

Have you heard about the man who found a wig in the street and took it to a psychiatrist because it was off its head?

★

Rick: Did you hear about the French horn player whose wig fell into his instrument at last night's concert?
Nick: Whatever happened?
Rick: He spent the rest of the concert blowing his top!

★

Why are a wig and a secret alike?
  Because you keep both under your hat.

Wild Duck

Customer: Have you any wild duck?
Waiter: No, sir, but we can take a tame one and irritate him for you.

Will

The family gathered around in the solicitor's office to hear him read the last will and testament of Archibald Able. He came to the last paragraph and read: 'I always told you, Adeline, that I would remember you in my will. So, hello there, Adeline.'

A rich old man was nearing the end of his days and the doctor who had attended him for years suggested he put his affairs in order.
'Oh, I've done that already,' said the old man. 'It's just my will I have to see to. And I'm going to leave all my money to the doctor who saves my life.'

Will Knot

Have you heard about Will Knot?
  He signs his name Won't.

Wind

What is wind?
  Air in a hurry.

What did the North wind say to the East wind?
  Let's play draughts.

Window

What is the definition of glass work?
  What a window does for a living.

How can you see through the thickest walls?
  Look through the window.

Window Box

Why did the window box?
  Because it saw the garden fence.

Window Cleaner

Bill: Did you hear about the stupid window cleaner who put a sign at the top of his ladder?
Ben: What did the sign say?
Bill: Stop.

What's soft and wet and goes around 'When I'm Cleaning Windows'?
  Chamois Davis Jnr.

A man got very tired of nosey neighbours staring through his windows and suggested to his wife that she clean the inside of the windows only.
'What good will that do?' she asked.
'Well,' replied her husband, 'if we clean the insides we'll be able to see out, but the neighbours won't be able to see in.'

Window Shopping

Mrs Able: I'd like that dress in the window.
Mr Able: But, dear, it is in the window already.

Winning

What does *every* winner lose in a race?
  His breath.

Paul: Mum won a saucepan in a competition.
Saul: That's what I'd call pot luck.

Winston Churchill

Teacher: Billy, can you tell me what Winston Churchill was famous for?
Silly Billy: His memory.
Teacher: Why do you say that?
Silly Billy: Well, there's a statue erected to it.

Winter Wear

Mrs Able: Last winter I wore white all the time so that the traffic could see me.
Mrs Cable: That must have kept you safe.
Mrs Able: No, a snow-plough knocked me down.

Wishbone

Jenny: Mum, can I have the wishbone?
Mother: Not until you've finished your greens.
Jenny: But I want to wish I won't have to finish them!

Wishing

Mother: The trouble with you, Jenny, is that you're always wishing for what you don't have.
Jenny: Well, what else is there to wish for?

Wit

Adam: I spend half my time trying to be witty.
Eve: I know, half-wit!

Witch

Why couldn't the young witch write a decent letter?
  Because she couldn't spell properly.

★

Witch in hospital: I'm feeling much better.
Doctor: Well then, you can get up for a spell this afternoon.

★

Why does a witch ride on a broom at Hallowe'en?
  So that she can sweep the sky.

★

What do you call a wicked old hag who lives by the sea?
  A sandwitch.

Why does a witch ride on a broomstick?
  Because a vacuum cleaner is too heavy.

★

What's the difference between a very small witch and a deer running from the hunter?
  One is a stunted hag and the other is a hunted stag.

★

Why do little witches always get A's at school?
  Because they're so good at spelling.

★

If a flying saucer is an aircraft, does that make a flying broom a witchcraft?

★

1st witch: I'm off on my motorbike, then. Goodbye!
2nd witch: Mind how you go on your br-oo-oo-mm stick.

★

1st witch: I'm so sorry, I've just run over your cat on my broomstick. Can I replace it?
2nd witch: Thank you for offering, but do you think you'd be able to catch rats and mice?

★

What did one witch say to another witch?
  Snap, cackle and pop!

★

What sort of music do witches like playing best?
  Hagtime.

★

1st witch: Is it the witching hour yet?
2nd witch: I don't know – I've lost my witch-watch.

Witch Doctor

A witch doctor was called in to see a very sick man in the jungle village. He examined him carefully and after much consideration said, 'I'll make you a medicine of river water, croco-dile tongue, snake skin and ground insect wing.' And the medicine man went away to make up the potion, brought it back and gave it to the man.

In the evening the villagers called the witch doctor back because the man was no better. 'Oh, well,' said the witch doctor, 'let him take two aspirin every four hours.'

Witness
Judge: Did you actually see the defendant bite off your neighbour's ear?
Witness: Not actually, your honour. But I saw him spit it out.

Judge: How can you continue to plead not guilty to theft when there are six witnesses to your action?
Prisoner: Because I can produce hundreds of people who weren't witnesses.

Wives
When a man gets married, how many wives does he get?

Sixteen – four better, four worse, four richer, four poorer.

Wizard
What do you call a wizard who only casts good spells?

A charming fellow.

Wizard of Oz
The wonderful Wizard of Oz.
Retired from business, becoz
What with up-to-date science,
To most of his clients
He wasn't the wiz that he woz.

Wolfman
What did the wolfman eat after he had his teeth taken out?

The dentist.

Wolves
Why are wolves like playing-cards?

Because they both live in packs.

Why is a woman on a desert island exactly like a woman in a shop?

Because she is always looking for a sail.

Wombat
Jack: What's that?
Jill: A wombat.
Jack: What do you do with that?
Jill: Play wom, of course.

Wood
Mr Wood and Mr Stone were waiting at the bus stop when a lovely girl walked round the corner towards them. Stone turned to Wood, Wood turned to Stone, and the girl turned into a shop.

Did you hear about the car with the wooden wheels and wooden engine?

It wooden go.

What is a boy with a wooden head called?
Edward.

Wooden Leg
Mother: Who's that at the door, Sam?
Sam: A man with a wooden leg.
Mother: Tell him to hop it, will you?

Two friends were boasting as usual to each other one day.
'My grandmother had a wooden leg,' said one.
'That's nothing,' said the other. 'My grandfather had a cedar chest.'

Which animal has wooden legs?
A timber wolf.

328

Woodman

What did the woodman's wife say to him one day?

Not many more chopping days until Christmas.

Woodworm

What did the woodworm say when he walked into the pub?

Is the bar tender here?

★

1st woodworm: How's life with you these days?
2nd woodworm: Oh, really boring.

Wool

Why did the little girl give her old neighbour all the wool left over from her craft class?

Because her mother had told her the old lady was always wool gathering.

★

Little Boy Blue: Baa, baa, black sheep, have you any wool?
Black sheep: Well, this certainly isn't nylon!

★

Top scientist: I've just made the most amazing discovery – I have discovered how to make wool out of milk!
Friend: That's wonderful news. But won't it make the cow feel a little sheepish?

★

Amy: Why do all your summer clothes have labels saying 'wool'?
Zoe: Mum's trying to fool the moths.

Words

When does a man never fail to keep his word?
When no one will take it.

★

What is the longest letter in the English language?
S — M — I — L — E — S, because there is a mile between the first and last letters.

Teacher: Can anyone in the class use 'fascinate' in a sentence?
Silly Billy: I can, miss! My coat has twelve buttons, but I can only fasten eight!

★

Which words can you pronounce quicker and shorter by adding another syllable to them?
Quick and Short.

★

What word allows you to take away two letters and get one?
Stone.

★

What do horses love that always comes in boats?
Oats.

★

Which word is always pronounced wrong?
W — R — O — N — G.

★

Bill: What's the longest word you've ever heard?
Ben: Whatever comes after, 'And now for a word from our sponsor.'

★

Where can you always find happiness?
In the dictionary.

Work

Workman: I throw myself into everything I do.
Foreman: Go and dig a big hole.

★

Why was the physicist exhausted?
Because he had too many ions in the fire.

★

Jack: What kind of work do you do?
Jill: My boss says it's sloppy.

★

Rick: I'm going to get a job where every day is a day off.

Nick: How's that?

Rick: Well, there are 365 days in a year – 366 this year because it's a Leap Year. If the working day is eight hours long, that's a third of a day which is 122 days. No one works on Sundays, so that's 52 days off, making 70 working days. Add two weeks' holiday, which leaves 56 days. There are four bank holidays, which leaves 52 days. There'd be no work on Saturdays, and as there are 52 Saturdays in the year, it would mean I had every day off!

★

Mr Able: How are you? Haven't seen you for ages. Still working for the same people?

Mr Cable: Yes . . . the wife and kids.

★

A young man who was out of work asked a friend if he knew anywhere he could get a job. 'Yes, I think I do,' said the friend. 'I read that there's a job going at the Eagle Repair Shop.' 'Well, I'll go along,' said the young man, 'but I don't know anything about repairing eagles.'

★

ALBERT BROWN, chairman of Blotto Blotting Paper Company, announced at the Annual General Meeting yesterday that he would not be retiring this year after all because he found his work totally absorbing.

★

Clerk: I can't live on this salary.

Boss: I'm sorry to hear that. I was about to promote you to the head of the Economics section.

★

One lunchtime a workman sat down with his mates to eat his lunch. He opened his box of sandwiches and took out a sardine and lettuce sandwich.

'Oh dear,' he said, 'I don't really like sardine and lettuce sandwiches, but never mind.'

The next lunchtime exactly the same thing happened, and the man said,

'Oh dear, more sardine and lettuce sandwiches.'

The next lunchtime he went through the same procedure and one of his workmates said,

'Why don't you ask your wife to make you sandwiches that you like?'

'Oh, that wouldn't make any difference,' said the man. 'My wife doesn't make the sandwiches – I do.'

★

What happens if 200 workmen fall off a mountain?

There's a navvy-lanche.

World

Soppy Poppy: Mum, is it true that the world is getting smaller?

Mother: Yes, I think so, dear. Why?

Soppy Poppy: Well, the postal charges have gone up again.

★

Teacher: How can you prove that the world is round?

Soppy Poppy: I never said it was, Miss!'

★

Teacher: Billy, when I asked you what shape the world was in, I meant 'flat' or 'round', not 'rough'!

★

Why is the world like a faulty jigsaw?

Because a piece (peace) is missing.

World Cup

Who won the World Cup in 1919?

No one – the first World Cup competition was played in 1930.

Worm

Mother: Billy, why are you bringing that worm indoors?

Billy: Well, we were playing outside and I thought he'd like to see my toys.

Visitor: What's that you're eating, Sam?
Sam: An apple.
Visitor: Watch out for worms!
Sam: Oh, no – when I eat an apple the worms have to look out for themselves!

★

What did Mrs Worm say to Mr Worm when he came home late?
  Why in earth are you late?

★

How can you tell which end of a worm is his head?
  Tickle his middle and see which end smiles.

★

Customer: Waiter! There's a worm on my plate.
Waiter (having a look): Oh, no, sir. That's your sausage.

★

Why was the worm in the cornfield?
  He was going in one ear and out the other.

★

Amy: I've just swallowed a long, fat worm.
Zoe: Shouldn't you take something for it?
Amy: No – I'm going to let it starve!

Mother worm: Let me give you some good advice.
Baby worm: What's that?
Mother worm: Never get up before the end of the dawn chorus.

★

Wrestling
How can a wrestler tell he's 'king of the ring'?
  When he sits on the thrown.

Writing
A teacher was finding out about her new class's abilities. 'Billy,' she asked, 'do you write with your left hand or your right hand?' Billy thought for a moment, and then said, 'Neither, Miss, I write with a pencil.'

★

Sam: Dad, can you write in the dark?
Father: I should think so, Sam. Why?
Sam: Would you sign this report card, please?

★

Saul: What are you doing?
Paul: Writing a letter to my brother.
Saul: Don't be silly – you can't write!
Paul: So what? My brother can't read.

★

Why is it bad to write on an empty stomach?
  Because paper is better!

Wrong
Nothing is ever all wrong.
  Even a stopped clock is right twice a day.

Strictly speaking, only the first two jokes belong in this chapter, but because they looked a little sad all on their own we found some company for them: hundreds more jokes that didn't seem to belong in any of the other chapters. This chapter is really a Lucky Dip. Have fun!

X-Ray

Patient: Well, what does my brain X-ray show?
Doctor: Nothing.

★

What is an X-ray?
  Bellyvision!

★

Wheeler: The horse you sold me is a fine animal, but he won't hold his head up.
Dealer: That's because of his pride. He'll hold his head up as soon as he's paid for.

★

Bill: Do you know that all dogs, no matter how vicious, will come up and lick my hand?
Ben: They wouldn't be so friendly if you ate with a knife and fork.

★

Farmer: Where's the mule I asked you to have shod?
Farm boy: Oh! I thought you said *shot!*

★

Diner: I'd like a cup of coffee and a muttered buffin.

Waitress: Do you mean a buffered muttin?
Diner: No, I mean a muffered buttin.
Waitress: Wouldn't you please have dough-nuts and milk instead?

★

Teacher: Give me a sentence with an object.
Pupil: You are very beautiful.
Teacher: What is the object of that sentence?
Pupil: A good mark.

★

What's worse than a giraffe with a sore throat?
  A centipede with sore feet.

★

Why are clouds like people riding horses?
  Because they hold the rains.

★

Bill: Just think – nothing is impossible!
Ben: Oh yes? Have you ever tried to ski up an escalator?

★

Andy: Your cough sounds very much better.
Zak: Good – I've been practising all night.

★

What bird is present at every meal you eat?
  A swallow.

★

Doctor: I don't think anything's wrong – your pulse is as steady as a clock.
Patient: That's because you've got your hand on my watch.

Why is doing nothing so tiring?
 Because you don't stop to rest.

★

What's the easiest way to catch a fish?
 Get someone to throw it at you.

★

Adam: What did the doughnut say to the cake?
Eve: I don't know. What did the doughnut say to the cake?
Adam: If I had as much as dough as you, I wouldn't be hanging around this hole!

★

Wife: I baked two kinds of cake today – take your pick!
Husband: No, thanks – I'll use my hammer.

★

Diner: Is this tea or coffee? It tastes like kerosene.
Waiter: Tea – our coffee tastes like turpentine.

★

Saul: What has eight legs, two arms, three heads, and two wings?
Paul: I know – a man on a horse with a chicken.

★

Teacher: Poppy, your typing has improved! You only have ten mistakes.
Soppy Poppy: Thank you!
Teacher: Now we'll look at the second line.

★

What's the difference between a tiger and a comma?
 A tiger has claws at the end of his paws and a comma is a pause at the end of a clause.

★

Adam: How much do you weigh now?
Eve: One hundred and plenty!

★

Sardine to a friend as a submarine passes overhead:
 'There goes a can of people.'

What's a kangaroo's favourite year?
 Leap year.

★

Policeman (taking out notebook): Name?
Speeding motorist: Amadeus Heinrich Garfunkel.
Policeman (putting away notebook): Drive more slowly next time.

★

Why is a baseball game like Yorkshire pudding?
 Because they both depend on the success of the batter.

★

Bookseller: Here's a book that will do half your work.
Customer: Wonderful – I'll take two.

★

Judge: Have you ever been up before me?
Burglar: I don't know – what time do you get up?

★

What's a wisecracker?
 A smart cookie!

★

Mother: Well, what did your father say about your smashing up the car?
Johnny: Leaving out the swear words?
Mother: Of course!
Johnny: Nothing.

★

What sort of house weighs the least?
 A lighthouse.

★

Judge: £50 fine or ten days in prison.
Silly Billy: £50 please, Judge.

★

Policemen chasing a burglar through a supermarket lost him when he jumped on a scale and got a weigh.

★

Johnny was given a plateful of jelly for the first time.

'Eat it up,' said his mother.

'Eat it!' said Johnny, 'But it's not dead yet!'

★

Patient: Doctor, I think I've got amnesia.

Doctor: Have you had it long?

Patient: Had what long?

★

Sam: Johnny's mother wouldn't let him keep his frogs at home, so he found somewhere else safe to put them.

Mother: Where did he put them?

Sam: In our bathtub.

★

Waiter: Here's your coffee, madam – a special blend all the way from Brazil.

Customer: Oh, is that where you've been!

★

Adam: Haven't seen you for ages – where have you been all this time?

Eve: In college, taking medicine.

Adam: I'm sorry to hear that – are you feeling better?

★

What do you get if you cross a sheep with a porcupine?

An animal that can knit its own sweaters!

★

Juliet: Romeo! Romeo! Wherefore art thou?

Romeo: Down here in the flower bed – the trellis broke!

★

A new army recruit was on guard duty at the camp gate with orders to admit only those cars with security badges. He stopped a car which hadn't got a badge, but which did contain a four-star general. The recruit heard the general order the driver to carry on, so he bent down to the open window and said, 'I'm new at this job, sir. Do I shoot the driver or you?'

★

What do you get if you cross a wild bird with a hiccup?

Wild Bill Hiccup.

★

What's the difference between a hill and a pill?

A hill goes up and the pill goes down.

★

Paul: I've just seen a strange yellow vehicle with flashing red lights – and it was full of little people.

Saul: Was it a UFO?

Paul: No, the school bus.

★

Which travels faster – heat or cold?

Heat. You can catch cold.

★

Visitor: Has your baby learned to talk?

Mother: Oh yes – now we're teaching him to be quiet.

★

Jack: What's a volcano?

Jill: A mountain that blows its cool.

★

What's a gnu?

Nothing much. What's a gnu with you?

★

What must you always keep after you have given it to someone else?

Your word.

★

Teacher: Tell me what you know about 18th century scientists, Sam.

Sam: They're all dead.

★

What is the difference between men and women?

Men have a sense of humour and women have a sense of rumour.

★

Why did Humpty Dumpty have a great fall?
To make up for his rotten summer.

★

Paul: What's the difference between a conductor and a teacher?
Saul: I don't know. What is the difference between a conductor and a teacher?
Paul: A conductor minds the train and a teacher trains the mind.

★

Boss: Did you leave that note for Mr Webb where he would be sure to see it when he comes in?
Office Boy: Yes, sir! I stuck a pin through it and put it on his chair.

★

Amy: Did you know that the animals went in to Noah's Ark in pairs?
Zoe: All except the worms. They went in in apples.

★

Maid: While you were out, madam, your son swallowed a bug. But don't worry, I sprayed him with insect repellant.

★

The boy stood on the burning deck,
His feet were full of blisters;
The flames came up and burned his pants,
And now he wears his sister's.

There was an old lady of Chertsey,
Who made a remarkable curtsey;
She twirled round and round,
Till she sunk underground,
Which distressed all the people of Chertsey.

★

There was an old man from Peru,
Who dreamt he was eating his shoe,
He awoke in the night
In a terrible fright,
And found it was perfectly true!

★

What sits on a lily pad and goes, 'Cloak, cloak'?
A Chinese frog.

★

As a beauty I am not a star,
There are others more handsome by far;
But my face – I don't mind it,
For I am behind it;
It's the people in front that I jar.

★

What's hot, greasy, and makes you feel bad?
A chip on your shoulder.

★

What's bright orange and shoots out of the ground at 100 mph?
An E-type carrot.

★

A Londoner stopped on his journey northwards at a pub in Stoke-on-Trent. He was boasting about how many famous and great men had been born in the south, in London especially. The publican made no reply, until the Londoner said,
'Well, then, have any big men been born in Stoke?' to which he replied, 'No, only little babies.'

★

What's yellow and goes 'slam, slam, slam, slam'?
A four-door banana.

What's round, purple or green and used to rule the waves?
    Grape Britain.

★

Sam: Dad, how long does it take to get from London to Norwich?
Father: About three hours.
Sam: And how long from Norwich to London?
Father: The same – you should know that!
Sam: Well, it's not the same from Christmas to Easter as it is from Easter to Christmas, is it?

★

What carries hundreds of passengers and squirts water at Tarzan?
    A jumbo jet.

★

What's brown, shiny, and flies at twice the speed of sound?
    The Anglo-French Conker.

★

Who's short, scared of wolves, and swears?
    Little Rude Riding Hood.

★

What starts with P, finishes with E and has thousands of letters?
    Post Office.

★

What happens when Japanese car spare parts fall out of aeroplanes?
    It rains Datsun cogs.

★

What's green, hairy and drinks from the wrong side of the glass?
    A gooseberry with hiccups.

★

What's green, curly and plays pop music from the heart?
    A transistor lettuce.

★

Mother: Answer the telephone, please, Sam.
Sam: But it's not ringing.
Mother: Oh, Sam! Why do you have to leave everything to the last minute?

★

Andy: My Dad's a big-time operator.
Zak: Oh really, what does he do?
Andy: He winds up Big Ben.

★

Mrs Able: Who's that lady with the little mole?
Mrs Cable: Sshh, that's her husband.

★

What do animals read in zoos?
    Gnus papers.

★

Adam: Did you miss me while I was gone?
Eve: Were you gone?

★

Judge: But I still don't see why you broke into the same shop three nights running.
Prisoner at the bar: Well, your honour, I took a dress home for my wife and had to go back and change it twice.

★

A spoilt little boy was annoying other passengers by lying in the aisle of the plane. One man was so irritated by the child that he shouted, 'Hey, kid! Why don't you go outside and play?'

★

Mrs Able: Remember there was a terrible storm like this the night you proposed?
Mr Able: Yes, it was a dreadful night.

★

Andy: I have an ambition to get my name in the papers.
Zak: That's easy. Just walk across Piccadilly Circus reading one.

★

Mrs Able: Can you lend me five pounds for a week, old dear?
Mr Able: Yes. Who's the weak old dear?

What made the field laugh?
Hoe-hoe-hoe.

★

Lady of the Manor: And what can I do for you, my man?
Tramp: I'd like a coat sewn on this button.

★

A customer in a restaurant decided to have ice cream for dessert and asked the waitress what flavours were on the menu. She whispered hoarsely, 'Chocolate, coffee and vanilla.'
The customer wanted to appear sympathetic, so he said, 'Do you have laryngitis?'
'No,' croaked out the waitress, 'only chocolate, coffee and vanilla.'

★

Visitor: So you'd say this is a healthy place to live?
Local resident: Certainly. When I came here I couldn't walk or eat solid food.
Visitor: Oh! What was wrong with you?
Local resident: Nothing – I was born here.

★

What's the difference between a man who has signed a legal document and a man who has eaten a good meal?
One has signed and dated, the other is dined and sated.

★

Sam: Mother, you promised to take me out today to see the orang-outangs.
Mother: Sam, why would you want to go out and see the orang-outangs when Grandpa's here!

★

Bill: You're wearing my brand new anorak!
Ben: Well, you wouldn't want me to get your new Nike T-shirt wet, would you?

★

Mrs Able: Well, I don't know which card to choose. Tell me, dear, do you ever have trouble making up your mind?
Salesgirl: Well, yes and no.

Paul: Did you hear about the man who couldn't play, even though he had a full deck?
Saul: What was he trying to play?
Paul: Shuffleboard.

★

Who make the most noise when they're doing their nails?
Carpenters.

★

How can you walk into a room with six legs?
Take a chair with you.

★

What day of the year is an order to go forward?
March 4th.

★

Why were Elijah's parents good business people?
Because between them they made a prophet.

★

What happened to the lord who had to give up his castles because he was so rude?
He lost all his manors.

★

What did one eye say to the other?
Between us, there's something that smells.

★

Mother: Poppy, why are you tiptoeing past the medicine cabinet?
Soppy Poppy: Because I don't want to wake up the sleeping pills.

★

What musical note makes a good army officer?
A sharp major.

★

Did you hear about the florist who had two children?
One is a budding genius and the other's a blooming idiot.

★

A drunken man went racing after a fire-engine, but fell exhausted before he caught up with it. 'All right,' he shouted as it disappeared up the road, 'keep your rotten ice cream.'

★

A man who was driving past a farm stopped because he saw a most beautiful horse in the field. He went to the farmer and said, 'That horse looks very good, and I'd like to buy her. Name your price.'
'She doesn't look so good and she's not for sale,' replied the farmer.
'I think she looks great, and I'll give you £1,000,' said the man.
'I tell you she doesn't look so good,' said the farmer, 'but if you want her that much, I'll accept the £1,000.'
And the man went away very happily with the horse. The next day, however, he went back to the farm in a furious temper.
'You're a cheat and a thief,' he shouted at the farmer. 'You sold me a blind horse.'
'I told you she didn't look so good, didn't I?' replied the farmer.

★

Knocked down pedestrian: What's the matter with you? Are you blind?
Motorist: Blind? What do you mean, blind? I hit you, didn't I?

★

Paul: How did you come to fall into the canal?
Saul: I didn't come to fall in the canal. I came to fish.

★

Bill: Excuse me, I think you're sitting in my seat.
Ben: Can you prove it?
Bill: I think so. I left a custard tart on it. . . .

★

Mother: Sam! Did you fall down in your new trousers?
Sam: Yes, Mum. I didn't have time to take them off.

★

Mrs Able: Is it all right to make breakfast in my dressing gown?
Mr Able: Yes, but it would be less messy in the frying pan.

★

Guest: What are the weekly rates here?
Hotel manager: I don't know, sir. Nobody's ever stayed that long.

★

Bill: You remind me of a man.
Ben: What man?
Bill: The man with the power.
Ben: What power.
Bill: The power of 'oo-do'.
Ben: Who do?
Bill: You do.
Ben: I do what?
Bill: Remind me of a man.
Ben: What man?
Bill: The man with the power. . . .

★

Mr Able: My wife must be really ashamed of me.
Mr Cable: What makes you say that?
Mr Able: For my birthday she knitted me a jumper with no holes.

★

Princess to knight in shining armour:
Don't just stand there! Slay something!

★

What would you get if you crossed a man with a goat?
Someone who's always butting into other people's affairs.

★

Husband: I can't think where all the grocery money goes each week.
Wife: Stand sideways, dear, and look in the mirror.

★

Terrible Tim: I guess it's time for me to go home now. Don't trouble to see me out.
Aunt Adeline: It's no trouble. It'll be a pleasure.

Jack: My little sister's just fallen down the laundry chute. What shall I do?

Jill: Quick – go to the library and get a book on how to raise a child.

★

Customer: Waiter, you've got your thumb on my steak.

Waiter: Well, sir, I don't want it to fall on the floor again.

★

Johnny: Do you feel like a glass of wine?

Jenny: No! Do I look like one?

★

Mr Able: Imagine! I've just met a man whom I haven't seen for twenty years.

Mr Cable: That's nothing. I've just met a man whom I've never seen before in my life.

★

What has sharp teeth and hair all colours of the rainbow?

A punk family's comb.

★

Mrs Able: I'm just going to the doctor's. I don't like the look of my husband.

Mrs Cable: I'll come with you. I hate the sight of mine.

★

Which British town sells bad meat?

Oldham.

★

What's big, grey and goes about muttering?

A mumbo-jumbo.

★

What has twenty-two legs, two wings and is yellow?

A Chinese football team.

★

What's purple and conquered the world?

Alexander the Grape.

★

What did the laundry man say to the impatient customer?

Keep your shirt on!

★

What always succeeds?

A canary with no teeth.

★

What happens when you throw a black rock in the Yellow River?

It gets wet.

★

Jenny: Daddy, there's a man at the door with a bill.

Father: Don't be silly, it must be a duck with a hat on.

★

Why wouldn't the girl take a job in a clothing factory?

Because she was too young to dye.

★

What animal has two humps and is found at the North Pole?

A lost camel.

★

What can you put in a mug but never take out?

A crack.

Where would you post a letter when you're asleep?

In a pillow-box.

★

What has two hands but no arms?

A clock.

★

Two met met after not seeing each other for many years. One said to the other, 'I hear your first two wives died of eating poisoned mushrooms, and now your third has just fallen off a cliff. That's a bit odd, isn't it?'

'Not at all,' said the second man, 'she wouldn't eat the mushrooms.'

★

What's the easiest way to mount a horse?

Take it to a taxidermist.

★

Who does everyone listen to, but no one ever believes?

The weatherman.

★

Policeman: Madam, it's been reported that your dog has been chasing the postman on his bicycle.

Mrs Cable: That's ridiculous, officer. My dog can't ride a bicycle.

★

Jack: I want to see the world!

Jill: I'll buy you an atlas for your next birthday, then.

★

What is boiled, cooled, sweetened and then soured?

Iced tea with lemon.

★

Mr Able: I didn't know your wife was such an energetic dancer.

Mr Cable: She's not. The waiter just dropped a bucket full of ice cubes down her back.

★

Polly: Mum, I feel as sick as a dog.

Mother: Don't worry, I'll call the vet.

★

Mother: Why is Jenny crying?

Johnny: Because she's just come down the stairs without walking.

★

What comes from trees and fights cavities?

A toothpick.

★

How long should a person's legs be if she's 5ft 5in?

Long enough to reach the ground.

★

Why was the lady's hair angry?

Because she was always teasing it.

★

Rick: Everybody laughed when I sat down to play the piano.

Nick: Why?

Rick: No stool.

★

Jenny: Mum, why are your hands so soft?

Mother: Because I use new improved Clean 'n' Shining for washing up.

Jenny: But how does that make your hands soft?

Mother: Because the fee Clean 'n' Shining pay me for this advertisement means we can buy an automatic dishwasher.

★

Paul: Did you hear about the two blood cells?

Saul: No, what happened?

Paul: They loved in vein.

★

What goes through a door, but never goes in or out?

A keyhole.

★

Why did the woman jump in the sea?

To get a wave in her hair.

340

Why are boarding-house keepers called landladies?

Because they charge the earth.

★

What can you hold without your hands?

Your breath.

★

What do you call a little clam who won't share his toys?

Shellfish.

★

There was once a little boy with a turned-up nose.

Every time he sneezed he blew his cap off.

★

What has a black cape, crawls through the night and bites people?

A tired mosquito with a black cape.

★

On the street stood an old man, a dog and a horse. The dog was playing an accordion while the horse sang, and the old man was collecting money from passers-by. One lady stopped and remarked on what an amazing sight the three made, 'And how talented you all are. You should be in the circus.' 'Oh, no, madam,' said the old man, 'my conscience wouldn't let me do that. I'll let you in to a secret, though. The horse can't really sing. The dog's a ventriloquist.'

★

A trainer and his talking dog were speeding along in a brand new sports car on their way to a special show at the seaside. Suddenly a police car overtook them and signalled for them to stop.

'Pull over, then,' said the dog. 'And remember – when he gets here, let me do the talking!'

★

Mr Able: My dog doesn't eat meat.
Mr Cable: Why is that?
Mr Able: Because I never give him any.

★

A man went in to a doctor's crowded waiting-room, fell on the ground, rolled himself into a ball and started tumbling around the room. Patients, furniture and magazines were soon flying everywhere. The commotion brought the doctor running from his surgery.

'What on earth is the matter with you,' he asked the man.

'I'm a billiard ball,' replied the man.

'Oh, well,' said the doctor, 'you'd better come to the head of the queue.'

★

What is purple and 5,000 miles long?

The Grape Wall of China.

★

There was once an Indian Chief whose name was Shortcake. He lived with his wife Squaw high up in the mountains. Sadly, one day Shortcake died and a very sympathetic Indian asked Squaw what she was going to do with him. She answered mournfully,

'Squaw bury Shortcake.'

★

Why did the man have a funny voice and funny teeth?

Because he had a falsetto voice and a false set o' teeth.

★

Adam: Are you sure you want me to put my head into the lion's mouth?
Eve: Yes, we had a bet!
Adam: But I thought you were my friend.

★

Two ants went exploring in a supermarket. They climbed on top of a box of cornflakes and suddenly the first ant went wild, running away as fast as he could.

'Hey! Wait for me!' cried the second ant. 'What's your hurry?'

'Can't you read?' shouted back the first ant. 'It says here: "Tear along the dotted line".'

★

What goes through water, but doesn't get wet?

A shaft of sunlight.

How do you write 'fifty miles under the sea' in just four words?

the sea
———————
fifty miles

★

What can you always count on when things go wrong?
    Your fingers.

★

What horse can you put your shirt on but be sure of getting it back?
    A clothes horse.

★

A city dweller went for a drive in the country and, passing a farm, saw a beautiful horse. He decided that he must have the animal, and although the farmer was reluctant to sell, the man finally persuaded him. He decided to go for a ride straight away, jumped on the horse and shouted, 'Giddyup!' but the horse didn't move.
    The farmer explained that it was a very special horse: 'He used to work in a circus and will only go if you say "Praise the Lord!" To stop him, you have to shout, "Amen!"'
So the city man said, 'Praise the Lord!' and off trotted the horse, going faster and faster towards a cliff. The rider was terrified but remembered just in time to shout, 'Amen!' and the horse screeched to a halt right at the cliff's edge.
The city man was very relieved, raised his eyes to heaven and exclaimed, 'Praise the Lord!'

★

Jenny's mother thought she was beginning to show off too much, so one night when there were guests for dinner, Mother said:
'If Jenny comes in and does anything to attract your attention, please don't take any notice of her. She's not supposed to be up.'
Sure enough, Jenny came downstairs during dinner and paraded around the room. The guests pretended not to see her and soon Jenny went back upstairs, looking very pleased with herself. The following morning Mother overheard Jenny saying to a school friend, 'I tell you it does work! Last night I rubbed Mum's vanishing cream all over me and nobody saw me.'

★

A man was out riding on a horse one day when a little dog trotted up behind him, and said, 'Hello, there!'
'Well, I never,' said the horseman. 'I never knew dogs could talk.'
The horse turned his head towards his rider and said,
'You learn something new every day, don't you.'

★

What can travel at the speed of sound, but has neither wheels, wings, nor an engine?
    Your voice.

★

Rick: Why are your hands shaking?
Nick: I suppose they must be glad to see each other.

★

Tramp: Will you give me some money for a cup of coffee?
Man in street: No, thanks, I don't drink coffee.

★

What do you get if you cross a young goat with a pig?
    A dirty kid.

Why does a mother carry her baby?
   Because the baby can't carry its mummy.

★

Where can you find cards on a ship?
   On the deck.

★

Rick: I fell and hit my head against the piano.
Nick: Did you hurt yourself?
Rick: No, I hit the soft pedal.

★

The animals in the jungle were playing a fiercely competitive game of football. Boris the Beetle was just about to score what would have been the winning goal when Ernie the Elephant, playing on the defending side, squashed him flat.
The referee blew his whistle and shouted, 'You've killed him! I'll have to send you off! Off you go!'
'But, ref!' said Ernie, 'I didn't mean to kill him, I only meant to trip him up!'

★

What did the elephant think of the grape's home?
   De-vine.

★

What is worse than a turtle with claustrophobia?
   An elephant with hay fever.

★

What fruit would a chimp most like to sleep on?
   An ape-ri-cot.

★

Where do you learn how to work for an ice cream company?
   At sundae school.

★

What has a neck, two sides, a bottom, and often a broken life?
   A bottle.

Why should you stay calm when you meet a cannibal?
   Because you don't want to get into a stew.

★

If there were ten cats in a boat and one jumped out, how many would there be left?
   None, because they were all copy cats.

★

Scientist: I've invented a new pill that's half glue and half asprin.
Assistant: Who's it for?
Scientist: People with splitting headaches.

★

Sam: Dad, where was I born?
Father: In London.
Sam: Where were you born?
Father: In New York.
Sam: And where was Mum born?
Father: In Rome.
Sam: Isn't it amazing that we all met up?

★

What should a girl wear if she wants to end a fight?
   Make-up.

★

How many chimneys does Father Christmas have to climb down?
   Stacks.

★

Customer: I have a complaint – when you sold me this cat you said it would be splendid for mice. But he won't go near them!
Pet shop owner: Well, isn't that splendid for the mice?

★

Doctor: Why are you holding that sardine in front of your mouth?
Patient: I've just swallowed a cat!

★

What kind of cup can't hold water?
   A cupcake.

★

Did you hear about the writer who dropped five stories in to a wastepaper basket and lived?

★

A man who was about to make his first parachute jump was very nervous, despite weeks of training. 'What happens if the parachute doesn't open?' he asked.
'That,' said the pilot, 'is what we call jumping to a conclusion.'

★

How did the world's tallest man become short overnight?
His best friend borrowed £100.

★

Twelve men were sheltering under one umbrella, but none got wet. Why?
Because it wasn't raining.

★

Did you hear about the cargo ship with 20 tons of yo-yos that crossed the Atlantic?
It sank 44 times.

★

Jack: Keep that dog away from me!
Jill: Don't you know the old proverb, 'A barking dog never bites'?
Jack: Yes, but does your dog?

★

Jenny came home from school one afternoon and said to her mother,
'Mum, is that stuff in the yellow bottle in the cupboard hair mousse?'
'No, dear,' replied her mother, 'that's super glue.'
'No wonder I couldn't get my hat off at school today.'

★

Mother to daughter: I don't care if the kitchen wall *does* have a crack in it. Will you please stop telling everyone you come from a broken home!

★

Paul: How do you know your Mum wants to get rid of you?
Saul: Why else would she pack a road map with my lunch every day?

★

What lurks at the bottom of the sea and makes you an offer you can't refuse?
The Codfather.

★

What moves around a bus at 1000 mph?
A lightning conductor.

★

Guard: Halt, who goes there?
Voice in the darkness: Well! How did you know my name?

★

What has tiny wings and is related to the camel?
A hump-backed midge.

★

Teacher: If there were a dozen flies on my desk and I swatted one, how many would be left?
Smart Alec: Only the dead one.

★

Sam went shopping with his mother, and the greengrocer gave him an apple.
'What do you say, Sam?' said his mother.
'Would you peel it, please, mister?' replied Sam.

★

If Ching Chong went to Hong Kong to play ping pong with Ding Dong and died, what would they put on his coffin?
A lid.

★

Mother: Sam, you've *got* to tell me where you buried Dad in the sand. He's got the car park ticket.

★

An insignificant-looking little man went into a

cafe for a cup of tea. Serving in the cafe was a most peculiar-looking man with a huge spot on the side of his nose. Nudging the man sitting alongside him, the little man said, 'Just look at the size of the spot on that man's nose!'

The other man stood up, grabbed the little man by his tie and shouted, 'That man is my brother!'

'Oh,' said the little man, 'doesn't that spot suit him!'

There was a young lady from Crete
Who was so exceedingly neat,
When she got out of bed
She stood on her head.
To make sure of not soiling her feet.

A man called on a married couple whom he had not seen for years. The wife opened the door.

'How lovely to see you again!' she exclaimed.

'It's good to see you, too,' said the man. 'And how is your husband Jack?'

'Oh, you don't know,' she said. 'Jack died last year.'

'Oh, I'm so sorry,' said the man. 'Was it sudden?

'Yes. One Saturday morning he went to the allotment to get a cabbage for lunch and dropped down dead.'

'How awful,' said the man sympathetically. 'Whatever did you do?'

'What could I do?' answered the woman. 'I opened a tin of peas.'

There was a young lady named Sue
Who carried a frog in each shoe.
When asked to stop
She replied with a hop,
'But I'm trying to get into Who's Zoo!'

★

A famous magazine editor was once dining in a very smart Mayfair restaurant. As each course arrived he praised it to the skies, and he finally asked to see the chef to compliment him in person and try to discover how he produced such delicious dishes. The chef was highly delighted with the praise, but shook his head when the editor asked him for one of the recipes. 'I'm so sorry, sir,' he said, 'but good chefs, like good journalists, never reveal their sauces.'

Once upon a time an Inca tribe found a beautiful throne in the jungle. It seemed to be made of solid gold and was encrusted with jewels. They carried it to their village and built a special grass hut to keep it in. The hut was guarded day and night and no one was allowed to enter it. A year later, at the end of the rainy season, the tribal chief decided to look again at the throne. He was terribly upset to discover it covered with green mould, and went out of the hut to sob on his wife's shoulder. She was very sympathetic and said quietly, 'Well, it just goes to show, people who live in grass houses shouldn't store thrones.'

Billy, in one of his nice new sashes,
Fell in the fire and was burnt to ashes;
Now, although the room grows chilly,
I haven't the heart to poke poor Billy.

There was a young student of Crete
Who stood on his head in the street.
Said he, 'It is clear
If I mean to stop here
I shall have to shake hands with my feet.

Last night I slew my wife,
Stretched her on the parquet flooring;
I was loth to take her life,
But I had to stop her snoring.

There was an old man of Vancouver
Whose wife got sucked in to the hoover.
He said, 'There's some doubt
If she's more in than out
But whichever it is, I can't move her.'

There was a young lady named Hannah
Who slipped on a peel of banana.
She wanted to swear
But her mother was there
So she whistled 'The Star-spangled Banner'.

Here I sit in the moonlight,
Abandoned by women and men,
Muttering over and over,
'I'll never eat garlic again!'

An Englishman was playing cricket in Australia. Facing a very fast Australian bowler in a tense test match, the ball bounced high and hit him straight in the eye. The next thing he knew, he was lying in a Sydney hospital bed after an emergency operation and one side of his head was totally covered in bandages.

The cricketer asked the surgeon who had performed the operation what the situation really was.

'Well, I did manage to save your eye,' said the surgeon.

'That's wonderful news,' said the Englishman.

'We'll give it to you when you leave as a souvenir,' said the surgeon.

A husband and wife were going through a very bad patch in their marriage. It lasted a long time and life seemed to be one long battle. One evening the husband was walking home from work when he was knocked down by a hit-and-run driver. As he lay in the road a policeman rushed up and asked, 'Did you see who it was?'

'Not really,' said the man, 'but I know it was my wife.'

'How do you know it was your wife if you didn't see who was driving the car?'

'I'd recognise that laugh anywhere.'

★

Jack: What does t-e-r-r-i-f-y spell?
Jill: Terrify.
Jack: And what does t-i-s-s-u-e spell?
Jill: Tissue.
Jack: Put them both together.

Jill: Terrify tissue?
Jack: Not at all – carry on!

There was an old man in a hearse
Who murmured, 'This might have been worse;
Of course the expense
Is simply immense,
But it doesn't come out of my purse!

There was a party going on in a flat in a large apartment block and an angry man knocked on the door.

'Do you know my wife is ill in bed upstairs? he said.

'No,' said the folk singer, strumming his guitar, 'but if you hum the tune I'll pick it up in no time.'

A chimpanzee walked into a bar and asked for a gin with two slices of lemon. The barman poured the drink and gave it to the chimpanzee who sat down with it at a corner table. A by-stander who had watched all this commented, 'Now there's something you don't often see.'

'That's right,' said the barman, 'most people are happy with one slice of lemon.'

A well-built old fellow named Skinner
Said, 'How I do wish I were thinner!'
He lived for three weeks
On a grape and two leeks –
We think of him Sundays at dinner.

★

Teacher: Who shot Abraham Lincoln? Can you tell me, Billy?
Silly Billy: I'm not going to, miss.
Teacher: Why not, if you know who did it?
Silly Billy: Because I never split on anyone.

★

A coal mine in the mid-west was in danger of flooding one spring with the thaw of the winter's snow and only one man could crawl through the narrow tunnel to close the hatch which would stop the water. The miners sent for 'Slim' Smith, a slight, short youth who could possibly avert the disaster.

He arrived at the mine and the foreman explained the situation to him. 'Sure, I'll go down,' said 'Slim'. 'It's a case of a titch in time saving the mine, isn't it!'

★

Teacher: Speak up, Jenny! We can't hear your answer.

Jenny: Confucius say, when in doubt, mumble.

★

Voice on phone: Can I speak to your mother, please?

Little boy: Mummy isn't home.

Voice on phone: Can I speak to your father then?

Little boy: Dad isn't home either.

Voice on phone: Is anyone besides you at home?

Little boy: Yes, my sister.

Voice on phone: Then can I speak to her, please?

Little boy (after a minute): No, I'm sorry, you can't speak to her.

Voice on phone: Why not?

Little boy: Because I can't lift her out of her playpen.

★

A lady was waiting for a bus with her hands held straight out in front of her about six inches apart. When the bus came along and she got on, she asked the conductor to take the fare out of her coat pocket, and she sat down still with her arms outstretched six inches apart. The conductor was more than a little puzzled, and said to the lady gently,

'Have you had an accident?'

'Oh, no,' replied the lady. 'I'm going to the shops to buy a piece of fringe this long for my lamp.'

★

A shepherd was herding his sheep through a country town when a policeman stopped him. 'What's the matter?' asked the shepherd. 'I was just taking the sheep down this side street.' 'Can't you read?' said the policeman. 'That sign says no ewe turns.'

★

Paul: Could you tell me the time, please? I've been invited to a party and my watch isn't going.

Saul: Why? Wasn't your watch invited?

★

Girl: I'd like three scoops of chocolate ice cream with hot fudge sauce, chopped almonds and whipped cream, please.

Waitress: With a cherry on top?

Girl: Oh, no! I'm on a diet.

★

A man went to a fair one evening and was fascinated to see a medicine man selling a bottle of 'magic potion'. The medicine man was singing the potion's praises:

'Ladies and gentlemen! The medicine in this bottle is a miraculous liquid which I guarantee will help you to live longer. Your life will be healthier and happier, too. Why, look at me! You'd never think to look at me that I was over 200 years old, would you? And the secret of my long life is right here – I take a dose of this potion *every* day.'

The man listened and thought the medicine sounded like an excellent idea, but on hearing that it cost £5 a bottle he decided to ask the medicine man's assistant if it really worked. Quietly he asked the assistant if the medicine man was really over 200 years old.

'Well, I honestly don't know,' answered the assistant. 'I've only been with him for 150 years.'

★

A mother ran in to the baby's room when she heard her three-year-old's screams coming loud and clear from the room.

'What's happened?' she asked.

'The baby's been pulling my hair,' howled her daughter.

'Don't worry,' said the mother, 'he doesn't know that it hurts.'

A few minutes later she heard the baby

screaming and ran back in to the room.

'What's happened to the baby?'

'Nothing,' said her daughter, 'but now he knows.'

★

A gorilla walked into a hamburger restaurant and ordered a quarter-pound cheeseburger with extra relish, a plateful of French fries and a large banana milk shake. The waiter brought the order and watched the gorilla eat the lot. The gorilla thought that the waiter had been staring at him, so to be friendly he said, 'I suppose you think it very odd that a gorilla should come in here and order a quarter-pound cheeseburger with extra relish, a plateful of French fries and a large banana milk shake.'

'Oh, no,' said the waiter, 'I had that for lunch earlier.'

★

Father: What are you looking for, Sam?

Sam (on hands and knees): The pound coin pocket money you gave me. I've lost it.

Father: Don't worry, it'll turn up. A pound doesn't go very far these days.

★

Nick and Rick went for a walk and they came across a high wall.

'How shall we get over?' asked Nick.

'Easy,' said Rick. I'll shine my torch over the wall and you climb up the beam.

'Oh, no!' said Nick. 'I'll get half-way over and you'll turn the torch off.'

★

Three men were sitting on a park bench. The two on the outside were acting as if they were fishing, baiting hooks, casting out their lines, and reeling them in. The man in the middle was reading a newspaper.

A policeman walked by and stopped when he saw what the two men were doing. He was a little surprised and asked the man in the middle if he knew the two men sitting on either side of him.

'Oh, yes,' said the man, 'they're my friends.'

'Well get them out of here,' said the policeman.

'Yes, sir!' said the man, and he began to row frantically.

★

Why did the girl sit in the sun all day?

Because she wanted to be the toast of the town.

★

Paul: When visitors arrive in my town, they always come to see me.

Saul: I'm not surprised, the sight you are!

★

Paul: Can I join you?

Saul: Why, I'm not coming apart!

★

Paul: Why did the chicken cross the road?

Saul: I don't know. Why did the chicken cross the road?

Paul: To get a Russian newspaper. Do you get it?

Saul: No.

Paul: Neither do I. I get the *News* myself.

★

A father, mother and little boy were out shopping one day and the little boy was getting tired of all the walking up and down stairs and in and out of shops. He tugged at his father's coat and as the father bent down the little boy whispered in his ear. The father straightened up and shook his head. A little while later the boy tugged his mother's coat, and she bent down as he whispered in her ear.

'No,' she said.

So the little boy tugged at his father's coat again, obviously pleading.

'No!' shouted the father. 'I don't care how Superman does it, we're using the stairs!'

★

Defence counsel: Now, Mrs Able, please tell the court why you stabbed your husband 120 times.

Mrs Able: I didn't know how to switch off the electric carving knife.

★

What can you eat all the way from London to New York?

A 3,000-mile hot dog.

Yacht

What did the yacht say to the dock?
 Yacht's up, dock?

Yak

What do you get if you cross a yak with a parrot?
 A yakety-yak!

Yard

What yard has four feet?
 A backyard with a dog in it.

Yawn

Mother: When you yawn, Sam, you should put your hand to your mouth.
Sam: What, and get bitten?

Year

How many weeks belong to a year?
 Forty-six. The other six are Lent.

Yeast

A bus conductor helped a very fat lady on to the bus.
'You want to take some yeast, my dear!' he said. 'It will help you rise better.'
'You better take some yourself,' replied the lady. 'Then you'd be better bred.'

Yeast and Polish

Paul: What happens when you eat yeast and polish?
Saul: You rise and shine.

Yellow

What's thick, yellow and dangerous?
 Shark-infested custard.

★

What is yellow?
 A cry of pain!

★

What's yellow and black and has red spots?
 A leopard with measles.

★

When is a yellow book not a yellow book?
 When it is read.

★

What is yellow outside, grey on the inside, and has a superb memory?

An elephant omelette.

★

If the yellow house is on the left-hand side of the road, and the green house is on the right-hand side of the road, where is the white house?

In Washington.

Yes

Boss: I don't like 'yes' men. When I say 'no' I expect them to say 'no' too.

★

Why is the word 'yes' like a mountain?

Because it is always an assent.

Yokel

What is the difference between a country yokel and a Welsh rabbit?

One is easy to cheat and the other is cheesy to eat.

Yoo-Hoo

The phone rings. A lady picks up the receiver and a man's voice says, 'Is that you, darling?'

'Yes,' says the lady, 'who's calling?'

Young Joker

Who wrote jokes and never grew up?

Peter Pun.

Young Lady

What's the difference between a young lady and a fresh loaf?

One is a well-bred maid and the other is a well-made bread.

★

An elderly lady was complaining about today's youth:

'They don't know how to behave! And as for their clothes! Why, look at that girl over there – she's wearing boys' jeans, a boy's shirt, and her hair is cropped as short as a boy's! You would hardly know she was a girl at all, would you?'

'Yes, I would,' came the reply, 'she's my daughter.'

'Oh,' said the old lady, blushing with embarrassment. 'I'm so sorry – I didn't realise you were her father.'

'I'm not – I'm her mother.'

Young Love

Mother: Jenny, whatever is the matter? Why are you crying?

Jenny: I've just had a letter from my boyfriend, with two kisses on the bottom.

Mother: Well, dear isn't that nice?

Jenny: No! No one double-crosses me!

Zebra

If a quadruped has four legs and a biped has two legs, what is a zebra?
  A stri-ped.

★

What's black and white and red all over?
  A blushing zebra.

★

What do you get if you cross a zebra with an ape man?
  Tarzan stripes forever.

★

Did you know that scientists crossed a zebra and a donkey?
  They called it a zeedonk.

Zebra Crossing

Policeman to pedestrian: Why are you crossing the road at this dangerous spot? Can't you see there's a zebra crossing only 50 metres away?
Pedestrian: Well, I hope it's having better luck than I am.

★

What goes, 'Now you see me, now you don't; now you see me, now you don't'?
  A snowman walking over a zebra crossing.

Zero

Teacher: Why are you shivering, Johnny?
Johnny: It must be the zero on my test paper.

What would you get if you crossed a zero with a pigeon?
  A flying none.

Zinc

Paul: What's zinc?
Saul: Where you wash zaucepans after dinner.

Zoo

A man went for a job interview and was asked to explain what his previous work had been.
'I used to be at the zoo,' he said.
'Oh, really,' said the employer, 'what cage were you in?'

★

A little boy was telling his friend about his trip to the zoo.
'The elephants were the best,' he said. 'What do you think they were doing?'
'I don't know,' said the friend, 'tell me!'
'Picking up their peanuts with their vacuum cleaners.'

Mother: If you were a good father, you'd take your son to the zoo.

Father: If the zoo wants him they can come and get him.

★

There were ten lions in the zoo. All but nine escaped. How many were left?

Nine.

★

What do the animals read in zoos?

Gnus papers.

Teacher: Your essay is very interesting, Billy. But I wonder how you and your twin managed to produce exactly the same essay after our visit to the zoo.

Silly Billy: Same zoo, Miss.

★

Why did Silly Billy get into trouble for feeding the monkeys at the zoo?

Because he fed them to the lions.